SEX AND THE CITY

THE CULTURAL HISTORY OF TELEVISION

SEX AND THE CITY

A Cultural History

NICOLE EVELINA

ROWMAN & LITTLEFIELD
Lanham • Boulder • New York • London

Published by Rowman & Littlefield
An imprint of The Rowman & Littlefield Publishing Group, Inc.
4501 Forbes Boulevard, Suite 200, Lanham, Maryland 20706
www.rowman.com

86-90 Paul Street, London EC2A 4NE, United Kingdom

British Library Cataloguing in Publication Information Available

Library of Congress Cataloging-in-Publication Data Available

ISBN 978-1-5381-6567-6 (cloth : alk. paper)
ISBN 978-1-5381-6568-3 (electronic)

To Mitzi, my *Sex and the City* twin—
Thanks for spending our Carrie years with me.

CONTENTS

ACKNOWLEDGMENTS

My first thanks must go to Bob Bachelor, without whom this book wouldn't exist. Thank you for the opportunity, for listening to my thoughts, and for allowing me to pitch this book. Thanks to my editor, Christen Karniski, for her guidance and having faith in me, and to my copyeditor, Niki Guinan, for cleaning up my messes throughout the book—especially in the citations.

I must also admit my debt of gratitude to all the people who have written about *Sex and the City* before me. Your insider information, interviews with the cast and crew, and deep insights helped me have a solid jumping-off point for my own opinions and research. I hope that everyone reading this book consults your work, as well. I list your names in the bibliography with the greatest respect and thanks.

Thank you to my agent, Amy Collins, for her support during the entire drafting process and to all the fans I interviewed or talked to during my research. Whether your name is used or not, you are as much a part of this book as I am.

I would also like to thank everyone involved in *Sex and the City*—Sarah Jessica Parker; Cynthia Nixon; Kristin Davis; Kim Cattrall; Darren Star; Michael Patrick King; Candace Bushnell; and all the writers, crew, and others behind the scenes. I realize I have been critical of your show and, in some cases, your work in this book. As a fellow artist, I don't take that lightly, nor do I do it with malevolent intent. I hope you take it in the constructive spirit in which it was intended.

Lastly, thank you to everyone who reads this book. Without readers, a book isn't really finished. I hope you find useful points of thought and discussion within these pages. If so, then I have done my job.

INTRODUCTION

On June 6, 1998, history was made with the initial eight-count notes of a jazzy theme song and a grown woman in a tutu walking the streets of Manhattan. Unusual? Yes. Unexpected? Certainly. But in the forty seconds of its opening credits, *Sex and the City* told viewers exactly what it was about, even if they didn't understand it yet. They were about to experience New York and life itself through the eyes of this woman, who is whimsical enough to wear a pink tutu in broad daylight yet worldly enough to "know good sex" and be willing to spill her secrets. And, no, she isn't perfect; she gets drenched by a bus rolling through a puddle to prove it.[1]

Sex and the City is a show with a clear premise expertly laid out in the first episode by Samantha: "This is the first time in the history of Manhattan that women have had as much money and power as men, plus the equal luxury of treating men like sex objects"—in other words, exploring the emerging freedoms of women, especially regarding sex, granted to them as part of third-wave feminism. With the combination of witty writing, superb acting, often outrageous fashion, and a keen sense of the times, it became one of the most iconic shows of the noughties and was the first cable show to ever win an Emmy for outstanding comedy series when it was honored in 2001.

As this book shows, *Sex and the City* was groundbreaking in many ways, but what the show came to be known for was its frank discussion of women's sexuality and pleasure. Sarah Jessica Parker, who played the main character of Carrie, explains,

> Carrie was writing about sexual politics and relationships, and men and women's roles socially, so the conversations were often about intimacy and the role it plays in these women's lives. That's what was so new—it involved language that made it new for women to be having these conversations. What was equally as important as the sex, is the way they were sharing and revealing truths of their lives.[2]

NEW YET PART OF A TRADITION

Despite this unique approach, the show was part of a long tradition of "single women" TV shows. "Upon its debut in 1998, the HBO series *Sex and the City* delivered a . . . bold protagonist four decades in the making," writes scholar Cameron Michael Tufino.[3] The first iteration of this character was arguably *That Girl* (1966–1971), starring Marlo Thomas, in which an aspiring actress moves to New York and works as a temp while awaiting her big break. Toward the end of its run, another hit premiered, *The Mary Tyler Moore Show* (1970–1977), in which Mary Reynolds moves to Minneapolis after breaking up with her boyfriend and takes a job as an associate producer on a TV news show. Both shows were groundbreaking in their portrayals of young, single women with jobs—they moved female television heroines out of the perfect mother and perfect mate roles of June Cleaver and Lucy Ricardo (who at least tried to get a job performing on Ricky's show), bringing the television heroine more in line with the lived reality of female viewers.

Susan Faludi, a former *Wall Street Journal* reporter and Pulitzer Prize winner, notes that Mary Tyler Moore's character was shocking in many ways because she was "not only unwed, she was more than thirty years old. Marriage panic did not afflict her. She had real male and female friends, enjoyed a healthy sex life, turned down men who didn't appeal to her, and even took the pill—without winding up on a hospital bed in the final scene"—very much like the women of *Sex and the City*, only twenty years earlier.[4]

However, television critic Emily Nussbaum points out a fatal—at least to today's mind-set—flaw in these characters, writing, "[T]he vast majority of iconic 'single girl' characters on television . . . had been you-go-girl types—which is to say, actual role models. . . . They were pioneers who offered many single women the representation they craved, and they were also, crucially, adorable to men: vulnerable and plucky and warm."[5] That is, they were a version of a male fantasy of the perfect woman, you know, if she *had* to have a job. They lacked the flaws and full spectrum of emotion that would make them more than two-dimensional.

Thankfully, as the years progressed, the single women on television grew in strength. Starting with *Rhoda* (1974–1978) and continuing on with *Laverne & Shirley* (1976–1983), these women began to have not only more realistic personalities but also a bit of venom on their tongues. Rhoda's comment in episode 1.7 of *The Mary Tyler Moore Show*, "Toulouse-Lautrec Is One of My Favorite Artists," could have been spoken by any of the *Sex and the City* gals: "There are no men friends when you're thirty. They're either fiancés or rejects." Likewise, in the first-season episode of *Laverne & Shirley*, "The Dating

Slump," a man tries to touch Laverne's breasts (through her iconic sweater with her initial emblazoned on it) without her approval and she threatens, "Touch my *L*, sweetie, and your teeth go to Peoria!" These are women who can not only survive on their own but stand up for themselves, as well.

In the 1980s, we began to see single women in foursomes, much like the women of *Sex and the City*. While this dynamic of friends as family is discussed in depth in chapter 10, it must be acknowledged that the two most iconic foursomes of the 1980s were the *Golden Girls* (1985–1992) and *Designing Women* (1986–1993). "The women of *The Golden Girls* may well be the future iterations of the women of *Sex and the City*," writes Dr. Wendy Burns-Ardolino of the University of Houston-Downtown.[6] They are just older and facing the problems that come with aging instead of with youth.

Similarly, the ladies of *Designing Women* could be their southern counterparts. Not only are they whip-smart, successful, and independent, but the show also takes on subject matter that television has difficulty dealing with even today. Melanie Hamlett of *Glamour* magazine writes,

> In [one] episode, Julia takes down a man for invading women's personal space and time because he can't fathom why they'd want to be alone. One of her most famous speeches was when she schooled her boyfriend and his buddies for blaming women for the world's problems when men are the ones who built and reign over this world they complain about. From AIDS and homophobia to slut-shaming and condoms in school, *Designing Women* covered it all.[7]

This foursome—much like the *Sex and the City* ladies after them—juggle relationships, careers, and societal expectations with dignity, poise, and more than a bit of caustic in their southern charm.

Finally, *Living Single* (1993–1998) can be seen as the direct precursor to *Sex and the City*.[8] The show involves six Black friends in their twenties, two men and four women, who face such issues as racism, sexism, and harassment and who struggle to live and love in Prospect Heights, Brooklyn. The four female friends, Khadijah, Synclaire, Max, and Regine, are clearly the immediate past patterns for the four friends in *Sex and the City*, something *Living Single* rarely gets credit for. "In a 90s kind of world Black women had depictions of themselves on the tube, which at best made them proud and at worst at least didn't cause them to shake their heads in shame," Bene Viera writes for *Vibe*. "When *Living Single* wrapped its final season in 1998, *Sex and the City* debuted, later becoming a major hit for the network. Had *LS* not existed *SATC* may not have been possible."[9]

UPDATING THE FAIRY TALE

"Once upon a time, an English journalist came to New York." With this opening narration by Carrie, *Sex and the City* establishes itself as a modern fairy tale, albeit for more mature audiences than traditional tales.

But then it flips the idea on its head as it carries on with the story of this English "princess." Instead of finding her Prince Charming, she gets ghosted by him. But perhaps this shouldn't be all that surprising. When Samantha asserts that women can now "treat men like sex objects," Miranda points out that there is a sexual double standard present because "men in this city . . . don't want to be in a relationship, but as soon as you only want them for sex, they don't like it." Women are stuck in a catch-22; no matter what they do, the man will disappear.

"Fairy tale or anti-fairy tale, which is it?" the show tauntingly asks the viewer. While the show's edginess and casual approach to sex, dating, and even marriage seem to want to push it into the "anti" direction, the full length of its run bears it out as a traditional fairy tale. Missouri Southern State University (MSSU) lists the following elements of a fairy tale.[10] By examining each, we can see how *Sex and the City* clearly fits this mold.

I. Short Story

This is the opening of the story, a story-within-a-story that provides background on the characters, what happened before the story begins, and what the stakes are. In *Sex and the City*, this is borne out through Carrie's opening conversation with the English journalist Emma, in which Emma tells Carrie of her heartbreak and experience with a man she met shortly after arriving in New York. By using this tale as an introduction to the series, the creators are telling the audience that they are about to experience a story of modern love, betrayal, and heartbreak in New York City, centered on the age-old quest for "the one."

2. Hero/Heroine

Every story must have its main characters that the audience roots for. In this case, we meet both our heroine (Carrie) and hero (Mr. Big) within the first eighteen minutes of the first episode. Interestingly, Carrie displays many characteristics common to heroes: "simple, naïve, innocent. Believes in miracles."[11] While in many ways these characteristics better suit Charlotte than

Carrie, she still has enough of them to make her the "fool" who undertakes a journey without having any idea what lies before her.[12] Compared to world-weary Samantha and cynical Miranda, Carrie still possesses her childlike innocence and belief in true love. While the course of the story will undoubtedly open her eyes, as it always does, it is her belief in magic (in this case, love and soulmates) that keeps her going.

In addition, we have Mr. Big, who is a typical fairy-tale hero. He may not bear the title of prince, but he is certainly a business tycoon and can partake of and provide the finer things in life. What's more, he "rescues" Carrie right off the bat, helping her retrieve the contents of her purse from the sidewalk that spilled out when the two literally ran into one another. Later in the episode, he "rescues" her again, pulling up in his black limousine like a knight on a black stallion when she needs a ride home after dark.

Moreover, the hero, or in this case the heroine, also has friends who offer her guidance and gifts, just as in traditional fairy tales. Often known as the sidekicks, these friends play a secondary role to the hero but are still important in their own right. Obviously, this role belongs to Miranda, Charlotte, and Samantha, who, in addition to providing love and moral support to one another, act as sounding boards to Carrie as she seeks answers to that episode's central question. In addition, they often make her continuing quest possible through financial gifts (remember when Charlotte gave Carrie her $30,000 engagement ring in season 5 so she could pay for her apartment?) or just a shoulder to cry on during heartbreak.

3. Evil Character

MSSU defines the villain as someone who "uses words and power and often abuses magic to exploit, control, imprison, and destroy—all for personal gain."[13] There is no single villain in *Sex and the City*, though it can be tempting to name as the evil element in the series Mr. Big and any of the many "toxic bachelors" on the show, the patriarchy, and even the idea of love itself. But overall, the women are their own worst enemies. What Carrie and the others struggle against most is themselves: their inner demons, their personal expectations for their lives, what society expects of them, and what they can and can't live with. They are the ones who use words—toward themselves and others—and the idea of love (magic) to exploit and control the men in their lives for what they believe to be personal gain. In so doing, most of the time, the only ones they hurt are themselves.

4. Magical Characters and Events

Most fairy tales have a fairy godmother or a similar character who fills the role of "donor and helper . . . [who] aid[s] the hero and the heroine at various points in the plot," says folklorist Jeana Jorgensen.[14] In the context of *Sex and the City*, Carrie's fairy godmother can be seen as the city of New York herself, for she always seems to provide exactly what Carrie needs. On the rare occasions that she dares to leave the city for the Hamptons, a cabin in upstate New York, or (God forbid) rival Paris, something always goes wrong—because her fairy godmother isn't there to help her.

For Miranda, her housekeeper, Magda, performs the same function.[15] From the beginning, she is a loving, cheerful presence, a light in Miranda's often cynical, bleak world. She clucks over Miranda like a mother hen, wanting what is best for her, even when she replaces Miranda's vibrator with a statue of the Virgin Mary. "Magda becomes an integral part of Miranda's life, evolving from a cleaning lady to a nanny and a permanent member of her household by season 6. Following the death of Miranda's mother during season 4, there's no doubt Magda fills the role of the surrogate maternal figure as well," notes Jennifer Lind-Westbrook of Screenrant.[16]

For Charlotte, her gay bestie Anthony fills the same role. We only see him when she needs him, often to dispense advice or a bon mot. Even years later, in *And Just Like That . . .* , Anthony is Charlotte's sounding board when her daughter Rose tells her that she doesn't identify as a girl.

On the surface, Samantha seems to be the character who has no need of a fairy godmother because she has the confidence and money to obtain everything she needs on her own, but it can be argued that Smith is Samantha's, especially after she begins chemo treatments. He helps her through hair loss, hot flashes, and other unpleasant side effects with the patience of a saint.

5. Overcoming Evil

Unlike many movies and TV shows, *Sex and the City* doesn't have a specific "big bad" or evil force to be vanquished. Rather, it follows the trials and tribulations of each woman as she faces her own fears, shortcomings, and need for change. These are detailed in the chapters on each character, but examples include Carrie's seeking of external validation, Charlotte's need to feel perfect, Miranda's lack of faith in herself, and Samantha's reluctance to show vulnerability of any kind.

These are played out in small ways in every episode as well as in their character arcs across the seasons. For example, in 1.8, "Three's a Crowd," we see all four dealing with their own reactions to the idea of having a three-some. Carrie is haunted by Mr. Big's admission that not only has he had a threesome in the past but also it was with his ex-wife. Carrie didn't know he was married, and so she grapples with how to handle the idea that her main source of identity and validation, Mr. Big, had shared himself so intimately with another woman. Miranda feels rejected and undesirable when none of the women say they would have a threesome with her, so she answers a personal ad from a couple seeking a third, only to ditch them after getting the validation that they want her. Charlotte tries to have one because her boyfriend wants it, only to get squeezed out of what becomes a twosome be-tween the other woman and her boyfriend; this is okay with her because it al-lows her to keep her pristine status, which is what she really wanted anyway. Samantha, on the other hand, willingly admits to having had threesomes and enjoying them and in so doing confirms her sexual power.

6. Moral Message

Sex and the City could be said to have many moral messages, but perhaps the strongest is that women deserve to be able to be sexual creatures just like men can. This goes for the way they talk about sex, the way they engage in it, and the way they think about it. For generations, women have been taught to be "good girls," pure and chaste and connecting sex only with mother-hood. Forget that they have sexual needs and urges and feel and wish to express passion. As chapter 12 shows, *Sex and the City* taught us that it is okay for women to speak candidly about sex, not just with one another, like the women do, but publicly, as well, because it was on television and gave them permission. It also empowered women to embrace all types of sexual expression, from masturbation to different types of sex and kink.

7. Predictable Language/Structure

Every fairy tale begins the same way: "Once upon a time." Those are literally the opening words of the first episode as well as three others: "Once upon a time, . . . a guy and a girl kept running into each other" (1.4, "The Valley of the Twenty-Something Guys"); "Once upon a time, in a magical land called Manhattan, a young woman fell in love" (1.8, "Three's a Crowd"); and "Once upon a second time around" (2.8, "The Man, the Myth, and the Viagra"). The traditional ending is "and they all lived happily ever after." While that isn't in Carrie's final narration, it is certainly implied.

Sex and the City follows a typical fairy-tale structure, wherein its heroines are rescued (sometimes multiple times) by potential white knights. In 3.7, "Drama Queens," Charlotte is rescued from being run over by a cab by Trey; in the first episode, Big rescues Carrie from having to walk home; in 3.1, "Where There Is Fire," politician Bill Kelly rescues Carrie from being stuck on Staten Island when she misses the ferry and loses her shoe like Cinderella—a gesture she calls her "Staten Island Ferry Tale"; and of course, in the finale, Big rescues Carrie from Paris.

8. Oral Tradition

While *Sex and the City* is obviously a visual medium, Carrie's narration places it squarely in the realm of oral tradition. She is our guide for each episode, providing exposition, asking questions of herself and the audience, and generally moving the storyline along. "Carrie is chatty. She's also brash, opinionated, and cynically optimistic. . . . We crawled into her head, guided through the changes, the inner thought processes of all of the characters through Carrie's narration. . . . Its primary purpose is to tie together the storylines and weave plot points into a single narrative," writes Kim Handysides for the Blast.[17]

9. Generally Has a Happy Ending

As is covered many times throughout this book, the ending of *Sex and the City* is a classic fairy-tale ending. Not only do Carrie and Mr. Big end up together in what appears to be a committed, long-term relationship, but Mr. Big also takes on the role of white knight by rescuing Carrie (our princess) from the terrible experience Paris had become for her.

REINVENTING THE ROM-COM

Sex and the City has also been characterized as a romantic comedy. According to screenwriter Michael Hauge, rom-coms, as they are often called for short, all follow a specific formula: "[A] romantic comedy hero must pursue his or her love interest, a crisis must precipitate a breakup at the end of Act 2, and the ending must always be happy."[18] Based on these three elements, *Sex and the City* clearly fits this mold. Carrie pursues Big throughout the series, they break up and make up and break up again several times, and the ending (of the series at least) is a happy one, with all four women blissfully paired off.

However, there is a fourth element of conflict where *Sex and the City* doesn't follow traditional rom-com lines: "[A]lmost all Hollywood romantic comedies are built on deception," Hauge writes. He classifies this conflict into six categories: secrets and lies (in which the hero is withholding information); the imposter (in which the hero is not who he or she claims to be); the magic spell (in which magic changes the hero's life, causing them to fall in love); Peter Pan and Wendy (in which immature men learn responsibility in order to win the more mature woman); slumming it (in which the conflict is based in class differences); and the long haul (in which the conflict comes from an unusual situation and covers a long period of time).[19]

None of these fit *Sex and the City*, even if they are mixed and matched, as often occurs in storytelling. It is possible, though, that the deception in *Sex and the City* isn't external but rather internal. Each of the four main women, in their own way, is lying to herself. As this book shows, at its core, *Sex and the City* is about female identity, both for each character and in general: as in, How do women of the mid- to late 1990s fit into a changing society? The obstacles the women face are often of their own making, whether consciously or not, something that sets the show apart from many others, where female characters face external obstacles in the form of men: cheating boyfriends, disinterested husbands, unrequited love, and the types of conflicts Hauge lists. While some of these things still happen, they are more often than not the result of thoughts, desires, or actions taken by the women.

This internal struggle is best exemplified by Carrie's weekly column, which is ostensibly her job but also provides her a vehicle through which to explore her inner thoughts and feelings (and those of her friends) about their lives. This question is rarely about something trite; this is the audience's chance to understand what Carrie is pondering existentially and an invitation to ask themselves the same question, thereby providing yet another avenue for the audience to identify with her and the other main characters. Scholar Cindy Royal writes, "One could argue that Carrie's preparation of her column is a type of journal in which she, and ultimately the audience, work out their own issues of identification as single women."[20]

So, does hitting three out of four characteristics a rom-com make? For this show, yes and no: yes because it checks the most important boxes of structure, and no because this is a new kind of romantic comedy, as shown in its conflict. "Noted as a show about sex and the single girl, it features an active engagement by its female protagonists in the renegotiation of the classic romance fantasy," writes film critic Joanna Di Mattia.[21] They will have their romance and eat it, too, as it were. These sexy, independent women are going to live their rom-com on their own terms; even if the ending is rather traditional, the journey sure as hell won't be.

ARCHETYPES: ARE YOU A CARRIE, A MIRANDA, A CHARLOTTE, OR A SAMANTHA?

If the women of *Sex and the City* are living in a fantasy version of real life in 1998-ish New York City, then why do women continue, even twenty years later, to want to sort themselves by the character(s) they most identify with? Because they relate to them on a basic level.

Carrie, Charlotte, Miranda, and Samantha are relatable because they are based on archetypes—"characters built on a set of traits that are specific and identifiable . . . [and] recurrent across the human experience," just as nearly all characters in drama are, dating back at least to the ancient Greeks.[22] How identifiable the archetype is depends on the subtlety of the characterization, but they are always present in some way. According to psychologist Carl Jung, there are twelve archetypes, which can be interpreted a number of ways.[23] Anyone who has studied writing will recognize them from his protégé Joseph Campbell's "Hero's Journey"[24] method of storytelling. Others may know them from the tarot, or if you've seen major movie franchises like *Star Wars* or *Lord of the Rings*, you'll be able to associate them with your favorite characters. Here is the list and definitions as interpreted by Masterclass:

The main characters of *Sex and the City* (from left): Miranda Hobbes (Cynthia Nixon), Charlotte York (Kristin Davis), Samantha Jones (Kim Cattrall), and Carrie Bradshaw (Sarah Jessica Parker). Photofest/*Sex and the City* (HBO), season 6 (summer 2003–winter 2004)

1. **The Lover:** "The romantic lead who's guided by the heart." *Sex and the City* character: The four women. All the women play this role to some degree throughout the series, but the ones who exemplify the archetype the most are Carrie in her quest for romance and Charlotte in her naïveté and belief in true love.

2. **The Hero:** "The protagonist who rises to meet a challenge and saves the day." *Sex and the City* character: Big. Given that Carrie is the main character, it is tempting to place her in this role, but the level of self-confidence that it takes doesn't fit her. In the end, it is Big who meets the challenge of changing to be worthy of Carrie and saves the day.

3. **The Magician:** "A powerful figure who has harnessed the ways of the universe to achieve key goals." *Sex and the City* character: Carrie. Masterclass defines this archetype as someone who is omnipotent (like Carrie is in her narration of events where she wasn't present) but also arrogant, which she certainly can be. You could also argue that Samantha's sexual power over men and her extreme confidence place her in this role.

4. **The Outlaw:** "The rebel who won't abide by society's demands." *Sex and the City* character: Samantha, without a doubt. She doesn't care what anyone thinks and lives life the way she wishes, consequences and rules be damned.

5. **The Explorer:** "A character naturally driven to push the boundaries of the status quo and explore the unknown." *Sex and the City* character: Carrie. Through her column, she is always seeking answers, and she certainly fits the traits of being "curious, driven, motivated by self-improvement, restless . . . [and] never satisfied."

6. **The Sage:** "A wise figure with knowledge for those who inquire. The mother figure or mentor is often based on this archetype." *Sex and the City* character: Miranda, Samantha, and Carrie. Many characters could be seen in this role, especially those cast as the previously mentioned fairy godmother. But it could be argued that Miranda, Samantha, and Carrie all fit this archetype. Miranda is Carrie's best friend and so often advises her; Samantha has a wealth of sexual knowledge she imparts on all the women; and Carrie is the one many of the women confide in, and in return, she advises as best she can.

7. **The Innocent:** "A morally pure character, often a child, whose only intentions are good." *Sex and the City* character: Charlotte, no question. She prefers to live in a world of romance and perfection rather

than sully her hands in the real world. Although she isn't virginally pure, she is the least sexually experienced of the four women and prefers to see the good in everyone, even when they don't deserve it.

8. **The Creator:** "A motivated visionary who creates art or structures during the narrative." *Sex and the City* character: Carrie. Both literally and symbolically, her roles of narrator and columnist make her the creator.

9. **The Ruler:** "A character with legal or emotional power over others." *Sex and the City* character: The male love interests. Because of their ability to affect the women's lives, all the male love interests fit this archetype at various times but especially Aleksandr (he has the traits of "aloofness, [being] disliked by others, [and] out of touch") and Mr. Big and Richard (they both have some of that aloofness, as well, but more importantly they have "status and resources").

10. **The Caregiver:** "A character who continually supports others and makes sacrifices on their behalf." *Sex and the City* character: Aidan and Miranda. Here again, the fairy godmothers could apply. Aidan has some of this in him, as demonstrated by his desire to have a family and take care of Carrie. Miranda evolves into this archetype as she learns to put others' needs before her own through motherhood and taking care of Steve's aging mother.

11. **The Everyman:** "A relatable character who feels recognizable from daily life." *Sex and the City* character: Carrie, Steve, Aidan, and more. Many characters are based on this archetype, including Carrie, which is why so many women identify with her. But it can be argued that all four women fit this role because most of us know women like them. Steve is certainly an everyman, and one could say Aidan is, as well—they are just normal guys. In their own ways, Skipper, Harry, and Berger are, as well, especially in comparison to larger-than-life characters like Mr. Big and Aleksandr.

12. **The Jester:** "A funny character or trickster who provides comic relief but may also speak important truths." *Sex and the City* character: Carrie. For her many puns and zippy one-liners, Carrie is the jester. But Stanford and Anthony, who are Carrie and Charlotte's BFFs, also act as foils for the women's drama by being over the top and humorous, just when the girls and the audience need it.

Scholars and critics have taken these basic personality types and expanded on them to fit the characters of *Sex and the City*. Literary critic Anne Kaler identifies the "four dominant stages of a woman's life—as virgin, spouse, mother and wisewoman," as the pattern for the "complete woman."[25] If defining "virgin" to mean not physical virginity but as a symbol of innocence and purity, then you could easily apply that label to Charlotte; the spouse is usually associated with sexual activity, so that would be Samantha; the mother is the caring, nurturing one, which, despite her sometimes-caustic tongue, is Miranda (she is not only the sole character to actually become a mother, but she also is often the one to take care of the others when they are ill or depressed, especially Carrie); and finally, the wise woman, the one with the advice and answers, is sex columnist Carrie. Put another way, as author and scholar Janet Cramer sees it,

> [T]he women represent particular images of women: Miranda is the successful, serious one; Samantha is the lusty vamp; and Charlotte represents a restrained prudish viewpoint. These, of course, are gross generalizations, but they provide a shortcut to understanding the way these characters are portrayed. Carrie is the one who holds the group together, and her narration is the thematic glue of the program as well.[26]

Chelsea Fairless and Lauren Garroni add to this list: "There's the fashionable one, the traditional one, the hedonistic one, and the smart one who occasionally eats cake out of the garbage."[27] (For those keeping score at home, that is Carrie, Charlotte, Samantha, and Miranda, respectively.)

These archetypes are important because they give viewers a touchstone when getting to know the characters. We gravitate toward the ones we identify with, but by having so many represented on the show, we get to experience what the world is like for others, as well. "These female foursome characters encourage the viewer to broaden and deepen her understanding of different worldviews and perspectives while providing a comfortable safety net through self-identification with the character who best reflects her values and tastes," writes Burns-Ardolino.[28]

And perhaps that is one of the most important contributions of the series, especially today. Back when *Sex and the City* first aired, people were still able to talk to others of differing viewpoints and opinions, have a conversation, and perhaps learn from one another. Sometimes they would have to agree to disagree, but the dialog could still take place. But now, even with civil discourse all but dead in America, the show still offers viewers that same opportunity to step into another woman's Manolos and experience life for a while.

PART I

THE CHARACTERS

I

CARRIE

"I will never be the woman with the perfect hair, who can wear white and not spill on it."

—Carrie, episode 3.3, "Attack of the Five-Foot-Ten Woman"

Let's be honest—Carrie Bradshaw is a mess. But aren't we all?! That's a huge part of what makes her so relatable and why so many fans identify with her.[1] For advertising expert Bonnie Fuller, "it wasn't really the glamour or the glitz that made 'Sex and the City' a winner, although they helped. . . . It was the 'she could be me' or 'she could be my best friend'-ness of the Carrie Bradshaw brand that worked big time."[2] Dan Clay, whose drag alter ego is Carrie Dragshaw, recalls his first encounter with Sex and the City after he had come out and realized it was okay for him to like the show: "It was like a complete Carrie love-fest. I was like 'She is me! I am her! I've never seen myself so mirrored!'"[3]

As Sex and the City's narrator and main character, Carrie has received the most analysis of any of the female characters. She is the bridge between the audience and the show, so understanding her is key to understanding the show. "The biggest misconception about Carrie is that she was somebody who was only interested in pursuing a sex life, when really she was interested in the conversations about sex and relationships. . . . Carrie didn't really sleep around and she definitely wasn't casual about sex," Parker said about her character.[4]

For all her sexual curiosity and her willingness to cheat with Big even when he was married, Carrie had values and knew them well. In episode 2.4, "They Shoot Single People, Don't They?" a very drunk Carrie meets a su-perhot guy at a club but refuses to go home with him because, as she narrates, it would be the only time in her life that she slept with a guy to validate her feelings, and that was a line she wouldn't cross. "You can say a lot of things about her, but she has a moral compass," Parker said. "Someone who only cared about sex would not have told her boyfriend that she had an affair. She would have said, 'I can get away with it.' But it haunted her—and that says a lot about who she is."[5]

Duality is an essential part of Carrie's character; she is a lot of "this" but also "that." For example, she's romantic yet cynical about modern love; she's smart and witty but also sometimes so incredibly daft; poised yet clumsy; sexually open yet cautious. Carrie is the rare combination of brains and heart, according to writer and executive producer Michael Patrick King: "Writing Carrie is about opening up your heart and your head at the same time. With her intelligence, loyalty, mind-boggling fashion sensibility, and open heart she is the best friend every girl wants and the girlfriend of every guy's dreams."[6]

But yet, she isn't perfect, and she's the first to admit it. She spent an entire episode worried that Mr. Big would dump her because she farted in front of him—the ultimate sin of imperfection in her mind. The amount of concern she has over this is also revealing of her self-centeredness and lack of self-confidence. "Although a lot of things were done right with the character," writes entertainment columnist Saim Cheeda, "one of the mistakes that *Sex and the City* made repeatedly was to make Carrie a conceited person right when she was on the cusp of showing genuine character development."[7] And most often, this happened around or in reaction to Big. Amy Sohn, author of the show's companion guide Sex and the City: *Kiss and Tell*, explains, "With Big, Carrie was at her most extreme, yet somehow her most real—belligerent, pained, sexy, naïve, protective, posturing, and caring."[8]

In many ways, Carrie tried to make herself into what she thought the men in her life wanted her to be. Nussbaum likens her to a kaleidoscope: "In the first season Carrie is 'neurotic.' Then she tried being 'the marrying type' with Aidan. In season 3 she became 'the other woman' to Natasha's 'perfect little woman'. . . . She got more honest and more responsible; she became a saner girlfriend. But she also became scarred, prissier, strikingly gun-shy—and, finally, she panicked at the question of what it would mean to be an older single woman."[9]

These personas that Carrie tries on like a DNKY dress—"you know it's not your style, but it's right there, so you try it on anyway" (1.3, "Bay of Married Pigs")—often have detrimental effects on her life. "It's pretty shocking the way Carrie messes up her life over and over again between the cheating, the smoking, the losing the dog, and the lying," said King. In doing this, Carrie isn't just disappointing those around her; she's also letting herself down. King explains, "The idea of failing loving yourself is a big thing in my own life—when something fails, learning to be OK with it and honoring what you tried to do."[10] This is a lesson that Carrie tries and fails to learn over and over throughout the series.

Even into the final season, she tries to be the aloof sophisticate who would fit in with Aleksandr's Paris society friends. But the result isn't the bliss she hoped for; she finds herself lonelier than ever and on the verge of a breakdown. It isn't until she trusts her instincts and is ready to flee back to New York that she finally knows who she is. Because of this, she is ready for Big's grand gesture and the commitment that comes with it.

CARRIE'S SEARCH FOR IDENTITY

In 1972, art critic and novelist John Berger (not to be confused with the *Sex and the City* character Jack Berger) wrote in his classic essay "Ways of Seeing,"

> To be born a woman is to be born, within an allotted and confined space, into the keeping of men. The social presence of women is developed as a result of their ingenuity in living under such tutelage within such a limited space. But this has been at the cost of a woman's self being split into two. A woman must continually watch herself. She is almost continually accompanied by her own image of herself.[11]

As a result of our patriarchal culture, then, according to Berger, all women live with a split sense of self: the one she reflects to others and the one she feels on the inside, which don't always match.

This alignment of selves is exactly what Carrie—like many of us—is searching for. Her "both and" personality is the result of her ongoing quest to find and shape her own identity. She's a thirty-something still trying to figure out who she wants to be when she grows up. She admits to her crisis of identity in the first season (1.11, "The Drought"), when she says to Miranda, "I'm not like me. I'm, like, Together Carrie. I wear little outfits: Sexy Carrie and Casual Carrie. Sometimes I catch myself actually posing. It's just—it's exhausting." She's talking about who she is when she is around Mr. Big, but she could just as easily be referring to any moment of the show. After all, we've also seen "Heidi Carrie" dressed for a picnic in the park (complete with dirndl, one of the show's most oft-scorned looks) and "New Carrie" after she broke up with Big for the first time and started dating a Yankees player (2.1, "Take Me Out to the Ball Game"), which makes her sound like a line of 1980s Barbie dolls that have different occupations and outfits to match.

Like Barbie, Carrie's clothes reflect this quest to figure out who she is. This is why she is often seen pairing vintage and designer duds and wearing outfits that no one else on the planet would wear. "Few characters in the history of television have been defined as sartorially as Carrie, whose psyche was on display each week via her dresses, shoes, and accessories," writes Ron Simon, curator of television at the Museum of Television and Radio.[12] She's not so much getting dressed for the day or for an event as she is "trying on" an aspect of her personality or who she might wish to be.

A 2015 study by the Association for Psychological Science showed that what we wear really does affect how we think and act. "It's . . . about what you're communicating intentionally or unconsciously through your fashion choices. Just as the actor in the right costume moves and speaks differently, so does the everyday person," writes Molly St. Louis for *Inc. Magazine*.[13] This is also why Carrie is so identified by her clothes and her closet. In fact, her closet is much more than a place to store her clothing. For Carrie, it is her safe space. She often goes there when she is upset, which is natural because it is where she feels whole. For example, in episode 2.5, "Four Women and a Funeral," Carrie carries her phone into her closet and stands in it while talking with Big for the first time after their initial breakup. Even in *And Just Like That . . .* , Carrie's closet is where she stores Mr. Big's ashes until

Carrie's closet and the clothes within are inextricably linked to her search for identity. Photofest/*Sex and the City 2* (2010), directed by Michael Patrick King

she figures out where he would want them to be scattered. She feels safe there because it is the only place where all the aspects of her identity are together. "Carrie and her closet are one and the same," writes Lynn Gibbs for Screenrant.[14]

This explains her strong reaction in episode 4.13, "The Good Fight," when Aidan suggests she clean out her closet to make room for him as they prepare to move in together. He is basically asking her to make room for him in her life, not only literally, but also to make room in her identity for him (i.e., as his girlfriend, fiancée, or wife). Beatriz Oria, film analysis lecturer at the University of Zaragoza in Spain, explains,

> This fight is over Carrie's "access" of clothes and shoes, but taking into account the important role played by fashion in the show and how it is used to express Carrie's personality it becomes clear that what is really at stake in this scene is her identity. Aidan's inability to understand Carrie's love of fashion emphasizes the differences that separate them, while his taking over of her wardrobe represents not only the invasion of her private space, but an all out threat to her independent single self.[15]

When the first *Sex and the City* movie was being promoted and Cynthia Nixon (Miranda) was on *The Wendy Williams Show*, she told a story about how the first time she saw the film, the "women around her began cheering after 'Mr. Big' showed Carrie the closet he had built her." This didn't sit well with Nixon because she felt the audience was missing the female empowerment message in favor of their fashion fantasy.[16] But what the audience was responding to was the idea that here, finally, is a man who understands what Carrie needs. Instead of asking her to make her identity smaller for him, as Aidan does, he actually gives her a larger closet than she's ever had before and, symbolically, the freedom to be whoever she wants, in addition to his wife. He gets her. The fact that he proposes to her using shoes instead of a ring just cements that idea.

Anna König, senior lecturer of textiles history and theory at Arts University in Bournemouth, England, speculates that Carrie's "walk-in wardrobe . . . give[s] the audience permission to similarly indulge in their fashion fantasies."[17] Given that it is the seat of her identity, it also acts as a kind of Narnia-like entrance between her world and ours, drawing us into her outrageous life. In her Manhattan apartment, it is literally a passageway from one part of her apartment to another, from the public part (her living room/bedroom area) into the private (the bathroom), one she has to traverse every time she gets ready to go out, giving her an opportunity to pick her identity and take us, the audience, with her.

A Column and a Conundrum

As the first episode illustrates, Carrie has no illusions about who society expects her to be. She says in a voiceover, "Welcome to the age of un-innocence. No one has breakfast at Tiffany's, and no one has affairs to re-member. Instead, we have breakfast at 7 a.m. and affairs we try to forget as

Carrie's weekly column is both a way to voice the theme of each episode and a way for Carrie to untangle a thread in her life. Photofest/*Sex and the City* (HBO), season 2 (summer–fall 1999)

soon as possible. . . . Cupid has flown the co-op." In other words, women in New York are expected to sleep around (yet mostly regret it), not open their hearts to anyone or even dream of romance. Those things are passé. Yet when Samantha and Miranda get into a conversation about men only wanting women for sex, Carrie gestures to them and says that as soon as the right guy comes along, "This whole thing, you two right here, this whole thing, right out the window," showing she is a romantic at heart.

This is only one of the tensions—but the one most relevant to the ongoing series storyline—that Carrie embodies and tries to understand through her writing and her interactions with her friends. Her column is not only her source of income and a large part of her identity—ask most people about themselves, and they will tell you what they do rather than who they are—but it is also her lifeline. It's written more like a personal journal than like something meant to be consumed by the public. "During the voiceover moments in which she frames the central question, one gets a sense of her insecurity, self-consciousness, and subjectivity," writes Royal.[18] It is perhaps her most vulnerable moment of each episode as she allows herself—and the audience through her—to question something vital.

"Carrie's writing provides a deeper understanding of her identity, and her column is pivotal to the character because Carrie organizes her life largely through her writing, as it serves as a way for her to reflect on her own life experiences and examine and consider other perspectives, which are offered by her friends during their conversations," Delaney Broderick, scholar at Wake Forest University, notes.[19] So central to her life and identity is this weekly chance to reflect, question her friends, and form her own conclusion, that if it was taken away, Carrie would have a loss of identity stronger than if her entire wardrobe burned to ashes.

CARRIE'S CHARACTER ARC

When characters are created, if they are done well, they have intwined inner and outer journeys, just as people do in real life. The outer journey is what happens to them from outside forces: for example, Carrie's many breakups and makeups with Big and the other men in her life. The inner journey is the evolution, hopefully to greater maturity, that she goes on over time.

Hauge identifies a distinct pattern to this character arc that all main television, play, novel, and movie characters experience over the course of their story. A character begins their journey wearing a mask or "persona" they have created and present to the world in order to feel safe and deal with a traumatic incident in their past, which he terms their "wound." He explains, "The heroes of these stories always carry some wound from the past—a deeply painful event or situation that the character believes she has resolved or overcome, but which is still affecting her behavior. . . . These beliefs that grow out of past wounds are never true. But they are ALWAYS logical."[20] For Carrie, this persona is that of the fun, quirky, inquisitive sex journalist. She's a little edgy, a little sweet, and always charming. So what was she trying to hide from the world and from herself with her seemingly free-spirited life?

Sex and the City gives us precious little to go on regarding any of the four main characters' pasts, but what we need to know about Carrie is revealed in episode 4.17, "A Vogue Idea," when we learn that Carrie's father left her family when she was five.[21] Like many children who suffer abandonment early in life, as an adult, Carrie thinks she had long ago dealt with her feelings of betrayal, when what she had really done is fashion for herself a personality that pretends such things don't matter. But what she shows us through her actions is that while she may have convinced herself of that, deep down, she is still the heartbroken little girl whose father left—likely because (in her mind, at least) she wasn't good enough. In episode 3.1 of *And Just Like That . . .* , Carrie reflects on her younger years, saying to Miranda that she feared that she "wasn't enough" for Big. Therefore, she tries on all these different personalities in an effort to find the one that will finally make her worthy of a man staying with her.

With Aidan, Carrie gets a glimpse of what life would be like without her mask, and it scares her. That's one of the reasons she falls for Big's siren song over and over again. Every time she gets close to really loving, free of drama and guilt and all other distractions, she retreats back into what is safe and familiar: sabotaging her good relationship—usually with Big—in order to reinforce the idea that she's not enough.

Carrie's black moment, the one in which it seems like nothing will ever be right again, comes in Paris, when Aleksandr abandons her at the museum the weekend before his show opens. She has hit rock bottom and no longer has anything to lose, so she may as well gather up her courage; tell Aleksandr exactly what she thinks; and go back to New York, where she belongs. She doesn't even need Big's help; he is just along for the ride and for one final grand gesture. Once back in New York, Carrie is fully in her essence, ready to see what the next stage of life will bring.

WHAT DOES IT MEAN TO BE A CARRIE?

In light of all this, what does it mean if the *Sex and the City* lady you most identify with is Carrie? Likely that you are still a work in progress and you're on a personal journey to uncover who you are. And that is just fine—actually, it's more than fine; it's a healthy, liberating adventure, which is what life is all about. Keep looking, even if you don't like everything you uncover (Carrie surely doesn't) because the more you seek, the more you learn about yourself and the better the person you become. And as Carrie would say, "I couldn't help but wonder if that wasn't the point all along."

2

CHARLOTTE

"I'm pretty and I'm smart. I'm a catch."

—Charlotte, episode 3.1, "Where's There's Smoke"

Sometimes it seems like Charlotte York would have been more at home in the 1950s than in the late 1990s. After all, in that period, she would have had her MRS long before her thirties, and her dream life of a marriage and family would have been easier to obtain. Plus, more people would have shared her old-fashioned values, which would have made it easier for her to force her perfectionism on others. (And oh, did she try, beginning with a dog in season 2 and continuing on to her daughters in *And Just Like That . . . .*)

But that wasn't the world she was meant to live in, so Charlotte bravely navigated the "anything goes" waters of the end of the twentieth century with good-natured aplomb. For all her seeming prudishness, she is remarkably open to the strange or gross (in her mind) things her boyfriends want to do, such as oral and anal sex, both of which she ultimately turns down. But at least she considers them, asks her friends, and goes into her decision well informed.

Sohn is right to characterize Charlotte as a love-her-or-hate-her kind of character: "When it comes to Charlotte, people tend to have strong opinions. Because she so often espouses a traditional view of men, marriage, and commitment, those who agree with her cheer her on—while those who disagree with her want to throw things at the television." Charlotte is the dewy-eyed optimist who always believes things will work out and she will get what she wants if she just tries and pushes hard enough. And it is that tenacity that makes viewers sometimes want to call her "sweet summer child" and shake some common sense into her. "On one level her needs seem impossible to meet and utterly unrealistic; on the other, they are what

Kristin Davis played the conservative of the group, Charlotte York. Photofest/*Sex and the City* (HBO), season 2 (summer–fall 1999)

any woman expects and deserves: love, stability, devotion—and a little trifle called sex," Sohn writes.[1]

When compared to Samantha, Charlotte can seem staid and even frigid, but she's really not. In fact, she often "slut shames" Samantha for having one-night stands, despite doing the same thing herself.[2] The difference, though, in Charlotte's mind, is one of intent. She goes into every sexual relationship thinking she has found the man she is going to or at least could marry; Samantha, however, goes into her one-night stands knowing that they will be just that. To Charlotte, her intent to stay with the men long term negates any sluttiness that might ruin her pristine reputation if the man chooses to leave.

And they usually do. As a result, Charlotte has a fair number of sexual partners throughout the show, tying the seemingly more adventurous Carrie at eighteen.[3] So much for the theory that she was meant to be a "less cynical and more conservative foil to Carrie."[4] To Samantha, definitely. To Miranda, quite possibly. But Charlotte and Carrie, for all their outward differences, are really two peas in a pod with different ways of approaching the same goal: finding Mr. Right.

CHARLOTTE'S "RULES" OF DATING

While Carrie approaches dating (and life) in a rather haphazard, "come what may" way, Charlotte is very methodical. "Every man she meets is sized up as a potential husband. Dating is regarded as a competitive sport and Charlotte plays to win," writes feminist scholar Beth Montemurro.[5] It is clear Charlotte has been preparing for this her whole life. She has positioned herself, perhaps better even than Samantha, to meet the type of man she has always dreamed of: a John F. Kennedy Jr.–esque figure who has the wealth, status, and power to bring with him her dream mansion, summer home in the Hamptons, and the requisite 2.5 perfect children.[6] As an art dealer, she regularly comes into contact with the type of man she might date or who may know someone who would fit her high standards. Yet she also admits in the first episode, "Most men are threatened by successful women. If you want to get these guys, you have to keep your mouth shut and play by the rules."

And Charlotte means that literally. Once she accepts a date, she is a devotee of *The Rules: Time-Tested Secrets for Capturing the Heart of Mr. Right*, a *New York Times* best-selling how-to guide for dating that was spectacularly popular in the late 1990s. Called *The Rules* for short, it lists literal rules for how a woman should behave: "Above all, women were to be passive (Rule No. 2: 'Don't Talk to a Man First'), undemanding (Rule No. 17: 'Let Him Take the Lead'), and above all happy and busy, breezy, and lighthearted."[7]

For Charlotte, it is a playbook to be followed religiously, even when experience teaches her that her rules don't always work. In the premiere, Charlotte tells Carrie about her rule to never sleep with a man on a first date, only to have her date share a cab with her while she goes home, and he heads to a local club to get laid—by Samantha. Yet Charlotte doggedly persists. Later in the series (3.7, "Drama Queens"), she is reading yet another advice book, this time the fictional *Marriage, Inc.: How to Apply Successful Business Strategies to Finding a Husband*, which advises, "If you really want to get married, you shouldn't be spending so much time around dysfunctional single women." Thankfully, that is advice she chooses to ignore. Otherwise, our favorite foursome would have become a threesome much sooner than *And Just Like That . . .*

For two seasons, Charlotte sets her sights on finding the man she has constructed in her fantasies, only to be disappointed again and again by some of the show's strangest men: Ned, the guy who hangs out by his wife's grave to get sympathy dates (2.5); Jack, the threesome guy (1.8); Bram, the guy who falls asleep during sex (2.16); and Stefan, the gay-straight man (2.11), to name only a few.[8] Just when all hope seems to be lost, she meets the man of her dreams, totally by accident. Having stormed out of a bar where she was supposed to meet a blind date, Charlotte trips and falls right into the street. A cab nearly hits her, and out pops Dr. Trey MacDougal, with the perfect timing of a storybook prince.

Unfortunately, Trey cannot live up to Charlotte's expectations or even her basic requirements, try as she may to make her marriage work through his sexual dysfunction, overprotective mother, and other issues. For a woman who used to live by rules that literally told her not to talk too much or be the first one to make a move, she now has no choice; therapy and the open dialog that goes with it are the only things left to save her storybook romance.[9]

But even that isn't enough, and in the end, she makes the heartbreaking decision to end their marriage. That has to be a great source of pain and embarrassment to someone whose whole life was, to that point, focused on perfection. Divorce is not only a huge blow to Charlotte's ego and the end of her carefully constructed dreams but also a very public admission of failure. She married into her desired social set, and now she has to face all of them and admit that (at least in her mind) she isn't perfect enough to make her dream life work.

Richard Lawson of *Vanity Fair* claims that "after Season 3, Charlotte is never fully human again."[10] If he considers her starry-eyed, puppy-dog, almost-Stepford-like adherence to an outdated moral code human, then yes, he's correct. But if not, the opposite is actually true. In divorcing Trey, Charlotte faces her biggest fear and comes out the other side. No one emerges from trauma like that unscathed, and neither does she. But to call her inhuman is to say that all women whose eyes are opened to reality and who grow and mature beyond their youthful fantasies are somehow less, when in fact they are so much greater than they were before. Dreaming is the easy part; living in reality is hard.

One thing that doesn't change as a result of her divorce is Charlotte's determination. She may have been burned by an on-paper Mr. Right, but she refuses to give up on her dreams of becoming a mother. "She learns how to not compromise what is important to her sexually and emotionally and walks out of her divorce with a sense of self-worth and value she did not have before," writes Princess Weekes for the *Mary Sue*.[11] And if that isn't the sign of a strong woman, what is?

INFERTILITY AND ISSUES OF FAITH

From the outside looking in, Charlotte seems to have it all: an impressive career, two wealthy husbands, an enviable Park Avenue apartment, good friends, and health. But even *she* can't have the one thing she wants most: a baby. According to the Centers for Disease Control and Prevention, an estimated 6.1 million women aged fifteen to forty-four in the United States have difficulty getting or staying pregnant, but that is something we rarely talk about in our baby-obsessed society.[12] On *Sex and the City*, these women found a voice they so often lack in Charlotte York.

There was a little foreshadowing to this storyline in episode 2.11, "Evolution," when Charlotte reveals she has a tilted uterus, so sperm have to jump in order for her to get pregnant. Later, she finds out that her body is literally attacking sperm, so she has only a 15 percent chance of getting pregnant. Charlotte endures everything our procreative society has to throw at a woman suffering in her own private hell of infertility: baby showers, one of her best friends getting pregnant when she didn't even want to, and a husband who changes his mind halfway through their fertility treatments.

An article on WebMD explains, "In her quest to have a child, Charlotte tried hormone treatments, acupuncture, and considered adoption. The show deftly illustrated that there are not necessarily quick fixes to this problem."[13] It takes a toll on her mental health, too. "Coming up against infertility can really shake a woman's core belief in herself," fertility expert Dr. Devora Lieberman says. "Many of my patients will feel like they've failed, and it's quite shattering to self-esteem."[14]

In Harry Goldenblatt, a bald, loud, sweaty Jewish lawyer—pretty much the polar opposite of everything Charlotte thinks she wants—she finds exactly the man she needs. A man who puts up with her fussiness and finds it charming, one so laid back not even her perfectionism can ruffle him. If her divorce taught Charlotte anything, it is that shedding her rigid rules of life and learning to be flexible has its benefits; had she not gone through that experience, there would have been no way she would give Harry enough of a chance to fall in love with him. She certainly wouldn't have been willing, like her idol Elizabeth Taylor did for Eddie Fischer, to shed her Upper East Side Protestant identity to convert to Judaism for him.

The same love for Harry is what sees Charlotte through at least two rounds of IVF, Chinese herbs, and a painful early pregnancy miscarriage (that Charlotte bounces back from also with inspiration from Elizabeth Taylor). It strengthens both of them through countless adoption forms, months of waiting, a near miss with a prospective adoptive couple, and finally getting the wonderful news that they would be the parents of a little girl from China.

CONSERVATIVE FEMINISM

There is no doubt that Charlotte is the most conservative in her values of all four women. Unlike the others who seek independence, she wants to be the traditional image of a woman: wife, homemaker, mother. "Traditional feminine expectations fall heavily on Charlotte's shoulders as the other three women are mostly portrayed as happily inept at or uninterested in cooking, cleaning, and other homemaking tasks. For Charlotte, fulfilling traditional roles is a fantasy to be realized with elegance," Montemurro writes. With Carrie using her oven to store sweaters and messing up cooking a simple fondue, Miranda hiring a housekeeper, and Samantha dining out at every meal, Charlotte is likely the only one of the group to pass on these conservative values to the next generation.

If we assume that *Sex and the City* is a third-wave feminist show, then does this mean that Charlotte isn't one? That is a debate that has been going on for as long as women's rights has been an issue (more on that in chapter 9), and the answer depends on who you ask. Leah Thomas of *Marie Claire* believes Charlotte deserves to be blacklisted by fans for her unthinkable antifeminist mind-set: "She claims that women need to be 'rescued' by men, and believes females should change for their partners 'because we are more adaptable.'" Because of this, "among millennials, Charlotte has replaced Miranda as the most loathed character."[15] This argument only holds water if you hold to a liberal definition of *feminism*, one that eschews the traditional model of woman as helpmeet for man, espousing instead an extremely independent and woman-centered model of feminism. While the vocal majority hold this opinion, not all do.

Broderick sees Charlotte as a postfeminist: "Charlotte's old-fashioned perspective derives from a postfeminist notion in which women looked back to traditional standards of womanhood and femininity."[16] Postfeminism, a concept with several definitions, was a popular form of discourse in the 1990s, "reflecting a reaction against the feminist theories of the 1970s and 1980s, often on the basis that the 'battle of the sexes' is over."[17] While it is true that postfeminists did harken back to traditional ideas of what it means to be female, it is questionable if Charlotte would self-identify as one. For all her dreams of becoming a lady who lunches, she is well aware of the world she lives in and would at least support the ongoing need for feminism for pay equity and an end to the types of harassment that all women face, if nothing else.

There is a type of feminism that critics seem to be unaware of when trying to toss Charlotte out of the feminist circle all together. Conservative feminism dates back to the early 1980s during the second stage of the so-called second wave of feminism and is often credited to Betty Friedan and Jean Bethke.[18] According to scholar Judith Stacey, conservative feminism rejects the politicization of sex in favor of the family; celebrates the differences between male and female by emphasizing the traditionally feminine, especially motherhood; and believes that the liberal struggle against male dominance takes away from more important issues. Charlotte would certainly agree with Friedan that "almost all women and men need and want family *and* equality."[19]

This definition, as we have seen, fits Charlotte to a tee. She doesn't like to talk about sex openly—she has to whisper the word *penis*, after all—so she is definitely not one for making it a political issue; she is the ultimate trophy wife and openly celebrates that as her ambition; and she doesn't see why the other girls are focused on men all the time, when they should be celebrating themselves and their accomplishments instead. After all, the goal of conservative feminism is not female domination over male; it is "to achieve the new human wholeness that is the promise of feminism."[20]

That human wholeness is different for every person. For Charlotte, it is to be found in the roles of wife and mother. Despite her unrelenting quest to become a mother, she doesn't force that mind-set on her friends, who face the idea of childbearing with strong reluctance (Carrie and Miranda) or outright disdain (Samantha). "For Charlotte, motherhood is her personal choice and not a requirement to every woman's life. Thus, she is a progressive representation of real women," writes Tufino.[21]

That Charlotte willingly, if a bit reluctantly, gives up her dream of owning her own gallery after marrying Trey in order to become a homemaker (and hopefully a mother) is something her close friends cannot understand. Montemurro emphasizes how "inconceivable" this is to them: "By making Charlotte the minority voice in this situation, the writers and producers of *Sex and the City* have done something interesting and novel. They allow the traditional feminine voice to be rejected rather than rewarded, while the voices of the career-focused workers-not-wives dominate," placing the show itself clearly in liberal-feminism territory and showing that Charlotte, once again, has a view of the world different from the others.[22]

However, if you boil down feminism to its most basic tenet, encapsulated in Susan B. Anthony's famous quote "Men their rights and nothing more; women their rights and nothing less," then a woman's political leanings have nothing to do with whether she is a feminist or not, so long as she supports women attaining and keeping their full rights, including the sexual freedom the show fights so hard for. In this way, whether Charlotte should be considered a feminist is a moot point because by this definition, she is, conservative or not.

CHARLOTTE'S CHARACTER ARC

While *Sex and the City* is notoriously stingy with its backstory for the main characters, we learn more about Charlotte's background than of the three other women. In season 2, she mentions being from Connecticut, a state often associated with wealthy families, and indeed her wedding invitation in season 6 reveals her father is a doctor and her mother a socialite.[23] This apparently upper-class background is further shored up by Charlotte having attended Smith, a prestigious liberal arts women's college in Northampton, Massachusetts, where she majored in art history and minored in finance.

This background sets Charlotte up for the wound that is very obvious in her character: She had to have been taught from a young age that in order to be loved, she had to be perfect. That explains why Charlotte wears a mask of prim perfection, when it is obvious there is an inner wild woman buried deep inside and waiting to get out—Charlotte's true essence isn't as innocent as she would like others to believe.

When Charlotte marries Trey, she gets a small glimpse of what her life could be like if she dropped her quest for perfection when she is forced to admit her marriage isn't the happily ever after she wished for. In trying to keep her dream life alive, she is forced to become more malleable and grows tremendously, even though she fears more than ever that everyone will know that she isn't perfect.

That fear is realized in her "black moment," when she has to admit to the world that she wasn't enough to keep a seemingly storybook marriage together. Unlike lesser women, Charlotte faces this bravely and doesn't let it get her down. Instead of turning bitter, like so many other women, she leans into who she really is by retaining her positive attitude and continuing on her quest for true love.

Before she knows it, Harry Goldenblatt is in her life, a strange, sweaty man who is completely not Charlotte's type. But she is attracted to him anyway. When Charlotte meets Harry, she is forced to confront her greatest flaw, the last vestige of the mask she has been wearing for so long: her superficiality.[24] She nearly loses Harry for good over it, yelling at him with uncharacteristic venom during their first Shabbas dinner, "Do you know how lucky you are to have me? Do you know how we look? Do you know what people out there think when they see us together? Do you?" implying that she is far superior to him in appearance and in every other way.

In the time that she and Harry are apart, Charlotte comes to realize how meaningless are the things that used to matter to her. At a Jewish singles mixer, she meets a guy who should be exactly what she wants—he's handsome and wealthy and has a Yale pedigree—but she isn't interested in him. She finally realizes that she likes Harry's imperfection and admits as much to him, asking him to forgive her. He does her one better; he proposes. "The proposal was Charlotte's finest moment," writes Sohn, "Just when we thought Charlotte had lost him forever, after she had told him bluntly that he wasn't nearly as attractive as she, Charlotte finally understood that it wasn't a wedding or even a husband she wanted—it was Harry. And even though Harry didn't look like perfection, he was."[25] Charlotte proves that she is living fully in her essence at her wedding when everything that can go wrong does, and she "takes it in stride, because she is a woman who has learned that superficial perfection does not equal love."[26]

SO WHAT DOES IT MEAN TO BE A CHARLOTTE?

To be a Charlotte is not, as some people believe, to be a "Park Avenue Pollyanna" or a naïve dimwit, as critics may claim. Charlottes are optimists and hopeless romantics, yes, but they are also people who know their own value and refuse to compromise. Being a Charlotte means being open to new possibilities but understanding deep down which ones fit with who you are and which are just not right for you. People who identify with Charlotte may be more conservative than those around them, but they are comfortable with that. Charlottes are individuals of grace, strength, and conviction, who over the course of life's trials learn that rigid inflexibility isn't going to get them anywhere, so they learn to give a little when it counts—all the while staying true to themselves. And no matter what the haters may say, the world needs more Charlottes, not fewer.

3

MIRANDA

"Sexy is what I try to get them to see me as after I win them over with my personality."

—Miranda, episode 4.2, "The Real Me"

Miranda Hobbes may well be the most divisive of the female characters on *Sex and the City*. When the show originally aired, she was generally considered the least likeable of all of the women, but in the last few years, she has seen a renaissance, becoming something of a cult hero to millennials.[1] "As it turns out, Miranda was the feminist icon all along and Carrie merely catered to viewers on an exclusively aesthetic level," writes Eva O'Beirne, student at Trinity College in Dublin and deputy life editor of *Trinity News*, Ireland's oldest and most successful student newspaper.[2]

She is certainly the most realistic of all the characters. While she has a high-powered job, Miranda is most down to earth. Instead of spending her free time up to her ears in designer fashion like Carrie, obsessing over finding "the one" like Charlotte, or dating up a storm like Samantha, Miranda eats takeout, rents movies from Blockbuster, reads historical biographies, and goes on the occasional date.[3] Like a normal woman. Ron Simon calls her a "successful lawyer searching for a personal life," which is an apt description, considering she was the "least active in the dating scene" of the four friends, having the lowest number of sexual partners over the course of the show (seventeen) and spending nearly half the series with Steve.[4]

"With her quick wit, pragmatism, and deeply held opinions, Miranda represents the realist in all of us," writes Amy Sohn. "A Harvard Law educated lawyer, she is always the first of the four women to point out the sexual double standard. Her favorite coffee shop topics are sexism, power, and hypocrisy—and she is utterly unafraid to say what she thinks."[5] This attitude likely stems from the fight she has had to endure to get to where she is in a profession mostly dominated by men. Her determination is what brought her this far; in season 1, she declares her goal of making partner at her firm, even if she has to pretend to be a lesbian to do it. "Miranda understands her identity through her career," writes Broderick. "Miranda is unwilling to compromise her job because of her gender and is upset when she is looked down upon for being a woman in a male-dominated occupation."[6]

Or a woman alone. In episode 2.5, "Four Women and a Funeral," she faces a sort of social discrimination when she applies for a mortgage to buy her own apartment, with everyone from her real estate agent to her bank asking, "It's just you?" as in "No boyfriend or husband to vouch for you?" as though she were living in the Victorian era, not on the cusp of the twenty-first century. At the bank, she is even asked if her father is going to cover the down payment and asked to "check the 'single woman' box" several times when signing her mortgage papers.[7]

These are the types of situations that enrage Miranda. "I want to enjoy my success, not apologize for it," she says in episode 2.10, "The Caste System." She has worked hard to get to where she is, and to be questioned and invalidated simply because of her gender is unthinkable. If asked, she would likely say this—along with a mile-long list of other reasons, complete with legal citations—is why she is a proud, card-carrying feminist. Like the women's rights pioneers before her, Miranda "feels she is making a place for women where there wasn't a place before."[8]

In the postfeminist era of the late 1990s, many viewers couldn't handle the biting edge to Miranda's attitude, and that soured them toward her character. "Our Carrie-normative culture has perpetuated the myth that embodying the characteristics of a Miranda (blunt, sarcastic, career focused) are undesirable qualities for a woman," write Fairless and Garroni. "It's textbook sexism and it doesn't take a genius to realize that [such] oppression only benefits the patriarchy."[9] By not appreciating these qualities, society reinforces an outdated notion of what a woman should be.

From early on, girls are taught to be likeable—that is, kind, quiet, and biddable. Those who express strong opinions are called "precocious" at first and humored, but if the behavior continues, they become "bossy" and are told to be polite and consider others. If this goes on unchecked into adulthood, they are labeled "bitches" and are often seen by men as intimidating. The terms *ball-busters*, *man-eater*, and several not fit for print are applied to them. Men shy away from dating Mirandas in favor of more pliable, less intense women they feel they can control, like Charlotte.

Girls who can stand on their own rarely play the "follow the leader" game demanded by classroom queen bees and, therefore, are often shunned by schoolyard cliques. As a defense mechanism, they develop a tough exterior that manifests itself in sarcasm, as the girl seeks to protect her vulnerable and lonely heart. "Sarcasm is actually hostility disguised as humor," explains *Psychology Today*. "It can be used as a subtle form of bullying."[10] It's not surprising, then, that with sarcasm comes a reputation for negativity and even anger. Friends who are stung by a sarcastic woman's tongue rarely stick around for long, and men pass them over in favor of women like Charlotte and Samantha who have honey dripping from their lips instead of vinegar.

Girls who show natural intelligence, like Miranda, are often passed over in school in favor of boys. A decades-long study conducted by David Sadker and Karen R. Zittleman finds evidence of clear bias in the classroom against girls and in favor of boys:

> [T]eachers spend up to two thirds of their time talking to male students; they also are more likely to interrupt girls but allow boys to talk over them. Teachers also tend to acknowledge girls but praise and encourage boys. They spend more time prompting boys to seek deeper answers while rewarding girls for being quiet. Boys are also more frequently called to the front of the class for demonstrations. When teachers ask questions, they direct their gaze towards boys more often, especially when the questions are open-ended.[11]

Even those who overcome these disadvantages have a harder time breaking into male-dominated professions. Miranda attended Harvard Law School. In the second season of *Sex and the City*, which aired in 1999, she is thirty-three, so we can reasonably assume she graduated law school at the age of twenty-five, which would have been in 1991. According to records kept by the American Bar Association, average law school enrollment for the class of 1991 across the country was 42.7 percent for women and 57.3 percent for men.[12] Given that Harvard is a prestigious school known for its low admission rates, it is safe to assume that a woman like Miranda would have had to fight even harder to get in than her counterparts across the country.

On top of that, a 2015 survey by the American Bar Association's Commission on Women in the Profession and the Minority Corporate Counsel Association finds that female lawyers make 44 percent less than their male counterparts, and a 2017 study by McKinsey and Company finds that "women in the legal industry receive first-time promotions 11 percent less often than men; female lawyers are 29 percent less likely to win promotion at the first level of partnership than men."[13] And these numbers would have been even worse in the late 1990s/early 2000s, when *Sex and the City* aired.

Given this, is it any wonder why Miranda seems bitter and cynical? Some of it could be attributed to the personality she was born with, but society certainly isn't helping foster positive attitudes among women who are naturally confident, assertive, and bright, especially in the legal profession. "For better or worse, the Miranda personality type is typically characterized by a mild distrust of the world and the norms set upon it by society," and it is easy to see why.[14]

THE RISE OF MIRANDA

Back in the late 1990s, "Miranda was too abrasive, too cynical, and too completely lacking in fashion sense to be considered cool. She was, for all intents and purposes, the odd one out."[15] She was the one no one wanted to be on the "Which *Sex and the City* Gal Are You?" quizzes. "She is basically Hufflepuff," explains writer Harling Ross.[16] Miranda just didn't fit in with the time. Young third-wave feminists were quick to embrace the girl power of Lilith Fair and stop shaving their armpits like Fiona Apple—things Carrie might have done—but had little time for deeper issues.[17]

It was a time when the sexual power of women like Pamela Anderson, Carmen Electra, the Spice Girls, Victoria Beckham, and even Buffy the Vampire Slayer was valued over the intellectual and activist contributions of Ruth Bader Ginsberg, Madeleine Albright, and Janet Reno.[18] That was the contradiction of the third wave. It brought us great strides toward sex positivity and helped women reclaim their identities as sexual beings, but it also objectified our bodies with crop tops, low-rise jeans, and the stripper/pole-dancing exercise fad. It was certainly the time to be a Samantha or a Carrie, not a Miranda. "The presence of this feminine contradiction indicates uneasiness with popularised images of women, caught between traditional and contemporary ideals of femininity," writes Georgina Isbister of the University of Sydney's Gender and Cultural Studies Department.[19]

Miranda and other "serious," radical feminists were written off as "feminazis" by the media. As the new millennium dawned, it was no longer cool to identify as a feminist, which is why some women's studies scholars add a period of "postfeminism" between the third and fourth waves. "A prevailing characteristic of popular post-feminism is a trend towards women reclaiming traditional ideals of femininity, following a presumption that the ideals of feminist politics have now been met, opening up a perceived flexibility of subject positioning as a matter of individual choice rather than political necessity," writes Isbister.[20] So choose to be a feminist if you want, but that's on you because not everyone thinks it's necessary anymore.

However, times have changed. If the last six years of growing conservatism and attacks on women's rights in America have proven anything, it's that we have more need for feminism now than we have in decades, so postfeminism seems silly. As awareness of attacks on women's rights has grown, so has public perception of Miranda. In fact, Fairless and Garroni wrote an entire book about the character, who is their hero, titled *We Should All Be Mirandas: Life Lessons from* Sex and the City's *Most Underrated Character.* They would certainly applaud *Marie Claire*'s assessment of the change in attitude toward her:

> Today, most women are not "Charlottes," but rather "Mirandas"—liberated, career-driven females who, while desiring romantic relationships, have not built their life goals around them. Among millennials, Charlotte has replaced Miranda as the most loathed character, as Miranda's once "annoying" qualities of independence, intelligence, and—for lack of a better word—ballsy-ness somehow look much more admirable.[21]

Raised with women like Hillary Clinton, Elizabeth Warren, and Alexandria Ocasio-Cortez as role models, today's "fourth-wave" feminists are much more likely to embrace a woman who is well educated and speaks her mind, even if her pantsuits are "slightly awkward."[22] In fact, her lack of interest in fashion and superficial things—beyond looking professional for her job—is part of what now makes this kind of woman so attractive. "By [today]'s standards, Carrie is the equivalent of an overly edited Instagram. She is the idea of a person. A snapshot. A fragment. Miranda's authenticity is radical in comparison, and far better suited to our present-day hunger for 'realness,'" Ross explains.[23]

Fairless and Garroni write of their own personal experiences in converting from "Carries" to "Mirandas,"

> We had been gaslit—by society, and the series itself—into believing that Miranda was the least aspirational character. . . . We thought that adopting a Carrie-esque lifestyle would lead us down the path of enlightenment. . . . However, after a considerable amount of soul searching, we were proud to say that Miranda Hobbes is the only icon we needed. Beyond her six-figure salary and designer wardrobe, Miranda's fierce intelligence and drama free approach to living are the real things worth coveting. She speaks her mind, stands her ground, and refuses to apologize for her success—or the contents of her bedside drawer. Ms. Hobbes eschews repressive gender norms with style and grace, all while serving up the greatest menswear looks you've ever seen.[24]

As gender fluidity has become accepted—something that couldn't have happened during the show's original run (the culture just wasn't ready)—Miranda has also become a hero for nonbinary fans of the show, who see themselves reflected in her. "Physically, Miranda is not shown to dress in a conventionally feminine way and often is shown in styles that are traditionally worn by men, such as a pantsuit or trousers. Additionally, Miranda does not conform to the gender roles that have restricted women throughout history," explains Broderick.[25]

In addition, with the revelation that Nixon is queer, Miranda's popularity with *Sex and the City*'s LGBTQIA+ audience was bolstered. The character of Miranda affirms her heterosexuality in the third episode of the show by first posing as a lesbian at a party thrown by her boss and then kissing her actual lesbian date just to be sure. "Even though she insisted that lesbianism wasn't for her, queer fans of the show have always felt that Miranda was one of their own. Perhaps it's her hair, or the fact that she famously berated the entire squad for their singular focus on men. Or maybe it's because within her social circle, Miranda was the least reliant on the opposite sex," speculate Fairless and Garroni.[26] Whatever the reason, LGBTQIA+ fans finally found the representation in the show that is so lacking for them.

MIRANDA'S CHARACTER ARC

Very little is revealed about Miranda's background in the original *Sex and the City* series. All we really know is that Miranda attended Harvard Law, so we have to guess at what her wound was. Given the earlier analysis about what she likely went through to become a high-powered woman and her attitude toward men in general, it seems safe to say she had her heart broken in a bad way at some point in the past. Fairless and Garroni explain Miranda's cynical take on men:

> Miranda's thesis is thus: men are like cabs, and when they are ready for a serious relationship—one that could culminate in marriage—their metaphorical light is turned on. Whoever enters the cab next (i.e. the next like-minded woman he meets) will swiftly become his bride. Miranda's theory challenges the notion that these bachelors have finally found their soulmates; instead their sudden desire to get married is a survival instinct, motivated by the sudden realization that they do not want to die alone.[27]

This attitude is the armor Miranda has constructed to protect her heart. Unfortunately, it has rusted with repeated heartbreak. She is definitely the "most brutal of the women," especially toward men.[28] When she meets Steve, she is so mean that it's a small miracle he ever allows her in his bar again, much less wants to date her. But he seems attracted to her spunk, calling her a "real pisser" and repeatedly going back for more.

Miranda gets a good look into what her life could be if she took off her armor during her multiple makeups with Steve. That is when we see glimpses of her softer side; on the rare occasion she accepts Steve for who he is and lets herself be less rigid, "that cute, reluctant smile . . . creeps out whenever she finds herself charmed. And although it takes a lot to charm this woman of steel, underneath her hard exterior beats a soft soulful heart."[29]

Miranda's "black moment" begins in season 4 with the death of her mother. Here, we see her allow the love and support offered by her friends to begin to seep into her heart. Not long after, her "moment of truth" takes place when she accidently gets pregnant by Steve. It is in her struggle to decide what to do and the subsequent nine months of her pregnancy that Miranda realizes how much she will have to change. She has to reevaluate her singular goal of being a career woman; somehow it would have to fit in alongside the role of mother. More importantly, she has to drop her tough

David Eigenberg played the man with the heart of gold, Miranda's boyfriend, then husband, Steve Brady. Photofest/*Sex and the City* (2008), directed by Michael Patrick King

mask and live in her vulnerable essence; having a child depend on her would mean being open to all the joys and sorrows that go with life. With her heart on the outside of her body after the birth of baby Brady, Miranda now lives a much more authentic life. She is able to admit to Carrie that she is in love with Steve. But as so often happens in life, her timing is off. Steve is in a relationship, and Miranda soon finds herself in one with Dr. Robert Leeds.

It is only after both try to make it work with someone else that Steve can admit that Miranda is "the one." Now firmly in both love and commitment, Miranda faces the ultimate test of identity versus essence: This self-proclaimed "Manhattan girl" must decide if she can give up all she has worked for and identifies with by moving to Brooklyn in order to help take care of Steve's ailing mother.[30] Whereas in the past she may have let her selfishness and self-protective tendencies rule, with her heart now opened as a mother, she is able to make the choice that, as Carrie's voiceover says, "was best for her family . . . so she negotiated her way into her future."

Blair Underwood played Miranda's season 6 love interest, Dr. Robert Leeds. He is one of only three people of color to appear on the show. Photofest/*Sex and the City* (HBO), season 6 (summer 2003–winter 2004)

Having completed her cycle of growth, Miranda is now 100 percent living her true self as a mother—to both Brady and Steve's mom. Women and Hollywood explains,

> She started *Sex and the City* as a woman who was paralyzed and angry by the prospect of pain. She ended the show open to the possibility that she was capable of great joy, even that she had her fair share of it coming to her, but vindicated in the understanding that it would sometimes be accompanied by great hurt. Instead of being overwhelmed by that possibility, as she was so many times in the past, Miranda, more so than any of her friends, finally opened up to the full force of both of those emotions.[31]

WHAT DOES IT MEAN TO BE A MIRANDA?

Identifying with Miranda means you are a smart, driven, and goal-oriented person who isn't going to take any crap or let anyone get in your way. This is a good thing, and don't let anyone tell you otherwise. Mirandas are the individuals who change the world. But you are also a person with a very loving heart, which is why you protect it so fiercely. Be aware that if you guard it too closely, life may force you into opening it in ways you never expected. If you can find a healthy balance between your goals and your ability to love, then there is no stopping you.

And as the women who wrote the book on Miranda say,

> Charlottes may label us as pessimists, but being a realist in an age of insanity has helped us to preserve what little dignity we have left. This go-to defense mechanism does not make us heartless, despite what our exes may shout as they leave. On the contrary, Mirandas love fiercely. We are very attentive in our friendships, occasionally at the expense of our own sanity. . . . Being self-sufficient and living life authentically are essential for maintaining one's mental health. . . . Mirandas are driven and resourceful people. We can accomplish anything with enough time [and] determination.[32]

4

SAMANTHA

"Yes, I am harsh. I'm also demanding, stubborn, self-sufficient, and always right."

—Samantha, episode 6.3, "The Perfect Present"

If there is one word that defines Samantha Jones, it is *sex*. And she's proud of it. Even though she's in her forties, she has never let go of the wild party girl of her twenties. In fact, she's managed to integrate it into a classy-yet-just-a-little-bit-trashy persona. She's bold, brash, and upfront about who she is—a sex-positive woman who is up for just about anything—and what she wants—great sex. She calls herself a "try-sexual" because she will "try anything once," and she means it. She's done sex swings, tantric celibacy, more than 1,001 sexual positions, being a lesbian (or perhaps bisexual is a better term), and Viagra and knows how to turn all the "massagers" at Sharper Image into sex toys. She's also slept with a dildo model, an actor half her age, and a guy who was basically the male version of her.

Why? Because Samantha lives by the mantra "I get what I want" and does whatever she pleases, damn the consequences. She is driven by pleasure and sensuality and therefore has no room in her life for typical models of femininity that involve propriety, marriage, and children. She is the one who articulates the show's central question of whether a woman "can have sex like a man": that is, without feeling. While we may be left to wonder if the others can (okay, we know Charlotte can't), there is no question that Samantha can and does. "This erotically adventurous woman in her 40s embodied the revolutionary sexual freedom and independence that *Sex and the City* stood for when it premiered," the Take writes.[1] Simon asserts, "Samantha exemplifies total experimentation in fulfilling her sexual desires."[2] Drugs are also no big deal to her, though she rarely does them. There is some indication that she may have taken cocaine in the '80s, she does ecstasy once, and she is seen smoking a joint on more than one occasion.

Kim Cattrall played the sex-positive PR exec Samantha Jones. Photofest/*Sex and the City* (HBO), season 6 (summer 2003–winter 2004)

And she certainly doesn't lack in confidence. According to Carrie, Samantha has the "ego of a man trapped in the body of a woman" (2.11, "Evolution"). She has few body issues, but we do see a brief moment of vulnerability when she goes to the plastic surgeon in episode 2.3, "The Freak Show," and the doctor marks up her body to show what she might like to get done in the future. When Samantha looks at herself in the mirror, she lets out a very Lucille Ball kind of wail.

Samantha wields power in all aspects of her life, from her eponymous PR firm, where she is the boss, to the bedroom, where she works hard to please the men she's with and demands satisfaction in return. She's also the most opinionated of the women and is not afraid to say what she thinks, even when it will be unpopular or offend. In episode 5.6, "Critical Condition," she says, "If I worried about what every bitch in New York said about me, I'd never leave the house."

Kim Cattrall, the actress who played Samantha, is proud to have brought such a brazen woman into American homes. Initially, she didn't think she could play such a sexual character at her age, but Star convinced her. Now she's grateful for the role, both for what it did to help people accept older women and for what it did for her personally. "People started to look differently because of shows like *Sex and the City* about 40. Now to have one of your main characters at the end of a big Hollywood movie say, 'I'm 50, and I'm fabulous,' it really gives me a lot of hope for the next decade," she said.[3] Cattrall also told the *Boston Herald*, "I've been a part of something that has contributed to the quality of women's lives and men's lives, in the respect that these subjects are no longer taboo. It makes them easier to talk about and solve."[4]

SLUT-SHAMING

Thankfully, our culture no longer burns or stones the sexually liberated woman, but that doesn't mean she's accepted for who she is. Samantha has been shamed out of a high-end apartment by her judgmental neighbors (3.6, "Are We Sluts?") and nearly lost a lucrative job because she slept with someone at the firm (4.10, "Belles of the Balls"), and while the show itself may not "level any kind of moral judgement against Samantha's behavior," her friends certainly do.[5]

In many ways, it is only natural that Charlotte would be the one to treat Samantha the worst because the two truly do not understand one another. It's like they are from two completely different moral planets. "Charlotte and Samantha represent ideologies from opposite sides of the spectrum: Charlotte being generally conservative and Samantha radically liberal. While Charlotte is optimistic, innocent, and insecure at times, Samantha is hyper-sexual, self-assured, and unapologetic," Broderick explains.[6] Charlotte is both morally outraged and threatened by Samantha's sexual freedom because it goes against everything she was raised to believe, but she is also threatened by it because it is something she knows she will never let herself have. Charlotte may get drunk on occasion, and she has sex with her husband on the regular, but she is too uptight to ever let herself go like Samantha does.

Samantha, however, is both annoyed by Charlotte's prissy prudishness but also a little intimidated by her strong values. In many ways, Samantha sees Charlotte as a little girl who has never grown up, still dreaming of princesses and castles when she should be looking for her next great lay. In episode 1.9, "The Turtle and the Hare," she tells Charlotte that her theory that a relationship should be based on honesty and communication is unrealistic: "If you were twenty-five that would be adorable, but you're thirty-two, so that's just stupid."

Somewhere along the way, Samantha learned that you have to give men what they want sexually if you are going to get ahead, and here is Charlotte who embodies the exact opposite of that. Because Samantha secretly fears being judged (and judges herself for her lifestyle), Charlotte is everything Samantha hates. "The two often argue about relationships, as Charlotte believes in the importance of monogamy and marriage while Samantha is more primarily interested in casual sex," writes Broderick.[7] The most famous example takes place in episode 2.15, "Shortcomings," when Charlotte, upset that Samantha has had sex with her brother, yells, "Is your vagina in the New York City guidebooks? Because it should be; it's the hottest spot in town: It's always open!"

While Charlotte is by far Samantha's biggest detractor, Carrie and Miranda are not above slut-shaming her, either. It is impossible to count the number of puns and zingers Carrie makes at Samantha's expense, even though she's supposedly a sex columnist. One that comes early in the show's run is at a couple's party, where a drunk Samantha realizes she's slept with most of the men in the room. Carrie responds by suggesting, "Well, maybe we should start tagging your married men, and that way you can keep track of them" (1.3, "Bay of Married Pigs"). Similarly, in 5.7, "The Big Journey," Carrie says to Samantha, "Sounds to me like you might be experiencing a 'been there, done them' existential crisis."

But the most blatant example is in episode 5.4, "Cover Girl." When Carrie arrives at Samantha's office for an appointment, she walks in on Samantha performing oral sex on the Worldwide Express courier. Later, instead of talking about it like adults, Carrie throws in one-liners instead. When Miranda asks Samantha, "Do you kiss a guy after a blow job?" Carrie quips, "No, she just signs the delivery slip and sends him on his way." When the two finally do talk, Carrie admits it isn't something she'd ever do, which Samantha takes as condemnation. She responds, "I will not be judged by you or society. I will wear whatever and blow whomever I want for as long as I can breathe and kneel."

Fans had their issues with Samantha, as well. "While the erotically adventurous forty-something quickly became a pop culture icon, fans of the series tend to enjoy Samantha but don't actually want to be 'a Samantha,'" the Take finds. "When a 2017 Buzzfeed quiz asked readers which of the four *Sex and the City* leading ladies was their favorite, Samantha won with 35% of the vote. However, when a different Buzzfeed quiz the following year asked which *Sex and the City* lady readers saw themselves as, Samantha came in fifth out of six places with just 8% of the vote."[8] This is likely because, as much fun as Samantha is to watch, our culture has trained most women to be good little Charlottes rather than raunchy, outsized Samanthas. No one wants to be looked down on or shamed for their sexuality, and—dare I say it?—no one wants to be called a slut. Samantha is not nearly as popular as she used to be, not because of her promiscuity, but because of her attitude. According to the Take,

> Samantha's character started as a fan-favorite and has slowly lost popularity. When the show aired, many viewers applauded Samantha's radically confident and overt sexuality. But in recent years, voices have focused more on shortcomings like her vanity and egocentrism, with Samantha being described . . . as "insensitive," guilty of some "pretty toxic behavior," and even "a cautionary tale." Rather than interpreting Samantha's promiscuity as a sign of her strength, modern viewers see it as a symptom of her fatal flaw: a lack of emotional vulnerability.[9]

Being open to love is a quality intrinsically related to femininity in our culture. Those who are not—often spinsters—have long been seen as dried-up old shrews, and no one wants to be labeled that way. While "Samantha defies societal expectations by . . . proving that a single, sexually active bachelorette of any age can be happy without having to outgrow her independence or promiscuity . . . viewers hesitate to identify with her."[10]

SAMANTHA'S CHARACTER ARC

As with the other characters on the show, we know precious little about Samantha's past. In episode 3.15, "Hot Child in the City," we learn that "at thirteen, [she] was selling Dilly Bars at Dairy Queen," which means she must have been raised in a lower to middle-class family, or she wouldn't have needed to work at such a young age. We also learn in episode 2.15, "Shortcomings," that Samantha was already having sex at this tender age. Whether this because she liked it or not is unclear, but it had to have some effect on her future view of herself as a sexual being.

Cattrall offers some additional insight into her character:

> Samantha is street smart. I imagine that she was an assistant to somebody like [famed public relations exec] Peggy Siegel and learned things the hard way. I think she might have gone to college and taken business or communications classes, but she never went to one of those Ivy League bullshit schools. She reads people and circumstances. I think she's the oldest in her family and was the trailblazer. She had a strong relationship with her father and mother, but was also the one that broke away. There's a feeling with her that she's always had to pay her own way.[11]

As the owner of her own public relations firm, Samantha is certainly a self-made woman, and as such, she enjoys her success. Unlike Carrie, who wears outrageous outfits, Samantha flaunts her wealth through her sometimes tasteful, sometimes tacky attire that always sends a message that she's the one in charge. This is the mask she's wearing when the show begins—the up-for-anything, no-inhibitions woman of every man's dirtiest dreams. But what made her that way? In episode 2.11, "Evolution," we find out that some years back she was in a serious relationship with a man named Dominic, who left her to marry a Swedish model, and it took her a year to get over him, something unheard of for the Samantha Jones we know and love.

Unless something happened to her earlier in life that we don't know about, this is most likely the wound that made her into the tough-as-nails woman who views monogamy as a disease. Unwilling to let herself get hurt again, she closes off her heart by only engaging in casual sex. Yet that soft heart is still beating somewhere deep down because as Sohn astutely notes, "each season she had a lover for whom she cared deeply."[12]

In the first season, it was James, and the two really seemed to hit it off. Unfortunately, in the end, Samantha couldn't handle that his penis was very small. In season 2, it was Dominic once again. She starts out wanting to get revenge on him for breaking her heart all those years ago but ends up falling for him a second time and getting her heart broken again when he leaves her. As Carrie's voice-over in episode 2.11, "Evolution," says, in the process, Samantha learns she "hadn't evolved past having emotions." This is a very important though painful step for her. From this point on, we see Samantha show emotions in the encounters that matter to her and risk her heart just a little bit more each time. She has remembered what it can be like to love, and for a special person, she is now willing to give a little bit of her heart.

In season 4, Samantha opens her heart (and her legs) for a short time to a lesbian artist named Maria, who teaches her "how to connect during sex. It's not just an animal act. It's about two people making love" (4.4, "What's Sex Got to Do with It?"). This, in turn, allows her to have a deeper connection with her next love, Richard. He is the first man we ever see her say she loves. "I think I have monogamy," she says to the girls in 4.15, "Change of a Dress." "I must have caught it from you people." Later in the same episode, Richard tries to convince her "we're not the monotonous, [pretends to correct himself] monogamous kind," but a few episodes later, he says he wants them to be exclusive. Samantha gives him a painting of three hearts as a symbol that she has also given him *her* heart, "[b]ut just as she was opening herself up, she discover[s] him in a compromising position with another woman. Furious, Samantha smashe[s] the painting and shout[s], 'now your heart's broken too!'"[13]

By season 6, Samantha is ready for love again, although she doesn't yet know it. She meets hot model Smith Jerrod, whom she finds she likes spending time with. Fearing her own vulnerability, she tries to screw it up by sleeping with Richard but then admits she hates herself for doing it. Smith quickly forgives her. It is good timing because Samantha is about to experience her black moment: a diagnosis of breast cancer. As a woman who prides herself on her looks and raw sexuality, the low sex drive that comes with chemo is worse than the cancer itself. While her friends try to be there for her, it is Smith who ends up caring for her the most. Because he sees her at her worst, Samantha finally sheds her tough mask and allows herself to be vulnerable with Smith, transforming into the woman she was meant to be: "Suddenly, Samantha found herself holding hands, of all things, and liking every moment of it."[14]

WHAT DOES IT MEAN TO BE A SAMANTHA?

If you relate to Samantha, rejoice! You are a confident, powerful person who is true to herself, no matter what others may say or think. You may enjoy sex like she does, or you may not; while that is the outward manifestation of Samantha, that is not all of who she is. For her, sex is symbolic of a deep inner joy for life and an appreciation of all the beauty and pleasure it can bring. Keep being who you are, no matter what anyone else says, and don't be afraid to open your heart to love, at least once in a while, so that you experience the fullness of this thing called life.

5

CARRIE'S TWO BIG LOVES

Mr. Big and Aidan Shaw

"I fucking love you alright, you know I do. It's just a tough thing for me to say, because it always seems to get me in trouble when I say it."
— Mr. Big, episode 2.10, "The Caste System"

"I love you, Carrie. There's no one I could love more. I want to live my life with you."
— Aidan, episode 4.12, "Just Say Yes"

Throughout the six seasons of *Sex and the City*, Carrie Bradshaw vacillates between two men: the flashy, drama addict who breaks her heart over and over again and the steady, kind-hearted man who just wants to love her. "Each man represents both an attractive and limiting archetype that compels Carrie to reconsider her fantasies and ask herself: 'who is my Mr. Right?'" writes Di Mattia. "Carrie makes a huge investment in a sexually charged fantasy with Big while desiring the rescue fantasy offered by Aidan, creating a paradoxical dilemma that is ultimately irreconcilable. That Carrie repeatedly reconsiders Mr. Big's Mr. Right credential reveals her addiction to a romance that never ends."[1]

In watching these two storylines develop and Carrie question her fate, viewers questioned theirs, as well. Who would they pick? Who did they want Carrie to end up with? Like any good love story, this burning question kept them tuning in week after week. By looking at both men, we can see the two very different types of romance on offer in the show and learn about what drives Carrie to choose one over the other.

MR. BIG: THE MAN, THE MYTH, THE ICON

When fans don't even learn your real name (John James Preston) until the last moment of the final episode of the series yet women across the world are in love with you, you are officially a male icon. Introduced in the first episode as the "next big thing," Mr. Big would wear that moniker for all ninety-four episodes and grow into it more with each passing week. He is a bigshot—a corporate financier who once took "something like $3 million and leveraged it to build a $100 million building"—and he has the wealth to prove it. Owner of a large Upper East Side apartment and employing his own driver, he is certainly a catch. But add to it a handsome face and charming personality, and Mr. Big has "heartbreaker" written all over him.

Chris Noth played the billionaire boyfriend role of Mr. Big. Photofest/ *Sex and the City* (HBO), season 4 (fall 2001–winter 2003)

Everything he does is big. He doesn't just go out for a night on the town; he attends the opera, gallery exhibits, the ballet, the symphony, and all the right parties and fundraisers. He knows everyone who is anyone and can get a girl anything she desires, whether that is a ride home at 2 a.m. or a Tiffany bracelet. Referred to as a "major tycoon, major dreamboat, and majorly out of [Carrie's] league," he haunts every moment of the show, from his first appearance across the room from Samantha and Carrie to Carrie's last goofy, lovelorn smile as her phone rings while she walks down the street in Manhattan—even when he isn't on screen. Professor Imelda Whelehan of De Montfort University notes, "Even his name is masculine. He is like this phallus at the centre of it all."[2] Di Mattia theorizes that his nickname also suggests that this man is the "big love" of Carrie's life, but he will also be "big trouble."[3]

TOXIC MASCULINITY

Fine scotch, red wine, a thick steak, a Cuban cigar, Mr. Big: all symbols of luxury but also things that can slowly kill you. Like any good snake, Mr. Big is shiny and attractive on the outside but deadly when you get too close. Yet somehow he is so mesmerizing you can't quite get away. He has a darker side that both attracts and repels. A serial cheater, adulterer, and commitment-phobe, he's not exactly the one you bring home to mama.

Fairless and Garroni call him the "emotionally unavailable biz bro," which is a nice way of saying he will charm you into his bed but never let you into his heart, even while he is bleeding yours dry. They continue,

> This asshole is not for the faint of heart. . . . You will always fall hard for this man. The balance of power is distinctly in his favor, yet you were oddly intoxicated by this progressive dynamic. The more withholding he is, the deeper you will dig in for any semblance of heartfelt intimacy. It's a vicious, vicious cycle of emotional highs and lows that you willfully suffered through because your inner Charlotte is convinced things will work out. . . . Even when you break things off "the Big" has an uncanny ability to reappear at the exact moment you are ready to move on.[4]

Yet, women the world over couldn't get enough of him. Why is that? The short answer: We really like those bad boys.

If his type sounds familiar, it's because you've either dated him or nursed the broken heart of someone who has. Mr. Big is the classic "alpha male."

You know him without even having to open a book or turn on your TV. He's buff, rugged, and tall. His very presence oozes testosterone. In the past, he always held a supermasculine job, like a firefighter, police officer, or soldier; now the corporate billionaire has somewhat replaced his blue-color counter-part. One thing is certain: He wears the pants in the relationship and will be the provider and protector of his woman. According to Di Mattia, the alpha male is "characterized by spectacular masculinity. This spectacular, unrelenting masculinity suggests phallicism beyond the body: every aspect of his being, whether his body, his face, or his general demeanor is informed by the purity of his maleness. Almost everything about him is hard, angular and dark."[5]

And don't even think about trying to crack that well-muscled exterior to curl up in his heart unless you are willing to put in a lot of work—"he is emotionally rigid, complex, and needs a heroine to transform him into a more perfect model of Mr. Right."[6] It is that challenge, the idea of fixing this otherwise perfect man, that draws women to him. He's flawed, he's hurt, and we're going to be the one to make him all better, even though hundreds of women have failed in the past.

Romance readers and authors will draw a distinction between the tradi-tional alpha male and the type that has risen to popularity over the last thirty years: the alpha hole—and this is important when dissecting the character of Mr. Big. Romance blog *Romance Rehab* describes the alpha hole as a "curdled, sour blend of a regular alpha-male, and an asshole."[7] The main difference boils down to how they treat their women. *Romance Rehab* elabo-rates, "[The alpha male] might get a little jealous from time to time, but he's never disrespectful of his lady because he's just as protective of her heart as he is of her body. Alphas might not be the greatest verbal communicators in the world which can cause some frustration in their relationships, but they demonstrate their love clearly through their actions."[8]

Exactly. What does Big ever do for Carrie? (Other than jerk her around and break her heart multiple times.) Granted, she *is* really needy, but he rarely shows his affection for her through actions; gifts, including the gift of his time, are rare. He can't even be bothered to let her keep things at his place or tell her when he is moving—either time! Similarly, at a fancy Upper East Side party, Carrie has a conversation with an old friend that is misconstrued by the host, and without even letting Carrie explain, Big tells her, "You're embarrassing me" (2.10, "The Caste System"). These are not the actions of an alpha male but of an alpha hole.

In contrast, an alpha hole is controlling and obsessive, "will pursue the heroine with a single-minded determination that would be scary if it hap-pened in real life. He refuses to go away, even when she tells him to. He basically wears her down until she lets him into her life. . . . This guy runs super hot and cold, and can fly into a rage at any moment."[9] He also is a "little too focused on [his] own goals, and [doesn't] understand the true meaning of negotiation or compromise."[10]

Sound familiar? In seasons 3 and 4, Big never leaves Carrie alone, even when she tells him to. The fact that he repeatedly calls her when he knows she is in a serious relationship with Aidan is not only childish but also frightening. He even has the nerve to track Carrie down at Aidan's cabin to complain about his movie star girlfriend, gets drunk, and imposes himself on their hospitality. The story of his life is being hot and cold. He either can't get enough of her or is off to some other city with some other woman. He also focuses on himself throughout their whole relationship and never bothers to consult her or take her needs into account.

King justifies the toxic masculinity of characters like Big by saying they have to be equally "magnetic and powerful," because the female characters would never tolerate men they can walk all over. He continues, "We've always tried our best to keep the guys palpable and as present as the women. The guys have to be really worthwhile opponents. That's why there are stars playing them—because our girls are superstars."[11] The part about giving them equals is noble, but King seems to have mistaken "overbearing" for "magnetic."

BIG AND CARRIE: A MATCH MADE IN HELL

They say the course of true love never did run smooth, but when you mistake a toxic relationship for "the one," you're in for more than a few bumps; buckle up because you're about to get the whole roller coaster.[12] Nussbaum succinctly describes the relationship between Carrie and Big: "A man practically woven out of red flags, Big wasn't there to rescue Carrie; instead, his 'great love' was a slow poisoning."[13] But it is the one love affair she couldn't get out of because of the fairy-tale nature of the story. Alice Wignall, executive editor at *Elle UK*, explains,

> The "right" couple were signaled in the first episode [Carrie and Big,] and in some ways the entire show has just been about them getting together. . . . But this central relationship is clearly problematic. Mr. Big is arrogant, egocentric, and apparently unable to see a good thing when she is standing in front of him in four-inch heels. Carrie's own inability to wake up and realise what a terrible cliche she is dating renders her, at best, pretty dumb and, at worst, passive and weak.[14]

Let's take a look at how this "great love" unfolds and pick out those red flags when Carrie could have and should have gotten out, shall we?

Season 1

Despite at first appearing as Carrie's handsome prince to help her pick up her purse after they collide on the sidewalk and then again to give her a ride when she can't find a taxi, Big repeatedly shows he has no respect for Carrie or her time. On what was supposed to be their first date, a "drink thing," he brings a friend along without telling her, making her feel like a third wheel (1.4, "The Valley of the Twenty-Something Guys"). When they do have their first official date and end up having sex instead, he doesn't call her for several days (1.6, "Secret Sex"), and then she finds out he is dating other women (1.7, "The Monogamists"). But yet somehow, she is still fool enough to say, "I've been on the merry-go-round, through the revolving door, and I feel like I can stand still with you," whatever that means.

Carrie finally gets concerned when she finds out he's been married before and he tells her he doesn't want to get married again. He physically moves her off his lap when she tries to seduce him while he's trying to watch a sporting event on TV. If that isn't bad enough, he refuses to introduce her to his mother. Despite all this, Carrie tells him she loves him and asks Big to tell her she's the one. He can't, even though they have been dating for about a year, so she breaks up with him. Carrie should just let him go here—but she doesn't.

Season 2

When Carrie sees Big again for the first time post-breakup (2.1, "Take Me Out to the Ballgame"), she turns into a mess—which she does a lot around him and isn't exactly the sign of a healthy relationship. She and Big start seeing each other again in secret because she is too ashamed to tell her friends that she has gone back to him after all the heartache he put her through (2.6, "The Cheating Curve"). Once they are accidently outed, Carrie tries to leave some of her things at his apartment, but he literally won't make room for her. Not long after, he weasels out of meeting her friends, as though he's either ashamed to be seen with her in public or is afraid they will see him for the asshat he is (2.8, "The Man, the Myth, the Viagra"). He proves that he's a pig multiple times in episode 2.9, "Old Dogs, New Dicks," by looking at other women, evading Carrie's request for a key to his apartment so she can wait for him to come home without the neighbors watching, and literally pushes her off the bed in his sleep. "Each time Carrie looked for signs that Big felt strongly about her, he shimmied ever so slightly away," Sohn points out.[15]

But in Carrie's mind, it's fine. Everything is fine. She realizes that she loves him in the next episode. He gives her an ugly purse, and instead of saying, "Thank you," she accidently blurts, "I love you." Seemingly unfazed, he tells her she can return the purse if she doesn't like it. Later that night, when she sees all the other upscale women carrying purses by the same designer, she realizes Big thinks she is interchangeable with any one of them; he has no idea who she really is, which is why he bought her a purse that is totally not her (2.10, "The Caste System"). Yet two episodes later he tells her he loves her.

Yes, he loves her so much he doesn't tell her he may have to move to Paris for a year. Carrie breaks up with him and has two powerful realizations: (1) Big is terrified of being tied down, and (2) she is addicted to the pain of being with him. She does nothing about either. Instead, she becomes so obsessed with talking about Big that her friends think she needs to see a therapist.

Toward the end of the season, Carrie finds out that Big is back from Paris with his new girlfriend, Natasha, who is twenty-six (2.17, "20-Something Girls vs. 30-Something Women"), and in episode 2.18, "Ex and the City," she learns they are engaged. If Big loved Carrie so much, how did he immediately fall in love with someone new in Paris, especially enough to ask her to marry him, when he told Carrie in no uncertain terms that he didn't want to get married again? "The move likely wouldn't have been the end of their romance if he hadn't made it abundantly clear that he had no plans to factor her into his life," writes Andrea Francese. "The relationship ended when Mr. Big went to Paris. After he left the city, the duo had no contact until they ran into each other in the Hamptons. Mr. Big had his new girlfriend at his side. That moment, at the very least, should have signaled that things were never going to be right between them."[16] But Carrie never learns.

Season 3

Things are relatively quiet, and Carrie seems to have moved on from Big until she sees his wedding announcement in the *New York Times* (3.3, "Attack of the 5'10" Woman"). She accepts that he is married and starts dating Aidan. Just when she is happy, she starts to run into Big all over the place. Then he starts being a creeper and shows up unannounced at Carrie's apartment when

Aidan runs to the store, proving that he is watching them. She tells him to go home to his wife, and he tells her that it is over between them and he loves her, "exactly what she needed to hear a year too late" (3.8, "The Big Time").

Then he jerks her around by being on and off with his divorce until she starts sleeping with him again (3.9, "Easy Come, Easy Go"). For the next two episodes, Carrie tries to break off the affair, but Big won't let her, charming her back into bed each time and once even threatening to come up to her apartment when he knows Aidan is there. Charlotte finds out about the affair, and Carrie realizes she can't keep meeting Big in hotels, so she breaks it off for the third time (3.10, "All or Nothing," and 3.11, "Running with Scissors").

Once again, just as Carrie seems to be moving on and is happy with Aidan, she finds out that Natasha has left Big and his marriage is over (3.17, "What Goes around Comes Around"). Francese explains, "Carrie should have cut all contact with her big love when she left him in the emergency room where Natasha was getting stitches. Natasha needed to visit the hospital after she caught Carrie in the apartment she shared with her then-husband."[17] Carrie has ample opportunity, but instead she just stands in the doorway, giving him chance after chance to make things right, which, of course, he doesn't.

Season 4

Carrie hasn't learned anything. Now that she knows that Big is available again, she can't stop thinking about him, even calling him at midnight on her birthday (4.1, "The Agony and the 'Ex'tacy"). When her friends end up missing her birthday party due to traffic, it isn't their impromptu coffee get-together after that makes up for it but Big sitting outside her apartment in his limo like a stalker with red balloons and champagne.

Carrie dates other people, the first of whom is Ray King, a jazz musician she meets while out for a "friends night" with Big (4.3, "Defining Moments"). Over the next two episodes, Big proceeds to insert himself into their relationship in any way he can to try to keep the two apart. "He even went so far as to join them in their cab ride home to further cockblock her and assert his control. . . . [I]t's just creepy. He didn't want her when they were together, then strung her along for years and prevented her from moving on," notes *Newsweek* journalist Emma Clarke.[18] Most women would have kicked him to the curb for such ludicrous behavior, but no, Carrie just keeps on taking it.

Things get even stranger—and more frightening—from there. Big keeps calling her like some obsessed high school crush or a psychopath, insisting on talking to her and meeting with her even when he knows Aidan is there. And she keeps doing exactly what he wants—classic behavior for someone who is being emotionally manipulated and abused. Big's calling and then coming to visit her at Aidan's cabin (4.10, "Belles of the Balls") should have been the last straw, if not for Carrie, then for Aidan, but Aidan is too nice, and she isn't strong enough to stand up to Big. Inexplicably, Big and Aidan end up as friends after beating the hell out of each other.

When Carrie tells Big she thinks Aidan is going to propose, instead of pretending to be happy for her and support her, as a normal person would do, even if he doesn't feel it, Big harshly tells Carrie that her marriage to Aidan is "never gonna happen" because she's "not the marrying kind." Besides being mean, this statement undermines Carrie's confidence, which is exactly what Big wants to do (4.12, "Just Say Yes").

Totally whipped, when Carrie needs money to buy her apartment after breaking up with Aidan, the first person she goes to after the bank turns her down for a loan is Big (4.16, "Ring a Ding Ding"). Though she doesn't ultimately end up taking the money he offers, this shows just how dependent on him she has become. Two episodes later, after waxing poetic about how safe she feels with Big (no, honey, it's not him; it's just that you are the kind of woman who needs a man at all times), he tells her he's moving to Napa, California (4.18, "I Heart NY"). Again, this is a perfect chance to end this abusive, codependent mess of a relationship, but instead of just parting as friends, Big leaves her plane tickets to Napa in case she gets lonely. What he's really doing is encouraging her to hang onto him, which she does.

Big's tendency to slip back in when least expected makes him as addictive to the viewers as he is to Carrie. By the end of the fourth season, some fans felt he had returned too many times, while others wanted him to stay for good. According to co-executive producer Cindy Chupack, "in those last episodes of season 2, he became so charming. Chris and Sarah Jessica had such good chemistry that no matter what we wrote or how much of a cad we wanted to make him or how impossible we wanted that relationship to seem, I would always think, 'how do we pull these two apart?'"[19]

Season 5

Just when we think we might get a Big-free season, Carrie's publicists send her to San Francisco for a book tour. Of course, Carrie isn't concerned about the thing that is making her money and paying for all those shoes—her book—but is obsessing yet again over Big. When he ends up in the audience at one of her book signings, she thinks she has it made. But then . . .

Big has read the book and now completely understands how bad he was to her. We're supposed to believe that he was so shocked by what he read (Didn't he read her columns before? Real supportive, dude) that he changed and grew as a man overnight. Now he's so much more sensitive to her needs that he worries about hurting her again. He understands perfectly well that Carrie "remains wedded to a belief that [he] will change for her," so that's what he does . . . kind of.[20] Master manipulator that he is, he protests just the right amount to keep her ensnared, even while he is away.

Season 6

Big is now clearly so bad for Carrie that the writers "had to introduce the likes of Jack Berger and Aleksandr Petrovsky . . . just to make Big seem half-decent in comparison and have fans rooting for him when he went to Paris to 'get our girl' in the final episode," writes Clarke.[21] The final season kicks off with Big and Carrie having occasional phone sex, but as things get more serious with Berger, she calls Big to "clear up the past" (6.3, "The Perfect Present") and then again to let Big know they are on a break (6.6, "Hop, Skip and a Week").

After Carrie and Berger break up, Big shows up in New York with the news that he needs to have an angioplasty, which sends Carrie into fits of weeping, even though it is a routine procedure. She visits him in the hospital and at home and nurses him back to health. Delirious with fever, he asks Carrie, "What are we doing? Life's too short. What are we doing?" That night, as she watches him sleep, she thinks, "Big's heart was finally unblocked; in fact, it was wide open." But by morning it has closed again, and that isn't enough for her (6.11, "The Domino Effect").

Later, when Carrie is dating Aleksandr, as if he can sense that they are happy, Big leaves three messages on Carrie's machine, all of which she deletes without calling him back (6.17, "The Cold War"). When she doesn't return his calls, he travels to New York and camps out in his limo outside her building. On her way to her farewell dinner with the girls, Carrie gets into the car to see what he wants. He apologizes for shutting down on her after the surgery, but Carrie won't let him say anything else. She tells him she is leaving for Paris in the morning and says goodbye.

Frightened by her sudden farewell, Big follows her out onto the street and asks when she was going to tell him she was leaving. There's a pregnant pause in which the viewer can practically hear her mentally yelling at him, "So how does it feel?" For the first time ever, Carrie realizes he's about to mess things up yet again and finds the strength to tell him off:

CARRIE: You do this every time! Every time! What, do you have, some kind of radar? "Carrie might be happy, so it's time to sweep in and shit all over it?"
BIG: What? No, no, look, I came here to tell you something. I made a mistake. You and I—
CARRIE: You and I nothing! You cannot do this to me again. You cannot jerk me around!
BIG: Carrie, listen. It's different.
CARRIE: It's never different! It's six years of never being different.
BIG: But this is.
CARRIE: I am done! Don't call me ever again! Forget you know my number! In fact, forget you know my name!

Several weeks later, while Carrie is lonely in Paris and thinking of Big, he meets with Miranda, Charlotte, and Samantha and lays out his case. He admits he "fucked it up—many times." He repeats that he loves Carrie, and if they think he has the slightest chance, then he'll be on the next flight to Paris, will roam the streets until he finds her. But if they think she is really happy, then he doesn't want to wreck that for her, and he'll be history. The ladies are all quiet, but then Miranda responds, "Go get our girl!" (6.19, "An American Girl in Paris, Part Une").

When Carrie is running from the museum to the party being thrown by the booksellers, Big is right behind her in a car, but the two don't see one another. It's not until Carrie has left Aleksandr that Big finds her in the lobby of her hotel, picking diamonds from her broken necklace out of her gown. She spots him, and they run into each other's arms. She tells him Paris is a mess and she shouldn't have come and accidently mentions that Aleksandr slapped her. This sends Big into a rage, and he charges up the stairs in full alpha mode, determined to punch Aleksandr. Carrie trails on his heels yelling, "I don't need you to rescue me. I took care of it myself." She trips him to stop him, and they both fall and giggle. Outside the hotel, he looks deep into her eyes and says what she wanted him to say at the end of season 1: "It took me a really long time to get here, but I'm here. Carrie, you're the one." They kiss, and she responds, "I miss New York. Take me home."

Once they make it back to Carrie's apartment in Manhattan in the middle of the night, Big reminds her he has nowhere to go because he lives in California, and the Four Seasons won't check people in at that hour. She asks if he wants to come up, and he responds with his classic line,

"Abso-fucking-lutely." The next day, we see her walking down the street, and her phone rings. Big's first name is finally revealed on her caller ID: John. He is calling to tell her his Napa house is on the market and he's on his way to New York. He's finally gotten her on his timeline. All's well that ends well.

AIDAN SHAW: THE HEART OF GOLD

Can the good guy ever win? This is the question posed by Aidan Shaw's character when he and Carrie meet in season 3. In opposition to Mr. Big, who can almost literally fly women to the moon, Aidan is more of a typical man. He has a steady job as a carpenter and furniture designer, so he's not hurting for money, and he is kind, caring, and patient with Carrie's commitment issues. He's the kind of guy who wants to settle down and have a family.

John Corbett played Carrie's second-biggest love, Aidan Shaw. Photofest/*Sex and the City* (HBO), season 4 (summer 2001)

A "stable contrast to the elusive Mr. Big," Aidan should be everything Carrie wants and needs.[22] He's the "embodiment of a good boyfriend, the one every girl wishes she had," writes Sohn.[23] He's accessible, where Big is only available to Carrie on his own terms; loyal, where Big has a wandering eye and a propensity to cheat; and devoted, where Big doesn't give his heart to anyone but himself. Star describes Aidan as a man who is "incredibly down to earth, and who was all about heart and not about anything superficial."[24]

Also unlike Mr. Big, Aidan doesn't have any time for drama, but he has all the time in the world for romance. The man can cook, and he draws Carrie a candle-lit bubble bath, for Christ's sake! He even waits to have sex with her because he wants it to be special. While she is having panic attacks over "nothing being wrong" in their relationship, he is trying to teach her how to remember romance before Big came into her life and tainted her view of what relationships should be.

Aidan will also happily "make room in his life" for his girl, going on dates with her and hanging out with her, something that Carrie, so used to being isolated by Big, considers smothering rather than normal.

AIDAN: THE ROMANTIC BETA MALE

If Mr. Big is the alpha male or alpha hole, then Aidan is a beta male. Rather than being seen as second best or some kind of wimp in comparison, the beta male should be seen as evolved. Amanda Diehl for Bookriot describes a beta male as a

> more mild-mannered type of hero. No bursts of unwarranted jealousy from these guys. For the most part, they've got their stuff together, and their relationship with the heroine is more complementary instead of built on constant conflict. Betas are comfortable with themselves and where the heroine is at in her life. They're just sweet, considerate guys who you want to bring home to mom and dad.[25]

Sound like Aidan or what? Di Mattia calls him the "archetypal postfeminist fantasy of masculinity: a reconfigured fantasy mixing the traditional phallic hero with a sensitive new man," and Isbister says he is the "contemporary Prince Charming—the more available, sensitive nascent feminist man."[26]

In many ways, Aidan is too good to be true. "He was devoted and crazy about [Carrie], calling her 'nuts' and 'love bird.' When she confessed she had

had an abortion, he didn't judge her. Carrie couldn't help but love someone who loved her unconditionally, and at times it was impossible not to envy her for having landed such a generous, caring man," Sohn writes.[27] Aidan is the ultimate knight in shining armor, there to rescue not only Carrie but her friends, as well. When her computer crashes, he buys her a new one, along with a zip drive to back it up; when Miranda hurts her neck but Carrie can't go to her because of a meeting, he takes charge; when Carrie finds out her building is going co-op, Aidan comes up with the idea to buy the unit next door and make them into one big space for both of them; plus, he is there as moral support when she needs it, like at Miranda's mother's funeral.[28]

However, Aidan takes his beta qualities too far over time, until he becomes a pushover, allowing Carrie to get away with her abusive side fling with Big too many times. He's just too nice, too tolerant, too in love with her. The prime example is when Big keeps bothering them. Most men would tell him (with a shove, if needed) to back the hell off, but Aidan just takes it like a puppy who is used to being abused. You would think that when Big calls the cabin, or at least when he shows up, Aidan would yell and tell him to go back to the city where he belongs. But no, he lets Big and Carrie talk and offers his couch when Big gets drunk. That is just too much for any real man, no matter how beta.

AIDAN AND CARRIE: A HEAVEN THAT JUST WASN'T ENOUGH

As with Carrie's relationship with Big, looking at her relationship with Aidan shows us all the opportunities Aidan has to get out but doesn't take. Carrie and Aidan meet when Stanford takes her furniture shopping. Sparks fly, and they go out, but Aidan backs out when he finds out she is a smoker (3.5, "No Ifs, Ands, or Butts"). This is his first opportunity to get out, and he takes it, but she surprises him. At first, Carrie is only disappointed, but the more she thinks about it, the more she realizes she wants to see where this might go, so she quits—or at least tries to. She has to wear the patch and sneak a few illicit smokes before she gets the hang of it, but Aidan is worth it. Too bad there is no patch for Big.

As their relationship progresses, Carrie is eager to have sex with Aidan, but he holds her off with romantic gestures, like that bubble bath and introducing her to his parents. Carrie freaks out at the prospect of meeting them and tells Miranda that Aidan is acting just like she wanted Big to, but now *she's* acting like Big. When the meeting goes well, and her relationship with Aidan is cemented by sex, Carrie starts waking up in the middle of the night, gasping for air, only to discover it is not because something is wrong but rather that everything is too right; she's addicted to the drama she was used to with Big, and without it, she's in withdrawal (3.7, "Drama Queens").

With Carrie already insecure, it is not good timing that she keeps running into Big. To make matters worse, he tells her that he's leaving Natasha (3.9, "Easy Come, Easy Go"). From this point on, Carrie is never comfortable in her relationship with Aidan again because that little voice in the back of her head keeps whispering that Big is available. Everything Aidan does starts to annoy her. "The more devoted Aidan acted, the more restless Carrie became (in typical New York neurotic style), until she finally started sleeping with Big again" (3.10, "All or Nothing"), repeatedly—all the while knowing she already has a perfect man at home.[29]

Eventually, Carrie feels so guilty that she has to confess. Unfortunately, she does so right before Charlotte's wedding, ruining the day for both Aidan and herself and breaking his heart. She tries to have her cake and eat it too by asking if he can forgive her, if whether her cheating can just be like a flaw in wood, but he says no: "I just know myself. This isn't the kind of thing that I can get over." And so they break up (3.12 "Don't Ask, Don't Tell").

Although Carrie runs into Aidan a few times on the street, they both appear to have moved on until they go on an ill-advised double friend date with Miranda and Steve (4.6, "Baby, Talk Is Cheap"). They part as friends, but later that night an obsessive Carrie throws rocks at his window and asks him if they can work things out. Despite yelling, "You broke my heart," Aidan gets back together with her the next day.

And you guessed it: Big is conveniently back, which he decides to announce to her answering machine while she and Aidan are having sex (4.7, "Time and Punishment"). This makes Aidan worry that Carrie and Big are going to get back together, and Carrie fears Aidan is going to cheat on her in revenge for her affair with Big. The trust between them is too frayed to continue, so they break up briefly but are back together by the end of the episode.

By now they have exchanged keys, and Aidan is practically living with Carrie. But Big is still calling, and when he comes to the cabin, they have their fisticuffs and then are friends (4.10, "Belles of the Balls"). Soon enough, Carrie's building goes co-op, so she and Aidan decide to move in together. Carrie finds an engagement ring in Aidan's bag and throws up—that is how unsure she is about their relationship lasting long term. By the end of the episode, he proposes, and she says yes, not because she really wants to, but, as she says later, "because that's what you do" (4.12, "Just Say Yes").

Trapped in an engagement she doesn't really want, Carrie does every-thing she can to signal her unhappiness without saying it, including oddly, taking off her engagement ring and wearing it on a chain around her neck so it can "be closer to her heart." If Aidan doesn't buy that excuse, he doesn't say anything. But they do fight when he asks her to make space in her closet—remember that it is symbolic of her identity—for him (4.13, "The Good Fight").

They make up, but for Carrie, the unwanted pressure is mounting. Aidan keeps dropping hints about the wedding, and Carrie can't take it. She asks him for more time, which he originally grants, but he soon runs out of pa-tience and gives Carrie the ultimatum she's needed all along: Marry him, or they are done (4.15, "Change of a Dress"). She can't commit to him.

Di Mattia writes that

> when Carrie and Aidan part for a second time, the inconsistencies between the two romantic quests—one toward marriage and happily ever after [Aidan], the other caught up in the ecstasy of pure romance [Big]—are transparent. Ultimately, Aidan offers a closure to romance that Carrie finds fundamentally disappointing, and in spite of her feminist proclivities, she wants that sexy feeling she learned to love with Big.[30]

In many ways, Aidan and Carrie's behavior in their relationships is the same. While neither are true victims (though Carrie thinks she is), neither have the spine to stand up to or for the person they truly love. Both keep taking punches from their abuser because they love them. While relation-ships are certainly about compromise, there is a point when working with your partner turns into losing yourself, and rather than being an example of selflessness, both become sad examples of misplaced devotion.

In not marrying Aidan, Carrie is essentially choosing Big, with all his paradoxes and drama, over Aidan's surety of a happily ever after. Because it's not *her* happily ever after. That can only be found in the uncertainty of life with Big, a flip-flopping stomach, a feeling she would later call "zsa, zsa, zsu." In the end, all that is left is Carrie's obsession with Big and his manipulation of her. Toxic for toxic. Maybe Carrie and Big do deserve one another, after all.

6

ALEKSANDR

Too Good to Be True

"How can you people still have questions? I got all of your questions answered. And they were good answers by the way."
                                        —Aleksandr, episode 6.18, "Splat!"

Carrie Bradshaw certainly has a type: older, handsome, rich, dark-haired, and controlling. In coupling with artist Aleksandr Petrovsky, she shows the same need for safety and protection that she has sought in her major loves throughout the series, but this time with an alarming willingness to submit to his will and sacrifice her very self for the man she loves and the drama she is so addicted to. If Big is toxic, then Aleksandr is downright radioactive.

Although only in Carrie's life for the final season, Aleksandr makes a big impression, perhaps because he is, on the surface, everything Carrie should want. He's cultured, wealthy, successful, creative, and an international jet-setter. He is bigger than even Mr. Big and far more manipulative. Fairless and Garroni call him like they see him: "Despite his bohemian qualities, Petrovsky is a control freak through and through."[1]

LOVE OR EMOTIONAL ABUSE?

Aleksandr comes into Carrie's life in the unlikeliest of ways. She is seeing a performance artist at a Chelsea gallery who is refusing to speak, eat, or sleep for sixteen days in order to change the vibration of the world. Unable to contain their laughter at the absurdity of the situation, she and Charlotte giggle, attracting the attention of a handsome older man Carrie noticed staring at her earlier.

Charlotte, as an art expert, recognizes him right away as a famous artist and introduces herself, fawning all over him in gratitude for his contribution

Mikhail Baryshnikov played aloof artist Aleksandr Petrovsky, whom Carrie dates and nearly loses her identity to in season 6. Photofest/*Sex and the City* (HBO), season 6 (summer 2003–winter 2004)

to both the art world at large and her own career. Aleksandr has no time for her; he is more interested in her companion, who cannot take the artist's performance seriously, joking that if they came back at 3 a.m. she would likely be around the corner eating a Big Mac instead of sitting at the 24/7 installation like she should be. Both confused and intrigued by this strange "comic," as he calls her, Aleksandr decides to see if Carrie is correct and arranges to meet her for dinner at 1 a.m. so they have time before checking on the artist. Carrie is intrigued by him, as well, though she has a hard time understanding his accent, so she shows up to the odd dinner date.

That's when the red flags begin to appear, but Carrie may as well be color-blind. As soon as she arrives, he informs her she is three minutes late. He shows her to a table already laden with a meal he has chosen—thus depriving her of making her own decision—and corrects her pronunciation of his name way more times than is necessary or polite. Already, he is reluctant to speak of his work or engage in conversation any more than is necessary (6.12, "One").

Of course, Carrie would be attracted to him. As we've seen, she's like a magnet when it comes to men who exude emotional unavailability, intensity, and the promise of heartache. Carrie doesn't hear from him for three weeks after their date, so she is shocked to receive a formal invitation on stationery inviting her to go for a walk. On that second date, Carrie finds out that, like Big and his business trips, Aleksandr couldn't be bothered to tell her he was going to be out of the country, even though he had her phone number.

Having learned a little something from her past heartaches, Carrie decides to make this a sex-only relationship, which Aleksandr seems fine with. When she wakes the next morning, she is wearing a sparkling necklace instead of her trademark "Carrie" nameplate, a sign that she is already losing her identity. (She won't be seen wearing her Carrie necklace again until the very end of the final episode.) Perhaps in an effort to make it easier to separate her head from her heart, Carrie starts calling him "the Russian," a name that sticks even after she realizes she can't do just casual sex with this man (6.13, "Let There Be Light").

By the following episode (6.14, "The Ick Factor"), Aleksandr is plying Carrie with European romance by reading her poetry in front of a roaring fire in the deep freeze of winter and gifting her with designer gowns from his famous friends. Carrie is not comfortable with this level of wooing but refuses to tell Aleksandr. This is the second sign that Aleksandr's form of love might be more abusive than it is caring. According to *Psychology Today*, "intense romance can be a form of grooming, a predatory tactic that is meant to build a deep emotional connection."[2]

As it does when Carrie sees the wedding ring from Aidan and when she puts on the wedding dress, Carrie's body betrays her, this time by causing her to faint outside the opera. Instead of attending as Aleksandr has commanded (not asked), they end up at McDonald's, where he is clearly uncomfortable but Carrie is happy as a lark. She successfully avoids an evening in his world by pulling him into hers.

But he's not all bad. In episode 6.15, "Catch-38," Carrie is splitting babysitting duty with Charlotte while Miranda is on her honeymoon. Much to Carrie's surprise, Aleksandr tells her to bring Brady over and shocks her by being good with children. But there is a reason for that: He had a child and a wife long ago and has no desire for more children; to ensure this, he has even had a vasectomy and refuses to even consider getting it reversed. He lays it out very plainly that if children are something Carrie desires, then he will let her go rather than deprive her of the joys of parenthood, but he is too old to have more children. Once again, Carrie faces a situation where it is Aleksandr's way or none; he has spelled out her future in such a way that she has to follow his will if she wants to stay with him.

Carrie decides to roll the dice with the Russian, and he begins to woo her with a storybook-like ardor that includes grand romantic gestures and adventures in parts of the city even this dyed-in-the-wool New Yorker hasn't experienced. In that way, he is beginning to open "Carrie's world in ways she never could have imagined."[3] During their conversations, though, it becomes increasingly clear that they are a case of "opposites attract." She is the light to his dark and the joy to his pessimism. At one point she tells him, "I need my relationship with a little bit of milk," meaning she can't take his Russian bleakness without a bit of levity (6.16, "Out of the Frying Pan").

The longer she is with him, the more Carrie realizes that Aleksandr lives two separate lives: one with his work and his art friends and one with her. And although he has introduced her to some of his art colleagues, she still feels shut out from his real life. So she tries to invite him into hers by planning a drinks night with the girls, whom she has been ignoring in favor of spending time with Aleksandr (6.17, "The Cold War"). He ends up not being able to make it due to some kind of art emergency but sends the ladies a bottle of champagne by way of apology. Later, they show up at his apartment/studio drunk, and he says to Carrie very coldly, "When I say I'm working, I'm working" (i.e., "Leave me the hell alone").

These two things—the isolation and his temper—are significant because they are ways in which abusers groom their victims to tolerate their abuse: "These are the weapons of coercive control . . . [which] strips away their independence, sense of self, and basic rights, such as the right to make decisions about their own time, friends, and appearance."[4] This idea becomes increasingly important as Aleksandr prepares to whisk Carrie away to Paris.

THE PARIS AFFAIR

If *Sex and the City* is a fairy tale, then Carrie's time in Paris is the "underbelly of the fairy tale, written as though the Ugly Stepsisters were allowed to finish Cinderella's tale."[5] It all starts out innocently enough, as these things usually do, with Carrie and Aleksandr preparing for the dinner party that will make up for his rude treatment of her friends. Just a few minutes before their guests are due to arrive, Aleksandr invites Carrie to Paris—not just for his show but to live for as long as they like. She would quit her job, and he would pay for her apartment in New York so she wouldn't have to worry about that. She would be a totally kept woman.

Before Carrie has a chance to react, the ladies and their dates arrive, cutting off any discussion. It quickly becomes clear that Aleksandr doesn't approve of Carrie's friends, with their lowbrow talk of Billy Joel, vibrators, and how they don't like Paris. When Charlotte, seeking to shift the conversation to a safer subject, asks about his sculptures, he quickly corrects her that they are not sculptures. Carrie quickly explains in a Stepford-like tone that indicates she has had the information drilled into her that they are "large-scale light installations integrated with video imaging." Her friends exchange worried looks because that reply did not come from the Carrie they know and love.

The subject of Paris comes up, and Aleksandr informs them that Carrie is moving with him, even though they haven't discussed it, nor has she made a decision. Naturally, her friends have a million questions, so Aleksandr allows the girls to take a tour of his apartment and talk, while the men gather for a drink. As soon as they are alone, Charlotte, Samantha, and Miranda pepper Carrie with questions like "What about your job?" and "How long will you be gone?" none of which she has any answers to.

Carrie relays her friends' questions to Aleksandr, who answers what he can, but he quickly grows annoyed that no matter what he says, she always has more questions. He asks, "Why are you always asking everyone else? What do you want? Think for yourself. You make the choices. Don't ask everyone else." There is a great deal of irony there because he is not allowing her to think for herself or make her own choices; he's always subtly manipulating things so that she will "choose" what he wants her to. It is telling that Carrie's final question for her column—there are no questions in the last two episodes—is "Is it time to stop questioning?" After looking at what she wrote for a moment, Carrie changes the question mark to a period, telling herself it is time to stop questioning.

Miranda is the only one brave enough to speak up and voice her dislike of Aleksandr. Though she doesn't mention it to Carrie, she told Steve after the dinner party that she was concerned about Carrie: "It's how she is around him. She's different and not in a good way. She didn't laugh all night—not once." She asks Carrie not to go to Paris, pointing out that she will have no job and no friends and doesn't speak the language, so she will be totally dependent on Aleksandr there, but Carrie doesn't want to hear her objections.

After attending a party where Lexi Featherston, a former friend and single woman over forty, falls to her death from a window, Carrie realizes Aleksandr might be her last chance of not ending up like Lexi, so she decides to go to Paris. "Carrie has never met anyone like Petrovsky, and with him she feels she can go anywhere and do anything," writes Sohn. "She gets swept away by him—his life, his opportunities, and his ideas of the world. She thinks, 'we'll go to Paris, will experience Europe, art, food, wine, and literature. New York is a hometown, just a little place to come back to.'"[6]

It is only Miranda, her best friend, who can see the danger Carrie is walking into. When Carrie informs them she is moving, Miranda asks,

"Why? Because you're afraid of going out a window [like Lexi]?" Carrie responds, "I can stay here and *write* about my life, or I can go with him and *live* my life." Miranda is quick to correct her: "You mean *his* life. You're living in a fantasy." But no amount of rationalizing with her will sway Carrie. She is determined to go (6.18, "Splat!").

IDENTITY LOST AND FOUND . . .

Carrie arrives in Paris under the dreamy impression that she is going to spend all her time with Aleksandr, but when she finds him in the hotel salon with his daughter, Chloe, he quickly disabuses her of that notion. He's going to spend the day with his daughter, then meet with some work people for a light dinner, and they can go out afterward. (Read: You are my last priority and always will be. Work comes first, then family, then you.)

Carrie is understandably disappointed, but her spirits are buoyed by the sight of her grand hotel room and its spectacular view of the Eiffel Tower. She puts on a beautiful designer ballgown, one just like a princess in a fairy tale would wear, and waits for her prince to come. But ten hours later, he is still not there and she, like Sleeping Beauty, has succumbed to sleep. When Aleksandr wakes her, she asks why he didn't at least call her, and he said he did, but she had "do not disturb" set on her phone. She doesn't recall this but takes his word for it. While she could just be fuzzy-headed from sleep, he could also be gaslighting her so he doesn't appear in the wrong.

After a week of waiting around for Aleksandr, only to be disappointed, Carrie decides to spend a rainy day shopping at Dior. However, when she takes down her umbrella, she unwittingly creates a puddle on the floor. With her next step, she slips and goes sprawling face first across the floor. In a much more dramatic replication of her fall on the sidewalk in the first episode, the contents of her purse go flying and a half-dozen sales associates have to help her pick them up.

That night, Carrie realizes her "Carrie" necklace—the symbol of her identity—is missing and assumes she lost it in the fall. The next day, she walks through Paris, thinking of what it would be like to be there with Big. Her eyes alight on a foursome of women, and she is suddenly homesick for her friends, so she calls Miranda from a pay phone. In true Carrie fashion, she doesn't ask how Miranda and the others are but proceeds to complain about her missing necklace and being lonely. "I'm just sort of lost," she says. Miranda tells her to come home, but Carrie insists she will be fine.

That night, Aleksandr surprises Carrie with a gift. She opens the jewelry box to find a thin gold chain with a string of diamonds threaded on to it. He says he knows it is not the same, but it is meant to replace the one she lost. While on the surface this is a kind gesture, it is yet another way Aleksandr is replacing Carrie's true identity with one more to his tastes, one that suits his world. Aleksandr's friends interrupt this rare quiet moment for the couple, sitting down and speaking in rapid French, with no one noticing or caring that Carrie needs a translator. Yet again, she is trapped in a situation she can't get out of and is all alone, in spite of being surrounded by her boyfriend and several people (6.19, "An American Girl in Paris, Part Une").

During her second week in Paris, Aleksandr arranges for himself and Carrie to have lunch with his ex-wife, Juliet. Not surprisingly, there is a crisis at the museum, and Aleksandr can't join them after all. This might be the very thing that saves Carrie because it gives her and Juliet time to speak openly. Upon hearing that Aleksandr isn't coming, Juliet sighs and says, "Nothing else exists when art does." She goes on to tell Carrie that when they were married, he was constantly telling her that he would have more time for her as soon as this or that happened, but it never did. She always came in second to his art, and he was never supportive of her work. "I believe a relationship is like couture; if it doesn't fit perfectly, it's a disaster," she says.

Over the next few days, Carrie spends nearly all her time alone, walking through the streets of Paris. By the time Aleksandr gets back to the room, she is always asleep. One day, Carrie walks past a bookshop and sees a French copy of her book in the window. She goes inside to look at it and is recognized by a few of the people working there, who are huge fans. They offer to throw her a book party that weekend, and she accepts. That night, she asks Aleksandr if he wants to come along, but of course, he can't. The museum curator is getting his first look at the art that night.

The night of the party comes, and Carrie is just about to leave, when she notices Aleksandr is having an anxiety attack over the curator seeing his work that night. "What if they think I am the old man with the light machines?" he asks plaintively. In the ultimate act of devaluing her as a person and putting himself first, he asks Carrie to come with him instead of going to her party. She stupidly agrees, yet again putting her man's needs ahead of her own.

When they get there, Aleksandr makes Carrie promise not to let go of his hand all night, as though he really needs her moral support. But as soon as the curator calls him a genius, he lets go and leaves her behind to pass the night sitting on a bench. "In some ways Carrie gives up her life for Petrovsky," writes Sohn. "As big as their love was, Carrie had lost a piece of herself along the way. The more time they spent together, the clearer it became that Carrie had compromised her life for his, and was losing her identity as a writer, a New Yorker, and an independent woman."[7]

While fumbling in her purse for a smoke, Carrie finds her necklace caught in its ripped lining. She has had it all along. Inspired, she decides to go to her own party. But she has waited too long; by the time she gets there, the party is over, and all that remains is the detritus of the meal and a copy of her book with wine stains on the cover—a visual "fuck you" from the bookstore staff for not showing up.

More confident now and livid that she let Aleksandr make her miss a party thrown in her honor, Carrie confronts him about abandoning her in the museum. He tells her he is tired and doesn't want to fight because he's had a stressful day—it's all about him as usual. Carrie tries to explain, and he cuts her off: "This is who I am. You always knew this." Then he tells her that he's going to take a shower and go to bed. Carrie reaches to stop him, and as he turns, he accidently hits her, and in the process, his hold over her—as well as the necklace he gave her—breaks. He apologizes, saying, "I thought I was clear all along about who I am."

Carrie's response reveals that after ninety-four episodes of searching, she finally knows who she is: "Well, maybe it is time to be clear about who *I* am. I am someone who is looking for love, real love, ridiculous, inconvenient, consuming, can't-live-without-each-other love. And I don't think that love is here in this expensive suite in this lovely hotel in Paris. It's not your fault. It's my fault. I shouldn't have come here." With that, she kisses him and goes down to the lobby to try to get another room, one only for her. And that is when Big finds her.

Once their reunion is complete and Big has declared his love, Carrie responds in an odd way. Instead of telling him she loves him back, she says, "I miss New York. Take me home," as in "Take me back to my one true home, Manhattan." She is done with Aleksandr's world and ready to get back to her own.

. . . AND LOST AGAIN?

Depending on how you feel about Mr. Big and the authenticity of his transformation, Carrie's story could end one of two ways. If you believe his love is genuine and that Carrie really does find her true self in Paris, then this is the happy ending you were waiting for. However, if you believe that Mr. Big will always be a manipulative jerk and that Carrie still lacks the willpower to withstand his negative influence on her, then she is stepping out of one nightmare and into another.[8]

7

THE OTHER GIRLS' MEN

"Somewhere out there is another little freak who will love us and understand us and kiss our three heads and make it all better."

—Carrie, episode 2.3, "The Freak Show"

They say we all have to kiss a few frogs before we find our Prince Charming. That is certainly true for the ladies of *Sex and the City*. While Carrie is the main character and her love story takes precedence over the others, Carrie's men aren't the only ones who matter. By looking at the men who break the hearts of Miranda, Charlotte, and Samantha (the misses) as well as those who mended them (the hits), we get a better insight into the ladies and what they really need.

MIRANDA

Miss 1: Skipper Johnston

Carrie introduces Miranda and Skipper, who resembles Napoleon Dynamite's older brother, with his tightly curled blond hair and glasses, in the first episode (1.1, "Sex and the City") after hearing that he hasn't had sex in the unthinkably long time of a year. Miranda doesn't like him, insists on calling him "Skippy," and is about to walk away when he kisses her. That must have been some kiss because they end up in bed together.

Skipper becomes obsessed with her, but Miranda's not having it. Then he dates someone else, and apparently that is enough to make Miranda jealous because she calls him and he comes running immediately—as in he doesn't even stop having sex with his girlfriend before he breaks up with her—to do Miranda's bidding. They are on again/off again for a while (1.12, "Oh Come All Ye Faithful"), and then he disappears until Miranda runs into him again in episode 2.14, "The Fuck Buddy." That's when she realizes she has a type:

angry and bitter, which Skipper is because girls keep breaking up with him, so she sleeps with him yet again. And that is the last we see of him.

No one seems to know what happens to Skipper, even Susan Seidelman, who directed the show's pilot and two other early episodes. "I thought Skipper was adorable," she said. "He was a really nice counterpoint to Miranda's no-nonsense behavior, him being so romantic and such a cuddly, teddy-bear kind of guy. Maybe [the writers] felt like that was not a relationship that was going to last too long because they were so different. . . . I don't know!" She also theorizes that he was written off as the show found its legs.[1]

Why he's a frog: Skipper gives all romantic men a bad name. First, he's a dweeb, which makes it seem like all romantic men are weak. Second, he's definitely not the model of mental health. Who breaks up with a woman "while he's still inside of her" (1.7, "The Monogamists")? Miranda is better off without him.

Miss 2: Dr. Robert Leeds

Miranda meets handsome Dr. Robert Leeds when he applies to buy an apartment in her building and she is on the co-op board (6.9, "A Woman's Right to Shoes"). The two hit it off right away and before long are doing the predating flirting dance, which is a fantasy come true for the *Jules and Mimi*–loving Miranda. They begin dating after he gives her courtside tickets to see the Knicks, for whom he works, and they flirt and share their first kiss at the apartment mailboxes the following day. Soon, they are sleeping together.

Dr. Leeds is quickly cooking for Miranda, and when he convinces her to take a day off—something she has never done in her whole career—their lovemaking is interrupted by Steve, who comes over to get something for Brady. Not long after, Dr. Leeds brings Miranda a cookie pizza that says "I love you" in chocolate chip cookies. She is so mortified that she can't say it back that she eats the whole thing. Later, after Miranda and Steve confess their mutual love (6.12, "One"), she tells Robert, who is very hurt and accuses her of using him for a "fast fuck." But as upset as he may seem, it's not long before he has another woman in his apartment and is on the road to recovery (6.13, "Let There Be Light").

Why he's a frog: He's not. Anything but. It is just bad timing. Miranda breaks his heart by finally getting together with Steve for sure. It's too bad Miranda hadn't found him sooner so he didn't have to be rushed through his story arc at the end of the series. Not only does his character give the series some sorely needed diversity, he also was a great guy.

Hit: Steve Brady

Sohn says it best: "Steve Brady is the quintessential good guy."[2] He's sweet, understanding, and emotional and always has Miranda's best interests at heart—whether he's disarming her anger by prompting her to be more polite or supporting her in raising their unexpected child. But there is something more lurking beneath the surface, or he wouldn't be able to put Miranda in her place when she is so mean to him upon their meeting, nor would he have the guts to flat out ask her, "Why do you hate men so much?" Miranda needs a guy like that because she has a tendency to be a man-eater, whether she realizes it or not.

As a bartender, Steve has learned to put up with a lot of BS over the years, and he uses that to good effect with a very bitchy Miranda on the night they meet (2.8, "The Man, the Myth, the Viagra"). They have sex and try for a relationship, but it ultimately fails because of their incompatible schedules and the fact that she makes more money than he does, which he can't handle as a matter of pride. He tells her she "needs to be with someone more on her level" and breaks up with her (2.10, "The Caste System").

The two run into each other multiple times and sometimes sleep together, but Miranda really tries to keep him at arm's length. She doesn't truly appreciate him until he helps her get back home after having Lasik eye surgery and stays the night to make sure she is okay (3.1, "Where There Is Fire"). Soon after, they get back together, and he tells her she is the "best woman he's ever met" and that he loves her (3.2, "Politically Erect"). Much like Carrie does with Aidan, Miranda's inner independent woman soon begins to feel cramped; her real problem is that she is scared Steve will see her as imperfect and vulnerable. He moves in, and despite some bumps along the way—like Miranda needing to support him more—they are happy for a while. That is, until he suggests they have a baby right at the same time Miranda is working her butt off because she is up for partner. They have a fight and break up again (3.8, "The Big Time").

They see each other on the street and even go out as friends a few times. When Steve tells Miranda he and Aidan are opening a bar together, she encourages him because that has always been a dream of his. "Each time Steve and Miranda broke up, this quiet chemistry pulled them back together," writes Sohn.[3] This time it is Steve's testicular cancer and Miranda's desire to show him, via a "mercy fuck," that he is no less of a man just because he has only one ball that reunites them (4.7 "Sex and the Country").

This is the turning point for them as a couple because Miranda gets pregnant. Steve tries to propose because it is the right thing to do, but Miranda knows they aren't in love, and a baby isn't the right reason to get married. So they negotiate a "time-share" agreement for the baby and establish that Miranda will be the primary parent. They have a rough go handling shared parenthood once Brady is born but ultimately find a comfortable rhythm.

That's when Miranda realizes she is in love with him. Unfortunately, their timing is off, and he's just started seeing someone else, so she has to keep her feelings to herself. Steve gets serious with his new girl, Debbie, but at Brady's first birthday party, he ends up declaring his love for Miranda. Just like Magda, we all secretly rooted for that moment in the laundry room midway through season 6, when Steve, suddenly serious, turns to a teary Miranda and says, "You're the one."[4]

Why he's "the one": Do you even have to ask? Steve is the ideal guy for any woman who wants children. He's devoted, easygoing, and kind. His gentle, sweet nature counterbalances Miranda's prickliness perfectly, and he has just enough spine to keep her from walking all over him. Steve might not be a runway model, but he is a role model, and for Miranda and Brady, that is way more important.

CHARLOTTE

Miss: Trey MacDougal

Trey rescues Charlotte from being hit by a cab, like a prince from a fairy tale (3.7, "Drama Queens"). What's more, he is Charlotte's perfect match on paper. She has always dreamed of marrying a rich, handsome man who can give her a Park Avenue apartment, and Trey delivers on all counts.

The first inkling that this love story isn't going to have a happy ending comes when Charlotte doesn't get the traditional, down-on-one-knee proposal of her dreams. Instead, caught up in the moment of thinking Trey is going to propose, she says, "Maybe we should get married," and Trey responds, "Alrighty" (3.9, "Easy Come, Easy Go"). Not exactly the romantic moment Charlotte has envisioned.

Unfortunately, their good breeding and desire to do what is "appropriate" leads them to abstain from sex until the day (after midnight) of their wedding. That's why they don't know until then that Trey can't maintain an erection long enough to have sex. Determined to do the right thing, they go through with their lavish and expensive wedding anyway (3.12, "Don't Ask, Don't Tell").

Kyle MacLachlan played Trey MacDougal, Charlotte's first husband. Photofest/*Sex and the City* (HBO), season 4 (summer 2001)

This would be a difficult situation for any couple, but for Charlotte it is especially hard (no pun intended) because she desperately wants children. Carrie suggests she find out if Trey's problem is physical or mental, so Charlotte wraps a line of stamps around Trey's penis at night, only to find it broken in the morning, meaning he can get an erection, just not for her (3.13, "Escape from New York"). This, combined with her walking in on him masturbating to a porno magazine (3.15, "Hot Child in the City"), convinces Charlotte that it is something about her that is causing Trey's problem. "Trey's Madonna-whore complex when it comes to Charlotte affects their sex life when he is unable to fully see her as a sexual being," writes Weekes. "Their lack of intimacy is not only just a storyline about them, but about how those puritanical ideas about sex can not only backfire on women, who have their sexuality stifled, but on men who don't know how to see women as fully realized humans with their own sexual needs."[5]

In order to fix their intimacy issues, Charlotte suggests they try couple's counseling and buys sexy lingerie in order to help him see her as desirable (3.16, "Frenemies"). Their slow progress toward marital union isn't helped any by Trey's strangely close relationship with his overprotective mother, Bunny. Over the course of their marriage, she helps them go shopping for a new marriage bed (and lays in it with them), sits in the bathroom and talks with Trey while he bathes, and even accidently walks in on them having sex. "Trey was everything Charlotte wanted, except for the umbilical cord tied tightly around his neck," jokes Sohn.[6]

Eventually, Trey and Charlotte solve their sexual problems and start trying to have a child. Charlotte finds out she has only a 15 percent chance of conceiving, so she starts IVF and puts them on a waiting list to adopt a Mandarin baby just in case the IVF doesn't work (4.11, "Coulda, Woulda, Shoulda"). Trey starts feeling a lot of pressure (4.13, "The Good Fight") and eventually admits to Charlotte that they aren't on the same page when it comes to having children, and he doesn't want to be together anymore because she is so angry (4.14, "All That Glitters"). They separate and later divorce.

Why he's a frog: Between his sexual issues and his mother, that should be obvious. Trey is better off sticking with his mother.

Hit: Harry Goldenblatt

In the course of Charlotte's divorce from Trey, she gets a rude awakening that even though Trey told her she could have their Park Avenue apartment, it is still in Bunny's name, and there is no way she is going to let Charlotte have it. Charlotte hires the most ruthless divorce attorney she can find so that she will win the apartment, but comes to realize he's too attractive; Charlotte can't be as vindictive as she needs to be around him. So she hires his unattractive partner, the bald, sweaty Harry Goldenblatt (5.6, "Critical Condition").

After he wins her the apartment, Harry tells Charlotte he loves her, and they have sex, the best sex Charlotte has ever had. While it's not clear exactly what attracts her to Harry, he believes she is the "sexiest woman he's ever met" (5.7, "The Big Journey"), and they declare their mutual love at a wedding in the Hamptons. There is only one problem: He can only marry a Jew, and Charlotte is Christian (5.8, "I Love a Charade").

After much thought, Charlotte decides to convert to Judaism for Harry. She also tells him about her fertility problems, and he is completely understanding. After an accelerated course of study, her conversion is complete, and she is anxious for him to pop the question. On their first Shabbas together, Harry would rather watch baseball than focus on the holy meal, so Charlotte gets upset that he isn't taking it more seriously. In a tirade, she lets her true feelings about them as a couple show, asking, "Do you know how lucky you are to have me?" meaning that she is way too attractive for a guy like him. Harry is heartbroken that she could be so conceited and leaves her (6.4, "Pick-a-Little, Talk-a-Little").

Evan Handler played Harry Goldenblatt, Charlotte's unexpected but true love. Photofest/
Sex and the City (HBO), season 6 (summer 2003–winter 2004)

Weeks later, Charlotte sees Harry at a Jewish singles event and apologizes, saying she doesn't care if he marries her; she just wants to be with him. To Charlotte's surprise, he kneels down and proposes (6.6, "Hop, Skip and a Week"). They get married, but everything that can go wrong, does: Harry spills ritual wine on Charlotte's dress; Samantha's bracelet breaks, interrupting the service; the glass won't shatter when Harry stomps it; Charlotte trips walking back down the aisle; one of Harry's groomsmen makes a very inappropriate toast at the reception; and Miranda's notecard for her toast gets too close to the candles and catches on fire (6.8, "The Catch"). But through all this, Charlotte finally learns her ultimate lesson: Perfection isn't nearly as important as having someone truly special to see you through all the imperfections of life.

Why he's "the one": Harry may not look anything like what Charlotte pictures as the perfect guy, but he is perfect for her. He is so kind and understanding and tolerant of her perfectionism. She needs a guy who is willing to go with the flow instead of also striving for perfection right next to her. As the *Rolling Stones* sang, "You can't always get what you want. But if you try sometimes, you just might find, you get what you need."

SAMANTHA

Miss: Richard Wright

Samantha meets Richard Wright when she applies for a public relations consultancy at his hotel chain. The two are immediately attracted, and Richard tells Samantha that he "likes that she's not afraid of him." They play at being a proper boss and employee for a short period before giving in and having sex (4.12, "Just Say Yes"). They are both players, so they vow to keep it simply a sexual relationship.

But it isn't long before Samantha, to her utter shock and horror, falls for him, something she almost never allows to happen (4.13, "The Good Fight"). Shortly thereafter, high on ecstasy, she accidently tells Richard that she loves him, but he knows she's on drugs and doesn't take her seriously (4.14, "All That Glitters"). Richard plies her with gifts, and she gives him a threesome for his birthday, before he declares that he wants to be monogamous: "Let's try this. Just you and me" (4.17, "A Vogue Idea"). No matter how much Samantha wants to trust him, she can't quite shake that something is wrong between them. She ends up walking in on him giving another woman oral sex and breaks things off (4.18, "I Heart NY").

James Remar played Richard Wright, the first man Samantha Jones ever dares give her heart to. Photofest/*Sex and the City* (HBO), season 5 (summer 2002)

Heartbroken, Samantha ignores Richard's incessant calls and pleas for her to give him one more chance. Finally, he wears her down, and they agree to give it one more try, but Samantha can't shake her mistrust of him (5.2, "Unoriginal Sin"). In Atlantic City, she keeps feeling like he is going to cheat on her and tries to catch him in the act. Finally, she decides that even he isn't worth the stress their relationship is putting her under, so she breaks up with him, saying, "I love you, Richard. But I love myself more" (5.3, "Luck Be an Old Lady").

Why he's a frog: In the words of Fairless and Garroni, Richard is a "sociopathic playboy" and an "asshole."[7] No matter what expensive gifts he gives or pretty words he says, he will always have a cheater's heart. No one, especially not Samantha—who is perhaps the most vulnerable of all the women, which is why she works so hard to hide it—deserves that.

Hit: Smith Jerrod

Samantha meets Jerry "Smith" Jerrod at Raw, a trendy new restaurant where he works as a waiter (6.2, "Great Sexpectations"). She initially sees him as just another conquest but then finds that she likes having him around. When she accidently gets him fired from his catering job by having sex with him while he is working, she tries to pay him, but he sees it as her treating him like a prostitute and says, "Lady, you are fucking out of your mind" (6.3, "The Perfect Present").

Jason Lewis played Smith Jerrod, the man who finally steals Samantha's heart. Photofest/ *Sex and the City* (HBO), season 6 (summer 2003–winter 2004)

They continue to see each other, playing sex-fantasy games, until he decides he wants to play reality with her and tells her he's in AA. That is too much for Samantha, who bolts (6.4, "Pick-a-Little, Talk-a-Little"). She still goes to see his play and, sensing a star on the rise, offers to be his public relations representative. She renames him Smith Jerrod (6.5, "Lights, Camera, Relationship"). Samantha's first order of business is to get her new client a nearly nude (except for a phallically placed Absolut vodka bottle) poster in Times Square. From this, he gains criticism but also fans and a movie part (6.6, "Hop, Skip, and a Week").

Even though he is twenty-eight to her forty-five, Smith is not afraid to show that he views her as more than a sex partner. He calls Samantha his girlfriend in episode 6.7, "The Post-It Always Sticks Twice," and tries to hold her hand in episode 6.11, "The Domino Effect." Samantha about loses it because both gestures smack of commitment, of which she is deathly afraid. Astute for one so young, Smith calls her on her fear, saying it is "horseshit," and from there on out, they are publicly together.

But rough times are ahead when Samantha reunites with Richard Wright at a Teen Posse event at which Smith is being honored. There, their age difference is thrown into stark relief, and Samantha regresses to her old ways. By way of a breakup, she tells him to go play with his friends (the teens), and she will play with hers (Richard). She goes upstairs and has sex with Richard, clearly regretting her decision. When she comes back down, Smith is still waiting for her, just to "make sure she gets home safe." She clings to him and cries, "I hate myself for doing this to you" (6.13, "Let There Be Light").

All is well with them before he leaves for his movie shoot. While he is gone, Samantha finds out she has breast cancer, has a lumpectomy, and begins chemo. Many men would be scared off by this much change but not Smith. He stands by her, even shaving his head (and hers) in solidarity when her hair starts to fall out (6.16, "Out of the Frying Pan"). He's willing to make a sex tape with her to prove that she's not a "fag hag" when the press accuses him of being gay (6.17, "The Cold War"), even though he doesn't care what people think of him.

After that, Samantha is finally confident enough to call him her boyfriend (6.18, "Splat!"), though she does give him permission to sleep with others on his eight-week movie shoot because she has no sex drive thanks to the chemo. He appreciates the gesture but refuses to go through with it. He tells her that her losing her sex drive will pass. It is like the trees in the winter, which aren't dead even though they appear to be; she will bloom again in the spring, just like they will. To reinforce his point, he sends her daffodils that will open in the spring, a gesture that touches Samantha so much, she calls and asks him not to sleep with anyone else.

When Smith gets home from his shoot, he tells her he loves her. In return, she says, "You have meant more to me than any man I've ever known," words so much more powerful coming from her than "I love you" could ever be (6.20, "An American Girl in Paris, Part Deux").

Why he's "the one": Smith offers Samantha a combination no other man ever has: love, sex, and support when she needs it most. Like Miranda, she needs a man who is not threatened by her strong personality and will call her on her "bullshit," which Smith does more than once. They may seem like an unlikely pair, but in the end, each has the other's best interests at heart, and for two people used to just sleeping around, that is a huge step.

PART II

THE ISSUES

8

THE SINGLE GIRL

"In New York, they say you're always looking for a job, a boyfriend, or an apartment. So let's say you have two out of three, and they're fabulous. Why do we let the thing we don't have affect how we feel about all the things we do have? Why does one minus a plus one feel like it adds up to zero?"

—Carrie, episode 5.5, "Plus One Is the Loneliest Number"

The late 1990s were an interesting time to be a single woman in the United States. It was generally accepted that more and more women were deferring marriage and motherhood in favor of college and careers, but it still wasn't quite the norm that it is now—and there was a definite cutoff: age forty. While single women looked at their married counterparts with jealousy over their steady life of commitment—as they say in *Sex and the City*, the wedding section of the *New York Times* is the "single woman's sports section" (3.3, "Attack of the 5'10" Woman")—married women looked back at the single women's independence with equal envy. Neither one "had it all," and both wanted it. So, how did we get here?[1]

Throughout history, there have been two expectations of women: that they would grow up to become wives and then, shortly thereafter, mothers. While some women managed such home-based businesses as sewing, laundry, and childcare from time immemorial, and some helped with their husband's businesses, like merchants, craftspeople, and so on, with the rise of the middle class in the Middle Ages, beginning in the 1800s, a new sphere emerged: that of working women in factories.[2] Now women were earning an income outside the home, even though her pay usually had to be forfeited to her husband. This put the first cracks in the age-old idea that the "public domain belongs to men, wives and their services belong to their husbands, and family life is the responsibility of women."[3]

Even as women began to enter the workplace in greater numbers in the early twentieth century as nurses, teachers, secretaries, and journalists, they were expected to give up those jobs after marriage to focus on their traditional roles of wife and mother. It wasn't until the 1950s that women began trying to balance work and the demands of home life.[4] "Women have been taught that they should be successful in both of these domains, which is extremely difficult because the demands of one conflict with the other," writes Montemurro.[5]

By the 1970s, more women were working than ever before, and within a decade they were beginning to shatter glass ceilings in law, medicine, academia, corporations, and government to rise into leadership in traditionally male occupations. But even as second-wave feminists fought for equality in the workplace, the cultural expectations of women to be wives and mothers didn't lessen. If anything, they increased as women tried to do everything. "She would live a temporary existence: a rented apartment shared with a girlfriend or two and a job she could easily ditch. Adult life—a house, a car, travel, children—only came with a husband," reports *Time* magazine.[6]

In the 1990s, the daughters of these "superwomen" came of age. They looked around at the struggle their mothers faced "trying to successfully balance work and family" and the results: "frustration, anger, and resentment given the impossibility of 'having it all.'"[7] Thanks to advances in education and a changing economic situation that meant they were no longer dependent on a man for their livelihood, they said, "Forget this," and increasingly chose to focus on their careers and delay motherhood.

While women were still interested in (and okay, some were—like Charlotte—obsessed with) finding a husband, there wasn't a looming deadline of thirty any longer. Thanks to the now infamous *Time* magazine cover (August 28, 2000) featuring the ladies of *Sex and the City* along with the headline, "Who Needs a Husband?" the characters and the show were forever linked with this new breed of independent woman. The accompanying article details the "growing number of US women who remain single by choice" and examines why this phenomenon was taking place.[8] "The single woman has come into her own," the article declares, citing, "Forty-three million women are currently single—more than 40% of all adult females, up from about 30% in 1960. . . . If you separate out women of the most marriageable age, the numbers are even more head snapping: in 1963, 83% of women 25 to 55 were married; by 1997 that figure had dropped to 65%."[9]

Sex and the City was on the cutting edge of that "seismic shift in American demography" and was one of the first to show what that life was like on television.[10] While the ladies on the show have financial means and privilege that many single American women did not, they still show that being a single female is not a source of shame but should be viewed as a source of pride. As Carrie says in episode 2.18, "Ex and the City," "Being single used to mean that nobody wanted you. Now it means you're pretty sexy, and you're taking your time deciding how you want your life to be and who you want to spend it with." This was a cultural realization decades in the making. To break through the stranglehold of tradition, it needed to be beamed into millions of American homes and become ubiquitous. Kristin Davis, who played Charlotte on the show, explains how fortunate her generation was:

> The show is really about a cultural movement, which we didn't realize at first. Our generation and those since have grown up with choices. We didn't have to get married by a certain age, we could be career women if we wanted to be. Our mothers didn't have these choices growing up. They were only presented to them later in their lives, when they were already on a certain path. My mother was married when she was 20 and had me when she was 21. I grew up with *Ms. Magazine* on the coffee table, but she had already committed to me and my father and to that life. So I think our show is about those choices and being able to create your life the way you want to create it.[11]

Creating the life you want to live and enjoying yourself while doing so might be the best articulation of the overall theme of *Sex and the City* and the movement it catalyzed. Through the lives of Carrie, Charlotte, Miranda, and Samantha, millions of single women found much-needed validation and courage to build their lives as independent woman.

REDEFINING THE SINGLE WOMAN

"The dictionary once defined a spinster as an unmarried woman above a certain age: 30. If you passed that milestone without a partner, your best hope was to be seen as an eccentric Auntie Mame; your worst fear was to grow old like Miss Havisham, locked in her cavernous mansion, bitter after being ditched at the altar," writes Tamala M. Edwards in that infamous *Time* magazine cover story.[12] But from 1998 to 2004, with *Sex and the City* on the screen, all that was changing. Star says that was a deliberate choice: "From the beginning I wanted it to be a show about independent women who were not looking to define themselves by a man. . . . They are women who are career oriented, sexually free, and always about putting themselves and their friendship with each other first."[13] He elaborates, "One of the big messages of the show is that it's okay for a woman to be single."[14]

And that was exactly what attracted audiences to the show. Women, gay men, and others tuned in and finally saw reflections of themselves, people who either don't want to get married or didn't feel pressured to get married right away, who wanted to focus on their jobs and make their thirties a decade of self-discovery. Maybe they would get married, maybe not.[15] But either way, they knew they could make it on their own. "My single friends have their own life and money to bring to the table," Parker told *Time* magazine in 2000. "It's the same as the characters on the show: my friends are looking for a relationship as fulfilling, challenging and fun as the one they have with their girlfriends."[16]

This attitude is encapsulated in episode 2.7, "The Chicken Dance," which takes place at a friend's wedding. As the four women are getting ready to leave, they hear the emcee announce that all single women are needed on the dance floor for the bouquet toss. They obligingly join the other singles in grouping behind the bride. When she throws the flowers, time slows down. Whereas just a few years earlier there would have been an all-out brawl to catch the bouquet—and thus be designated the next to get married—when the bouquet sails directly toward them, not a single one of the four reaches for it. They simply watch as it hits the ground, shrug, and step over it in order to go home. And just in case anyone thought that their ideas changed over time, the same idea is telegraphed at Charlotte's second wedding (6.8, "The Catch"). This time, Carrie and Miranda don't even go out on the dance floor for the bouquet toss. They are just standing up against the wall when the bouquet hits Miranda in the head. Neither one reacts any more than they did four seasons earlier.

THE STIGMA OF BEING SINGLE

"Single by choice—it's an empowering statement for many women," declares that *Time* magazine article.[17] But it is one that still came with its fair share of scorn and stigma, even toward the end of the twentieth century. Despite its empowering message for singles, the show doesn't sidestep the fact that being single is hard, especially in a culture where the idea that the world was built for two is still very much ingrained. "A great number of episodes addressed the pros and cons of single life, and the characters have many discussions about the institution of marriage," writes Henry.[18]

The show feels real because it was drawn from real life. The writers and directors have been very open about the fact that things they saw, experienced, overheard, or knew about through friends influenced every single episode. King said to Vulture in 2013, "When our show was good, it was always tethered to a writer's reality and then went fantastically up to where it should be."[19] Chupack shared how her personal life contributed to the show: "When I started on the show [as a screenwriter,] I was 32 and single and felt more of a stigma about being single because all of my friends were starting to get married and have kids. But now I feel these might have been the best years of my life—or at least the funniest and most fabulous."[20]

And those stigmas? Poor Miranda has to bear the bulk of them. From having to defend herself as a single woman buying her own apartment, every step of the way from the showing with the real estate agent to signing the mortgage papers (2.5, "Four Women and a Funeral"), to having to justify her choice to keep a vibrator in her bedside table to her housekeeper who believes no man will marry her if he sees it because it means she doesn't need him (3.3, "Attack of the 5'10" Woman"), she has seen it all. And she would certainly agree with her admirers Fairless and Garroni that, "If hell exists, it's probably an endless stream of stop and chats with married acquaintances who ask you if you're seeing anybody special—and you aren't."[21]

One episode that continues to resonate with single women even today is 6.9, "A Woman's Right to Shoes." In it, Carrie is invited to a baby shower for Kyra Bronson. When she gets there bearing gifts, she finds out the hostess has asked all guests to leave their shoes at the door to avoid tracking in dirt that the kids might be exposed to. Carrie reluctantly removes her Manolo Blahniks. Later, when she goes to put them back on, she finds that someone stole them. When she tells Kyra, she seems unconcerned. A few days later, when Carrie returns the tennis shoes Kyra lent her to walk home in, Kyra offers to pay for Carrie's shoes—that, is until she finds out they cost $485. She tells Carrie that she is willing to give her $200 for them. When Carrie points out Kyra used to wear them and therefore knows how much they are worth, Kyra snarks, "Yeah, but that was before I had a real life. No offense, Carrie, but I don't think we should have to pay for your extravagant lifestyle. It was your choice to buy shoes that expensive."

Carrie tells her friends that Kyra "shoe-shamed" her. When Carrie calls her a second time, Kyra once again implies that Carrie's life as a single, childless person isn't as valuable as her own as a married mother. Upset, Carrie mentally calculates that she has spent more than $2,300 on Kyra in wedding expenses and gifts for the wedding and baby showers. This causes her to give one of the best monologues in the series while talking to Charlotte: "If I don't ever get married or have a baby, what? I get bubkes? If you are single after graduation, there isn't one occasion when people celebrate you. I am talking about the single gal. Hallmark doesn't make a 'Congratulations! You didn't marry the wrong guy!' card. And where's the flatware for going on vacation alone?" Inspired by her own words, Carrie calls Kyra and says she's getting married to herself and is registered at Manolo Blahnik. Kyra finally relents and buys her the shoes.

Besides being a great story about revenge against a condescending mean mommy, this plot gives voice to a frustration so many single women have felt but were gagged by politeness from voicing: Why do we, who have less money because we have no partner, have to be the ones to spend money on people who are getting married and having babies when no one is willing to celebrate our life milestones in the same way? "Women loved it," Oria writes about not only the point that Carrie made but also the gesture. "Like so many *Sex and the City* accoutrements before, women rushed out to get this one: but this time, they didn't clamor for the shoes. They registered for whatever they wanted for their birthdays, or for no occasion at all—no occasion to do with men or procreation."[22]

In her article on this episode, Esme Mazzeo shares her own experiences as a single woman:

> The unspoken "rules" of society also still say after 18 years that it's ridiculous of me to celebrate non-romance related accomplishments with a list of gifts, too. I love my friends, but I guarantee that most of them would be too busy to attend my "I got a new job!" party—especially if it included a link to a gift registry filled with my dream wardrobe. . . . But if I don't attend their engagement parties, bachelorette parties, weddings, bridal showers, baby showers, or kids' birthday parties, eventually I'm just not going to be in their lives at all. The shift would be unintentional, perhaps even unconscious, but it's still not fair.[23]

Unfortunately, not even the cultural juggernaut of *Sex and the City* was able to make celebrating singleness via a party an acceptable practice. It did advance the discussion and help normalize "self-weddings," in which single women commit to honoring themselves as they would a spouse, but outside of television and movies, single people registering for getting a promotion, a publishing contract, or even the giant step of buying their first home hasn't yet materialized—this, while divorce parties are becoming more common. For all our progress, the world is still concerned with couples, whether they are getting together, expanding into families, or separating; single people haven't yet achieved equal status. As Carrie says at the end of the episode, "The fact is, sometimes it's hard to walk in a single woman's shoes. That's why we need really special ones now and then—to make the walk a little more fun."

THE NEW DEADLINE

"We've ended the spinster era," declares psychotherapist Diana Adile Kirschner in the *Time* magazine article.[24] But was that really true? Not according to *Sex and the City*. If anything, it was just pushed back a decade. In the first episode (1.1, "Sex and the City"), Miranda makes it clear that being single over forty is the ultimate death trap. To illustrate, she tells the story of a friend "who used to only date sexy guys, and then she woke up and was forty-one and couldn't get any more dates. She had a complete physical breakdown, lost her job, and had to move back to Wisconsin to live with her mother. Trust me, this is not a story that makes men feel bad."

At one time, spinsterhood began between ages of twenty-three and twenty-six; then the term *thornback* kicked in.[25] Now we reserve our scorn for single women over forty. If there was only one instance of this age limit in the show, it would be easy to dismiss it, but the idea is reinforced with gusto in the show's final season, in the third-to-last episode, almost like a bookend reminding the audience of Miranda's declaration in the opening of the show.

In episode 6.18, "Splat!" Carrie attends a party thrown by her former editor at *Vogue*, Enid Frick. There, she runs into an old friend, Lexi Featherston. Lexi is the only single woman there, and she is doing cocaine in the bathroom. She is also loud and very out of place, the only remaining party girl in a room full of people suited for a high-end soiree. Lexi "paints a rather pathetic picture of singleness at 40."[26] When Enid tells her she can't smoke inside, something no one does anymore, Lexi opens a large floor-to-ceiling glass window to smoke next to it and goes on a tirade about how no one is fun anymore, New York is over, and "I'm so bored I could die." And she does. She trips on her own shoes and falls out the window, eighteen stories to her death. King explained how the character came about: "Lexi is what Carrie was in season one. She's carrying a Fendi bag with poker chips on it, wearing a Versace dress. And smoking. . . . We needed to scare [Carrie] with what her life could be like if she stayed [in New York], which is why Lexi was created."[27]

In case the symbolism of Lexi's death might escape the audience, at the funeral, Carrie, seemingly for once unaware of the pun hidden in her words, says, "Ladies, if you are single in New York after a certain point, there is nowhere to go but down." That is it; if you are single after forty, the best you can hope for is death. "It seems as if the show is finally drawing the line in its celebration of singleness," writes Oria.[28]

REDEFINING DATING AND MARRIAGE

While *Sex and the City* "puts forward the possibility that women's 'happily ever after' may lie in something different from traditional marriage," it also rightly acknowledges most women still wanted to get married eventually.[29] Hence, all four women played the dating game.

The late '90s and early '00s were a period when, for the most part, couples still met in person, at work, in bars, at parties, or through mutual friends. Internet dating, while it did occur, was still frowned upon with strong messages of "stranger danger" attached to it. Therefore, dating was a lot more work than it might be today, when you can sit on your couch and swipe left or right on a dating app or even get the first few awkward dates over with via Zoom. Yet, even without apps and social media, *Sex and the City* revolutionized dating by making it fun. To all the women except Charlotte, the point was no longer just to find the right guy and settle down; it was to have fun, and if you found him, wonderful. It gave women permission to date for themselves, not just with their future family in mind. "The very fact that we're able to so overlook *SATC*'s impact is proof of how truly transformative it was," says Liz Tuccillo, a writer on the show. "These women were the first on television to say, 'We are in our 30s, we want love, but we're also going to have fun, have sex, go out.' They allowed this time of singleness to not just be a frightening time of not knowing when or if he would show up, but also of glamour and joy and friendship."[30]

However, "singlehood does not yield itself to a simple, blithe embrace. It's complicated, messy terrain because not needing a man is not the same as not wanting one. For all the laughs on *Sex and the City*, one can feel the ache that comes when yet another episode ends with the heart still a lonely hunter," writes Edwards. Single, hopeless romantics everywhere related to Charlotte's frustrated cry in the season 3 opener: "I've been dating since I was fifteen. I'm exhausted. Where is he?" "He" being her soulmate, Mr. Right, whatever you choose to call it.

Fairless and Garroni understand why women still chase the fantasy of a soulmate but caution that eventually we may have to accept reality:

The concept of "the one" gives all of us hope. It makes us feel like all of our failed relationships and unfortunate sexual encounters will ultimately culminate in a Hallmark Channel–esque romance that will solve all of our problems. But in reality none of us are guaranteed love. Some of us will have fairy tale marriages, while others will die alone and be eaten by their cats. Even more of us will settle for a romance that is less than perfect because we can't stand the prospect of being alone. . . . Contrary to popular opinion, ditching our overly romantic notions about the way [the world] operates is an act of agency—not defeat.[31]

Those two very different mind-sets—romantic fantasy and reality—are perfectly illustrated in episode 4.12, "Just Say Yes," when Carrie finds an engagement ring meant for her among Aidan's things. Upon seeing the diamond, Carrie runs to the sink and vomits. She then calls Charlotte, freaking out that she isn't ready to get married. Charlotte happily squeals, "You're getting engaged!" totally ignoring everything else Carrie has just said—after all, for her, marriage has always been the end goal.

Later, when Aidan does propose, Carrie's physical reaction is a panic attack accompanied by a serious case of hives. Unlike the romantic Charlotte, Carrie is very much grounded in reality and what all marriage would entail, and her body is telling her she's not ready. She says, "My body is literally rejecting the idea of marriage. . . . I'm missing the bride gene." At one time that would have been a travesty for any woman, but thanks to those who fought for women's rights, it no longer had to be. As *Sex and the City* shows, it is now not only okay to date with yourself in mind, but it is also acceptable to turn down a proposal that doesn't feel right—an option previous generations of women often didn't have.

THE AFTEREFFECT

Sex and the City's impact on American culture lasted far beyond its six-season run and even the two movies. Not only did it reignite interest in Candace Bushnell's original books the series is based on, but also other books about the very subjects Carrie writes in her column became hits with readers and publishers alike. "Books on the single woman, her history, and her habits became a mini-publishing phenomenon," says Jones.[32] The show itself spawned *He's Just Not That into You* by Greg Behrendt and Tuccillo, both of whom worked on the show. It is an award-winning self-help guide for single women based off a line in episode 6.4, "Pick-a-Little, Talk-a-Little."

But that is only commercialization. The bigger impact is that despite the power of its message about singlehood and the "fact that this realization seemed so groundbreaking at the time it aired . . . [there is] a bigger problem with the way society treats single women. It's nearly two decades later, but we've barely made much progress at all," Mazzeo notes.[33]

Single women, especially over forty, are still the lepers of American culture. They are still the "crazy cat ladies" who must have something wrong with them, or they would have been snapped up in their prime. While social media has given these women a much more public way of celebrating their accomplishments and the highlights of their very single lives, the gifts have yet to materialize. Plus, it is difficult for some women to feel like their big news is equal to that of married women.[34] Not everyone can, like Carrie Bradshaw, treat the career milestone of publishing her book like other women do their weddings: "There is one day even the most cynical New York woman dreams of all her life. . . . She imagined what she'll wear, the photographers, the toasts, everybody celebrating the fact that she finally found . . . a publisher. It's her book release party" (5.5, "Plus One Is the Loneliest Number").

But for those who can, it is a wonderful way to remind the world, and their mothers, that there are multiple paths in life, and not everyone is called to take the same one. For some, the "road less traveled" leads to a sustained single life punctuated by career successes and pet adoptions rather than weddings and baby showers. While others mark the years by children's birthdays, extracurricular activities, and graduations, these women count them in passport stamps, awards won, and hobbies learned. As Carrie says, "Maybe some women aren't meant to be tamed. Maybe they need to run free until they find someone just as wild to run with" (2.18, "Ex and the City). And even if they never find that someone, they'll always have their friends.

9

FEMINISM

"Is there a 'white knight' for every woman, or should we simply save ourselves?"

—Carrie, episode 3.1, "Where There Is Fire"

Is *Sex and the City* a feminist show? That is the million-dollar question, one for which no one seems to have a good answer. Feminists have been debating it since the show first aired. "Like any other 'hot' marketable topic, feminism has become an issue that can be opportunistically pimped by feminists and non-feminists alike," warns feminist scholar bell hooks.[1] This means that any answer must be understood with careful analysis of the intentions behind it. And indeed, there are many different arguments, some that take on the show as a whole and others whose answer hinges on the series' ending and some that depend on your definition of *feminism*. But before we get to that, let's address another commonly asked question: Does it matter?

The answer is a resounding yes, regardless of whether you identify as a feminist or feel like you are involved in the fight or not. As Julie D'Acci, professor of media and cultural studies at the University of Wisconsin, writes, "Television's schedule, its information, and its stories [play] active roles in shaping the ways TV viewers think about themselves and feel about themselves and their worlds, including how they think and feel about themselves as gendered human beings."[2] Television has a huge impact on how we see ourselves, from the commercials that play on our fears (or try to give us new ones) to sell products to the way characters are portrayed and what storylines are addressed. That is why representation is so important. When women see themselves represented on television in strong female roles and in situations they can relate to, their lives immediately take on greater importance. They are empowered to examine and discuss the issues raised in the show and how they affect their lives, regardless of whether they call themselves feminist or see the show as such. *Sex and the City* was one of the first to offer this representation, which has since led to a "contemporary environment [in which] popular feminist discourse is constructing as a golden age of television for women."[3]

Feminism, simple as it may appear on the surface—the fight for equal female rights in a society where they have traditionally been viewed as inferior—is very complex, and even ardent adherents sometimes face contradictory viewpoints and situations. This is especially true when it comes to heterosexual relationships.

Feminism has long existed in tension between female independence and evolving ideas of love and romance with the opposite sex. Can a woman like Charlotte, for example, call herself a feminist when she is focused on finding Mr. Right, even if she believes she has to give up a little of the progress women have made in order to do so? There's no easy answer to that question or a million others because the answers all depend on the definition of *feminism* you espouse. The characters in the show are "attacked for being too feminist or not feminist enough, they hate men, yet are still looking for Mr. Right, they enjoy sex but wonder if they are sluts," explain Kim Akass, professor of radio, television, and film at Rowan University, and Janet McCabe, lecturer in media and creative industries at Birkbeck, University of London, in their book *Reading* Sex and the City.[4]

These contradictions are exactly why there is no clear-cut answer to the question of if the show is a feminist one. Journalist Alice Wignall writes that on one hand, it is feminist because

> [n]ot only is it a programme about women, but one about women who like each other. They identify as each other's soul mates and provide emotional, practical and moral support. They don't compete with each other for male attention. They make each other laugh. It is probably the best depiction of the genuine nature and importance of female friendship ever to win an Emmy. . . . [On the other hand, it] seems churlish to be bitter about the fact that Carrie et al. do not offer a fail-safe model for emancipated womanhood when nor, frankly, has real-life feminism.[5]

In order to try to get some answers, let's take a look at both sides of the argument.

BUT FIRST, WHAT IS FEMINISM?

Before we get in too deep, let's take a brief look at what feminism is. Historian Estelle B. Freedman offers a concise and simple definition in her book *No Turning Back: The History of Feminism and the Future of Women*: "Feminism is a belief that women and men are inherently of equal worth. Because most societies privilege men as a group, social movements are necessary to achieve equality between women and men, with the understanding that gender always intersects with other social hierarchies."[6] Or put more simply by scholar Angela Chiang, "Feminism as a whole, regardless of its sub-issues of examination, works toward one primary objective—that is defining what a woman's role in society is and debating what it should be."[7] This is the principle that has been at feminism's core since Abigail Adams entreated her husband in 1776 to "remember the ladies" when shaping the country's laws and Susan B. Anthony made the motto for her suffragist newspaper *The Revolution* (1868–1872) "Men their rights and nothing more; women their rights and nothing less."[8]

Of course, the definition of *feminism* in the United States has changed over time as women's focus and values have shifted. Though now falling out of favor, the history of feminism has been traditionally defined in terms of "waves" or periods of intense activity: The "first wave" encompassed the suffrage movement, which ran from the 1848 Seneca Falls convention through 1920, when women were granted the right to vote through the Nineteenth Amendment; the "second wave" began in 1963 with the publication of Betty Friedan's *The Feminine Mystique* and lasted through the late 1980s, focusing on women's calls for legal and workplace equality; the "third wave" began with the 1991 Anita Hill/Clarence Thomas hearings and lasted into the late 1990s and was a much more sex-positive, intersectional movement.[9] This is where things get mushy. Some say that the postfeminist movement—or the belief that feminism was over because it had achieved its aims—came next, even though women still had not legally been guaranteed equal pay or equal rights.[10] Others believe we are still in the third wave, while still others—myself included—believe that a "fourth wave" began in 2016 with the presidential campaign of Donald Trump and its implications for women or in 2017 with the #MeToo movement.[11]

YES, *SEX AND THE CITY* IS A FEMINIST SHOW

While "none of the creators, writers or directors associated with the programme has directly referred to it as 'third wave,' or even 'feminist' for that matter, from its inception the show has addressed many of the key issues and themes discussed by third wave feminists," and so many—myself included—call it a feminist show.[12] After all, as Tufino writes, "in this series,

Carrie and her friends do not search for solutions to female inequalities; they become opinion leaders and activists for real American women in discovering the solution."[13]

This is especially true with the issue of sex—third-wave feminism was very much concerned with empowering women to own their sexuality and embrace it. "For third-wave feminists, therefore, 'sexual liberation,' a major goal of second-wave feminism, was expanded to mean a process of first becoming conscious of the ways one's gender identity and sexuality have been shaped by society and then intentionally constructing (and becoming free to express) one's authentic gender identity."[14] In keeping with this attitude, *Sex and the City* works to assert "women's sexual autonomy" and debunk the "traditional view of female sexuality as subordinated to men's."[15]

Weekes offers the personal experience of her friends with *Sex and the City* as an example of how the show embraces many types of feminism, from the hard-line, sometimes anti-male attitudes of stereotype to the sex-positive:

> One of the things I find when I talk to my friends about love is that we all find ourselves talking about how we have had to harden ourselves because "men will hurt you" and "you can't expect anything" while also denying the fact that we do, in many ways, want companionship. It is hard, as women, to figure out how to live in that place. The place where we can cry over a break up without feeling deep shame for caring that much in the first place. The place where we can admit that for some of us, casual sex doesn't mean as much. That place where you aren't scared to admit you want to get married and have kids someday.[16]

As women living in that same space—one that Rachel Moseley, reader in film and television studies at the University of Warwick, and Jacinda Read, lecturer in media studies at De Montfort University, describe as the "experience of being female, feminist, and feminine"—the characters of *Sex and the City* all come at feminism from different perspectives and embody different "types" of third-wave feminists.[17] While it makes sense to examine the show from the third-wave viewpoint, when looking at it through its characters, the show also harkens back to the second wave, in which the characters would have grown up, and is even prescient of the fourth wave, in which we are living now.[18]

One of the unique things about *Sex and the City* as a feminist show is that no one type of feminism is judged above another. Even while they are sometimes contradictory, all are seen as valid. Davis says it well: "I love that the four of us are so different, that we can have the variety of choices displayed without saying, 'this is the right one' or 'this is the wrong one.'"[19]

THE TRYING BUT NOT PERFECT FEMINIST: CARRIE

It isn't by accident that this book characterizes Carrie as a "mess" in chapter 1. It's not only a fitting descriptor, but it also illustrates Carrie's brand of feminism, as articulated by Catherine Harnois, chair of the Department of Sociology at Wake Forest University: "Third wave feminists have emphasized the 'messiness' of their own lives in terms of identities, beliefs, and actions, and have repeatedly called for feminisms that address the complexity of real lives."[20] Carrie's messy life—her yo-yoing quest for identity, her inconsistency in love, and even her mismatched outfits—are all symbols and reflections of a generation of women seeking to find their voice and their place.

As the show's narrator and the character most viewers identified with at the time, Carrie is therefore the one best positioned to show what feminism meant in the '90s through her experiences and her life, which she does in each episode through her column and her conversations with her friends. This is why she has been called the "first female thinker in [television] pop culture" and "our first pop-culture philosopher" by feminist author Naomi Wolf, who also named her an "icon of the decade," on December 21, 2009. Wolf explains, "Carrie showed audiences week after week that a lively female consciousness was as interesting as female sexuality or motherhood or martyrdom—the traditional role model options."[21]

Instead, Carrie was presented as a successful woman with an impressive—albeit unrealistic—shoe collection and wardrobe, who had a fun job and fabulous friends and was living life to the fullest, although within her own personal boundaries. Yes, she might be a bit of a fantasy, but she is also presented and accepted as a role model of third-wave feminism. "Teenage girls watching each episode were taking in a clear message," writes Wolf. "Not only can I dress up and flirt, seduce and consume, overcome challenges, yield to temptations, take risks, fail, try again—I can think about it all, and what I think will matter."[22]

Carrie is remarkably progressive on several topics near and dear to the hearts of third-wave feminists. Though not as adventurous as Samantha (but really, who is?), she is sexually curious, and while not as verbal about her feminism as Miranda, she is constantly questioning the status quo and women's roles in changing it. She is open on the issue of reproductive rights, having had an abortion herself in the past and supporting Miranda through her own decision-making process while not judging her.

However, Carrie has strong room for improvement. One of the things that third-wave feminism was known for was its inclusion of women who "come in many colors, ethnicities, nationalities, religions, and cultural backgrounds."[23] In this regard, Carrie is definitely not a good representation of a third-wave feminist. A later chapter covers this in depth, but her massive freak-out over having a bisexual boyfriend (3.4, "Boy, Girl, Boy, Girl"); her casual racism in making the joke "she's not so dim, that Sum" (2.10, "The Caste System"); and calling jewelry "ghetto gold" are only a few examples of how she doesn't fully align with the tenets of intersectional feminism.

It's interesting that most of the criticism aimed at Carrie "not [being] the feminist icon we want her to be" is aimed at her being too consumerist to be a feminist.[24] "For 10 long years, Carrie couldn't decide, and we couldn't decide, so we all went shopping," writes Camilla Long of the *Times of London*, as though that was all the show was about, and "dilemmas about relationships and starting a family were tossed in the trash alongside a mountain of credit card bills."[25] If that is all Long saw in the show, then she clearly wasn't watching with her eyes or mind open. While this subject is discussed again in chapters 13 and 14, this is actually a false assumption that one cannot be a feminist and an avid consumer because, as Broderick notes, a "postfeminist perspective allows for Carrie to be addicted to shopping and fashion without being considered less of a woman for these traditional feminine qualities."[26]

So while she is no Rebecca Walker, Kathleen Hanna, or even Alanis Morrisette—all icons of the third wave—Carrie tries her best, as can be said for most feminists of the time.[27] It is easy to judge but harder to be perfect ourselves. And perhaps that is why Carrie deserves to be called a third-wave feminist—she tries and fails just as much as the rest of us.

THE POWER FEMINIST: MIRANDA

While we have never seen Miranda engaging in a protest or picketing any location, she is definitely the most active in the feminist movement of all the characters, even if only in her thoughts and words. In episode 2.1, "Take Me Out to the Ballgame," a visibly annoyed Miranda confronts her friends with a verbal Bechdel Test:

> All we talk about anymore is Big or balls or small dicks. How does it happen that four such smart women have nothing to talk about but boyfriends? It's like seventh grade but with bank accounts. What about us? What we think, we feel, we know? Christ! Does it always have to be about them? Just, you know, give me a call when you're ready to talk about something besides men for a change.[28]

Chiang says Miranda "represents the feminist who still fights for equality."[29] She may be characterized as a bitch, but she doesn't care. She wants equality in the workplace (as evidenced by her drive to be named partner); in the bedroom (in episode 1.7, "The Monogamists," she tells Charlotte, "I only give head to get it"); and everywhere else—especially for single women.

Because of her own personal experiences, Miranda is the character who is the most aware of the stigmas single women face.[30] From being judged when making large purchases on their own and being harassed by construction workers for walking down the street alone, to being verbally sexually assaulted by a street performer and not having a date to her mother's funeral, she acutely feels that the world was made for couples, not for single people.

Her career-oriented focus, panache for power suits, and enjoyment of her success have led some to classify Miranda as more of a second-wave feminist because that wave was more focused on the workplace and related women's rights. In episode 2.10, "The Caste System," she bemoans the fact that it still matters to men if women make more money than them: "None of this matters to me. I just don't want it to matter to him. It's like when single men have a lot of money, it works to their advantage. But when a single woman has money, it's a problem you have to deal with. It's ridiculous." She tired of the power dynamic that requires men to have the money and the power and women to be subservient—and this is where she differs from second-wave feminists who still felt like they "can succeed but only on men's terms in a man's world."[31]

Instead, Miranda embraces what Wolf calls "power feminism." First proposed in Wolf's 1993 book *Fire with Fire*, power feminism bridges the gap between second-wave-feministic ideas that alienated some women and third-wave ideas of individualism by declaring that rather than being victims of the patriarchy, women are responsible for their own lives. "Power feminism is based on tolerance and respect for women's individuality," Wolf said to the *Chicago Tribune* in December 1993. "It's free thinking and pleasure-loving. It's about hating sexism without hating men, being able to call ourselves feminists without sacrificing our femininity. It says that women matter as much as men do and have the right to determine their lives."[32]

Nowhere is this attitude more evident than when Steve proposes to a pregnant Miranda out of a sense of duty in episode 4.12, "Just Say Yes." Her first response to the proposal is "What? Are you fucking crazy?" When Steve tells her he thought this is what she wanted, she tells him, "I don't want to marry you, Steve," and he admits to not wanting to marry her either. Later in the conversation, when Steve asks how they are going to raise a child together without being together, she answers, "We'll figure it out." Two seasons later, Miranda ends up proposing to Steve and marries him. That is the essence of Miranda in a nutshell: even in the hardest of situations, she insists on living life on her own terms, not on those expected by society.

THE CONSERVATIVE FEMINIST: CHARLOTTE

Charlotte's brand of feminism is detailed in chapter 3, where I call her a conservative feminist. At its heart, conservative feminism is a reaction to the perception that the liberal feminists of the current wave have gone too far in an outrageous or scandalous direction. It is a way to allow more traditional, and perhaps demure, voices to remain a part of the movement.

Though the phrase wasn't coined until the early 1980s, conservative feminism has been around since 1869, when Lucy Stone and her friends broke with Susan B. Anthony's radical National Woman Suffrage Association (NWSA) to form a more conservative arm of the women's suffrage movement, the American Woman Suffrage Organization. In addition to advocating for a state-by-state approach to female suffrage (as opposed to the NWSA's national approach), these women preferred more subtle forms of agitation, like letter writing, to the often-loud demonstrations and controversial tactics of the NWSA.

In the early 1980s, Betty Friedan and Jean Bethke created the idea of conservative feminism, which favors femininity and family over politics and the struggle against a male-dominated society. This fits well with Charlotte's seemingly irreconcilable throwback attitudes toward the role of men and women in society and her often-astute awareness of the world around her. However, it was also one side of a deep divide that developed in the feminist movement, pitting those with more traditional values against those with liberal ideas. In the mid-1990s, though, feminists tried to heal that rift and sought

> to reunite the ideas of gender equality and sexual freedom that came apart during the "sex wars." Because third wave feminism insists that each woman must decide for herself how to negotiate the often contradictory desires for both gender equality and sexual liberation, it sometimes seems to uncritically endorse behaviors that appear problematic. . . . However, the third wave approach actually exhibits not a thoughtless endorsement of "choice," but rather a deep respect for pluralism and self-determination.[33]

This is the feminism invoked by Charlotte in episode 4.7, "Time and Punishment," when she tells the other women that she has decided to quit her job and stay at home now that she is married to Trey. The women are all confused, but Carrie and Samantha support Charlotte no matter what because it is the right decision for her. Miranda, however, has a problem with it, and Charlotte has to demand Miranda stand with her. Charlotte uses Miranda's own feminism against her, saying that the women's movement has given her the right to choose whether to work or be a homemaker. "I choose my choice!" she yells several times. Montemurro explains the significance of this phrasing:

> When Charlotte refers to the women's movement, she seems to be referring to the idea that women have been "liberated" or freed from the constraints of patriarchy and are able to work and attain success at levels similar to those attained by men. Thus, she has the right to decide for herself what will make her happy and satisfied as an individual. If she chooses not to work, then she is not succumbing to traditional feminine expectations; rather, she is doing what she sees as right for her and thus she should not be judged for this.[34]

In addition, choice is one of the linchpins of third-wave feminism, not only in terms of reproductive rights, but also in all aspects of life. In the third wave, a "movement that is largely defined by freedom of choice, independence, and personal freedom, . . . a woman who has a career is not considered any different than a woman who stays home as a housewife because a woman's experience is never rejected or discredited," writes Broderick.[35]

In this way, *Sex and the City* is very in keeping with third-wave ideals: "The show does not criticize the idea of traditional gender roles. . . . [It] also does not reject the narrative that mothers *can* work . . . suggesting that both choices face scrutiny, and both should be accepted."[36] Similarly, the women (though they rarely understand Charlotte and often make jokes at her expense), love, support, and accept her as having a different though equally valid outlook on life and sex.

THE SEX-POSITIVE FEMINIST: SAMANTHA

While Charlotte might be seen as too conservative to be a feminist, Samantha is controversial because she is the exact opposite and proudly so. She embraces the "sempiternal archenemies of traditional feminism: pornography, prostitution and perverse sexuality."[37] From the get-go she declares her ability and desire to "have sex like a man" (1.1, "Sex and the City"), willingly has sex on camera for an "artist" who usually only records models (1.2, "Models and Mortals"), and is shown unapologetically enjoying the opening of a kink-themed restaurant a few episodes later (2.12, "LaDouleur Exquse!"). In episode 6.17, "The Cold War," she even makes a sex tape with her boyfriend, Smith, with the sole purpose of leaking it online to get attention, hoping for the same outcome experienced by Paris Hilton.

Samantha's sexual openness is reflected in this quote from author Anna Quindlen: "I like guys, but my body is home to me. That was the point of feminism: I got custody of myself."[38] As a woman with custody over her own body, she asserts her right to do with it what she pleases, with whom she pleases, whenever she pleases. To her and many other third-wave feminists, the right to sexual freedom is as natural as the right to vote.[39]

And this right doesn't just apply to her; it applies to all women. Unlike their second-wave foremothers who questioned if sex workers could be included in the feminist movement, third-wave feminists insisted they should be. In the show, Samantha defends the rights of the workers at the LaDouleur Exquse! S&M restaurant (2.12, "LaDouleur Exquse!"), and when Carrie questions whether she's akin to a prostitute because her latest sexual partner leaves her money the morning after, Samantha indirectly defends prostitutes by asking, "What are you getting so uptight about? Money is power. Sex is power. Therefore, getting money for sex is simply an exchange of power" (1.5, "The Power of Female Sex"). Unfortunately, her openness doesn't extend to transgender sex workers, whom, as explained in chapter 11, Samantha regularly berates and calls them names that are seen today as slurs. Samantha may be a *very* open feminist, but her feminism is far from perfect.

Samantha is an important character to feminism because she was one of the first to be shown on television not being denigrated for her openness about sex. "The history of English—and one might say western—culture, when it comes to female sexuality, is the history of sluts getting punished for their lust," writes Wolf.[40] Unlike Tess of the d'Urbervilles or poor Hester Prynne, the writers didn't give her HIV or kill her off with breast cancer—though they did scare us for a minute with both! Much like Moll Flanders, Samantha is able to have her adventures and conquests and be "bad" and still find a happy ending.

NO, *SEX AND THE CITY* IS NOT A FEMINIST SHOW

Some critics and viewers feel like *Sex and the City* doesn't go far enough into the feminist realm to be considered as such. "It's babe feminism—we're young, we're fun, we do what we want in bed—and it has a shorter shelf life than the feminism of sisterhood," writes author Anna Quindlen.[41] While the third wave is specifically characterized by an independence that turns away from the idea of collective sisterhood as demonstrated in the first two waves, Quindlen has a point. We know and even feel that the four women are friends, but we don't necessarily see a true bond of sisterhood, at least in the feminist sense, among them. And part of that is because we only see such a small sliver of their lives. "While these four characters are undoubtedly bright and accomplished, they also spend all their time together talking about men, relationships, love, and to a lesser degree, sex. The fact that the show never bothers to develop their friendship outside of these areas is both telling and disappointing," writes journalist David Caballero.[42]

At first glance, this might seem to be a hard thing to believe, but when you think about it, he's right. Unless Samantha is hosting an event that doubles as a night out or Charlotte is doing the same at her gallery, we rarely see the women working. When we see them on vacation in the Hamptons, it always ends up revolving around a guy. When we see them out shopping, they are talking about their love lives. What are their hobbies, outside of shopping and exercising in Central Park? We know Miranda likes to read, but that's only because she met a guy at a bookstore. It takes two movies and *The Carrie Diaries* to give us a glimpse of how they met. With the exception of Miranda's mother's death, when we witness them confiding in one another, their conversation always has something to do with their relationships.

Another argument is that the show never uses the word *feminist* and so cannot be called by that label. Montemurro writes,

> Feminism seems to be a dirty word. Even though HBO is no stranger to "strong" language, this one appears to be on the "do not use" list. While Carrie, Samantha, Miranda, and sometimes Charlotte, act in ways that are decidedly feminist. . . . [R]arely, if ever, are the women or their actions labeled as feminist. When a show avoids using the word feminist—seemingly because of its still-stigmatized connotations in the age of postfeminism—it is difficult to interpret the show as such.[43]

However, many critics are willing to admit, that while *Sex and the City* is not itself a feminist show, it did initiate an important discussion around feminism and women's issues.[44] Akass and McCabe explain,

> In this sense, HBO gives representation to our complex age of troubled emancipation—and may in fact offer more realistic female characters—fallible,

inconsistent, complicated, virtuous, troublesome, and both emotionally strong and fragile. Steering clear of feminist agendas, but valuing individuality, these women have much to tell us about the contradictions we all live with each and every day.[45]

So by making a point around a feminist issue in each episode, the show gave women something to talk about when they gathered around the water cooler at work or at the bar for happy hour. The fact that those issues were directly related to their real lives gave them gravitas and begged for more serious consideration than a recap of Sunday night TV usually called for. In this way, *Sex and the City* certainly spreads a message of women's empowerment without using the word *feminist*.

This idea of the show being a dialog about feminism but not feminist raises an important question: If talking about feminism isn't enough, then what *would* make a show feminist? By this logic, the consciousness-raising sessions of the 1960s would not have been labeled feminist, though they were an integral part of the second wave. Is it action that the audience can see that is missing? Perhaps these critics are looking for female characters who actively engage in public protest or wear the title of feminist loudly and proudly? Such a show couldn't have been made in the period of *Sex and the City*. The country wasn't ready. Even today, this kind of show would have to be written, directed, and acted with great care and subtlety to avoid being called over-the-top, preachy, and part of the liberal agenda.

WHOSE FEMINISM?

Another reason some refuse to label *Sex and the City* as feminist is because it doesn't represent all feminists—not by a long shot. As chapter 11 details, the lack of diversity in both race and sexual orientation is one of the show's biggest blind spots. The fact that it is about four White, well-educated, affluent women aligns it more with the racist and classist attitudes that kept nearly all the first wave of feminism and much of the second limited to a small, privileged group of White women, which is not what the third and certainly not the fourth waves of feminism are about. "A central tenet of third wave feminism is to include women who have previously been excluded from social movements [read: second-wave feminism] due to race, class and sexual orientation prejudice," writes Harnois.[46]

According to hooks, calling a show such as this feminist could do more harm than good to the movement: "Coalition building that broadened the movement [in the 1960s and 1970s] may be in danger in the 1990s: 'that work now risks being undone and undermined by some of the current feminist writing by young white privileged women who strive to create a narrative of feminism (not a feminist movement) that denies race or class differences.'"[47] Nixon is very cognizant of the show's failings. *"Sex and the City* started twenty years ago, and I'm very keenly aware of this," she says, adding that one of the chief deficiencies of the show was its focus on a "very, very thin slice of an extremely white and extremely affluent part of New York." And while she calls it a feminist show, she says that the "flaws of the feminist movement are reflected in *Sex and the City*, too."[48]

One of these flaws that is often overlooked in early periods of the movement but is glaringly obvious in the show is its classism. Not only are the women well off, but also the "truth is that Carrie never falls for 'poor' men. Even though she has dated men who were not particularly well off, the three men she has had serious relationships with (Big, Aidan, and Petrovsky) were far above her in the economic and social ladder, and Carrie's conception of her partners' suitability seems deeply shaped by their 'provider' status," writes Oria.[49] Not only is this socially problematic, but it also sends a distinctly antifeminist message that women still need to be financially rescued by men. Carrie might be intelligent, employed, and a "semi-celebrity," in New York (3.1, "Where There's Fire"), but she certainly can't manage her own finances. This fact alone, plus her luxury shoe addiction, does nothing to add to her street cred as a feminist, firmly placing her in the realm of the stereotypical woman and requiring her to marry above her station to support her lifestyle.

Oria also points out that she isn't alone in that behavior pattern. With the exception of high-powered Miranda dating and eventually marrying working-class Steve—which causes plenty of cringe-worthy problems throughout the series—the other women all seem to aspire to marry or at least "date up," as well. Charlotte is very open about her desire to marry into wealth, which could possibly be excused because she grew up in an upper-class family and wishes to maintain the only lifestyle she has ever known. But Samantha has no excuse. She seems to have come from a middle-class background, worked her way up, and set her sights even higher. She is only attracted to rich, high-powered men—they are the only ones she sees as capable of being her equal, which is pretty much the definition of classism.

All this means that *Sex and the City*, if it can be called feminist, is reflective of only a small cross-section of what it means to be feminist in America. Excluded are people of color, any sexual orientation other than heterosexual, and those of low to average income levels. That's a hefty majority of the country. Yes, the show is a product of its time, but critics who label the show as not feminist have valid complaints.

ABOUT THAT ENDING

On February 22, 2004, fans gathered with cosmos in hand at watch parties across the country to find out the answer they had waited five and a half years and ninety-three episodes to know: Would Carrie end up with Mr. Big? And if not, how would the writers choose to end the show? What would happen to Miranda, Samantha, and Charlotte? That evening was a cultural phenomenon all its own, with 10.6 million viewers tuning in to the final episode, the most-watched of the series.[50]

Love it or loathe it, much of the debate over the show's feminism surrounds the series finale, specifically Carrie's ultimate coupling with Mr. Big. Viewers and critics fall into two general camps: those who love the ending because it completes the fairy tale of the show with a happily ever after—at least until the movies came along to muck things up—and those who feel betrayed by an ending they believe goes against everything the show has been about from its first episode.

For those rooting for Carrie to end up with Mr. Big, the finale is about as perfect as it can be. "It honored the wishes of its heroine, and at least half of the audience, and it gave us a very memorable dress"—another fairy-tale attribute—and most importantly, a happy ending.[51] It gave viewers a fantasy high, that moment of pleasure—the sigh of the hopeless romantic, a heartbeat in which they could believe that love really does conquer all—before turning back to face a harsh real world in which love isn't guaranteed. The heroine gets the guy in the end, the princess in Manolos is rescued by the prince with a black limousine, and viewers finally find out his real first name: John.

What's more, each of the women ends up happily paired off like the show is a Shakespearean comedy: Carrie with Big, Charlotte with Harry, Miranda with Steve, and Samantha with Smith. The women have their reward, their men, for all they have gone through in the rest of the series.[52] All's well that ends well, even in the rough and tumble urban jungle of New York City. "At that point the TV show had become so big. Viewers got so invested in the storyline of Carrie and Big that it became a bit like Mr. Darcy and Elizabeth Bennett," Bushnell says, implying this was the only ending the series could have had.[53]

For all its fairy-tale attributes, King swears up and down that this ending was never meant to be the bookend to the show's "once upon a time" opening. Although he always planned for Big and Carrie to end up together, he didn't want it to end with a clichéd marriage proposal.[54] "The moral was never, 'find a man to love you so you'll be whole. It's 'love yourself and your girlfriends, and maybe somebody will come along and enjoy the party,'" he says.[55] That is why the show ends with Carrie's narration, "The most exciting, challenging, and significant relationship of all is the one you have with yourself."

Yet for those who followed the show because it was about building a life contrary to societal expectations, this fairy-tale ending rings hollow. It betrays exactly what Carrie says in her final narration. They felt that if Carrie had walked down the streets of New York alone (or with the other ladies) with her newfound confidence, it would have served the show, her character arc, and the audience so much better—and her actions would have fit the narration. Taking on her own Carrie-like tone, Nussbaum writes, "And I can't help but wonder: What would the show look like without that finale? What if it were the story of a woman who lost herself in her thirties, who was changed by a poisonous, powerful love affair, and who emerged, finally, surrounded by her friends? Who would Carrie be then?"[56] Even Bushnell admits, "In real life, Carrie and Big wouldn't have ended up together."[57] Yet the show panders to a typical Hollywood ending that caves to conventional culture and "[shows] a failure of nerve, and inability of the writers to imagine, or to trust themselves to portray any other kind of ending—happy or not."[58]

Star was livid about the ending, saying that it "'betrayed what [the show] was about.' The series, he said, was supposed to be about women not being defined by men. 'They could fall in love with men, but the message should not be about finding fulfillment with one. Alone on the streets of New York would have been fine. Reunited with her friends, sure. Why did Mr. Big have to be such a big part of it?'" he asks.[59] And he wasn't the only one. Feminists looking for a strong, female-centric ending were disappointed that the show "pulled its punches" after spending so long emphasizing the power of individuality and "that a friend can be the love of your life."[60] The show spends its entire run telling viewers that they have choices "outside stereotyped destinies" and that women's "'happily ever after' may lie in something different from traditional marriage."[61] By placing the happily-ever-after above the personal transformations of the show, the writers "not only [diminish] the girls' story together, [but they] perhaps also invalidate the show as a whole, because it sends the message that, at the end of the day, all a woman really wants, and needs, is a man," writes Caballero.[62]

That is especially true for Carrie, whose whole quest for identity is lessened, if not erased, by her fairy-tale ending. If you need proof, just look at her completely clashing final outfit, which reveals her true, contradictory feelings on ending up with Big (more on that in chapter 14). She has worked for the last five years to shed her mask of not being good enough, worthy enough of love, only to realize in Paris that what she thought she wanted all along isn't what she really needed. Now back in New York, she should be relying on herself and her friends to see her into a new, promising period of life in which she lives in her essence, but she can't seem to quite let go of her mask, which is embodied in her toxic relationship with Mr. Big.

In that way, the show fails the very viewers who had supported its feministic underpinnings. They watched Carrie come *so close* to a true transformation, only to fail by succumbing to convention at the last moment. What could have been a truly groundbreaking ending that gave women across the globe a role model for a new kind of single living, even into their forties, still crumbles under the weight of cultural pressure. At the beginning of a new millennium, it would have been empowering to see a woman choosing to live on her own terms rather than on those expected of her for centuries. That is not to say that Carrie couldn't have found love—there is by all means a much-needed place for that in the lives of modern women—but it should have been either a mystery to come or with a Mr. Big whom we saw truly transformed, not rushed into a quasi-maturation for the sake of a happy ending. That would have cemented *Sex and the City*'s reputation as truly a revolutionary feminist show.

10

FRIENDSHIP

"The most important thing in life is your family. . . . In the end, they're the people you always turn to. Sometimes it's the family you're born into, and sometimes it's the one you make for yourself."

—Carrie, episode 2.15, "Shortcomings"

If *Sex and the City* is best known for its advancements in sexual empowerment, its second-biggest contribution to American culture is its portrayal of strong, positive female relationships. Over the years, stories based in the male perspective have portrayed women as competitive, conniving, and willing to stab one another in the back in a heartbeat, especially over a man. But not *Sex and the City*—it was written with women in mind and tried to reflect the world as they saw it.

It was the latest in a small but mighty handful of shows that emphasized the importance of female friendship and pointed out the wrongheadedness of the idea that women only view one another as threats. *The Golden Girls*, *Designing Women*, and *Living Single* are all its predecessors—shows that said what needed saying for their core demographic. *The Golden Girls*— who incidentally were the same age as the ladies of *And Just Like That . . .* —showed that older women still have value and vibrant lives; *Designing Women* focused on the career woman and her problems as reflected in the 1980s; *Living Single* made great strides in portraying positive Black friendships on television and brought a fresh, early-'90s perspective; then *Sex and the City* showed how women can be sexual beings at the dawn of a new millennium. And they all have one thing in common: the foursome of friends at their core.

THE "CHAT AND CHEW"

Sex and the City has so many scenes where the women discuss something over a meal that the crew came to call these scenes "chat and chews." The nickname may minimize these scenes for the sake of production, but they are actually the most important element of the series. As Gail Markle, sociologist at Kennesaw State University in Kennesaw, Georgia, writes, "[W]hat is different about *Sex and the City* is the portrayal of committed friendships between the main characters. The highly valued relationships the women have with each other are the foundation of the series. Their conversations with one another are often more intimate than the sex they have with men."[1]

This idea of female intimacy is one that is rarely explored in modern culture; instead, we focus on the individual. But like the women of Anita Diamant's novel *The Red Tent*, the ladies of *Sex and the City* understand the value of coming together regularly to talk about things only other women understand, share their problems, discuss possible solutions, and simply revel in being female together. By the end of the series, even Big understands how close they are: "I know you are the loves of her life, and a guy is just lucky to come in fourth" (6.19, "An American Girl in Paris, Part Une").

Many of the show's most important discussions take place between the ladies over a meal, emphasizing the power of female friendship. Photofest/*Sex and the City* (HBO), season 5 (summer 2002)

For Carrie, Miranda, Charlotte, and Samantha, this gathering is almost always over a meal, whether it is a leisurely Sunday brunch, a quick bite at lunch, a nice dinner, a postdate nightcap, or just a get-together at one of their apartments. But the most important time of the week is their "Saturday morning ritual: coffee, eggs, and a very private dish session" (2.1, "Take Me Out to the Ball Game"). This is a time just for the ladies. While they may—and often do—talk about the men in their lives, that is secondary to the way this gathering reinforces the bonds between them. These meetings "function like consciousness raising sessions where each character expresses her thoughts and the group processes them, often by challenging each other's viewpoints," writes Henry.[2]

These get-togethers are almost always accompanied by good-natured ribbing, Carrie's ubiquitous puns, and laughter. Henry points out that "*Sex and the City*'s regular depiction of women's laughter is worth noting for its rarity on TV and for its implicit feminism. As one feminist critic noted, 'the threat to male dominance isn't women laughing at men; the threat is women laughing with women.'"[3] They show women having fun together in an environment where there is no thought of competition. Even when they are discussing models and the impossible standards of beauty they represent (1.2, "Models and Mortals"), there is no competition over who is the prettiest. Rather, they compliment one another—Samantha tells Miranda, "Oh, honey, you are so cute"—and openly discuss what they each dislike the most about their own looks: Charlotte hates her thighs; Miranda doesn't like her chin; Carrie's insecurity is her nose; and Samantha, well, she "loves the way [she] looks." (Would you expect anything less?)

In this way, the women not only express what is on their minds, functioning as healthy outlets and sounding boards for one another, but also reinforce the bonds that keep them together. Oria posits that this is the show's "whole ethos: lovers and husbands may come and go but the girls' bonds are here to stay."[4] Even as they face various conflicts, "themes of sisterhood and solidarity resurged as anchors for the principal characters and their friendship during the series. When one sister is in need there is frequently a group response. . . . [T]he theme of just showing up to support one another becomes a cornerstone of sisterhood for the women of *Sex and the City*."[5]

DYNAMICS OF THE FRIENDSHIP

As important as the four main characters are as individuals, their greatest strength can be seen when they are together. While each woman has her own flaws and weaknesses, together they balance one another out, becoming an unstoppable force. For example, whereas Charlotte is old-fashioned and sees the world through rose-tinted glasses, Samantha is progressive and realistic; while Miranda is judgmental, Samantha rarely judges; Miranda's cynicism is countered by Charlotte's never-ending hope. "*Sex and the City* emphasizes the differences of these four characters and the importance of female friendship and conversation in offering a perspective that accepts both conventional and non-conventional angles on what it means to be a woman among friends in a relationship where no friend's outlook is considered better than another," writes Broderick.[6]

These women grow more from their relationships with one another than they do through all the heartbreak they endure. Over the course of six seasons, Miranda learns to be more caring and kinder from their love for her; Samantha learns to accept her vulnerabilities by bolstering them in theirs; Charlotte learns to accept her imperfections by showing them that theirs are part of what makes them beautiful; and Carrie learns to trust herself because of the way they trust her. As Sohn points out, "while Carrie's relationships with men may be charged and difficult, her relationships with Charlotte, Miranda, and Samantha are always strong and vibrant."[7] The same is also true for the other women.

That doesn't mean that they don't fight, however. And when they do, they are typical female fights, complete with yelling, name calling, and biting words. Even though Carrie and Miranda are clearly best friends and have known each other for more than a decade—the first movie tells us they met while Carrie was working at Bloomingdale's in 1989, but the book says Miranda was protesting outside of Saks Fifth Avenue when they met—they still have their knock-down, drag-outs on occasion.[8] In episode 3.18, "Cock-a-Doodle-Do," they have their "first big fight." They are out shopping at a vintage store, when Carrie confides in Miranda that Big called her and said Natasha left him. He wants to have lunch with her at the Boathouse restaurant in Central Park, and she is thinking about going. Frustrated to her limit with Carrie constantly running back to Big, Miranda explodes, "Wake up, Carrie. How many more times are you going to go through this? He's bad for you. Every time you get near him you turn into this pathetic, needy, insecure victim, and the thing that pisses me off the most is that you're more than willing to go back for more." When Carrie tries to protest, Miranda says she doesn't want to hear it. A stunned Carrie replies, "The first sign of any little weakness or flaw, and you just write people off. My God, Miranda, you are so judgmental." Miranda walks off, leaving Carrie alone in the store.

In the same way, Charlotte and Samantha have their share of blowouts—perhaps more so than the others because of their extreme differences. They are almost always instigated by Charlotte judging Samantha's sex life. In episode 2.15, "Shortcomings," Charlotte is appalled that Samantha had sex with her brother, whom she considers off-limits, especially from her friend. Upset that neither of them understood her wishes (she never told them), Charlotte yells at Samantha, "Is your vagina in the New York City guidebooks? Because it should be! It's the hottest spot in town. It's always open!" A visibly hurt Samantha gathers her clothes and goes home.

Similarly, in episode 3.16, "Frenemies," Charlotte says she doesn't like the cavalier way Samantha talks about sex and voices her opinion: "Sex is something special. It's supposed to happen between two people who love each other." Samantha retorts, "Or two people who love sex." An enraged Charlotte yells, "Oh my God! You're such a—" Samantha cuts her off, daring her to slut-shame her yet again. "A what? What am I, Charlotte?" Instead of answering, Charlotte storms out of the restaurant.

However, no matter how hurt their feelings or how deep the rift seems to be, in the end, they always come back to one another. Carrie and Miranda solved their differences with a phone call; Charlotte bakes Samantha muffins by way of apology the first time, and Charlotte calls Samantha the second time to confide in her about her sex life, the ultimate compliment to Samantha. "They yelled and even got into fights, but when push came to shove they were always there for one another," writes Sohn.[9]

FRIENDS AS FAMILY

The idea that friends can be family is nothing new, but the way *Sex and the City* emphasizes it is. The show "regularly suggested that this family of four could be enough to make up a life, a life still worth living without the husband and baby, a life led outside the historic feminine and feminist script," writes women's studies author Jane Gerhard.[10] We see this played out quite literally in episode 2.5, "Four Women and a Funeral," when Miranda buys her own apartment. After the girls support her through many stigmas of being single and taking such a big step, the episode ends with Miranda placing a photograph of the four of them on her fireplace mantle, which is, as Oria reminds us, a "spot usually reserved for family pictures."[11]

Because none of the women seem particularly close to their parents—the only times we see them interact is when Miranda's mother dies and Charlotte's parents attend her second wedding—they have to rely on one another for the love, advice, and support one would otherwise turn to biological family for. Oria writes, "[F]riends are consistently presented as a consistent safety net in times of crisis. . . . [Friends are] a support system for scary situations."[12]

This is evident when Miranda's mother dies, Charlotte faces infertility, and Samantha battles cancer. No matter the situation, the women are quick to gather, hug, listen, cry, offer advice, or simply be together, whatever is best at the time. Nixon says, "*Sex and the City* is about how important friendships are when you're not married and you don't have a family. It's a gay thing, and the single person thing, where your friends are your family. . . . Whether or not these women end up getting married, marriage is not the only measure of their lives."[13]

Being a group of single women, there are times when each of them doesn't have a man in her life when one is traditionally required. In those instances, they "replace the roles normally filled by men."[14] This can range from something as simple as Carrie acting as Charlotte's date to the opera when she is stood up (3.7, "Drama Queens") and as Miranda's to her mother's funeral (4.8, "My Motherboard, Myself") to the much more profound gesture of Charlotte offering her financial help to Carrie so she doesn't have to rely on Mr. Big for money. Oria explains, "In a moment rife with symbolism, Charlotte offers Carrie her beloved engagement ring to make a down payment for her flat. Carrie has just broken up with Aidan, and Charlotte recently divorced Trey. The episode ends with a literal exchange of vows, with Charlotte asking if Carrie will accept the ring, and Carrie saying, 'I do'" (4.16, "Ring a Ding Ding").[15]

Burns-Ardolino explains this dynamic:

> In a moment of personal illness, crisis, or tragedy, each individual woman in the female foursome may feel isolated, alone, and lost; however, the bonds of their alternative family through sisterhood and collective solidarity transcended the cultural pitfalls of single them, and these independent women actively choose interdependence within the framework of their sustained female relationships. . . . Members of the female foursome, the sisterhood, serve to protect, nurture, comfort, encourage, and defend one another against the onslaught of an androcentric world in which women's identity is hinged on their relationship to the men in their lives and in which the political economy of the heterosexual couple supersedes the value of the single woman.[16]

Henry astutely notes that the show "routinely concludes with the four women together, laughing and talking, supporting each other," a natural way to reinforce the bonds between the women and the importance of female friendship to the audience.[17] This is also done through voice-overs and lines

The women of *Sex and the City* (from left: Samantha, Carrie, Charlotte, and Miranda) are role models of female friendship, there for each other in good times and bad. Photofest/*Sex and the City* (HBO), season 2 (summer–fall 1999)

that draw the women together. For example, in episode 2.1, "Take Me Out to the Ballgame," Carrie tells us that the most important rule of breakups is "no matter who broke your heart or how long it takes to heal, . . . you'll never get through it without your friends." Later, in 3.12, "Don't Ask, Don't Tell," she narrates, "It's hard enough to find the people who will love you no matter what. I was lucky enough to find three of them."

As touching as those lines are, there is another that is even more germane to the central premise of the show. In episode 4.1, "The Agony and the 'Ex'tacy," Charlotte, who is married, says to the women, "Maybe we could be each other's soulmates. And we could let men just be these great nice guys to have fun with." This harkens back to the show's original premise of having sex without emotion; emotion is reserved for your female friends. It also supports Samantha's assertion that "women are for friendships; men are for fucking" (2.18, "Ex in the City"). While this may make them seem like misandrists, it has nothing to do with hating men and everything to do with the power of female friendships. No matter how much a man and a woman love one another or how close they become, this bond is different from than the one that runs between women. Nothing can or should ever attempt to replace it. As Carrie says in episode 6.8., "The Catch, "I survived because I have a good safety net": that is, her friends.

MIRRORED IN REAL LIFE

The show's popularity with women encouraged them to gather in groups to watch it and to discuss it over the following week. It wasn't uncommon for these friends to share stories with one another about how what took place in the show was reflected in their own lives or how they would act if it was. In this way, the viewers "mirror[ed] the 'coming together' of the women in the programme" to create their own sisterhood that, hopefully, would endure well beyond the run of the show.[18]

Star was talking about Carrie, Miranda, Samantha, and Charlotte when he said, "[N]o matter what kind of adventures these girls go on, they are able to come back to the group, re-collect themselves, and touch base," but he could also have been talking about any number of the show's fans who found strength and solidarity in shared love for the show.[19] For all the ink spilled over its coverage of sex, *friendship* is the lasting legacy of *Sex and the City*.

11

LGBTQIA+ AND RACE ISSUES

"Gay men understand what's important: clothes, compliments and cocks."
—Samantha, episode 4.14, "All That Glitters"

"**L**adies, you have some 'splainin' to do." With all apologies to Ricky Ricardo, *Sex and the City* really does need to explain—or perhaps *atone* is a better word—for the way it treats characters in the LGBTQIA+ community and characters of color, especially given that its creator, Darren Star, is a gay man. Even Parker admits the show isn't a great representation of LGBTQIA+ people: "There were no women of color [in the main cast], and there was no substantial conversation about the LGBTQ community."[1]

Granted, the show was of its time, one in which all-White casts and homophobic humor in sitcoms was commonplace—look at *Friends* or even the groundbreaking *Will & Grace* for contemporary examples—but that doesn't excuse the sheer volume of instances of blatant disrespect for people of color and those who identify as LGBTQIA+. Nor does it excuse the lightheartedness with which many of the "jokes" made at their expense are treated. As Cassie Da Costa notes in *Vanity Fair*, "*Sex and the City*'s most reactionary perspectives are never portrayed as a source of shame for the characters or their acquaintances; they're always meant as light entertainment," as though it is okay to make fun of others as long as you're "just kidding."

We know now that how people are portrayed on television has a great impact on how they are accepted by society and how they feel about themselves. D'Acci writes that rather than functioning as a mirror of society, as it should, television often is "selective about what it chooses to represent and how."[2] This is especially true in the lack of representation in *Sex and the City*. As Da Costa points out, "Its quippy, city-girl tone has aged unevenly. Though that approach was well-suited to a story about proudly imperfect women, the show also used it as a cheap excuse to center a very specific viewpoint: straight white affluence, as written by straight white women and gay white men."[3]

Sex and the City was both groundbreaking for White women and painfully familiar for those of color and in the LGBTQIA+ community. "It was a show that was simultaneously progressive and regressive, where people of colour were either stereotypes or punchlines," wrote journalist Hunter Harris in 2016.[4] The lack of representation is especially troubling today because it is viewed by a whole new generation in syndication. "The oppressive misconceptions that existed when the show first aired 20 years ago persist even now—and that's why it's important to highlight its problematic moments that undermine the lived experiences of marginalized people," writes Tari Ngangura of *Fashion Magazine*.[5] We can hope that the younger viewers of today, with their acute sensitivities for all manner of cultural injustice, will see the show for what it is, just as my generation was able to spot the obvious racism in *All in the Family* but still enjoy the show. But the more we call a spade a spade, the less likely it is that those negative attitudes will be passed on.

ISSUES OF RACE AND REPRESENTATION

The silence of the people of color who should have been part of *Sex and the City* is so loud, it's deafening. The fact that there are only really four examples of characters of color in ninety-four episodes and only two of those lasted more than a single episode speaks volumes.[6] Out of the sixteen pages of notes for this chapter, issues of race take up only four. That is how few examples the show gives us to work from. "[Carrie] didn't have any Black friends, but in the 2008 movie, she had a Black assistant. The optics of that power imbalance are not insignificant," writes Harris.[7]

And this from a show set in one of the most diverse cities in the world. Anyone who has ever walked down the streets of Manhattan can attest to the number of languages being spoken; the volume of people representing perspectives other than White; and the number of ethnicities represented by neighborhoods, stores, and restaurants. Yet somehow, the ladies of *Sex and the City* manage to live in a nearly all-White bubble for six seasons. "Sure, plenty of white New Yorkers, especially in tony neighborhoods like Carrie's Upper East Side, surround themselves with other white people," writes Jill Filipovic for CNN. "But in a city that is less than half white, it's a choice to have one's whole social circle be so homogeneous."[8] Perhaps it was a case of "write what you know," but that is what consultants are for. And it is difficult to believe that *everyone* involved in the show lived such White-centric lives, as most of them were New Yorkers. Yet "during the first and second seasons of the show, our wealthy cisgender heroines live and operate within an entirely white bubble. In the third season that all changes, albeit not for the better."[9]

The most often-cited—and most blatant—example of racism comes in episode 3.5, "No Ifs, Ands, or Butts," which is the "first episode of *Sex and the City* to feature black actors in any meaningful way": that is, as more than extras, a truly sad commentary on the show and the times.[10] The episode opens with Carrie, Charlotte, Miranda, and Samantha dining at a hot new fusion soul food restaurant run by a Black chef named Adeena. Adeena introduces her brother, Chivon, to the group, and he realizes he and Samantha have met. They have chemistry right away and begin dating. One wouldn't think that in the late 1990s an interracial relationship would be worthy of mention, much less the subject of an entire episode of a show, but it was. In a twist on the usual *Guess Who's Coming to Dinner* trope, Samantha is the one to have to adapt to Chivon's Black world. In so doing, she wears some truly terrible "Jennifer Lopez–looking outfits" and begins saying words that should only be used by the Black community. And it only gets worse from there.

Soon, Adeena, who was nice enough to the ladies when they were patronizing her restaurant and would be okay with Samantha if she was just "fucking" Chivon, becomes frighteningly racist in her own right at the idea of her brother seriously dating a White woman. Her portrayal as an angry, bitter Black woman plays off an overused and insulting stereotype, placing her in the wrong and making Samantha, the White woman, virtuous in comparison, which is just a shade away from the equally problematic White-savior-complex narrative.[11]

As if not trusting the audience to understand the racial dynamics at play, the episode devolves into Samantha and Adeena yelling about race in the middle of a crowded dance club. This is followed by them getting into a literal hair-pulling cat fight, initiated by Adeena, who is again shown as being in the wrong and playing off of another stereotype that Black women who are upset are not only violent, but they also go for the hair in fights. Plus, as Desta writes, "Adeena's hatred of white women isn't grounded in anything; when Samantha asks her why Chivon is off-limits, she replies by saying, 'It's a Black thing!' It's a shallow, inelegantly expressed line" and lazy character development on the writers' part.[12] If they were trying to say something about how racism can work in reverse, too, then they certainly didn't do a good job of building it into Adeena's character or backing it up with any real evidence.

On top of all this, when Samantha is telling her friends about how much she likes Chivon—"Chivon is the sweetest man. We have great sex. And he happens to have the biggest . . ."—instead of letting her have a moment of genuine feeling, the writers have Charlotte interrupt, yelling, "Black cock. We know! He has a big, Black cock!" Not only does this make the viewer wince, but Samantha also makes it worse by replying, "I was about to say heart, but now that you're so interested, yes, he does have a big Black cock!" Yet another racist stereotype and completely unnecessary to the plot.

Sundra Oakley, the actress who played Adeena, has said about the role, "When I was looking at it through the lens of 20-years-ago Sundra, I was happy to have this job and work on this fabulous show. Even a few years later . . . it's like, oh man, why did it have to be that way? Why couldn't it have been a different story?" She does say that the racism in the script did not translate when the cameras stopped rolling. "There was not one negative experience on that set."[13]

Another cringe-worthy example comes in a subplot of episode 2.10, "The Caste System," in which Samantha dates a rich man who has an Asian servant named Sum. She is portrayed as a stereotypically subservient woman who speaks in broken English, keeps her eyes on the ground, and bows to her employer. When Samantha finds out that the meekness is all an act (which is bad enough because that means Sum is an Asian woman playing into the image painted onto her race by White people), Sum takes on yet another racist trope: that of the scheming Asian servant. She kicks Samantha out of bed, calling her all sorts of lewd names and pretending that Samantha struck her to evoke pity from her employer—whom her expression tells us she loves—and gets him to kick Samantha out so she can have him all to herself. If the writers had left it there, it would have been worthy of criticism, but no, they had to have Carrie make one of her witty puns: "She wasn't so dim, that Sum." Shon Faye, writing for Dazed Digital, puts it best: "The pun is as woeful as it is racist, and typifies many examples of the ways in which the show uncritically rejoiced in the prejudices of the affluent straight white women at its core."[14]

And then there are the random acts of racism sprinkled throughout the show. In the first movie, Miranda is trying to locate an available apartment in a "nice" (a.k.a., supergentrified) neighborhood and instructs those with her to "follow the White guy with a baby." Then there is Samantha's unexplainable Afro wig that she proudly wears in a blatant instance of cultural appropriation after losing her hair to chemo (6.17, "The Cold War"). And who could forget the comments by Bunny, Charlotte's mother-in-law, on Mandarin culture and its "daughters of the South Pacific" (4.12, "Just Say Yes")?

The writers seem to have learned at least a little from their early mis-steps because two later characters of color are treated with much more re-spect—and longer story arcs. In season 4, Brazilian actress Sônia Braga portrayed Samantha's girlfriend, Maria, and in season 6, Black actor Blair Underwood starred as Dr. Robert Leeds, Miranda's love interest for five episodes. In 2003, Nixon said everyone in the cast could see the lack of diversity was "irresponsible."[15] In another interview around the same time, she added, "We, all of us, and no one more than Sarah Jessica, had lobbied for this for a long, long time. . . . I'm a huge fan of the show, but if we had area in which we really could use improvement, it's certainly this one. . . . I think it's about time."[16]

HOMOPHOBIA AND TRANSPHOBIA

For a show about sex, with a sex columnist as the main character, *Sex and the City* is remarkably tone-deaf and at times aggressively negative about its portrayal of LGBTQIA+ characters. Even for its time, when there were very few queer characters on television, its negative message sometimes out-weighs the good it did through visibility. "If *Sex and the City* were on TV now, it'd probably be considered harmful for its extremely narrow view of queerness," writes Kasandar Brabaw for Refinery29. "But this was the '90s when the LGBTQ+ community was just coming out of the AIDS crisis, and there was relatively NO representation of queer lives on TV. *Sex and the City* pushed the envelope and showed those narratives at least. . . . It's a taste of queerness in its most diluted and digestible form."[17]

The country had to start somewhere, right? That's what Willie Garson, the straight actor who played Carrie's gay BFF, Stanford, said that the show did for the gay community. "[Gay characters] were kind of hushed or in the shadows on TV, or talked about in a dark way," he told Pink News in 2016. "I think it was a darkness that the producers wanted to bring out and say, 'Hold on, this character is fun, and is just one of their friends, it's not a 'thing.'"[18] However, having the subplot of an episode (2.16, "Was It Good for You?") revolve around two gay men who decide they want to have sex with Samantha because they are curious and she is the "hottest woman [they] know" is per-haps not the best way to go about it. Even though the two guys decide they can't go through with it after getting a look at Samantha's vagina, this subplot reinforces dangerous ideas about gay men. The first is that being gay is not a real sexuality because after all, even these two gay men are choosing to be with a woman. Second, it appears to give credence to the misinformed idea that if a woman is attractive enough, she can turn a gay man straight. And third, it seems to validate the childish notion that all gay men are repulsed by the female genitalia—though some likely are—and that the vagina is something to be scared of, an idea that harms both men and women.

STANFORD AND ANTHONY

Thankfully, this isn't by far the only episode to show the love lives of gay men. Most of the dating adventures in the world of gay men are portrayed through the characters of Stanford Blatch, Carrie's best friend from the beginning of the show, and Anthony Marentino, whom Charlotte meets and befriends in season 3. They embody the first non-negative stereotype of gay people commonly seen on television: the now clichéd gay best friend. As Carrie says, "The gay guy is the single girl's safety net" (5.5, "Plus One Is the Loneliest Number"). These are characters who have no real backstory or lives of their own but function solely as support and sounding boards for the female main characters. "They're accessories that Charlotte and Carrie use whenever they need a pep-talk, or a friend to hang out outside their inner circle," says Caballero.[19]

Mario Cantone (left) played Charlotte's gay best friend, Anthony, while Willie Garson played Carrie's gay BFF, Stanford Blatch. Photofest/*Sex and the City* (2008), directed by Michael Patrick King

Star, who is gay, explains the inclusion of this type of character: "It's something that, to me, was such a fabric of New York and friendships that was very, very organic."[20] If that is truly the case, then you would think they would have written more original and fully fledged characters, but no. As *Harper's Bazaar UK* points out, "there are only two types of gay men in *Sex and the City*—the camp man with a finesse for style and the bitchy gossip who doles out sharp one-liners": Stanford and Anthony, respectively.[21]

Stanford represents the harmless but fun gay male trope. He's Carrie's "other girlfriend," her confidant and guardian angel.[22] He's adorable and clearly on the lookout for love, just like the women are, which makes him a perfect addition to their world. "He wins our heart with his mischievous sense of humor and perseverance in the face of the often bizarre and brutal gay dating world," writes Sohn.[23] He is Carrie's life preserver when she is adrift after her breakups with Big, Aidan, and Berger. But he is never fully developed as a character. All we ever really learn about him is that he (1) is a talent manager, (2) is gay, (3) sometimes falls for his clients, and (4) is just as likely as Carrie to pick the wrong man. In limiting his character to those qualities, we can only see him in relation to Carrie, not as a person in his own right. This is demeaning to all members of the LGBTQIA+ community because it implies they are somehow less than the heterosexuals who populate the show with more dimension, there just when they are useful to the straight characters.

In episode 4.14, "All That Glitters," Carrie makes a new gay friend, Oliver, and Stanford's position as Carrie's BFF is threatened. While anyone might feel jealous of a friend's new bestie, because his only purpose in the show is to be Carrie's friend, Stanford reacts as though he is being erased, which he kind of is. When Carrie realizes this, she makes a comment that, while funny, leaves no doubt that she sees both gay men only in relation to herself: "I've been so preoccupied with my gay boyfriend, I kept forgetting about my gay husband."[24]

Anthony, however, is the stereotypical loud-mouthed queen. He's bitchy, self-centered, negative, and not afraid to spout his biting opinion to anyone who will listen. Given that, one would think he would be hard to get along with, but not for Charlotte. His flamboyance is the perfect counterpart to her conservatism. She wouldn't have become the character that she is at the end of the series without him. "Anthony brought out Charlotte's spontaneous side. It was he who pushed Charlotte to get back in the game when her marriage to Trey fell apart, and he helped her to design the 'new York' she became," writes Sohn.[25] Anthony is the one who encourages Charlotte to act on her undesired attraction to Harry. Even though he is far from her ideal image of the perfect man, Anthony tells her to go for it. From his experience, "ugly sex is hot sex" (5.7, "The Big Journey"). "If Anthony hadn't applauded that hot, ugly sex, he might never have gotten to design the Goldenblatt-York wedding," Sohn points out. "And that, as Charlotte might say, would have been a real *shundah*, a tragedy."[26]

Speaking of tragedies, the fact that the writers chose to pair up Stanford and Anthony in the second movie is a mistake. When they meet, Anthony is so repulsed by Stanford that he leaves the fashion show where Charlotte had invited them both, hoping to set them up (4.2, "The Real Me"). Throughout the show, they have little interaction, and when they do, there isn't any attraction between them. In fact, in episode 5.5, "Plus One Is the Loneliest Number," Stanford is so petty to Anthony that Anthony just walks off. But then in *Sex and the City 2*—seemingly just because they are both gay—the writers decided to have them get married. As Anthony says in episode 4.2, "Why? Because he's gay and I'm gay? Charlotte, let me clear something up for you. . . . I could do a lot better."

Yes, Anthony, you both could have. But the writers gave into yet another stereotype, the idea that all gay men are interchangeable: that is, that attraction and personality have nothing to do with whom they end up with, unlike in heterosexual relationships. What if the writers had said, "Hey, Aidan and Charlotte both like dogs, so they should end up together," even though they have nothing in common and barely know one another? That is how ridiculous and disingenuous the Stanford-Anthony pairing is. No wonder they end up in major fights and then get a divorce in *And Just Like That . . .* There is no other possible ending for such a forced couple.

EXAMPLES OF HOMOPHOBIA

Beyond the ongoing inclusion of the two stock gay characters of Stanford and Anthony, *Sex and the City* has several specific episodes and a few ongoing plotlines that show a distinct homophobic attitude. Even the fact that Samantha describes herself as "try-sexual" because she'll try anything, while a funny joke, is demeaning of actual sexualities because it implies— like songwriter Mark Ronson describing himself as a sapiosexual—that sexualities can be created at will rather than being ingrained from birth, and it mocks the experiences of those who are truly part of marginalized communities.[27]

Bisexuality

Despite 52 percent of the LGBTQIA+ community identifying as bisexual, bi-erasure has been a real problem both in the heterosexual community and inside the LGBTQIA+ community for years.[28] Defined by GLAAD as a situation "in which the existence or legitimacy of bisexuality (either in general or in regard to an individual) is questioned or denied outright," it is any attitude, comment, or assumption that implies that bisexuality is not a valid form of sexuality.[29] "Identifying as bisexual often feels like you're stuck in limbo—not 'gay' enough for some, and not 'straight' enough for others," writes openly bisexual journalist Kyli Rodriguez-Cayro.[30]

For those struggling to justify or discover their own bisexuality, episode 3.4 of *Sex and the City*, "Boy, Girl, Boy, Girl," can be especially painful and even harmful. In the episode, Carrie dates a younger man, Sean, who reveals that one of his three previous serious relationships was with a man. Instead of acting like the "sexual anthropologist" she claims to be—or even just an open-minded human being—Carrie flips out and starts obsessing over whether he is checking out every guy in the room. "She is it seems, the most sheltered and naïve sex columnist in the history of writing about sex," quips journalist Kayleigh Dray about Carrie's massive overreaction to the news.[31]

A sampling of the problematic and offensive comments in this episode that reinforce negative stereotypes about bisexuals include the following:

- **Miranda says that being bisexual isn't fair because "he's double-dipping."** This is harmful because it is just another way of saying that bisexual people are lucky because they have twice the number of people to be attracted to. That is about as realistic as a heterosexual woman thinking that she is going to be attracted to every man she meets. The reality is that bisexual people have tastes and proclivities and are attracted to and repelled by men and women based on looks, personality, and more, just like straight people are. Plus, bisexuality is a spectrum, so not everyone is 50/50.
- **Carrie calls bisexuality a "lack of sexual orientation."** This is bi-erasure in its purest form. It is a complete denial that bisexuality exists and is very hurtful to those who identify that way because it invalidates a very significant part of who they are, one they cannot control. Imagine having red hair from birth and being told that because you don't have either blond or brown hair, you don't have a hair color. That is what Carrie's comment feels like to a bisexual person.

- **Charlotte utters the words, "I'm very into labels. Gay. Straight. Pick a side and stay there."** This is also bi-erasure, only in very blatant terms. She is saying that there are only two sexualities and nothing exists in between, so all bi people need to decide if they are gay or straight and stick to their choice. In reality, bi people are attracted to at least two genders, perhaps more, depending on the person. To continue with the hair color analogy, it's like being told, "There are only two hair colors, blond or brown. You have to pick one and keep dying your hair that color, and you can't ever change it."

- **Carrie calls bisexuality a "layover on the way to gay town."** This assumes that bisexual people are just confused and eventually they will realize they are really gay. While some gay or lesbian people do start out thinking they are bisexual before realizing they are actually gay, to assume this is the case for all is to once again invalidate bisexuality as a valid sexual expression. Carrie's cavalier use of this phrase is offensive because she treats bisexuality "like no more than an invention. . . . [S]he treats it like a curiosity, something to be judged, not understood," writes Caballero.[32]

- **When Carrie is at the party with Sean's friends, many of whom are bi, she thinks, "I was Alice in confused-sexual-orientation land."** Again, this reinforces the idea that bisexuals are confused and will eventually figure out if they are gay or straight, like Charlotte's misguided idea of clear black-and-white sexual labels. Comments like this dismiss the notion that while some people may know for certain that they are gay or straight, others may know for certain that they like people of more than one gender.

- **Carrie asks herself, "Was sexual flipping the wave of the future?"** First, the phrase *sexual flipping* makes it sound like bisexual people can change who they are attracted to at will, which is not the case any more than it is for straight or gay people. Second, it has a connotation that bisexuals are somehow like swingers who swap partners. While this may occur in select groups, overall, bisexuals are not any more or less likely to be unfaithful to their lovers than any other sexual orientation. It is very possible to be bisexual and be in a monogamous relationship with either sex. Polyamory (having multiple romantic relationships at once, usually with the full knowledge and consent of everyone involved) is not the same as bisexuality. A person can be polyamorous and be of any sexual orientation.

- **Carrie declares to herself, "I was too old to play this game."** Even if we give the writers the benefit of the doubt and say the word *game* was referencing the game of spin the bottle going on at the party—which it clearly wasn't—Carrie's comment still makes light of bisexuality. She is implying that it is something people invoke for fun, like a fad or something they do when they are bored, not a core part of who they are. In addition, saying she was "too old" implies that there is an age limit by which people have to discover (or, in her mind, choose) their sexuality, which isn't true. Whether you know from childhood what your orientation is or don't discover it until late in life, it is equally valid. Finally, Carrie implies that bisexuality is really sexual experimentation rather than an orientation you can't change and that it is "only the new generations that are open to these options. This strategy allows the series to hold onto a heteronormative heterosexuality while maintaining its 'hip' open minded spirit."[33]

- **Carrie asks herself, "If women can transform into men and men can become women and we can choose to sleep with everyone, then maybe gender doesn't even exist anymore. If we can take the best of the other sex and make it our own, has the opposite sex become obsolete?"** There is so much to unpack here. First and foremost, no one "chooses" their sexuality. Period. End of story. Second, it is Carrie's turn to be confused here. She is conflating sexual orientation (who you are sexually attracted to) with gender (how you identify; i.e., male, female, gender fluid, trans, etc.). They are not the same thing. In fact, gender and sexuality have very little to do with one another. A person can be straight and gender fluid, trans and a lesbian, female and bisexual, or any other permutation. Third, no one is saying that bisexuality has anything to do with erasing gender. Even people who identify as gender fluid don't deny that others may identify as male or female; gender inclusiveness simply means that the old theory that there are only two genders is obsolete. It asks people to consider that gender is a spectrum, not that it doesn't exist. And yes, Carrie, the term *opposite sex* is obsolete for those who are gender fluid, but that has nothing to do with your boyfriend being bisexual.

In addition, the narrative around bisexuality in this episode centers Carrie's "anxiety" about male bisexuality; female bisexuality isn't even discussed, although some of the women at the party, such as Dawn, the woman Carrie kisses playing spin the bottle, are identified as bisexual. To Henry, this suggests "that women's sexuality is more open to change and experimentation than men's."[34] But it can also be argued that this mind-set is really a matter of cultural conditioning, as (thanks to male fantasies of threesomes) we are taught that women being bisexual is hot, but because of male homophobia, we're also led to believe that men being bisexual is deviant. In reality, whether you are male or female, being bi is the same—you like more than one gender. That is it.

Lesbianism

As with bisexuality, *Sex and the City* doesn't have a very good track record with its portrayal of lesbianism, which is ironic for a show with four female main characters who live in a large city where, in reality, at least one of them is likely to be something other than straight and one is a sex columnist, who it can be assumed knows at least one lesbian. But no, as Akass and McCabe write, "Lesbianism emerges as a lifestyle choice to be dispensed with like last year's fashion, while gay male sensibilities are celebrated. With lesbianism put firmly back into the closet, gay male sexuality emerges as the identity of choice that informs the bodies and languages of the four women."[35]

The show's problems begin in the third episode (1.3., "Bay of Married Pigs"), when Miranda is mistaken for a lesbian and plays along in order to get ahead at work. Playing "dress-up" with a sexuality many people identify with is extremely offensive in the best of circumstances, but doing so in order to be considered a minority and win brownie points at work is even more deplorable. What's worse is that she recruits her coworker, Syd, an actual lesbian, to be her accomplice in this little charade. In real life, it is unlikely that a lesbian woman would agree to such a thing—she would likely be deeply offended—perhaps unless she is as driven as Miranda and sees some value in appearing to have a girlfriend. But we can't make that judgment on behalf of Syd because she is completely dehumanized; the only thing she says after her initial meeting with Miranda is "Yeah, you are," after Miranda kisses her and says, "Yeah, definitely straight." Not to mention the fact that a single kiss is not necessarily enough to cement your sexuality—but that's an argument for another day.

In the second season, the issue of lesbianism is brought up again in episode 2.6, "The Cheating Curve," in which Charlotte befriends a group of "power lesbians"—who are "portrayed as exclusively white, rich, and power-hungry" and are nameless (with one exception) and therefore identity-less.[36] Aside from a tasteless comment from Samantha—"You can't expect to move to Wonder Woman's island and not go native"—Charlotte's friendship with the lesbians is portrayed as normal at first, until she is invited to go on a trip with them, which would mean entering their inner circle. When

Charlotte admits she's straight, Patty Austin, the queen bee of the lesbians, says to her coldly, "If you're not going to eat pussy, you're not a dyke."

There's a lot wrong with this situation. First, it implies that lesbians cannot be friends with straight women, which couldn't be further from the truth. Second, there are as many ways of being a lesbian as there are women; just because you don't like giving oral sex doesn't mean you aren't a lesbian if you are a woman attracted to other women. (Plenty of straight men don't like that particular sexual act, and no one questions their heterosexuality!) In addition, the word *dyke* can be offensive, though some lesbians have reclaimed the term. And finally, it plays on the stereotype of the cold, unfeeling lesbian, which any rational human being knows is not how all lesbians behave.

In season 4, for three episodes (4.3–4.5) Samantha engages in a lesbian relationship with artist Maria, whose apartment Carrie refers to as "casa del lesbo," a slur if there ever was one. "The show used lesbianism as a narrative device," writes Da Costa, "painting it as a strategy born out of dating fatigue; the possibility that Samantha was legitimately curious or bisexual was never explored."[37] This seems to imply that Samantha's relationship is "just a phase" from the very beginning. It is interesting that upon entering a relationship with another woman, Samantha immediately "declares herself a lesbian, instead of even considering the idea she might be bisexual."[38] As someone very sexually knowledgeable, Samantha surely knows about bisexuality, so the fact that she doesn't even mention it as an option is yet another example of bi-erasure in the show.

Carrie and Charlotte don't help matters by not taking Samantha's new relationship seriously. Once they are out of earshot of Samantha, Carrie asks the others, "How does that work? You go to bed one night, and poof, you're a lesbian?" To which Miranda responds that she is a fire hydrant, and Carrie says she's always wanted to be a shoe, as if those inanimate objects are the same as lesbians. Then Miranda uses the phrase *eat pussy*, and Charlotte and Carrie—a sex columnist, mind you—are so disgusted that they respond with a schoolgirl chorus of "Ewwwww!" like the class bully just presented them with a frog. You would think that as women with vaginas who receive oral sex from men regularly, they would have a more mature response, but because they are talking about two women, it is automatically gross. Later, Charlotte says, "Oh please, she's not in a relationship. She's just doing this to bug us," completely invalidating Samantha's relationship. Moreover, "her friends' sly, self-centered commentary about her new relationship . . . was framed not as gossip, but insight," as though these three women—none of whom have ever been in a lesbian relationship—are somehow experts.[39]

Samantha, however, has a short-lived transformation, putting off having sex right away because she wants the "first time to be special." This is unheard of for her. Later, she reveals to the women that her point of view about sex has shifted dramatically, saying, "Maria has taught me how to connect during sex. It's not just an animal act. It's about two people making love." Who is this woman, and what has she done with Samantha? When Samantha does finally initiate sex, Maria teaches her the difference between having sex with a man and having sex with a woman—with a woman it's about "connection" and "lovemaking," not pornography. This seemingly nice statement is a microaggression against heterosexual relationships because it implies that they cannot, and men cannot, include intimacy in lovemaking, which we all know is not true. It is also not fair to lesbian relationships because it implies that lesbians can't just have sex because it is fun and pleasurable, which, of course, they do.

By episode 4.5, Samantha's serious relationship is starting to chafe, and she is bored. "All we ever do is lie around, take baths together, and talk about feelings," Samantha says, painting a very boring and unrealistic image of lesbian relationships. Lesbians go out just as much as any other type of couple, so the fact that the show portrays Samantha dragging Maria out of the apartment to a bar is insulting. As a queer woman interviewed for an article on *Sex and the City* puts it, "Samantha's whole relationship with Maria is an exercise in cringing uncontrollably as a queer woman. It was basically a parody of lesbian relationships, capitalizing on the 'overemotional' stereotype of two women being together."[40]

This overreaction really comes into play when some of the men from Samantha's past come sniffing around, looking to get laid. As Samantha points out, Maria knows she had been with men—that isn't a secret. But Maria still gets violently jealous, yelling and smashing plates because she is upset about the men Samantha dated in the past. It is a complete overreaction and frankly a sign of psychosis, something that shouldn't be associated with a lesbian relationship because there are enough negative perceptions out there already without reiterating the idea that women, especially lesbians, are hysterical.

Maria and Samantha eventually break up because, as everyone who as ever met Samantha knows—yet Maria somehow couldn't figure out, despite multiple clues—Samantha has intimacy issues. But the writers couldn't let them go without one more lesbian gag: Maria's gift to Samantha of a ridiculously large strap-on. Here again, they are making fun of a very real way that lesbians can have sex by making it as (literally) outsized and outlandish as the rest of the storyline, proving none of it is meant to be taken seriously.

The Gay Straight Man

One very strange episode is 2.11, "Evolution," which could be seen as equally offensive to both straight and gay men. At the beginning of the episode, Charlotte is seen out with Stefan, a man she knows because he caters functions for the art gallery at which she works. She assumes they are just friends because she thinks he's gay. That is until he kisses her passionately. She's very confused because he's a pastry chef and likes art, Broadway musicals, cooking, and Cher—all things normally associated with gay men—yet he seems sexually attracted to her. When she explains her conundrum to her friends, they tell her that he is likely either a "gay straight man" or a "straight gay guy." Carrie's voice-over informs us that the "gay straight man was a new strain of heterosexual male spawned in Manhattan as a result of over-exposure to fashion, exotic cuisine, musical theater, and antique furniture." Samantha further explains, "A gay straight man means he's straight with great gay qualities. Whereas a straight gay guy is just a gay guy who plays sports who won't fuck you."

The idea of a "gay straight man" wasn't new; it just didn't have the same name. In the early 2000s, the term *metrosexual* rose to prominence in America to describe straight men living in urban areas who, according to Merriam Webster, were "given to enhancing [their] personal appearance by fastidious grooming, beauty treatments, and fashionable clothes."[41] The term was "coined in the mid-90s by the British journalist Mark Simpson, who writes about gay issues, to 'satirize what he saw as consumerism's toll on traditional masculinity.' Britain's Channel 4 had a show called *Metrosexuality* in 2001," according to the *New York Times*.[42] But in America, it came into the vernacular after the original iteration of the reality show *Queer Eye for the Straight Guy* made men caring about their looks, fashion, culture, and comportment cool among a large segment of the male population.

So Stefan's sexuality shouldn't really have been in question. It was more a matter of him having happily embraced his more feminine qualities. But Charlotte ultimately can't handle it. When a mouse gets stuck on a cruelty-free mousetrap in Stefan's kitchen, both he and Charlotte freak out in equal measure—squealing and flailing as one. Carrie's narration explains, "At that moment, Charlotte realized her masculine side wasn't evolved enough for a man whose feminine side was as highly evolved as Stefan's."

This portrayal of a tender straight man is insulting to both gay and straight men. For gay men, it is yet another reinforcement of a litany of traits, likes, and dislikes that are commonly associated with them, regardless of whether they hold true for most of the population or not. For straight men, it is a slap in the face to any who happen to enjoy things that are commonly associated with gay men as well as a definite message that men embracing their feminine side is to be frowned upon. It is a clear reinforcement of traditional masculine portrayals, or as we would call it today "toxic masculinity." Henry asserts that the episode reinforces the old idea that "women prefer their straight men on the butch side of the gender scale" and that the only way to get the girl is to be a man's man.[43]

Transphobia and Drag Shaming

Despite the inclusion of a drag queen in Miranda's birthday celebration in the pilot, the show's depiction of drag queens and transgender people is notoriously terrible. First, participating in drag culture and being transgender are two different things the show often treats as one and the same. Men who enjoy drag are just that—they are still men once they take off their costumes and shed their female personas. Transgender people's gender identity does not match the sex they were assigned at birth. Therefore, they may dress and sometimes even have surgery to make their appearance match what they feel.

In episode 2.9, "Old Dogs, New Dicks," Samantha encounters former boyfriend and semipro hockey player Brad at a bar. But to her shock and horror, he is now in drag, and his persona is named Samantha. He tells her that he started drag right after dating her, and because she was his inspiration, he took his name and look from her. Samantha's shock is understandable, but you would think that the notoriously vain woman would be honored by such an act; instead, she just looks like she is going to be sick.

The following season, in episode 3.4, "Boy, Girl, Boy, Girl," Charlotte hosts an art exhibit by a photographer who specializes in dressing women up in drag and photographing them as drag kings. The portrayal of Charlotte dressing as a man is done respectfully, but the problem is with her motivation. If she was doing this to truly explore her identity or even her sexuality, that would be laudable, but she books her photo shoot because she is attracted to the heterosexual photographer, whom she eventually sleeps with. Her newfound confidence is treated as an accidental side effect to establish her heteronomy through sex rather than an exciting discovery about her masculine side. This is a shame because the storyline has the potential to say a lot about gender and gender bending, but it caves to heterosexual binary norms. Still, the show gets some credit for using "real drag kings, but only as background players," instead of actors.[44] Too bad they didn't have bigger parts.

Another unfortunate choice on behalf of the writers is to make the normally "live and let live" Samantha into a transphobic person in season 3. Interestingly, when Samantha moves into the Meat Packing District in episode 3.6, "Are We Sluts?" she greets the trans prostitutes warmly, with no indication that she has any issues with them plying their trade on the sidewalk outside her building. Yet by episode 3.18, "Cock-a-Doodle-Do," she is spouting terms that were questionable at the time and are certainly considered slurs today. Yes, she is annoyed that they are making noise that interrupts her sexual conquest upstairs, but that doesn't justify her vitriol: "I am paying a fortune to live in a neighborhood that's trendy by day and tranny by night." And when Charlotte doesn't understand the term *tranny*, Samantha explains, "Transsexuals. Chicks with dicks. Boobs on top, balls down below." And when Miranda says she doesn't understand the appeal, Carrie helpfully quips, "It's the other white meat," thus comparing them to pork and pigs, insulting and dehumanizing them. Then they start referring to them collectively as the "up my ass players," which needs no explanation.

The next time they bother her, Samantha goes down to the street, introduces herself, and asks them to be quieter. They agree and move down the street. A few nights later, they are back and are making too much noise for Samantha to enjoy her latest conquest, so she pushes the guy off her, goes to the window, and yells at them to be quiet. They yell back, and she threatens to go down there and cut their dicks off for them. While meant in jest, this is a dangerous threat given the very real and very high rate of abuse and murder of transgender people, especially women. While filling up a pot of water, Samantha mutters to herself, "Seven thousand dollars a month, and I have to put up with a trilogy of fucking trannies out there—I don't fucking think so!" She goes to the window and dumps water on them. Two of them step away in time, but one is soaked. Nowadays, this would be considered a hate crime. In retaliation, one prostitute comes back and eggs Samantha's window. Carrie's voice-over tells us that Samantha realized she'd never win this fight because even though she was good with men, these men were also part women. This statement purposely misgenders the trans women. It also paints all women as devious, conniving, and vengeful.

Carrie's next voice-over is more problematic. "Samantha's friendly neighborhood pre-op transsexual hookers, half-man, half-woman, totally annoying" not only invades their privacy (How does she know they are pre-op? Or does she just assume? What business of is it of hers?), but it also invalidates their gender identity as women by calling them half-man because (she assumes) they still have penises.

REACTIONS FROM THE LGBTIA+ COMMUNITY

Sex and the City is known to have legions of fans within the LGBTQIA+ community, especially gay men, so asking real-life fans of the show who are part of that community about their thoughts is an important addition to any study of the show's portrayal and its effects. Brabaw interviewed several people for the article "How LGBTQ+ People Really Feel about *Sex and the City*," as did film journalist Grace Barber-Plentie for her article "The Conflict of Loving *Sex and the City* When You're Not a Straight White Woman," and I did, as well, for this book. Their testimonies show that the LGBTQIA+ community had mixed reactions to the show, just as the heterosexual community did.

Some, like Lauren, a cisgender bisexual woman, found great strength in seeing themselves in the storylines, flawed as they were. "*Sex and the City* definitely made me feel more comfortable experimenting with women as a baby queer. Samantha is my homegirl, even though the girls' reactions to her dating a woman were cringey. They could have had a great opportunity to normalize and destigmatize, but they didn't take advantage of it," she said.[45]

An anonymous woman who didn't give her sexual orientation wanted more: "I liked Samantha's quick trip to lezville, but I wish that there had been real representation of queer women in their dating experiences—especially since there was a lesbian [Cynthia Nixon, who identifies as queer] cast as a straight woman."[46]

Some held a more middle-ground attitude, like Katie, a cisgender queer woman: "*Sex and the City* was always a guilty pleasure for me. In terms of queerness, it's more of a cultural artifact now than a current representation. We have to look at it in terms of context, both the fact that it was 20 years ago and that the envelope at the time could only be pushed so far. Was *Sex and the City* perfect for queers? Absolutely not. Did it do what it could for us at the time? I think so."[47]

Dayna, a cisgender lesbian, felt like everyone was taking the show too seriously: "Of course there were problematic moments, but I wouldn't characterize them as harmful. It's not that deep! *Sex and the City* was an amazing, entertaining show! Although there was no regular lesbian character, *SATC* still helped me to unapologetically own my sexuality."[48]

Elizabeth, a cisgender bisexual woman, admits to not catching onto the problems on her first viewing:

At the time, none of it phased me in the least. I knew I was bisexual but—
and I'm ashamed to admit this—the homophobia went straight over my
head. It wasn't until I watched it again more than twenty years later before
And Just Like That . . . premiered that I realized how terrible the portrayal
was. Now I'm mad that a show I loved so much spouted so much harmful
rhetoric! They can try to correct it all they want, but the damage has been
done.[49]

Others were deeply affected by the show's missteps in its portrayal of the
gay community. Heather, a lesbian, said, "*Sex and the City* showed its queer
characters as gross stereotypes presented as accessories to cis-het women.
We're more than that and have value on our own. *SATC* was only helpful to
queer people in the very generic 'any visibility reminds people that we exist'
capacity."[50]

Suyin, a female who declined to disclose her sexuality, said that to her
it felt like anytime an LGBTQ character is introduced, "they're treated like
a punchline."[51]

An anonymous sexually fluid woman said, "I don't even know if I consciously understood the level it may have affected my psyche, but I *know* it
didn't help my straight girlfriends take my female relationships more seriously or as anything more than just some 'youthful phase.'"[52]

WHAT THE SHOW GETS RIGHT

Despite all its problems, there are some things that *Sex and the City* does well
regarding LGBTQIA+ people. Without *Sex and the City*, we wouldn't have
more progressive shows. "Despite its focus on heteronormative models of sexuality, it should be conceded that this was one of the first mainstream cultural
texts to allow the inclusion of 'peripheral' sexual identities and to explore the
questions of the electorate elasticity of gender categories," writes Oria.[53]

Plus, it was one of the first shows to portray gay people as something
other than cardboard characters or serial killers. They were also free to be
sexual beings. Michael Musto, a *Village Voice* columnist, praises the show
for allowing gay characters "to demonstrate their gayness: 'most gay characters in primetime aren't allowed to be sexual. They're only gay because they
say they're gay.'"[54] In 2002 in the *New York Times*, Alan James Frutkin called
Sex and the City the "best gay show on television" because "it has featured
storylines portraying contemporary gay life with a wit and a depth that the
more overtly gay *Queer as Folk* hasn't achieved."[55]

Even in episodes where bisexual and transgender characters are treated poorly, there are a few glimmers of hope. In 3.4, "Boy, Girl, Boy, Girl," Carrie's bisexual boyfriend Sean is written with great care. He is portrayed as a relatively tame character with only three serious relationships in his past, as opposed to the stereotypical bisexual person who sleeps with everyone they see. His attitude about his sexuality just being a part of him—"It's just me"—is also accurate; while television tends to define LGBTQIA+ people by their sexual orientation, in real life, it's just one facet of who the person is. Also, his explanation of not being attracted to anatomy but to the mind and soul is simple and spot-on: "It's about the person."

For all the shade thrown at the three transgender prostitutes in 3.18, "Cock-a-Doodle-Do," they are at least given the respect of being named people: Chyna, Destiny, and Jo. Unlike the "power lesbians," they are given identities and therefore are acknowledged. In addition, the fact that Samantha throws a "kiss-and-make-up party" to build bridges between them is huge. She is showing that with an open mind, one can learn, grow, and change and that tolerance—if not outright acceptance—can lead to friendships and fun.

Through Samantha, the show is also unintentionally but uncannily prescient about the future of sexuality and gender. In 2.16, "Was It Good for You?" Samantha shows that she is way ahead of her time in her concepts of sexuality. Sounding very much like a person of the 2020s rather than the late 1990s, she says to Carrie, "The new millennium won't be about sexual labels; it will be about sexual expression. It won't matter if you're sleeping with men or women. It will be about sleeping with individuals. . . . Soon everyone will be pansexual. It won't matter if you're gay or straight." This is such an insightful comment for a show that in so many other ways lacks sexual diversity; it makes one wonder why more attitudes like this aren't seen on the show; perhaps the writers felt the audience wasn't ready for them. It is also prophetic given the broadening of the gender and sexuality spectrum we've seen in the last decade.

In episode 3.4, "Boy, Girl, Boy, Girl," Samantha is the only character not fazed by Sean's bisexuality. She says to Carrie, "You know, I think it's great. He's open to all sexual experiences. He's evolved." In 4.4, "What's Sex Got to Do with It?" Samantha scolds Carrie that being a lesbian is "just a label, like Gucci or Versace," to which Carrie, trying to be funny but ending up being her stereotyping self, responds, "or Birkenstock." Samantha replies, "This is not about being gay or straight." While Carrie's comment serves to reinforce the image of the butch lesbian and her preferred footwear, Samantha once again shows great insight into the fluidity of sexuality and the pointlessness of labels.

Even Carrie—who is so often bigoted in her thinking—unintentionally presents a foreshadowing of today's gender-fluid culture when she muses, "If women can transform into men and men can become women, . . . then maybe gender doesn't even exist anymore." Though she means it in a negative way, as in gender is being erased rather than is no longer needed as a social construct, she is one of the first people to voice this kind of thought on prime-time television. For nonbinary people in the late 1990s, this comment had to be a surprising acknowledgment of their identity, even if it was accidental.

12

SEX AND MOTHERHOOD

"Easy?! You men have no idea what we're dealing with. Teeth placement and jaw stress and suction and gag reflex. And all the while bobbing up and down, moaning and trying to breathe through our noses. Easy? Honey, they don't call it a job for nothing."

—Samantha, episode 3.9, "Easy Come, Easy Go"

Sex and the City may have trod carefully in other areas but certainly not in its titular subject: sex. From the scene in the pilot at Miranda's birthday party—the first time we see all four women as an ensemble—the show makes it very clear what it is about. Appropriately enough, the show's thesis comes from the lips of sexual maven Samantha, who suggests "having sex like a man": that is, "without feelings."

Across the country, audiences gasped. Nothing like this had ever been said on television before by a woman. They knew they were witnessing history. "*Sex and the City* was not only the first show with a premise entirely based on sex on HBO, but on US television in general," Oria finds.[1] "It took sex out of the shadows," said King. "Before *Sex and the City*, whenever the word 'sex' was written in advertisements, it was always black and oily, and now whenever you see the word 'sexy,' it's usually pink. And that's us. We took the shame out of it and we made it fun. I'm very happy to have put a light—a very flattering and fun pink light—on a situation that society deemed as dark and shameful."[2]

They were able to get away with what, at the time, was shocking material, using words and nudity in a way no show, not even on cable, was able to before because they framed it as comedy. If the sex was treated seriously, the show never would have gotten the green light. "We are able to do things that are as outrageous and explicit [as on the Playboy channel] because they're funny," says Star.[3] Cattrall "elevated casual sex to a comedic art—those involved in the show referred to her as the 'Lucille Ball of the bedroom'" for her over-the-top sex-scene performances.[4]

Humor not only allowed the show to sneak a lot past the censors, but it is also disarms audiences so they are receptive to the show's racier elements. "Audiences are more comfortable with presentations of social change when they are infused with humor, which softens the blow, so to speak," writes Ashli LeeAnn Dykes in her doctoral dissertation. As a comedy, the show "employs humor to frame and partially diffuse the potentially radical representation of single women characters." Plus, humor is a great uniter; "by interjecting humor . . . [the] series avoid[s] being viewed (and disregarded) as polemical," Dykes adds.[5]

It also gives audiences permission to take the subject matter as they will. If people can laugh about the issues raised, then they don't have to take them seriously, if they don't want to. But the message is still there, and some part of it is getting through. Likewise, those who are receptive can use the laughs as a cover for their interest, if needed, and if not, they can share in the joy with likeminded friends.

WHAT NUMBER DOES A SLUT MAKE?

With all their talk, experimentation, and dating, the ladies of *Sex and the City* have very healthy sex lives. Over the years, they date men from all walks of life: "waiters, doormen, trainers, lawyers, yoga instructors, bartenders, writers, baseball players, ophthalmologists, realtors, artists, architects, furniture designers and unemployed actors."[6]

"By our count, the show's six-season run featured a total of 96 sex scenes—those that go just beyond the mere implication of sexual activity," journalist Andrew Thompson writes.[7] Another reporter, Christie Smith, also runs the numbers on the ladies' sexual activity: "We . . . calculated that during the course of 94 episodes and six seasons, the women of *Sex and the City* hit the sheets with a combined total of 94 men and one woman."[8] In case you're curious, Smith finds that breaks down to forty-two partners for Samantha, eighteen each for Carrie and Charlotte, and seventeen for Miranda.

How realistic is all that sex? That depends on where you live. A survey by Durex condoms finds that the average American woman has nine sex partners in a lifetime.[9] However, Karyn Bosnak, an author who has done extensive research into the sex lives of women, finds that New Yorkers have twice that many partners. "Women in other parts of the country tend to get married much younger. It's not a big deal to be single in your 30s in New York. There's also the anonymity factor. You can date men from different social circles here. If you have 20 sex partners and you live in a small, rural town, that's not good," she says, because where there are fewer people, there are more people to know whom you are sleeping with—and likely disapprove—and a greater chance the men will know one another.[10]

While Smith concludes the *Sex and the City* gals are "right on target," the numbers cited here are just for the five-year run of the show. They don't count the partners the women had before the show begins. Given that they are in their thirties and forties and most women start having sex as teenagers (from episode 2.15, "Shortcomings," we know Samantha was having sex at thirteen), their total lifetime numbers are likely much higher. When Miranda finds out she has chlamydia in episode 3.6, "Are We Sluts?" she has to make a list of all of her previous sexual partners. She later admits to Steve that her number is forty-two, while he admits his is higher than sixty.

While all this sex shows a "focus on women's pleasure with a healthy disregard for the accusation of selfishness that might have been made in previous decades," audiences didn't necessarily see it that way.[11] Reaction to the women's seemingly high number of sexual partners was swift and brutal. Chupack recounts, "One season I came back [from hiatus], and I heard so much feedback from people saying 'These women are sluts. How many men are they going to sleep with?' That notion eventually became an episode, 'Are We Sluts?'"[12] While that episode leaves the answer open to interpretation, men thought the answer was yes. "With the exception of Charlotte, men didn't find them likable," Nussbaum finds. "There were endless cruel jokes about Samantha, Miranda, and Carrie as sluts, man-haters, or gold-diggers."[13]

This situation is now called slut-shaming, a term that rose to the vernacular in the mid-2010s and is defined as the "practice of disparaging women, and occasionally men, for acting in a manner that violates 'norms' regarding sexually appropriate behavior."[14] Most of the time, slut-shaming involves a double standard in which "women who have casual sex [are held] to a different standard than men who do."[15] After all, men who bed lots of women are seen as virile studs, while women who have many partners are labeled sluts.

Slut-shaming of the show doesn't only come from viewers; it also takes place among the female characters. Usually, Charlotte is the perpetrator, and Samantha, the recipient. While many of Charlotte's judgmental asides can be ignored, two that certainly can't occur in episode 2.15, "Shortcomings," after Samantha sleeps with Charlotte's brother. Charlotte yells at Samantha, accusing her of being promiscuous, and later she says to Carrie and Miranda that Samantha "has so many notches on her bedpost, it's practically whittled down to a toothpick." Never mind that Charlotte has had her fair share of conquests, as well.

This attitude carried over with at least one cast member when the cameras were not rolling. In 2014, Chris Noth, who played Mr. Big on the series, made a problematic comment, calling the character of Carrie a "whore." He told an Australian news company that while Mr. Big "never tried to pretend he was anything other than what he was," it was Carrie

> who tried to pretend he was something he wasn't. He was always honest about himself—he never cheated on her. The relationship just didn't work, and he went on to get married while she went on to . . . how many boyfriends did she have? She was such a whore! [laughs] There's a misconception that Carrie was a victim of him, and that's not the case—she was a strong, smart woman.[16]

As *Sex and the City* writer Jenny Bicks points out, "Oh my God, that's such a 'Big' thing to say! . . . He seems to have forgotten that he may not have cheated *on* her, but he certainly cheated *with* her when he was married and Carrie was single."[17]

Eliana Dockterman points out the double standard of allowing male characters to have lots of sex with a wink and a nod but then condemning a female character for doing the same:

> Sure, Carrie bedded a lot of guys on *Sex and the City* (as did Samantha, Miranda and even the primmer Charlotte). But so did Barney on *How I Met Your Mother*, Don on *Mad Men*, Joey on *Friends*, Vince on *Entourage*, Nick on *New Girl*, Tony on *The Sopranos*. . . . [T]he list goes on and on. Hell, even Big is said to have had his fair share of conquests. To single Carrie out is simple sexism.[18]

At the time, Noth's comment was laughed off as an attempted joke that fell flat. However, with the sexual assault and harassment claims that have since surfaced against him, his comment can be seen in a whole new light that casts doubt on the lightheartedness of the situation.

TURNING THE TABLES

For decades, women have been seen on television and in film through the "male gaze"; that is, from a man's point of view. *Sex and the City* flips that idea and shows us life from the female perspective, allowing women to experience for the first time what it is like to be in the position of power. Not only do the women date and have sex for their own pleasure, but they also openly objectify the men they are with by giving them nicknames like Mr. Pussy, the Turtle, or Spring Roll Guy, instead of using their real names.[19] It is interesting to note one of the few times the ladies call a man by his name—Aidan—it is Big who objectifies him. In so doing Big neutralizes him as a threat by calling him at various times "Mr. Perfect" (3.8, "The Big Time"); "Paul Bunyan," "Daniel Boone" (both in 3.9, "Easy Come, Easy Go"); and "Country Bob" (4.12, "Just Say Yes"). We only hear him call Aidan by name once, and that is at Carric's insistence (4.12, "Just Say Yes").

Davis points out that men function in *Sex and the City* in much the same way that women have in shows for years: "I enjoyed watching male guest stars come on our show. What they have to do is something we as women actresses have had to do forever. It's always been part of our lots to come in and do the hot girl. But men aren't used to playing that role. Suddenly the women are in control, and it's about what they think is sexy. It's a complete turn of the tables."[20] She uses the key word: *control*. The role reversals in *Sex and the City* are all about power, and this time it is women who have the upper hand—something Oria calls a "radical turning of the tables in the gender struggle."[21]

SEXUAL EMPOWERMENT

That power shift was perceived clearly by the audience, which is one reason so many men felt the need to make fun of the show or of the characters; they were threatened by the idea of women rising, especially in the bedroom, long counted as the domain of men, where women were expected to be submissive. But not anymore. While *Sex and the City* brings "topics previously reserved for the bedroom into America's living room . . . [through] candid discussions about anal sex, bondage and sex toys," it also frees women to talk about what they desire from a sexual relationship and stand up for their right to experience sexual pleasure.[22] "It revolutionized the way many women conceptualized sex and talked about it, helping them foster a sense of entitlement to more egalitarian sexual relationships at the turn of the Millennium," says Oria.[23]

In addition, by adding some glitz and glamor, *Sex and the City* elevates the subject of sex from the gutter and our baser instincts to a gold- and diamond-encrusted affair to be enjoyed amid martinis and manicures. Writer Jennifer Wright believes that the show changed the way women viewed premarital sex in the late '90s and early 2000s in much the same way *Playboy* changed the way men viewed premarital sex in the 1950s. Just as Hugh Hefner pitched sex as something sophisticated men did between listening to jazz and drinking scotch, so *Sex and the City* made sex seem like a glamorous part of a single woman's life, to be sampled between shopping sprees and going to new restaurants.[24]

Sex became a pastime to look forward to and enjoy, not to be feared or feel ashamed of, something feminists have been fighting for since the 1960s and 1970s. This is also a core tenet of third-wave feminism: "sexuality, in all its guises, has become a kind of lightning rod for this generation's hopes and discontents (and democratic visions) in the same way that civil rights in Vietnam galvanized our generation in the 1960s," writes Henry. Finally, to be a sexual woman was to be free of accusations of wantonness and selfishness; it was to see sexual pleasure as a "fundamental right."[25]

One aspect of the open attitude toward sex and *Sex and the City* that is rarely talked about is that it serves as a kind of "sex ed" class for girls and women who were raised in conservative households. While obviously not the best place to get information on sex—especially because the show rarely addresses the importance of birth control or the risk of sexually transmitted diseases—it is for some a place they "could genuinely learn about sex" as a teen or even as a sheltered adult.[26]

ABORTION AND A WOMAN'S RIGHT TO CHOOSE[27]

While most television shows, especially sitcoms, shy away from the taboo subject of abortion, *Sex and the City* tackles it head on. In episode 4.11, "Coulda, Woulda, Shoulda," the four women have a frank and open discussion about abortion. Miranda, finding herself pregnant from a "mercy fuck" with Steve, is considering what to do. Without being preachy, the show gets across the idea that terminating her pregnancy is just as viable an option for a woman as having the baby. While Charlotte can't even remain at the table while they discuss abortion, Samantha matter-of-factly says she has had two, and Carrie reluctantly admits to having had one when she was twenty-two.

The episode was groundbreaking at the time for its frank discussion of abortion. While female television characters have been having them since the soap opera *Another World* broke that ground in 1964—nine years before abortion was legalized in the United States—had Miranda gone through with it, it still would have spelled serious controversy for the show. After all, it was less than fifty years prior that pregnancy couldn't even be talked about on TV—much less shown—and only six years before *Sex and the City* debuted, "Vice President Dan Quayle berated the sitcom character Murphy Brown for having a child out of wedlock."[28] Given that, this discussion was considered radical.

"Depicting controversial topics on television shows is often challenging; there is the risk of trivializing a subject, relying on lazy stereotypes, or falling into the dreaded 'very special episode' trap. Achieving the balance of simply telling the story, neither lecturing nor trivializing is tricky," writes Sarah Erdreich in an article on the history of abortion on television.[29] *Sex and the City* manages to find that balance while doing what it could in the culture of its time. Though she chooses to have the baby, Miranda's "choice doesn't feel like a copout," says Hillary Busis. "The series is supporting a woman's right to choose while acknowledging that abortion is complicated and fraught. . . . Miranda doesn't go through with her abortion because she's carefully weighed the pros and cons of having a baby."[30]

The show is also very progressive on the debate around whether the father has a right to know about a pregnancy, especially if it is aborted, by showing multiple viewpoints. In the show, Miranda chooses to keep news of her pregnancy from Steve until she decides what to do. Given that she doesn't make her final decision until she is called back in the doctor's office to have the abortion, it is almost certain that had she gone through with it, she wouldn't have told Steve until after the deed was done, if ever. Likewise, Carrie chooses not to tell the father of the fetus she aborted. But Aidan feels like Steve has a right to know.

While the show doesn't provide any answers, the fact that the father's feelings are even talked about is unusual. Television tends to show abortion as a female-only issue—and it certainly is, given that it is the woman's body and ultimately is her choice—but as Aidan points out, it is the man's baby, too. Had Steve been told sooner and had some input into the matter, it may have dulled the feminist message of reproductive choice, but it also would have been a powerful statement, one the country apparently wasn't ready for. While it had long been acceptable to show a father in the hospital or at the bedside while a baby was being born, he is rarely shown as part of the decision-making process, and in 2001 on TV, he had never accompanied a woman who chose abortion. That would have to wait another decade for 2011 and *Grey's Anatomy*, when Dr. Cristina Yang has an abortion "with her partner by her side."[31]

MOTHERHOOD

In keeping with its greater themes of independence and choice, the show gives women options when it comes to motherhood that are at odds with the traditional sitcom role of doting mother. Each character represents a different attitude toward motherhood: Charlotte is firmly pro-motherhood, Miranda is the reluctant mother, Carrie is the undecided, and Samantha is team "no way in hell." While Samantha seems to suffer from no guilt over her choice to have her abortions, Carrie is still haunted, wondering for the rest of the episode if she made the right decision so many years before. It's not until she visits the restaurant where the guy who got her pregnant used to work and finds him still working there—what's worse is that he has no memory of her—that she knows she did the right thing. After all, what kind of life would that child have been able to lead with a waiter for a father and her—clueless, poor, and way too young—as a mother? This gives her the courage to reveal her past to Aidan, who doesn't judge her.

Carrie is the only one of the four who doesn't appear to have a clear opinion on having children. While she says she wants one someday, she is also very worried in episode 1.10, "The Baby Shower," when her period is late. Later, when she finds out that she isn't pregnant, her expression reflects a combination of relief and disappointment, highlighting her ambivalence on the matter. It is possible that Carrie's mixed feelings stem from her unfinished quest to find her own identity. After all, if she doesn't know who *she* is, then how is she ever going to help another human being find and form their own identity?

Samantha's attitude toward her two abortions, likely the result of not using birth control (which we find out in episode 4.10, "Belles of the Balls," that she doesn't always do), may seem cold or shocking at first, but it is in keeping with her stand that she doesn't want children. While this may not seem like a big deal now—after all there are whole movements like "We Are Childfree" that aim to unite and celebrate women who choose not to have children—at the time for a woman to openly voice that she doesn't want children on television was revolutionary.[32] Not only does Samantha say it, but she also backs up her position by asking, "Why?" when she hears that others are having kids. She shows her disdain for children in episode 6.9, "A Woman's Right to Shoes," when they aren't controlled by their parents in public and one throws pesto pasta on her light-colored suit at a restaurant.

Samantha caught hell for her choice, with fans calling her a "smug asshole" for her "openly hostile attitude," which is in keeping with the "[depiction] of unmarried, childless women as scary witches" because they are going against a "woman's maternal destiny."[33] The fact that *Sex and the City* thought to offer childlessness by choice as an option for a single woman is rare on television.

Charlotte, though, is the one who embodies traditional female views about motherhood. She considers having children her sacred duty and has wanted to be a mother since she was little. She even has the perfect name picked out—Shayla—before her friend Laini steals it for her own daughter in episode 1.10, "The Baby Shower." "Charlotte's desire for marriage is expressed early on in the show, and unsurprisingly she is the first of the friends to wed. Not long after Charlotte *does* get married to Trey, she is disappointed with married life, and her romantic vision of marriage becomes tainted," writes Broderick.[34] But with good reason. First, she struggles with a husband who has impotency issues because he places her on a virginal pedestal—one that she certainly doesn't deserve—and therefore can't see her as enough of a sexual being to have intercourse with her. Then, once that problem is solved, she finds out she has only a 15 percent chance of having children and endures hormone shots that make her crazy, only for Trey to decide he isn't ready for a baby after all.

Motherhood is so important to Charlotte that it becomes all she can see. As Laura Tropp, communications associate professor at Marymount Manhattan College, writes,

> Charlotte succumbs to the biological fear discourse. . . . She represents the woman who desires having a child above everything else, including her career or her husband. For Charlotte, the right time to have a child is right now, before it's too late. . . . Charlotte has internalized the competing discourses for motherhood by reacting in an either-or fashion. Either she will be a successful career woman, or she will become a wife, and more importantly a mother. . . . [H]er quest for motherhood consumes her.[35]

When she marries the second time, Charlotte's struggle continues, but now, with a supportive husband to help bear the load, she handles the ups and downs much better. Eventually, Charlotte and Harry adopt a baby girl from China, and Charlotte gets her dearest wish.

As with most other things, like her career, her wardrobe, and her ability to afford the lifestyle she leads, Miranda reflects the most realistic view of motherhood. She has no plans to have children because she doesn't have time and is too focused on her career; she resists one attempt by Steve to have a baby on the grounds that one doesn't fit into their life. They get a puppy instead, and even that doesn't work out (3.8, "The Big Time"). Steve ends up taking custody of Scout and eventually names his bar after the dog.

But when she accidently ends up pregnant, Miranda rolls with the punches. Once she decides to keep the baby—"partly because she worries that she may not have another opportunity to conceive" due to her lazy ovary—she makes it clear to Steve that she will be the one raising the baby, and he will get to see it regularly, but that is it.[36] Ever the lawyer, she draws up a contract with a custody schedule. After that, Miranda continues with life pretty much as it was, well into her pregnancy, including her grueling fifty-hour-a-week work schedule. Soon, Miranda "finds herself sleeping under her desk and her law firm and thereby demonstrating her weakness, a betrayal by her female body that traps her and coopts her autonomy. . . . [I]t is Miranda's personal struggle as a superwoman that is explored," writes Burns-Ardolino.[37]

Like generations of women before her, Miranda is struggling to "have it all." Tropp traces this evolution: In the 1950s and 1960s, on television and in real life, this meant "managing a household and family while making it look effortless." The following two decades focused on "women trying to have it all in the workplace . . . achieving the same success at work as men." From the 1980s on, TV shows "define[d] having it all as mothers achieving a successful career while still remaining devoted to their families."[38]

Miranda is so busy with her work that she is nearly at her due date before she realizes she hasn't bought a stroller or a crib. Forced to admit she can't do it all, she accepts Charlotte's help in planning a baby shower to get the things she needs and, later, Steve's in putting together the crib. She even asks Carrie to be with her when the time comes—but no cheerleading or coaching her—because Steve is too emotional.

Not long before her due date, Miranda freaks out that she isn't going to be a good mother. She says to Carrie, "I'm going to be a terrible mother. I am! I have no maternal instincts, no patience. The way I yelled at Charlotte. She was just trying to point out what needs to be childproofed. [pause] Oh my God. I'm what needs to be childproofed!" (4.17, "A Vogue Idea"). She has a valid point: "Miranda does not exhibit a natural ability to be a mother. Throughout her pregnancy, she is not overly delighted but ambivalent."[39] At her baby shower, Miranda even endangers one of her coworkers' children when she is handed the boy and sets him on the couch next to her instead of holding him; he nearly falls off, but a sharp-eyed Carrie grabs him in time and picks him up. Even once Brady is born, Miranda's maternal instincts are slow in coming. She has trouble nursing and getting the baby to stop crying.

Tropp elaborates, "When Miranda has maternal moments, such as when she gives birth or finally successfully nurses Brady, the program does not imply that these moments come simply because Miranda is female. Miranda must work to become a mother rather than be one naturally."[40]

Miranda's life as a mother is realistic, as well. She struggles with her weight (5.4, "Cover Girl"), her friends react to her differently, and the baby quite literally interrupts her sex life. "Throughout season 5, Miranda struggles with the trauma of being a new mother surrounded by single childless women who seem patently unqualified to guide her through this particular maze," note Akass and McCabe.[41]

Despite her own personal struggles and even though Miranda is the most outspoken third-wave feminist on the show, it is interesting this doesn't seem to translate to her new role as mother; we don't see her advocating for "flexible work hours at the office or allowances for childcare," as a truly groundbreaking show would.[42] Still, "Miranda's journey conveys how there is no simple way to balance family, professional, and personal life," which has to be a great comfort to viewers also in this situation, just as the sex talk is for those who experience oppression in that arena.[43]

It is not until the very end of the series that we really see Miranda's maternal instincts bloom. Ironically, it is not for Brady that she comes into her own but for Steve's mother, Mary, who is suffering from dementia. Miranda rescues her when she wanders off and bathes her in a tub while Mary plays with Brady's bath toys, "car[ing] for her mother-in-law as a mother would a child. . . . Miranda has [finally] accepted the role that she fought against for so long."[44]

While some viewers found this ending unrealistic, it can also be seen as a heartbreaking depiction of Miranda's character arc and how she finally sheds her cynical exoskeleton and comes into her essence as a loving woman. As Akass and McCabe write,

> Over the course of the final three seasons Miranda has learned that there is more to being a mother than the idyllic and often sanitised versions offered to us in the media. She may perform the role of caretaker to Mary but this does not mean that she has embraced the whole romantic fiction of the "naturalness" of motherhood. Far from being contained in the role of mother and naturalised by it, Miranda's narrative shows us that it is possible to retain independence despite the constraints of caring.[45]

Just as Miranda learns, *Sex and the City* shows there is no one right way to approach motherhood. Women can choose not to participate like

Samantha, embrace it wholeheartedly like Charlotte, or feel their way through it like Miranda. It's even okay to not know where you stand, like Carrie, or to choose not to be a mother—right now or ever. That is the beautiful thing about modern life; it offers women a variety of options, and with each passing year, these choices are more and more accepted. And we have shows like *Sex and the City*, which aren't afraid to speak out and bring honest discussion into American homes, to thank for it.

13

BUILDING BRANDS
AND EXPECTATIONS

"'Cocktails at Tiffany's calls for classic charm. An Oscar de La Renta sleeveless silk full skirted dress with black patent leather bow belt.' Now that is pure poetry."

—Carrie reading from *Vogue*, episode 6.14, "The Ick Factor"

Manolo Blahnik. The cosmopolitan cocktail. Are there any more iconic images of *Sex and the City*? Over the course of its six years on television, *Sex and the City* built more brands than perhaps any other show in television history. Through a combination of superb product placement, a culture ripe to cash in, and an audience with a desire to live the fantasy, the show became a marketer's dream. Though Sarah Jessica Parker claimed in 2014 the show never engaged in product placement, that is likely a matter of semantics.[1] She went on to explain that the show's "partnerships often do not involve companies paying to have their products in the film," whereas traditional product placement is a pay-for-play situation.[2]

Still, as Reuters reported in 2008, the first *Sex and the City* "movie ha[d] 'promotional partnerships' with at least eight companies whose products appear in the film."[3] Back then, Sarah Jessica Parker told reporters, "It's a huge part of making a movie now, it's a huge part of financing and marketing in foreign territories and it would have been impossible, unfortunately, for us to make this movie without some partnerships."[4] In 2014, she said, "It's important to know that we never put on a shirt because a brand asked us to."[5] While it's possible that was the case for the fashion the women wore, the same cannot be said for all their accessories and other items associated with the franchise. Let's take a look at some of the brands *Sex and the City* made household names, starting with the most famous.

THE COSMOPOLITAN

The cosmopolitan—a relatively simple cocktail of vodka, Triple Sec/ Cointreau, lime juice, and cranberry juice—was *the* drink of the *Sex and the City* era, thanks to its popularity among the four women. While many 1990s viewers (myself included) thought *Sex and the City* invented the cosmo, that's not actually the case, though it certainly popularized it. Like many cocktails, the exact origins of cosmos are uncertain. Difford's *Guide for Discerning Drinkers* claims the recipe was first printed in the 1934 book *Pioneers of Mixing at Elite Bars*, though the ingredients were slightly different, using gin instead of vodka, lemon juice instead of lime, and raspberry juice instead of cranberry.[6]

Another origin story dates to 1968, when Ocean Spray was looking to increase sales of cranberry juice among adults. The result was the harpoon, the recipe for which—vodka, cranberry juice, and lime—was printed on the label of every bottle of Ocean Spray for quite some time. John Caine, the bartender many credit with popularizing the cosmo, dates the drink to the 1980s gay scene of Provincetown, Massachusetts, which is in cranberry-growing land. "I ran into the drink in Cleveland at the Rusty Scupper, a restaurant. It was very, very popular," he says. When he moved to San Francisco, he started selling it there. "It was light, clean, fast to make, pretty and cheap.... People said I invented the Cosmo. I just transported it."[7]

Two other contenders for the title of cosmo creator include Cheryl Cook—who supposedly invented the drink in Miami and claims to have served it to *Sex and the City* costume designers Patricia Field and Rebecca Weinberg—and Toby Cecchini, owner of Long Island Bar in New York, who worked at the Odeon in Manhattan's Tribeca neighborhood in the late 1980s. He claims he took a "terrible drink called the Cosmopolitan making the rounds at gay bars in San Francisco in the mid '80s" and improved upon it, like Cook, using Absolut Citron. "I went about reconstructing it, using what we were using at the time to make Margaritas—fresh lime juice and Cointreau . . . and to approximate the Rose's Grenadine I grabbed cranberry juice that was on hand from Cape Codders."[8] It became a favorite of the waitstaff, and then they introduced it to patrons. Both he and Cook claim to have served the drink to Madonna and Sandra Bernhard. From there, it spread to the Rainbow Room, where celebrities like Madonna were photographed with it in hand.

While there likely will always be arguments over the drink's provenance, one thing everyone can agree on is that *Sex and the City* is what made the drink a megahit. The first time the cosmo appears in the show is

Cosmopolitans were one of many brands *Sex and the City* helped build throughout its six-season run. Photofest/*Sex and the City* (HBO), season 5 (2002)

in episode 1.5, "The Power of Female Sex," when Samantha and Carrie are drinking at the bar of Balzac while waiting for their reservation. The drinks are first named two episodes later, when Carrie orders one at a party (1.7, "The Monogamists"). "The rest is history," writes Adam Teeter for Vinepair. "The cocktail appeared several more times throughout the show, leading people throughout the country to recreate the cocktail in order to sip along with their favorite characters."[9]

But how exactly did that specific cocktail make it into the show? According to mixologist Mikey Enright, "*SATC* cast and crew used to go to the Rainbow Room's bar in NYC after they wrapped from shooting and used to drink Cosmos—it was this that promoted their inclusion on the show, and hence gave rise to one of the most well-known cocktails around!"[10] Cindy Chupack, one of the show's writers, tells a slightly different story: "I feel almost certain that Michael Patrick King or Darren Star suggested it. Michael does not drink, but I remember he loved the look of the Cosmopolitan—this frothy, rose-colored version of the martini, the neck of the glass resembling the stiletto of a Manolo Blahnik shoe."[11]

As to why it became such a phenomenon, Jennifer Keishin Armstrong, author of the insiders' tell-all Sex and the City *and Us*, theorizes that it was one of the few things on the show within the reach of just about every viewer: "There's certain things on the show that you couldn't do, because the costs were prohibitive, but something like a cupcake or a Cosmo was something you could afford. . . . So you get a little piece of that, you get a little taste of it without having to take out a second mortgage or something in order to pay for it."[12]

But just as quickly as the cosmo craze began, it ended. By the time the average person was trying one for the first time, the New York club scene had already moved on. Bartenders quickly grew tired of the demand for them, and once the show ended—especially once the first movie disappointed fans—pretending you were in *Sex and the City* became no longer cool. "No longer associated with chic metropolitan women, cosmos became the unofficial beverage of what we lovingly referred to as 'the basic bitch,'" write Fairless and Garroni.[13]

In or out, no one can argue the lasting effects of the cosmo craze. "Much of the high-end cocktail culture we actually encounter today, the speakeasies, the high-end ingredients, and the drinks so complex only a mixologist can recreate them, can be seen as a direct response to the simplistic era the Cosmo embodied," writes Teeter. "We're probably in one of the richest and most interesting times to be a drinker, but if it weren't for the Cosmo, we might never have gotten here."[14]

JIMMY CHOO AND MANOLO BLAHNIK

In episode 4.16, "Ring a Ding Ding," Carrie estimates she has spent $40,000 on shoes. At $500 each, the price Manolos were going for at the time, that means Carrie owns around eighty pairs of designer shoes. But the Spanish designer wasn't Carrie's first footwear love. In episode 1.5, "The Power of Female Sex," we get our first look at designer heels when Carrie goes shopping at Dolce & Gabbana (D&G), only to have her credit card cut up. Luckily, her rich socialite friend Almalita comes to the rescue and gifts Carrie with the feathery pink confections.

Next there was Choo, Jimmy Choo. In episode 3.1, "Where There Is Fire," Carrie narrates, "With no man in sight, I decided to rescue my ankles from a life of boredom by purchasing too many pairs of Jimmy Choo shoes." In the late 1990s, they were only slightly less expensive than Manolos, going for $450 a pair, so that was not a cheap prospect.[15] In fact, these pricey shoes are the subject of an entire episode, when Carrie loses a blue and purple feathered shoe on the Staten Island Ferry. While chasing the ferry, her foot comes out of her shoe, and Carrie yells, "I lost my Choo!" instead of "I lost my shoe!" Tamara Mellon, cofounder of the brand, credits that episode with making them famous. "Before, you had to read *Vogue* and *Bazaar* to get it but suddenly we had this giant audience."[16]

Sex and the City also gave us the oft-quoted phrase "Hello, lover," when Carrie spots a pair of pink Jimmy Choos in a store window in the season 4 finale, a phrase she also uses in the premiere of *And Just Like That . . .* , when cooing over her closet full of heels.

But it was Manolo Blahnik who established a lasting association with the show. He had already been making shoes for nearly thirty years when *Sex and the City* made him a household name. Those shoes were already in the lives of people like Candace Bushnell before the show; they simply brought them into American homes. As a result, "Manolo Blahnik's success skyrocketed," said Paula Correri, accessory editor at Tobe Report, a retail consultancy. "The prices keep escalating, but women will starve themselves to score a pair of his shoes."[17]

It's little wonder why. For those with an eye for designer shoes, Manolos were the Holy Grail. The show features dozens of pairs of his shoes, including the "urban legend" Mary Janes and Carrie's iconic Hangisi stilettos, also known as her blue "wedding shoes," which are a prominent part of the premiere of *And Just Like That . . .* , as well. In season 3, Carrie is mugged of her beloved Manolos, which her mugger—a man—mysteriously is able to name by brand. Unless he had a shoe fetish or specialized in the high-end shoe fence, it isn't one of the show's more believable product placements.

In appreciation for all the show did for the brand, Manolo Blahnik designed a shoe called the SJP, in honor of the actress who played Carrie.[18] Parker admitted to Oprah in 2001 that she owned "well over 100 pairs of Manolo Blahnik's."[19]

OTHER BRANDS/TRENDS

"Sex and the City is unique in that it is a virtual how-to manual for New York style and leisure," writes Sohn.[20] Visibility on the show made it easy for Manhattanites to visit locations as soon as the show aired and tourists to plan them into their next visit. The result was a stratospheric rise in revenue for brands and locations lucky enough to be a part of the show. Here's a sampling of the places, items, and trends *Sex and the City* put on the map:

Accessories

- **Birkin bag:** This top-of-the-line Hermes handbag is known to be one of the most expensive in the world, regularly retailing for anywhere from $40,000–$500,000 each.[21] Its exclusive clientele—celebrities get preferential treatment—are usually the only ones to get their hands on the latest design. At the time one was the object of Samantha's desire on *Sex and the City* in episode 4.11, "Coulda, Woulda, Shoulda," the bag only cost about $4,000, and the brand had a waiting list, but today that is a thing of the past. Now women have to hope to be offered one and take whatever size, design, or color they are given. Or they can try to get one secondhand on resale websites like Poshmark or the Real Real.
- **The "Carrie" necklace:** Originating with Latino and Black cultures and popular in the 1980s, nameplate necklaces were nothing new to the fashion scene when *Sex and the City* aired.[22] Field sold them in her store long before the show, but it was the necklace's connection to the characters that saw it soar as a trend among White viewers.

  Was this a matter of cultural appropriation? Marcel Rosa-Salas, a New York University doctoral student in cultural anthropology, and her photographer friend Flower are documenting the cultural history of the nameplate necklace, and they say it depends on how the accessory is attributed. "The 'Carrie necklace' is, for some people, one entry point into nameplates that I want to honor and respect," Rosa-Salas says, "but I think we also want to push back on this idea that there is one sole originator for the style and also resist the continual erasure that specifically lower-income Black and brown creative producers often face when their specific aesthetic contributions are brought mainstream."[23]

- **Fabric flowers:** Carrie began wearing these brooch-like accessories in the show's second season, but they really took off as her "Jackie O.–like" signature after she dated local politician Bill Kelly in season 3. Piper Weiss reports that designer Patricia Field used it as a "symbol that spring had arrived for Carrie—and with it the possibility for new love."[24] It quickly became a symbol of cool, with retailers as high end as Chanel and as common as Claire's selling them for years to come.[25]

- **Horsehead bag:** An unusual wooden purse called Secretariat worn by Carrie to the racetrack became an unexpected success for designer Timmy Woods when it appeared in the show.[26] When HBO auctioned off items from Carrie's closet, the "horse head purse sold for $500 more than what costume designer Patricia Field paid."[27] The purse is still available to buy today on resale sites—expect to pay around $500—and animal head purses are now a trademark design of Timmy Woods.

- **Horseshoe necklace:** You may remember this trend from season 4 of the show, when Carrie wears a diamond horseshoe necklace. Created by up-and-coming designers Mia & Lizzie, the original was worth about $2,000. According to the designers, "Sarah Jessica liked the horseshoe because it was feminine, and as a fan of vintage, she loved our take on the Victorian charm."[28] This was fortunate because Sarah Jessica was the inspiration for the piece. It was a long-lasting relationship, as Field picked many of their other pieces for that season, as well.[29]

Food

- **Cupcakes/Magnolia Bakery:** Carrie and her pals eat cupcakes from Magnolia Bakery in the West Village in season 3. This seemingly innocent act started a nationwide trend that resulted in cupcakes being served in lieu of wedding cakes and Magnolia Bakery becoming so popular that they asked to be removed as a stop on *Sex and the City* bus tours because they couldn't handle the influx.[30] Still, the massive exposure has been good for the bakery. In 2018, they boasted six New York locations and satellites in three major US cities and seventeen international locations. Prepandemic, they were planning to open approximately two hundred franchises across the United States.[31]

- **Pret A Manger:** In one episode, Carrie and Miranda meet for lunch in the park, and they are seen eating from the British sandwich chain. This is not product placement but is due to Parker's personal preference for them. The food was donated for the scene.[32]

- **Tao Restaurant:** The day after an episode aired featuring a certain location, it was packed, according to Rich Wolf of TAO Group. Sales that first week soared 20 percent and then again the following week, he recalled. After they became part of the official *Sex and the City* bus tour, the location was forever linked in the minds of fans with their favorite gal pals.[33]

- **Tasti D-Lite:** This frozen yogurt company has been a New York staple since 1987 and has stores throughout the city. Though only shown prominently in episode 4.15, "Change of a Dress," in background shots a few other times, and named only three times, the frozen dessert company developed a cult following after being on the show.[34]

- **Various restaurants:** Cafeteria, Il Cantinori, and Sushi Samba are only a few of the Manhattan restaurants given "instant credibility" by filming there.[35]

Nightlife

- **Bungalow 8:** This exclusive California-inspired, members-only Chelsea club (which closed in 2009) was *the* it spot to see and be seen in the early 2000s. Despite is rarified status, owner Amy Sacco insisted the *Sex and the City* shout-out by Carrie is what "put us on the map worldwide. The brand recognition was epic."[36]

Pleasure

- **The Rabbit:** This female-centric sex toy not only normalized masturbation and gave people permission to experiment in the bedroom, but it also became a household name after Charlotte became addicted to hers. Sales increased 300 percent after the first airing of episode 1.9, "The Turtle and the Hare," something that Vibratex, the company that makes it, wasn't prepared for. For years after, the company could tell when the episode was rerun, just based on sales.[37] Today, thanks to the show, the word *rabbit* is a category of vibrators that features the original, its upgrades, and countless imitations. If creating a new category of sex toy isn't making branding history, then what is?

AND JUST LIKE THAT . . . : A MAJOR BRANDING MISSTEP

(Warning, major spoilers ahead.)

I would be remiss if I ignored the major faux pas of the Peloton product placement on the premiere episode of *And Just Like That* . . . The luxury workout brand is mentioned at least a half-dozen times and shown in a few scenes before becoming the cause of Mr. Big's ultimate demise—not exactly the kind of PR the brand was looking for.

As shocked fans dealt with the heartbreaking loss of one of their favorite characters, Peloton was scrambling in crisis mode. The company, of course, denied knowledge that "its product would be used as a prop that led to the death of Mr. Big, who dropped dead after a 45-minute ride," a spokesperson told Giles Turner.[38] They were quick to shift the blame from their product to Mr. Big's lifestyle, which may have been accurate earlier in his life but didn't reflect the salmon-eating, workout-obsessed man portrayed in the beginning of the episode. Dr. Suzanne Steinbaum, a preventive cardiologist and member of Peloton's health and wellness advisory council, said in a statement,

> Mr. Big lived what many would call an extravagant lifestyle—including cocktails, cigars, and big steaks—and was at serious risk as he had a previous cardiac event in Season 6. These lifestyle choices and perhaps even his family history, which often is a significant factor, were the likely cause of his death. Riding his Peloton bike may have even helped delay his cardiac event.[39]

Nevertheless, the company's stocks plummeted, more than 5 percent on Friday, the day after the episode aired, and 10 percent overnight on the Nasdaq, the lowest it had been in a year. This caused *Cycling Magazine* to quip, "If only they could hire Samantha to do some PR for them. Oh yeah. They can't."[40]

In a truly bizarre postscript to this story, on Monday, four days after the episode aired, Peloton aired a spoof ad engineered by Ryan Reynolds's ad agency Maximum Effort. It shows Mr. Big and his Peloton instructor, Allegra (played by Jess King, a real-life Peloton instructor who is also in the infamous episode), sitting by a roaring fire in a cozy, snowbound retreat. Sans drinks, they toast "to new beginnings," implying that he faked his death to run away with her. Reynolds is then heard in a very Carrie-esque voice-over extolling the benefits of exercise on the heart and declaring, "He's alive."

In a second postscript, about a week after it first aired, the ad was removed when allegations of sexual misconduct emerged about actor Chris Noth, who played Mr. Big. He denied them all categorically.

CARRIE BRADSHAW: THE FIRST INFLUENCER?

Sex and the City is a show that launched a thousand brands, but it became one because of its influence over female viewers. A study by communications company J. Walter Thompson reports that it "made haute couture 'popular,'" something it was never meant to be.[41] That is just one example of how *Sex and the City* is more than a television show; it is a lifestyle—one that millions of women were eager to emulate.

According to Antonio Marazza, CEO of the Milan office of Landor Associates, one of the world's leading branding consultancies, a brand becomes a lifestyle when it moves beyond its original product in symbolism and emotion.[42] It now evokes a desired feeling and a perceived lifestyle that one should live to get that feeling, which *Sex and the City* does—in spades. "Most of the female viewers saw *Sex and the City* as a holy Bible, and therefore imitated the characters," writes Clemence Dumoulin in *Circular*. "The series promoted certain lifestyles, which made the viewers familiar with products and habits before unknown. . . . [It] gave the series a loyal audience, who mirrored many of the protagonists' habits, to the great satisfaction of the advertisers."[43]

And all it needed to do that was a brand ambassador, which came part and parcel with the show in the character of Carrie Bradshaw. Bonnie Fuller spilled the secret to Carrie's success in *AdAge*: "The *SATC* brand recognizes what many marketers don't: that women connect with and will follow a woman or a brand that is friendly, relatable and likable vs. someone or something that is perfect and on a pedestal."[44] It could be argued, then, that Carrie (and Parker along with her) was the first modern influencer—long before YouTube and social media made it popular. While the history of being an influencer dates back to the 1920s and 1930s—and is often credited to style icon Coco Chanel—influencers as we know them today began popping up in 2004 or 2005, among a "small but growing group of independent creators [who] were beginning to have an unusually strong influence on public perception": so-called mommy bloggers.[45] Carrie is unique not only in predating them but also because she is their polar opposite. She lives a seemingly glamourous life that women the world over wanted to emulate. If mommy bloggers later struck a chord because they reflected American women's reality, then Carrie did the same years earlier by reflecting their fantasies.

She also had the same qualities that make influencers successful today, and we can thank HBO, King, and Star for that. *Forbes* lists these qualities as the following:[46]

1. **Relatability:** "By definition, these influencers are real people first, 'celebrities' second. Brands . . . look to capitalize on the so-called 'normalcy' of her life."[47] As detailed in chapter 1, Carrie is the most relatable of the four main characters. She has a confidence that can make the viewer believe that her lifestyle is attainable for them, too, if they only follow her lead.

2. **Knowing their audience:** "Lifestyle influencers . . . have a stronger connection to their community than a traditional celebrity. They know what their community likes, dislikes, and shares. As a result, they rate off the charts when it comes to authenticity."[48] Carrie and her friends *are* her audience, plus she is an astute, if informal, sociologist, so she knows them intimately, what they are talking about, what they desire, what they fear, what makes them feel good, and what keeps them up at night—and it isn't just sex. Not only does this help her curate an audience for her work, but it also helps the people behind the curtain at HBO market to its audience.

3. **Quality contact:** "Influencers bring [their] specialty to the table when creating branded content. . . . The influencer . . . can act as a legitimate collaborator and/or creator."[49] As a columnist, fashionista, and later author, Carrie certainly creates a lot of content. She may not have an Instagram (can you imagine if she did?), but her photo frequently makes it into the paper when she is dating someone note-worthy, her image is on the side of a bus, and she appears on the cover of *New York Magazine* (albeit not her finest moment) and in a Dolce & Gabbana runway show. Not bad for a sex columnist—she isn't even a fashion writer or critic, for Givenchy's sake!

4. **ROI (return on investment):** "If the goal of the campaign is to target a specific audience, then this type of influencer can provide a significant ROI through dedicated followings and an unparalleled

understanding of the platforms they leverage."[50] As the first part of this chapter illustrates, Carrie certainly provides "recognition and delivers a consistent financial return for all brands she mentioned and places she visited during the series," which is the definition of a successful influencer.[51]

If any more proof is needed, Wolf writes in the *Guardian* that Carrie "did as much to shift the culture around certain women's issues as real-life female groundbreakers," quite a bold statement given that those real-life counterparts include names like Gloria Steinem, Anita Hill, and Hillary Clinton.[52] They fought for women's rights; all Carrie fights for is a "woman's right to shoes."

LIFESTYLE OR UNREASONABLE EXPECTATIONS?

As we all know through experience, influencers sell products as part of their lifestyles, even when they aren't trying to. Anything Carrie wore, anywhere she or the other girls shopped or ate, become an immediate sensation. That is both the goal and the evidence of a successful influencer. "For a generation of wannabe Manhattanites, Carrie's life was a kind of Gatsby-esque platonic ideal. It wasn't maddeningly unrealistic; it was dreamy. Carrie wasn't tiresome, she was authentic," notes Harris.[53] Influencers also spin specific storylines around their lives, making themselves appear enviable so that their followers will emulate them and buy the products they are selling. While Carrie isn't a conscious influencer doing these things on purpose, the writers, creators, and producers were. They created the fiction that everything would work out if you had the right pair of designer heels or the season's latest handbag.[54]

As noted by Wolf in her book *The Beauty Myth: How Images of Beauty Are Used against Women*, "the stronger that women grow, the more prestige, fame, and money is accorded to the display professions: They are held higher and higher above the heads of rising women, for them to emulate."[55] This is exactly what the lifestyles of the women of *Sex and the City* ended up doing for the average American woman watching them with envy from her living room. The show's "protagonists have not only encouraged a new generation of women to find themselves a room of their own; it inspired them to set their sights on an Upper East Side apartment of their own, a highflying professional career of their own, Manolo Blahniks of their own, and maybe more importantly a sexuality of their own," writes Oria.[56]

Which is all well and good, but what happens when those expectations are out of reach for most people? After all, "Manolo Blahnik is considered the Michelangelo of footwear"; it's not like these ladies are shopping for shoes at Payless or getting their clothes from Kohl's, Macy's, or Target.[57] Carrie and her friends live in a world where high-powered women who supposedly have jobs (we only occasionally see Samantha and Charlotte on the job and never see Miranda in the courtroom) can meet up for long lunches regularly and attend VIP parties every weekend and brunch every Sunday. As Burns-Ardolino points out, the Manhattan of *Sex and the City* is one only a handful of women ever get to see—if it exists at all—because it is reserved for the White, wealthy, and privileged, which is definitely not the New York known to most residents—the working class, immigrants, struggling artists, single parents, and others just trying to get by—let alone across the entire nation:

> Charlotte, Carrie, Miranda and Samantha of *Sex and the City* are arguably the most affluent and privileged representations of women on television. *Sex and the City* shamelessly proffers a liberal choiceoisie lifestyle in the form of fetishized commodities, complete with Manolo Blahnik and Jimmy Choo shoes, Birkin handbags and Canary diamonds, signifying the attainment of the bourgeois bohemian or bobo lifestyle. The conflation of consumerism, privilege and independent working women obscures contemporary feminist visions.[58]

While it is not unusual for Hollywood to give characters living in New York huge apartments there is no way they could really afford (think Monica's apartment on *Friends* and that of the titular characters on *Will & Grace*), doing so creates unrealistic expectations for the audience. In February 2022, Bushnell revealed she made $5,000 a month during her stint at *Vogue* in the '90s because back then "people valued writing."[59] She admitted that her column at the *Observer*, on which Carrie's column is based, "paid less," but she could manage things because she had the two jobs. While that may be the case, Carrie doesn't get the *Vogue* job until later in the series, so how did she manage her lifestyle until then? Since *Sex and the City* first aired, numerous studies have been done asking if the characters could actually afford their extravagant lifestyles. Not surprisingly, the answers are mostly no, even if Bushnell's revelation about her salary is taken into account.

In 2018, Sara Nachlis of Girlboss asked what it would cost to live like Carrie Bradshaw.[60] She found that the average staff writer (remember that Bradshaw's column was for a fictional paper) in New York would make about $52,000 per year, or about $4,333 per month before taxes—and that is for a full-time writer. Given that we never see Carrie in the office, she is likely a freelancer. To use a real-life freelancing example, the *New Yorker* pays a flat fee of $325 for a two-thousand-word article, eight hundred more words than Carrie is required.[61] If a writer managed to churn that out every week, that would be only $16,900 per year before taxes, not very far above the 2021 federal poverty level of $12,880 for a single person. Regardless of what number you use, the point is that Carrie doesn't make much money on her column alone.

Her monthly expenses, according to Nachlis, would have included $2,116 for rent (in the show, Carrie's apartment is rent-controlled at an appallingly low $700 per month); $291.91 for utilities; $1,200 for all those cab rides; $464 for food (which seems low to me and I live in the much cheaper Midwest); $138 for drinks (very low, unless she got a lot of drinks paid for by men, based on my personal experience in the late 1990s); $392 for cigarettes; and $1,458 for shopping (calculated using price per shoe adjusted for inflation), bringing her total expenses to $6,059.91, or $72,718.92 per year. Even if we believe the show's rent and adjust down the cost of the shoes to their original $400 price, she'd still be spending more than $3,500 a month, which includes no extras, luxury upgrades, or emergencies like doctor's visits or the teeth cleaning excuse she uses in season 1 to hide from Miranda that she is back together with Big. If Carrie isn't massively in debt, which is likely according to any realistic calculation, then she's barely getting by.

Even Showbiz CheatSheet, which conducted an updated calculation based on Bushnell's $5,000-a-month salary, finds,

> Since Carrie's apartment ran just $800 per month, she would have had plenty of cash left over for sample sales, cocktails, and taking cabs. . . . While Carrie did have discretionary money, her income wasn't high enough for her numerous high-end fashion purchases and absolutely everything else. Does the math totally work? No, but it is certainly closer than a lot of us thought.[62]

Miranda's lifestyle, though, might actually be possible. Yes, she makes more as a lawyer, and yes, she buys a bigger apartment, but she also eats a lot of cheap takeout (and the occasional cake from the garbage) and isn't a clotheshorse like Carrie. So even factoring in her housekeeper, Miranda likely can afford the choices she makes.[63]

Charlotte's net worth is harder to calculate because she seems to have come from money, and we have no idea if she has a trust fund or other type of family inheritance to live off of in addition to her art gallery salary before marrying Trey. After him, she has the divorce settlement, which is valued at around $2 million.

Similarly, Samantha runs her own PR firm, so it is difficult to gauge how much money she makes and, frankly, how much she spends because many of her meals and much of her jewelry seems to be paid for by the men she dates.[64]

Regardless of which character you use as a barometer, unless you move to New York with a high-paying job in hand or another source of inherited or earned income, you aren't likely to live the *Sex and the City* lifestyle. And neither were the thousands of young, single women who flocked to New York during and after the show's run or tried to emulate their designer lives at home somewhere else. To show just how unrealistic the show's lifestyle is, *Cosmopolitan*'s sex and relationships editor Carina Hsieh and her editor decided Carina would celebrate the twentieth anniversary of the show by living like Carrie Bradshaw for a week.[65] After all, she was one of the many who moved there because of the show:

> I totally moved to NYC for college and thirstily chased after this exact job because of *Sex and the City*. I don't care if it's corny and basic, or if it's responsible for the great cupcake scourge of the early aughts—I love the show. It was extremely formative for me. Sure Carrie had some misadventures, but it seemed like every disastrous relationship just added more juice to her interesting life. As a shy and impressionable kid who craved attention, the lesson was clear. Move to New York, model your life on Carrie's, and then roll your eyes when you hear of other women your age doing the same.[66]

By the end of the week, Carina had found that cabs and Ubers cost a hell of a lot of money; she didn't make nearly enough money to rent like Carrie; buying *Vogue* instead of dinner just made her hangry, so she ordered KFC delivery; singles mixers, even when done for research, were more lonely than fun; she didn't have enough free time to shop like Carrie, even if she blew off work; and picking up sailors during Fleet Week is not nearly as easy as the show makes it seem. Her conclusion: "Carrie Bradshaw's life is fake as hell! No one has that much time on their hands, and for the first time in my life, I was happy not to be her. . . . But for all her insane fashion choices and self-absorbed behavior, Carrie deserves more credit than we give her. Going out there and trying to date every night is not only exhausting, but depressing AF."[67]

By the way, the magazine paid for Carina to recreate five of Carrie's classic looks, using a combination of designer duds and "reasonable" alternatives. The total price tag? Just over $15,300, based on the prices listed in the captions. But perhaps this isn't so shocking when you consider *Elle* magazine estimates that it cost $175,000 to outfit Carrie just for season 4.[68]

NETWORKS AND STARS BECOME BRANDS

Riding on the coattails, as it were, of *Sex and the City* and Carrie's superstardom were the network and its stars, who were natural benefactors of their own success. From the beginning, HBO strategically set out to show viewers that it was different from other television or even other premium cable channels with *Sex and the City*. Just a year before Star approached the network with his concept, HBO had launched a new branding strategy with the slogan "It's not television. It's HBO."[69] Then in walks Star with this fresh concept that would bring a whole new set of viewers to the traditionally male-dominated viewership of the network. Bambi Haggins, associate professor of film and media studies at University of California, Irvine, and Amanda D. Lotz, media studies professor at Queensland University of Technology, explain how:

> The breakout success of *Sex and the City* marks an important transition for HBO comedies and audience's expectations of them. . . . Although the revealing and frank depiction of four attractive women enjoying their sex lives unquestionably offered voyeuristic pleasure for HBO's long-targeted male viewers, *Sex and the City* ultimately became a "girls' show," particularly as the characters evolved and the series negotiated a careful balance of exploring dramatic struggles while maintaining a comedic edge.[70]

Star's deliberate choices were a big part of the branding strategy that made the show unlike anything viewers had previously seen. He jettisoned the age-old laugh track, gave the show a sense of verisimilitude by shooting on the streets of New York, and insisted that the "series be shot on film. Foregoing four video cameras and a live studio audience, he explicitly stated that he wanted 'to bridge the gap between a television series and a movie,' affirming HBO's premium subscription model."[71] HBO promoted *Sex and the City* as a "designer series" from its very first press release, hyping the show and itself at the same time.[72] Within two seasons, the show had helped HBO challenge NBC's "Must-See-TV" Thursday night lineup of hits with its own on Sundays, especially once it was followed by another megahit, *The Sopranos*.

Their brand strategy clearly worked. The company is notoriously tight lipped about monetary specifics but has admitted to making "hundreds of millions of dollars" from the show.[73] The real number is likely well into the billions. *Sex and the City* was the catalyst for HBO's global breakout into Central America, Europe, and Japan and syndicated programming in seventy countries. In 2004, HBO sold its first syndication cycle of the show to TBS and local broadcast stations for $350 million.[74] Not to mention that at the height of the show's fame, HBO's online store sold seventy-four *Sex*-themed items, including underwear named after the characters that retailed between $36 and $95 and themed martini glasses.[75] Today, that number is down to nineteen products ranging in price from $14.95 to $32.95.

In addition, *Sex and the City* made a brand out of some of its stars. While Cattrall tried to bring Samantha into the real world through two books, *Sexual Intelligence* and *Satisfaction: The Art of the Female Orgasm*, she had only moderate success, selling a combined 370,000 copies.[76]

It was Parker who became a name in her own right with the success of the show. She went on to become a clothing designer, with her ironically affordable line, Bitten, which only lasted a year (2007–2008), thanks to the collapse of its exclusive retailer, Steve & Barry's.[77] Undeterred, she went on to launch a "stiletto empire" with her SJP shoe and handbag line, which has since expanded to include a collaboration with Samsonite luggage; a beauty care line; and a dizzying array of accessories and gifts, including candles, water bottles, beach towels, wrapping paper, and, of course, a huge silk flower brooch.[78] Unlike Bitten, the items in this collection aren't cheap. Her shoes retail for $250 to $500 each, right about in the same price range that Carrie pays for her collection, and the purses will set you back $395 to $695.

In 2005, Parker also launched two perfumes, "Lovely" and "Covet," which earned $18 million in 2010.[79] She now has nine fragrances.[80] In 2019, she got into the wine business with Invivo X, an award-winning brand that has two types of wine bearing her name, a rosé and a sauvignon blanc.[81] In May 2022, she cofounded Thomas Ashbourne, a premixed cocktail brand, with fellow actors John Cena, Vanessa Hudgens, Rosario Dawson, and Ashley Benson and rapper Playboi Carti. Naturally, Parker's drink is a cosmo.[82] Then add what she earned for the show, its subsequent movies, and in royalties, plus her real estate investments. The result? Parker's net worth is estimated at $150 million.[83]

PROMOTING CONSUMERISM OR FEMALE FREEDOM?

With all this money and obvious consumption associated with the show, critics quickly accused it of promoting a lifestyle of consumerism. As the show went on and became more popular, the use of designer clothing and accessories increased. Stella Bruzzi, dean of arts and humanities at University College London, and Pamela Church Gibson, reader in film and cultural studies at the London College of Fashion, argue that this demonstrates a "growing preoccupation with designer brand names. Throughout, even when sunbathing poolside, there are self-conscious shots of various designer accessories: Chanel sunglasses, a Louis Vuitton visor and purse, and Fendi bags. This is a supreme exemplification of Thorsten Veblen's notion of 'conspicuous consumption.'"[84]

Veblen's theory applies to those who buy luxury goods as status symbols rather than because they actually need them.[85] It has been a hobby of the nobility and upper classes from time immemorial and in the United States dates back to before the founding of the country, when wealthy colonists went deep in debt to reflect the changing tastes of their European counterparts.[86] In that way, conspicuous consumption could be called an American pastime.

In fact, shopping was strongly linked to patriotism in New York in the months immediately following the September 11, 2001, terrorist attacks. It was seen as a much-needed way to get New York City's (and the country's) shocked economy back on track but also to bring Americans together. In episode 5.1, "Anchors Aweigh," the first to air after the attacks, Carrie tells her friends, "If you want to do your patriotic duty as New York women, you come shopping with me right now and throw some much-needed money downtown." Susan Zieger, associate professor of English at the University of California, Riverside, herself a native New Yorker, recalls seeing reflections of this attitude everywhere. "Merchants displayed a popular image of an American flag as a shopping bag, and the legend 'America: open for business.'"[87] In many ways, the city was looking to the show that made it culturally relevant again (not that New York is ever not relevant) to save it in its weakest hour. "*Sex and the City* was thought to be a useful instrument for stimulating the local economy, as boutique hotels, 'struggling to fill rooms since 9/11,' competed for guests by offering rival *Sex and the City* packages, including drinks, massages and hangover cures," Zieger writes.[88]

This idea highlights an important point. When analyzing the show, we have to be careful not to take it out of its context of the late 1990s and early 2000s. Looking back at the time from the pandemic-ravaged, inflation-weary

Sex and the City is often criticized for its glorification of consumption through shopping for designer and luxury goods. Photofest/*Sex and the City* (HBO), season 2 (summer–fall 1999)

early 2020s, it can be easy to forget that the 1990s were a different time. Like the Roaring Twenties, they were a boom time in America's economy, thanks to the rise of the internet and a strong stock market.[89] This heady mix created a culture of consumption the country hadn't seen since the "me generation" of the 1980s snapped up shoulder pads, luxury cars, and clunky car phones (and early cell phones) and built large homes (today referred to derisively as McMansions) like they all lived on *Dallas* or *Dynasty*. In a poetic twist of fate, the *Los Angeles Times* dubbed Donald Trump the poster boy for the consumption culture of the late 1980s, and the first episode of *Sex and the City* called Mr. Big the "next Donald Trump, except he's younger and much better looking" (1.1, "Sex and the City"), thus linking the two eras culturally.[90]

In the 1990s, a new generation of tech millionaires, workers flush with cash from signing bonuses, and high-powered working women needed an outlet for all that money, so they turned to luxury goods. As Samantha notes in the very first episode of the show, "This is the first time in the history of Manhattan that women have had as much money and power as men." Can they really be blamed for using that money and power to go shopping and enrich their lives in material ways like men have been doing for centuries?

In this way, it can be argued that the women's shopping is actually symbolic of their newfound freedom to not only support themselves but also thrive alone in what is still a male-dominated society. Broderick writes,

> A postfeminist perspective argues that this approach helps the characters become less dependent on men and helps them achieve individual freedom. To the postfeminist movement, consumption is a way to gain and assert one's power and dominance. Additionally, because women have not been able to make choices for themselves throughout much of history, purchasing material goods and participating in consumer culture is a way for women to understand themselves and receive gratification from others and society, thus boosting one's self esteem.[91]

Shopping was thus a way for women in the late 1990s to fashion independent identities. Like the "new woman" of the 1920s, the characters are "independent, self-fashioned consumer[s] whose sexuality is at once 'stylish, a source of physical pleasure, a means of creating identity, a form of body work, self-expression, a quest for individual fulfillment.'"[92]

As wonderful as that sounds, all the consumption can have a dark side, some critics argue. For example, the idea that you can just toss something away when it no longer serves you can bleed over into other areas of life. Broderick argues that the women of *Sex and the City* view their men as transient as the things they buy that are out of fashion the next season: "Aside from Carrie's obsession with shopping, each character discusses men similarly to the way they consider consumable goods: something they gain fulfillment from that is disposable."[93]

While this might be true for Samantha, who goes into her relationships with the mind-set that there will always be another one the following night, and maybe even Miranda, who often treats her lovers like something she found on the bottom of her shoe, the other women don't regard their men with casual disdain. Charlotte treats each of her men like Mr. Right until they prove themselves to be Mr. Wrong, and Carrie sees her boyfriends as intellectual curiosities and potential sources of something she needs mentally, emotionally, or both; neither drop their men easily or without thought and are often heartbroken when the men leave them.

Still, society has been connecting female sexual desire with consumerism for decades in a way that makes both seem negative and self-serving, as though women are ruled by avarice and lust that they can't satisfy and, like the biblical Lilith, will never be fulfilled until they are in total control. This is a double standard we can't seem to be rid of. When a man dresses in a bespoke Italian suit, dons a Rolex, and douses himself with expensive cologne, we call him successful and even place him on a pedestal, making him an object of envy for other men and of desire for women (just look at Mr. Big).

But when a woman wears a designer gown, drapes herself in diamonds, and slips on a pair of expensive shoes, there is no pedestal for her, only scorn. She is seen as showing off, and her motives are questioned. Is she a gold digger? What does she mean by drawing attention to herself like that? How dare she flaunt her success? For all our progress, we are still living in an age that wants women to conform to the old ideas that repress them even as they fight for expanded rights and freedoms—to no longer be seen as only virgins, mothers, or whores but as fully formed people with the same right to wealth, power, and desire as their male counterparts.

Women's quest for equality in the public sphere of the economy and the private realm of the bedroom is nothing more than a desire to be taken seriously as contributors, consumers, and sexual beings in society. Sharon Marie Ross, an associate professor of cinema and television arts at Columbia College in Chicago, argues that the "stories told [on *Sex and the City*] highlight a double bind still at work in American culture and society that often makes motherhood, career and sexual agency mutually exclusive, even as they also highlight the legitimacy of women wanting marriage and children."[94] In other words, women can want to "have it all," but society isn't yet willing to give it to them.

Ross locates women's agency in both consumerism and sexuality along a spectrum of choice, likening dating to window shopping, a seemingly innocent activity in which women look at the wares on offer, comparing them and weighing their options before making the decision which to purchase.[95] It's an apt metaphor that highlights the societal danger at work behind the "never satisfied woman." Whether looking at the woman with hundreds of pairs of shoes (ahem, Carrie) or the one with a long list of lovers (*cough* Samantha *cough*), the threat is the same: She has power—the power to choose her clothing and the power to choose her mate.

This at best threatens and at worst topples the centuries-old dominant structure in which men are the ones who do the selecting and women are the ones consumed. Thus, the quartet of women on *Sex and the City* represent a societal revolution in which women have taken the reins of power and aren't afraid to flaunt their choices. Plus, in being influential enough to build brands and make millions in the process, *Sex and the City* shows just how much untapped (at least until now) power women hold in the economy, in relationships, and in their ability to influence one another. If the female comradery on the show and among the audience is any indication, then women banding together behind a cause, as they have behind the products on the show, truly could change the world.

14

FASHION AND HOW WE
VIEW OURSELVES

"I like my money right where I can see it . . . hanging in my closet."

—Carrie, episode 6.1, "To Market, to Market"

Fashion. If there is a single word, other than sex, that *Sex and the City* has come to epitomize, this is it. The show has been called "television's hottest catwalk" and a "style Bible so transcending that its influence can be seen all over the country."[1] Fans and critics alike spent hours each week combing over every look to praise or vilify it. And even today, more than twenty years after the show first aired, there is an Instagram account, @everyoutfitonsatc, that continues this tradition by "dissecting" every bit of fashion ever shown on the show, "accompanied by irreverent captions," exposing the show and its fashion to a whole new generation of clothes horses.[2]

The media has always been crucial to *Sex and the City*'s sartorial success. "Fashion commentators . . . seem to note every shoe, frock, and bag, and turn these observations into fashion page copy," writes König. "It is a multimedia love affair between two consenting parties: the powerful, notoriously fickle fashion press and the sassy compelling *Sex and the City*."[3] This symbiotic relationship is, in part, what made the show not just a hit but also a cultural phenomenon. For its part, *Sex and the City* courted the fashion press through Carrie's love affair with *Vogue* magazine—already the Bible of the fashion world—which she in later seasons works for. In the pilot, Carrie narrates, "When I first moved to New York and I was totally broke, sometimes I would buy *Vogue* instead of dinner. I felt it fed me more." While certainly not a healthy habit, it is one that fans would come to understand as they strove to imitate Carrie's lifestyle. She is shown reading the magazine multiple times throughout the series, and even in the second episode of *And Just Like That* . . . , Charlotte brings a grieving Carrie three editions of *Vogue* to comfort her.

In turn, the magazine featured the show regularly, publishing hundreds of articles on it and creating an entire page dedicated to its coverage.[4] Parker appeared on its cover nearly a dozen times. "Most TV shows are happy to receive sporadic attention from TV critics, but *Sex and the City* has, at least theoretically, doubled its press coverage by consistently securing column inches on the fashion pages," König notes.[5] And through the show's fashion-obsessed audience, *Vogue* reached a whole new generation of subscribers eager to emulate their fashion icons.

"None of us knew that fashion would have an impact in any way beyond being an important part of the show," Parker said.[6] However, it wasn't a complete accident. "I wanted fashion to be really important in the show," Star recalls. "I wrote an episode of *90210* in its first season, I showed it to some friends, and was amazed to find that women watched the shows for clothes as much as the story."[7] And for many, that is completely true. "Do we really care if Carrie finally finds love and security?" asked *Evening Standard* reporter Emine Saner in 2003. "[All] we really want to know is what [she'll] be wearing in the 6th and final series of *Sex and the City*."[8]

This Versace dress, featured in part 1 of the series finale, is one of many garments *Sex and the City* helped to make famous. Photofest/*Sex and the City* (HBO), season 6 (February 15, 2004)

In most shows and movies, what the characters wear is based on the look they want to portray and the action of the scene. But in *Sex and the City*, that idea is reversed, with everything about the show serving the fashion. "[Costume designer Patricia] Field is signaling the spectacularity of this fashion and costume in *Sex and the City*, which the clothes, alongside the actors and the characters they adorn, are imposed on, or exist independently of script and narrative," write Bruzzi and Gibson.[9] The fashion has a life and identity of its own. And that is how—and why—the fashion became the phenomenon it did.

Star sees some irony in that: "Carrie is a character whose style is dictated by whimsy. She dresses distinctively and would not be wearing a flower if everybody else was. The funniest thing about fashion is that if real people are wearing something, the fashionistas won't because they can't be doing what the rest of the public is doing."[10]

THE WOMAN BEHIND THE WARDROBE

We can thank fashion designer Patricia Field for the show's quirky sense of style. Now known for dressing the spectacularly fashionable movie *The Devil Wears Prada*, for which she was nominated for an Oscar and a BAFTA for Best Costume Design, and as a *Project Runway* judge, it was *Sex and the City* that put Field on the map.[11] At the time she was hired, Field had worked as a TV and movie costume designer for more than fifteen years and was running an eponymous boutique in Soho. She was brought in "to lend the show the New York street credit needed."[12]

As in her shop, Field used a variety of pieces on the show, resulting in a freewheeling mix of vintage, designer, and items borrowed from cast and crew. She explains, "I find costumes in a variety of places. I would say that about 40% of the wardrobe is borrowed and the rest is bought. . . . The costumes on the show range from $5 to $20,000. . . . Any expensive pieces like that we have to send back to the designer when we're done. . . . When we finish an episode, the actresses can choose to purchase anything that has been bought."[13] Today, Field even has her own "As Seen on *SATC*" section on her website, where she sells replicas of a few of the pieces she helped make famous.[14]

CHARACTERS AND THEIR CLOTHING CHOICES

They say that clothes make the man, but they also reflect the woman. How and why are a matter of debate. Some believe woman dress up for men, while others say women dress more for one another, and still others believe clothing is an expression of the self or can be used as a weapon against the world. The women of *Sex and the City* would likely agree with all four.

In her famous book *The Second Sex*, feminist pioneer Simone de Beauvoir critiques the ideas of "dressing up" and "adornment" as reflections of a "woman's social station" as well as a way to "offer her as a prey to male desires." Only "once she has accepted her vocation as a sex object, [does] she enjoy adorning herself," de Beauvoir writes.[15] This is a philosophy that would sit particularly well with Samantha, given that she has no problem advertising herself as a sex object, but all the women accept this role at various times in their quest to find "the one."

On the other end of the spectrum is novelist Angela Carter, who in her 1975 essay "Notes for a Theory of Sixties Style" writes, "clothes are our weapons, our challenges, our visible insults."[16] She is speaking specifically of the seismic cultural changes of the 1960s, which were heavily reflected in the clothing of the period, but she could be speaking of any period in time. Women have long dressed in ways that show off to or try to outdo rivals, get back at exes, and entice. The right outfit can say, "See what you are missing?" as Samantha's daring black dress does for Dominic in episode 2.11, "Evolution"; "Look what you walked away from," as Charlotte's does in 5.3, "Luck Be an Old Lady"; or even "He's with *me* now," as Carrie's does in 6.18, "Splat!"

The famous Van Morrison song "Wild Night," which was covered by John Mellencamp in 1994 and was in heavy radio rotation when *Sex and the City* aired, contains one of the truest sayings about women and fashion ever uttered: "All the girls walk by/dressed up for each other." Any woman who has ever attended a party, gone clubbing, or been to any social event can tell you that she picks her outfit, at least in part, with other women in mind. Fashion is a constant game of one-upmanship with other women, as we, consciously or not, compete for mates. And this isn't just in our minds; science backs it up. A 2020 study published in *Social Psychological and Personality Science* found that "other women are always the sole intended audience for women's sartorial cues and/or signals."[17] And what we wear has a strong effect. A 2014 study published in the *Personality and Social Psychology Bulletin* finds that "women who wear red can make other women green with envy, putting them on the defensive and making them more protective of their partners."[18] So watch out for that "Lady in Red" when you're on a date, especially if her name is Samantha Jones.

But most importantly, when a woman dresses for herself, she embraces the "belief that adornment does not exist independently of the woman, but rather becomes a means of accessing and understanding her."[19] As explored at length in chapter 1, what a woman chooses to wear is a reflection of how she feels about herself and who she sees herself as being, which may change from day to day. *Psychology Today* emphasizes the difference between fashion—the clothing we wear—and style—our ability to pick and choose clothing that is "in keeping with how we see ourselves" when looking at fashion as a form of self-expression. "With style, we stamp our personal identity on an arrangement of things. And our closets always seem full of possibilities—it just depends on what aspect of our identity we want to make palpable in clothes that day."[20] With that in mind, let's take a look at the signature style of each of the ladies of *Sex and the City* and what it says about them.

MIRANDA

Miranda is the least traditionally fashionable of all the characters, especially at certain times in the series. While she can and does dress up for special occasions, like a night out or an office function, she is also frequently seen wearing the kind of outfits most Americans wear when running errands: blue jeans, overalls, hoodies, oversized sweatshirts, T-shirts, and the like—comfortable, casual clothing. When she first becomes a mother, she reflects new moms everywhere, with unwashed hair and baby puke on her clothing. She is not afraid to be a real person.

Field says that was a conscious choice: "Miranda has a lot of masculine aspects, like sweatpants. I would never wear them, but I think Miranda is either put together or she does not care at all."[21] Nixon says she liked Miranda's more laid-back style because it made her character more relatable: "I think that it is a great relief when you see Miranda at home and she's wearing sweatpants and a T-shirt."[22]

Miranda is hyperfocused on her career and doesn't have the time or energy to put into her wardrobe when she isn't at work, so she goes for function over style. Because she looks like the people watching the show, "Miranda quickly emerged as a fan favorite," writes Jonah Engel Bromwich. "A Season 2 shot of Ms. Nixon's character wearing a puffer coat with overalls and a baseball hat conforms strangely well to recent street wear trends. Miranda was a hypebeast all along; we just couldn't see it."[23]

When it comes to her job, however, Miranda dresses to the nines because she takes her work as a corporate lawyer very seriously. "Miranda's wardrobe is dictated more by her profession than any other characters," Field says. "Because she is a lawyer, it's very tailored. Cynthia's personal style is not so tailored, so we try to give her character a pop ethnic look with mixed patterns and colors when she's not at work."[24]

Surprisingly for fans who watched the show as it aired and often grumbled about Miranda's lack of fashion sense and how Field "did her dirty" with a plain wardrobe, millennials are embracing it.[25] Miranda is really about twenty years ahead of her time in many ways, from her take-no-prisoners attitude to her style. Jonah Waterhouse notes that Miranda, without anyone realizing it, is a "champion [for an] androgynous, no-bullshit style for a new generation of career women—which carried all the way from the pilot episode to the unforgettably problematic debacle that was *Sex and the City 2*."[26] Jessica Davis adds, "Her love of dungarees, puffer jackets, baseball caps and dorky sunglasses resulted in outfits that wouldn't look out of place in a modern-day Balenciaga campaign."[27] So Miranda doesn't deserve our pity; she's been a trendsetter all along.

CHARLOTTE

Charlotte's old-fashioned values are clearly mirrored in her wardrobe, which *Harper's Bazaar* calls "Park Avenue Princess style."[28] We rarely see her in pants, as she prefers more "ladylike" dresses and skirts. Her hemlines are much longer than the other ladies', usually landing just at or below the knee, and she is more likely to wear shirts that cover or hint at her breasts rather than exposing them. Her style is also more classic, favoring a 1950s, Jackie O.–inspired feel but without looking kitschy or like a costume.

The word *preppy* is used a lot when critics describe her style, but that is unfair because it often brings to mind a very different look—one from the '80s and early '90s of pastels, golf shirts, loafers with socks, and sweater vests—rather than Charlotte's elegant style. Yes, she does like her sweater sets, but on her, they are never cliché. Rather, they fit right in with the "neat tailoring, classic silhouettes and timeless accessories" that define her style.[29]

"Simone de Beauvoir was the first feminist to offer a sustained critique of fashion and femininity commenting on 'the woman of elegance' that 'what she treasures is herself adorned, and not the objects that adorn her,'" Bruzzi and Gibson write.[30] This could be said of Charlotte, who is more about the overall look she presents to the world than the individual objects that make up that picture.

Charlotte's signature is her love for all things Burberry. From a raincoat and a matching earmuff and scarf set to a luggage set and even a tiny bag to hold plastic waste disposal bags when she is walking her dog in *And Just Like That . . .* , she is a living, breathing advertisement for the luxury brand just as much as Carrie is for Manolo and Choo. And if Charlotte has a signature color, it is probably pink, followed by white, both of which emphasize her femininity and relative innocence.

Field says that when dressing Charlotte, she liked to mix "solids . . . with pretty patterns" to give her a "clean, sexy look." The result is a character who doesn't compete with the bolder styles of the other women but isn't overwhelmed by them either. Field explains, "When we started out we dressed her as a classic Americana girl. When she met Trey, that style became more pronounced, and when she married and became a housewife it became the more casual version of that."[31]

Many critics, like *Marie Claire UK* and *Harper's Bazaar*, argue that while Carrie is the one who gets all the attention for her fashion choices, Charlotte is the true style icon. Penny Goldstone sums up Charlotte's style and personality: "Sure, [it] was very classic, but that's precisely why it will stand the test of time, which can't be said for the others."[32]

SAMANTHA

Samantha always dresses to impress—and often to seduce. Like Miranda, for work, she is a fan of the power suit, but hers are more 1980s Joan Collins than Miranda's more stylish skirt- and pantsuits. Everything about her style is bold and proud—"brightly colored suits, fitted waistlines, low cut necklines, loud jewelry"—just like Samantha.[33] Everything she wears screams, "Look at me," because Samantha always aims to be the center of attention. "Samantha is a lot of fun to dress," says Field, "because she is such a vivid and sexual character, and she is very open about her attitude toward her sex life. And, because she owns her own company, she could dress how she chooses. . . . It's more theatrical than any of the other characters' wardrobes."[34]

For her dates, Samantha almost universally wears dresses—the more form-fitting, the better—as they are her weapon of choice in the dating game. They may end up on the floor at the end of the night, but Samantha chooses them with care, opting for pieces that show off her legs or breasts or sometimes both. But no matter what she wears, Samantha is always in style. She'd sooner be caught in one of Charlotte's conservative frocks than without hair, makeup, and designer duds like Miranda. As Meeta Agrawal of *Entertainment Weekly* writes, "from power publicist to sexy man-eater, Samantha Jones' wardrobe is always in control," just like Samantha.[35]

CARRIE

Chapter 1 discusses Carrie's style as a form of her identity at length, but it never hurts to revisit the closet of our favorite fashionista, which, while filled with some truly drool-worthy outfits, is also home to some that push the limits of suspension of disbelief, even for Carrie. "Her outfits, with their insistence on being the most extra in any situation, are really just an external manifestation of her extraordinary and toxic narcissism," writes Charles Manning for *Fashion Week Daily*.[36]

He isn't wrong. Carrie can be very narcissistic, even over small things. Who else would spend an *entire* episode acting like farting in front of her lover was the biggest calamity ever, especially when her friends are dealing with their own issues? And every time she breaks up with Big, it is over something to do with her. The first time it's because Big isn't ready to commit to her being "the one." The second time it's because he doesn't factor her into his life enough when he finds out he might have to move to Paris for up to a year because of work—even though he doesn't know that for sure yet. The man may have to uproot his entire life to move to a foreign country, but yes, it's all about you, Carrie.

But I digress. Carrie's outfits scream for attention. The getup that nearly every critic mentions as Carrie's most hated is season 2's "Heidi dress" that she wears to lunch in the park. "It became the example for when we've gone too far," says Parker.

> I take total blame for that, but I also stand by that. It's a great example of Carrie dressing for an occasion. She's going to a picnic in the park with her friends so she's got a big heavy brocade blanket, and she found a dirndl. I even had Kabuchi, the makeup artist, put freckles on my face. You have to take chances like that if you're going to have a character who is in love with silhouettes and colors and textures and fashion.[37]

And Parker had a lot of say in what her character wore, especially in the later seasons as her fame grew. "Sarah Jessica is very involved in what she wears," Field says. "She brings things in as ideas. She looks at every magazine. . . . She is a very fashionable person, and her interest helps us do our job.[38]

One of the most consistently scorned outfits is Carrie's quasi-cowgirl Hamptons beach party look, in which she pairs a striped orange sarong with a snakeskin tube top and an orange straw cowboy hat. The best thing that can be said about that look is that the sarong and the hat are the same color.

Another is the time she pairs pink and purple tie-dyed capris with a flouncy pink-and-white Chanel blouse that only kind of matches, and for some reason, she tops it all off with an electric blue bandana that makes her look like she's ready to clean the house—something we never see her do. There's also the ruched pink dress that Amelia Langas of *People* magazine says looks "like you're transported back to the homecoming dance circa 1986," which Carrie bizarrely finishes off with a silk headscarf that gives her a "1980s pirate bridesmaid" look.[39]

The only way these looks can be even remotely excused outside the high-fashion circles where they are the norm is to blame them on Carrie's psychological state, as Emily Alford of *Jezebel* does:

> Nearly all of the outfits that are commonly understood to be Carrie's borderline psychotic wardrobe fails come in instances where we most see her struggling with the bridge between who she is and who she'd like to be. . . . The more streamlined and by-the-lookbook, the more Carrie is trying to get her shit together. The more incongruous (and ultimately divisive among fans), the more Carrie is spiraling. As the series reaches the conflict that will become its core—Carrie's obsession with Big and determination to win Aidan to spite it, even if she's only interested in their relationship when she's on the cusp of destroying it—her outfits become the most reviled of the series.[40]

When thinking about the connection between Carrie's clothes and her identity, it is interesting to note her fashion choices in season 6. When she meets Aleksandr Petrovsky, she immediately conforms to a more Parisian sense of style, wearing generally more conservative looks that are much more at home with the diamond necklace Petrovsky gives her to replace her "Carrie" necklace than they would have been with the original, even if she hadn't "lost" it.[41] At first, while hanging out with Petrovsky's art crowd, Carrie keeps her quirky sense of style—who can forget the black-and-white Paris arrival dress that makes her look more like a mime than a fashionista?—but that is part of what alienates her from his crowd.

Unlike the Carrie of past seasons who clearly lives to stand out, this Carrie seeks to fit in. That is, until she understands she has lost all sense of herself. Upon finding her necklace, she realizes she wants to go back to New York, and when she does so, she switches back to her signature style. In the closing scene of the series, she is wearing a turquoise blue jacket belted over a metallic paisley skirt, a hot pink scarf, and her classic fur coat from season 1, accessorized with red heels and a shiny pink purse. She's clearly back home and back to herself again.

How to explain the messiness of this outfit, though? If we stick with the theory that the more scattered Carrie's mind is, the more disorganized her look, then this one could possibly reflect the divisiveness of the ending. It is possible that this strange choice of items is symbolic of Carrie feeling conflicted about her "happily ever after" with Mr. Big? Or it could just be a mismatched outfit? Sometimes a Fendi bag is simply a Fendi bag.

15

NEW YORK CITY

Place as Character

"11. Anything is possible. This is New York."

—Carrie, episode 6.10, "Boy Interrupted"

Sex and the City is as much a love letter to the city of New York as it is a story about four single women. In fact, Star calls the city the "fifth character" in the cast, and Parker says it was the "greatest character ever written."[1] While it is clear that the Manhattan of *Sex and the City* is not representative of the real city—as Simon writes, "the clash of diverse cultures, racial and ethnic, that make Manhattan unique, vital, and frustrating is largely absent from this HBO city. The juxtaposition of radically different economic groups, rich and poor living cheek by jowl, confronts every New Yorker every day, but almost never the women of *Sex*"[2]—it's not meant to be. Just as the show is the reinvention of a fairy tale, so is its location. New York is the Camelot of this legend, with Mr. Big as its King Arthur; Carrie as its Guinevere; and, for a while at least, Aidan as its Lancelot.[3]

This is the New York that has captivated writers and filmmakers for more than a century, the city of lights where dreams of romance and fame are as palpable as the steam from subway grates. It is the city of endless possibility. "New York City has long been associated with a romantic tradition as potent as that evoked by either Paris or Rome. In films like Woody Allen's *Annie Hall* and *Manhattan*, and the classics *Breakfast at Tiffany's* and *An Affair to Remember*, the city is a playground for lovers to wonder, their dreams embedded in its grand skyline, museums, autumn leaves, and smoky jazz haunts," writes Di Mattia.[4]

New York is one of those cities that has a mystique built up around it, like London, Rome, and St. Petersburg. It has a vibe all its own that isn't present anywhere else in the world. It represents at once a rich past and a present so current it is almost the future. Everyone is moving at once, propelled by ambition or basic need, and that creates the energy that people mean when they say the city never sleeps. Star puts it this way:

> There's something at the core that represents New York in that moment. The city is always a variation of the same—the experience of living here doesn't change. It's both a challenging place to live and an incredibly rewarding place to live. That equation of challenge versus reward is always present and it informs the lives of the characters. They chose to live here—the city is always in your face and a part of your world and daily experience for better or for worse.[5]

What better place to set a story that is both of its time and timeless than a city that is the same? "Every generation connects with the city in its own way," writes Marissa Blanchard for HBO.[6] Some were colonists who sought refuge from oppression in its vast wilderness. Others were immigrants who saw it as a place of respite and hope from the troubles of their homeland. Still more were descendants of those first settlers who inherited a sense of ownership from their ancestors and therefore ruled the city through money and power. Then came the artists with stars in their eyes who hoped to sing, dance, play, and act their way to fame and glory in Vaudeville and the Follies and then on Broadway. Following them were generations who didn't fit in, the mobsters and lawbreakers, the hippies and the hopefuls, all living side by side with hardworking average Americans and gays seeking community during the homophobia of the '60s and '70s and the devastation of the AIDS crisis in the '80s and '90s. And then, for six seasons, there were a group of four women and their closest friends who used the city to attempt to understand life at the dawn of a new millennium, with its unheard-of freedom and opportunities. *Sex and the City* is a "time capsule because New York is such an important part of the show, but it also continues to connect to a new audience because all of the questions Carrie explores are timeless. They're relevant to every generation," says Star.[7]

IT HAD TO BE NEW YORK

"New York presents itself as the only possible scenario not only for romance, but for the sexual utopia represented in the series," argues Oria.[8] And she's right. If the show used the stereotypes of other locations, it would be totally different. If it was set in Los Angeles, it would have a more sunny and sexed up vibe because of the body-consciousness of Hollywood. New Yorkers care about fashion and how they look, but it isn't the same unending quest for perfection as in California; it is more of a sense of identity and style. As Carrie says of Los Angeles in episode 3.13, "Escape from New York," "I can't believe how open and high about sex this place is. In New York, sex is so bottom shelf paper bag." Likewise, if it took place in Chicago, everything would be accented by Midwestern nice, and the women wouldn't be able to be as open about sex; the conservative values of the area wouldn't tolerate it, especially not publicly. No, as Parker says, "these women wouldn't be the same in Milwaukee, Boston, Chicago, or Cincinnati [because] if Carrie lived in a small town . . . she wouldn't walk out a door and not know what the future holds. In New York City you walk out the door and you do not know what's going to happen. There's such potential for poetry."[9]

The show is so very New York because so many of the cast and crew are native or longtime New Yorkers. They *are* the culture, so it can't help but shine through. Their real-life experiences, everything from roosters on the roof to having loud and proud sex workers as neighbors and ordering from the same Chinese place so much they know your order by heart, were reflected in the show. Tuccillo says, "I can see and hear so many things that can be transferred to the show. In general I feel that the city is so pulsing with life and drama and creativity and excitement that it's only natural to want to sit down and funnel all of that into something creative."[10] Amy B. Harris, a coproducer on the show, agrees. "Being a New Yorker shapes everything we do. . . . It's not enough that the women just walked down the streets of New York; it really is a particular headspace that makes you a true New Yorker, and I think living here just makes it all that much easier to tap into."[11]

That true New York mind-set is one of the reasons Carrie has such a hard time when she moves to Paris with Aleksandr. Not only would it be very difficult to chronicle the "New York sociosexual scene" from afar, but also, as Miranda says to her in episode 6.18, "Splat!" "You can't quit your column; it's who you are. Your column is all about New York. You're all about New York."[12] In many ways, Carrie *is* New York. Her identity is so intrinsically linked with the city that she can't exist anywhere else. In season 5, fresh off her final breakup with Aidan, Carrie swears off men and dates the city. What she is really doing is dating herself, getting to know who she is outside the men she dates. As Miranda points out several times throughout the series, Carrie changes when she is with a man, especially the toxic ones like Big and Aleksandr, so the "soul-searching loneliness" she experiences is to be expected because she not only doesn't know who she is but also doesn't know how to spend time with herself.[13] So she looks outside herself to the city and transfers the love she can't yet show herself onto it. She may be able to denigrate herself in a million different ways, but "I can't have nobody talking shit about my boyfriend" (5.1, "Anchors Away").

Another example of Carrie's twinning with the city takes place in Paris, just after Big declares his love for her, saying, "But I'm here. Carrie, you are the one." She doesn't respond with "And so are you," or "I love you," as one would expect. Instead, she says, "I miss New York. Take me home" (6.20, "An American Girl in Paris, Part Deux"). It is as if she can't say, "I love you," because her heart is already taken by the city, and no matter what they go through together, it will always be her one true love, even if, like Big, it can be "abusive and dismissive."[14]

FILMING IN THE CITY

According to crew members, "approximately 40 percent of every show consists of the women interacting with the city" by being out on the streets and filming on location.[15] They purposefully avoid the tourist attractions like Times Square that every show and movie uses in favor of "bars, clubs, and restaurants that feel authentically New York and of the moment."[16] That is what gives the show its verisimilitude.

They try to match the location to the scene in a way that feels like the characters would really go there to have that conversation or that the location is really where a certain event would take place. Co-executive producer John Melfi gives this example: "We will go to a historic location like the Old Town bar, where Carrie went on a date with the Yankee and will be careful not to damage the mirrors or booths because it's a staple of New York and we want people to know that that's a real bar. We're really proud to be able to shoot in these places."[17]

"You can't duplicate the texture of the city anywhere else," Star says. "With every point to camera you see something beautiful and unique and you are always getting the essence of the city. I would always have locations in mind while writing."[18]

Interestingly, even scenes that take place outside of New York City were purposefully shot within its five boroughs. Sohn notes, "The Hamptons episode in season one, when Carrie visits her married friends [1.3, 'Bay of Married Pigs'] were shot in a Manhattan brownstone; the season two Hamptons episode [2.17, '20-Something Girls vs. 30-Something Women'] was shot in Queens and Staten Island; and though the actual Staten Island Ferry was used [in 3.1, 'Where There Is Fire'], the fireman's bar was in the West Village."[19] This is not only a way the show can express its love for the city but also a way the creators infused it with a sense of New York–ness.

SEPTEMBER 11

It would be disrespectful to the show and to the city of New York to skip over the devastating terrorist attacks that took place on the World Trade Center on September 11, 2001, and changed the city forever. The attacks came between seasons for the show. While the second half hadn't aired yet—and wouldn't until January 6, 2002—it had already been filmed, wrapping only ten days before the tragedy. "They had finished the whole thing on a pre-911 mindset, [so] they were going to have to work with what they already had, and do what they could to make it feel appropriate to this astonishing shift in national mood. They had to switch their usual rose-colored lens on the city closer to the black of the moment," writes Oria.[20]

The first order of business was to remove the Twin Towers from all shots in the show and the opening credits. They were replaced by the Empire State Building and were erased from episode 4.13, "The Good Fight," where they would have been on the horizon.[21] The producers decided to keep the Twin Towers in a scene in the next episode, where Carrie looks at a souvenir snow globe with the lost landmarks inside and says in a voice-over that was filmed before the attacks but was chillingly resonant after: "That's the thing about relationships—sometimes they look prettier from the outside. And what's inside can be different than what it seems." It was an accident, but it felt more like a tribute.[22]

Similarly, the season finale appears to be an homage to the broken and battered town, even though it was already in the can before everything changed. Aptly titled "I Heart NY," it is "as much a love letter to New York as a farewell to Mr. Big," who was moving to Napa, California.[23] To mark this huge transition in both their lives, Big and Carrie go on a date where they celebrate "classic New York," including a carriage ride through Central Park and a musical nod to the iconic film *Breakfast at Tiffany's* through the nostalgic song "Moon River," which they dance to in Carrie's apartment. The episode ends with a voice-over from Carrie that seems tailor-written for the times, even though it was penned long before: "Seasons change. So do cities. People come into your life, and people go. But it's comforting to know the ones you love are always in your heart." A card before the closing credits tells viewers the episode is dedicated to "our city of New York . . . then, now, and forever."

SEX AND THE CITY TOURS

When a show places as much emphasis on its setting as *Sex and the City* does, it's only natural that fans will want to see the locations for themselves and walk in the footsteps (if not the shoes) of their favorite characters, if only for a few hours. Enterprising locals saw an opportunity to make some money while promoting their glorious city, and so tours of popular *Sex and the City* locations were born in 2001. At one time, Destination on Location Travel offered a luxury weekend in Manhattan that would set you back a cool $15,000 per person but offered groups as large as twelve the "fantasy that they're one of the four *Sex* characters."[24] Discover Card even sponsored a "Fun in the City Sweepstakes," in which a lucky winner got to spend "three days and two nights bustling around the Big Apple."[25]

Today, several tours are still available.[26] Free Tours by Foot offers free, self-guided *Sex and the City* walking tours.[27] If a bar crawl is more your style, strap on your Manolos and try out the *Sex and the City* Night Out.[28] But if you want the "official" experience and you're eighteen or older, then you have to take the 3.5-hour bus tour offered by On Location Tours, one of the first to bring *Sex and the City* to fans. It's even endorsed by Parker herself![29] At only $65 per person and more than forty stops at shops, eateries, and filming locations for the show, it's quite a deal. Shorter private tours and a limo option are also available at an additional cost.[30] All tours include cupcakes from Magnolia Bakery, and those twenty-one and older can enjoy a cosmopolitan at Onieals in Soho, which is the location of Steve and Aidan's fictional bar, Scout, in the show.[31] Other stops include

- Carrie's brownstone stoop in the West Village;
- the sex shop in the West Village that made the Rabbit famous;
- Equinox Gym; and
- boutiques along Bleecker Street, including Marc Jacobs, Ralph Lauren, Marc by Marc Jacobs, Toosh, James Perse, Brunello Cucinelli, Fresh, Lulu Guinness, Creed, Mulberry, Olive and Bette, and others.

They will also point out high-end retailers, like Jimmy Choo, Manolo Blahnik, Patricia Field, Jaime Mascaro, Bergdorf Goodman, Tiffany & Co.,

Henri Bendel, Takashimaya, Fortunoff, Saks Fifth Avenue, Lord & Taylor, Diane Von Furstenberg, and more, in case you want to give your credit card a workout and take home a special souvenir.

Or fans can always make their own tours using any number of guides to filming locations online. No matter how you do it, if you're a fan and can visit New York City, you'll be sure to see at least one location associated with the show, even if you aren't trying. Being there will make your next rewatch all the more special because you'll know exactly where the ladies are. Even if you can't make it in person, there are many video and virtual tours available online, so there's no excuse not to put on your favorite shoes and outfit; mix up a cosmo; channel your inner Carrie, Miranda, Charlotte, or Samantha; and take a *Sex and the City* tour from the comfort of your own couch.

PART III

THE LEGACY

16

AN ENDURING FRANCHISE

"They say nothing lasts forever; dreams change, trends come and go, but friendships never go out of style."

—Carrie, *Sex and the City: The Movie*

More than twenty years after the show ended, *Sex and the City* is still part of popular culture, a rare milestone achieved by only a handful of influential shows. This is due in no small part to DVD, syndication, and streaming deals. According to Oria, the show's "fan base extends through Latin America, Europe, the Middle East, Oceana, and Asia where the show was reported to be 'a smash among young professionals' in cities like Bangkok, Manila, Taipei, and Hong Kong." It's even got an illegal fanbase in Singapore and China, thanks to bootlegged DVDs.[1] But the bigger part of the ongoing franchise is thanks to the sequels and prequels it spawned to please fans who just couldn't get enough *Sex*.

THE MOVIES

The series finale was intended to be the end of the franchise, and King firmly believed that it ended as it should have. However, with audiences hungry for more, he got the band back together. One of the biggest questions they had to answer was, after spending six years exploring the issues of your thirties, how do you then expand the story to reflect life in your forties and, for Samantha at least, fifties? And how do you handle aging characters? For the cast and crew, the answer was simple: You don't. "Age is not avoided here. It is embraced and even savored, like, well, a nice, cool Cosmopolitan," according to Today.[2]

"For a Hollywood movie that's extraordinary," says Cattrall. "But I think it's the way the show has always been" unafraid to tackle controversial topics.

For a predominantly female cast, the issue takes on even more gravity. It's no secret that in Hollywood, roles for women over forty, especially leading roles, are rare. *Sex and the City: The Movie* proves that women of a certain age can carry a movie and command screen time in a franchise built around sex just as well as they can in their thirties.

The 2008 movie picks up three years after the series ends. When the movie begins, Carrie and Big are shopping for an apartment; Miranda and Steve are navigating marriage, children, and a constant state of overwhelm; Charlotte is dealing with the realities of being a mother; and Samantha is in Los Angeles, still managing Smith's career. The crux of the plot revolves around the idea that after Carrie and Big decide to get married, Big, in typical fashion, gets cold feet and leaves Carrie at the altar. Over the next two hours, we follow Carrie, Miranda, Samantha, and Charlotte as they deal with the fallout of this manufactured heartache over the ensuing year. We also find out that Steve cheated on Miranda, and they are unsure if their marriage will continue. Charlotte's storyline revolves around finally getting pregnant with Harry's child, and Samantha deals with her commitment issues to Smith, all of which are at odds with the way the series ends.

But the storyline is never really what the movie is about. It is about re-connecting with our four favorite ladies, and the producers knew that. The movie was billed as the "Super Bowl for women," so product placement was at an all-time high. *Forbes* magazine clocked contracts with at least eight companies for product placement, including VitaminWater, Mercedes Benz, and Skyy vodka, plus specially designed gowns, jewelry, and accessories for the characters.[3]

The gamble on a female-led blockbuster paid off, with the movie making "$26 million on its opening night in the United States and Canada, and $56 million in its first weekend, nearly twice what the studio had estimated for its entire run. It was the biggest opening ever for an R-rated film and a film with a female lead," notes Oria.[4] Just as the Harry Potter and Hunger Games franchises would do for teen moviegoers in the decades to come, *Sex and the City* proved to studio execs that female moviegoers are a force to be reckoned with.

But just because women sat their designer-clad bums in the seats and tapped their Manolo-shod toes in anticipation didn't mean they liked what they saw. Many fans were disappointed, especially because the movie breaks ranks with the ending of the series, taking many of the characters in directions they otherwise wouldn't have gone in; Cheeda describes this betrayal as "something that didn't feel right since established relationships were broken for the sake of an additional plot."[5] Steve never would have cheated on Miranda, and while a younger Big may have left Carrie multiple times, he wouldn't have done it at the altar and with no discernable reason. The only plotline with any viability was Samantha leaving Smith because she never was the committing kind. The two bright spots in the film are Charlotte's pregnancy and Carrie's gigantic closet (hello, luvah!).

The studio ignored critical and fan response, seeing only dollar signs. Though the sequel *Sex and the City 2* was "planned quickly, it took two years to make and distribute the movie," and what resulted is best left to the dregs of memory.[6] It was reported that King was aiming for a movie that had a women's liberation theme: He "planned the movie as a commentary on the Middle East's abominable treatment of women. His vision: these liberated American women would laugh in the face of such patriarchy. Samantha would throw condoms at religious men and yell, 'I have sex!' It would provide a broad, farcical take on America's volatile, era defining culture class clash with the region."[7]

There is a lot that can be said about that statement, and none of it is good. Perhaps setting this kind of movie in the Middle East wasn't the smartest move. What resulted is a movie that plays heavily on stereotypes, traffics in cultural and religious disrespect, and carries a strong White-savior-complex vibe, especially when the four ladies get up onstage to sing "I Am Woman, Hear Me Roar" at a karaoke joint in Abu Dhabi.

With only a 15 percent on the Rotten Tomatoes meter and negative reviews across the board from *Rolling Stone*, the *Wall Street Journal*, and the *Christian Science Monitor*, it's not surprising to see words like *stunted*, *aimless*, and *embarrassing* used to describe the film.[8] Legendary film critic Roger Ebert even said it made his skin crawl.[9] Fans didn't care much for it, either. "*Sex and the City 2* always felt like a relatively needless sequel, with the ending even rather ridiculous as it signed off with a gag rather than on a heartwarming note," writes Cheeda.[10]

THE CARRIE DIARIES

Perhaps realizing that *Sex and the City* was played out among its original audience, in 2013, the prequel series *The Carrie Diaries* premiered on the CW. Aimed at a much younger audience, it is based on a 2010 novel of the same name by Bushnell. The idea, besides appealing to the daughters of the original audience, was to fill in the backstory missing from the show by fleshing out the high school years of Carrie Bradshaw. The show is set in 1984 New York, two years before the movies tell us that Carrie moved to Manhattan for good, which means she never went to college, unless she managed to do so after moving to the Big Apple. But given that Carrie said she was so broke she sometimes skipped dinner to afford *Vogue*, that is unlikely.

But then again, it seems that all bets are off with this show. Besides lacking the spunk and verve of the original series, one of the biggest criticisms is that it contradicts information given in the series and subsequent movies about how the characters met.[11] Once you dishonor the source, there is no recovering.[12] Implicit in the bond between viewer and creator is that the rules of the world as originally established will remain so unless a very good reason is presented. Right off the bat, *The Carrie Diaries* has sweet, young Carrie living with her father, whom we are clearly told in the series left when she was five. With mistakes that huge, it's not surprising the show barely lasted two seasons.

AND JUST LIKE THAT . . .

As this book was being finalized, the *Sex and the City* reboot *And Just Like That . . .* aired. In the eleven months between the announcement that it was going to be produced and the premiere, fans and critics alike engaged in speculation about what the new series would be like. Just like Carrie, they asked many questions to figure out where this unexpected news fit into their world and the world created in what was now a full-fledged franchise. Cassie Da Costa of *Vanity Fair* asks with equal hope and cynicism, "Could a reprisal force [executive producer Michael Patrick] King to examine how his characters' flaws were often rooted in an anti-queer mentality? Or will the new series simply paper over the show's history by making Carrie, Miranda, and Charlotte paragons of midlife emotional and moral growth?"[13]

Some were hopeful by the possibilities. Saim Cheeda with Screenrant took a cautiously optimistic approach: "Since the revival is supposed to be a limited series, it's placed well to wrap everything up and send fans off feeling satisfied. More importantly, the characters themselves can rest well with their individual endings."[14] But there were plenty of people who asked a simple question: Why? Did we really need a reboot, especially when so many in the last few years proved that hits are the exception rather than the rule? Princess Weekes of the Mary Sue didn't think so, quipping, "And I couldn't help but wonder . . . what the hell are they thinking? . . . The new chapter is titled *And Just Like That . . .* , and honestly that ellipsis speaks volumes for me."[15]

Many others questioned how the show could take place without the spiciest of the fab four, Samantha. Cattrall adamantly refused to be in the reboot, saying, "It's a great wisdom to know when enough is enough. . . . I just thought to myself, 'No, this is right.' And you can't go against that feeling."[16] She elaborated that she had no desire to play Samantha at sixty-five but "feels powerful" that she "left something behind" that she's "proud" of.[17] Because the show has kept Samantha tangentially part of the story line through occasional text messages with Carrie, many fans hoped Cattrall would change her mind, but when asked if she would ever consider being on *And Just Like That . . .* , she responded, "That's a no," adding, "It's powerful to say no."[18]

To account for her loss—those involved with the show were very clear they were not replacing her—*And Just Like That . . .* introduces not one but four new female characters: Che Diaz, Carrie's nonbinary, bisexual boss; Lisa Todd Wexley, Charlotte's new BFF; Seema Patel, Carrie's real estate broker; and Dr. Nya Wallace, Miranda's Columbia law professor. All are women of color, so that is a huge improvement over the original series, but Che's gender and sexual preference feel like a box the producers needed to check.

Although they (Che's preferred pronoun) quickly became one of the most hated characters on television, Che is also the only one of the four new characters with any real personality or backstory.[19] The other three have one defining trait: Lisa is as perfectionistic as Charlotte, Seema is of a certain age and still single, and Dr. Wallace wants a child but cannot conceive. It is possible that they will be given more depth in the second season, but because the show was marketed as a limited-run production and not a series, that shouldn't have been an expectation.

SO HOW DOES IT LIVE UP?

(Warning, major spoilers ahead.)

Cheeda's insight, "Considering the revival is titled *And Just Like That . . .* , a whole new name might entail different turns in storytelling fans aren't prepared to experience," turned out to be prophetic and not in the way the show may have wanted.[20] *And Just Like That . . .* is nothing like *Sex and the City*, and fans like me who were looking forward to revisiting the fun, flirty series were sorely disappointed. It has its moments of artistic merit, but the general feeling of the first season is at best depressing and at worst traumatizing, even if you had read the spoilers or had an intuition what the big shocker in the first episode might entail. The series lacks all sense of joy and hope until the finale, and even then, those emotions are tepid and rely on anticipation of possible future changes in storyline rather than on what takes place in that episode.

One big problem is that overall, the show makes aging seem like a terrible rapid decline—like you go from thirty-something party girl to decrepit octogenarian overnight—even though the characters are only in their fifties. Between Carrie's bad hip, Steve's overdramatized hearing loss, and everyone's obsession with gray hair and wrinkles, you'd swear the Grim Reaper was coming for you the moment you hit 50, even though the average life expectancy of a woman in the United States was 78.79 years in 2019. And while the body aches that come with age are overemphasized, the biggest change of that part of life, menopause, is given barely a passing mention on a show with six females and one gender-fluid character.

Yes, it is nice seeing our old friends again, and Carrie gets a few good puns in there—for example, when Miranda complains about stepping on a used condom on Brady's floor, Charlotte says, "At least he's using protection," to which Carrie quips, "Now that is seeing the condom as half-full."—but it isn't nearly enough to buoy up the sinking ship or make fans want to keep watching. Maybe Samantha is the spark the show is missing or maybe it is something else, but the only thing that kept me watching was the ongoing prayer that the show just needed to find its feet and would get better. That prayer went unanswered.

To better analyze what went wrong, let's take a look at the first two episodes in detail. We need to get the "big" shocker out of the way first: Mr. Big dies. If you didn't know that from spoilers going in (I managed to avoid them), you had to have realized at least that something bad is going to happen to him pretty early on in the episode. The writers were pretty heavy-handed with the hints, from Carrie's insistence that they must have a certain type of salmon for dinner and the mention of Big's nitroglycerine pills to Carrie just happening to choose to wear her wedding shoes to the concert that night. For those still in the dark, they amp up the drama by cutting between Lily's piano recital and Big on his Peloton. By now it is very obvious what is going to happen—he has a heart attack after his triumphant one thousandth ride.

One thing that really bothered me—to the point that I was yelling at the TV—is that upon returning home to find Big dying on the shower floor, Carrie behaves like an idiot. While she could have been acting out of shock, she should have at least turned the water off and called 911 before attempting to take Big in her arms. But that wouldn't have been as dramatic as her ruining her wedding shoes in a last bid to hold her beloved. With as fast as he died, the paramedics couldn't have made it in time to save him, but she would have shown more concern by trying to call them rather than clumsily hefting and then dropping his bulk in a final semi-embrace. As *Rolling Stone* writer Alan Sepinwall writes, "If King wanted Big to die in Carrie's arms, rather than for her to return to find him already gone, there were ways to do it that wouldn't so thoroughly distract from the emotions of the moment."[21]

Parker said in a February 2022 interview with Andy Cohen on *Watch What Happens Live*, "Of course she called 911! Didn't you see the people behind [her, later], moving the body out? . . . It's suspended animation. It's this moment where everything stops, and then whatever collapsing of time that happens does not stop her from taking care of somebody in a fashion that you would want and expect from your partner or husband or wife."[22] Personally, I don't buy it. As my generation likes to say, "Pics, or it didn't happen." We don't see it onscreen, so as viewers, in our minds, it didn't happen. It isn't even referenced later in conversation. If it had been, then all could have been forgiven.

This excuse feels too much like backpedaling. The cast and creators have clearly heard the fan outcry and are trying to minimize it. It's a move out of a bad PR 101 playbook. But people are more media savvy than that—they can sense when an explanation is inauthentic; that's why all crisis managers are taught to begin by apologizing for their client's/company's mistakes.[23] It would have been better for everyone if they had said, "Look, we messed up." That's what Samantha Jones would have advised had she been around to act as counsel.

Because of its heavy subject matter, many critics compare *And Just Like That . . .* to season 4 of *Sex and the City*, which takes a decidedly darker turn with Miranda's mother's death and Miranda's unexpected pregnancy, but that is a natural progression for a series that grows more serious as its characters gain depth. *And Just Like That . . .* starts off that way, with no warning and no logical storyline excuse, other than a hint that this was the fate planned for Big in the never-greenlit *Sex and the City 3* and that Noth didn't want to return to the reboot but was convinced to at least do this one episode.[24]

While the premiere begins in seemingly familiar territory, with the remaining three girls meeting up for lunch, that is about where the similarities between this show and its predecessor end. As the *Guardian* notes, "It reduces the original characters to a baffled trio trying to negotiate a strange new world, as if the only thing ageing has to offer us (or women at least) is confusion and failure."[25] My first question as a viewer was, Who exactly is this new gray-haired Miranda, and what have they done with the caustic lawyer I loved? While it is true that many women embraced their gray hair during the pandemic and that, as Miranda says, she doesn't need to be a "spicy redhead" to help women in need, it's not just her hair that has changed. First, Miranda can be forgiven, if not lauded, for deciding to change her career from corporate law to human rights law, given how much the world has changed in the last twenty years, but the way it is explained feels more like the writers were trying to imbue Miranda with some of Nixon's own experiences rather than keeping true to the character. This becomes even more apparent as the season goes on (I won't spoil why), and by the end of the series, Miranda has dyed her hair back to red, negating the whole point made in the first episode.

As a lawyer, Miranda is excellent at arguing a case, and the series shows many times how logical she is even when debating a topic with her friends. However, in *And Just Like That . . .* she can't even open her mouth without a "Karen"-like speech falling out. That is not a good look for someone who claims to want to fight for those who can't fight for themselves. While it is clear the writers tried to make her into the fish-out-of-water, tone-deaf White woman who doesn't understand wokeness at all, that role would have been so much of a better fit for Charlotte than Miranda. (There is a reason the meme is Woke Charlotte and not Woke Miranda.) Miranda's resulting bumbling feels like a betrayal of all the character is built on: her intelligence, her career, and her wit. On top of that, by the end of the season, Miranda gives up her dream of getting her degree, passing up a highly coveted internship to run off to LA for the sake of a relationship that is tenuous at best.

Nixon defends the changes in her character, saying, "A feminist show shouldn't be agitprop, it shouldn't be propaganda showing women as these sensible, wise, kind, attractive people. First of all, who wants to watch that? I don't want to watch that. It's to show women and our struggles and our dreams and our foibles."[26] Her point is well taken for a new show, but when you are dealing with characters already created—and much beloved—consistency is expected. If major changes are made—and they can be; after all, people do change over time—you have to give a reason for it, and that is where the show falls short. These four women, Miranda especially, seem to have emerged from a 1990s time capsule in 2022 without a clue of what happened over the last twenty years, which isn't realistic. No reason is given for them not having evolved with the times, at least a little bit.

Back to the characters. Charlotte is still . . . Charlotte, but even more high strung, if that is possible. Instead of letting her daughter Rose be her tomboy self like Harry does, she goes into a screaming rage when Rose refuses to wear the designer dress she purchases for her. Her other daughter, Lily, is already a mini-me, so Charlotte's meltdown over the other is excessive. To her credit, though, later in the series, when Rose comes out as gender fluid, Charlotte, after understandable shock and confusion, shows uncharacteristic open-mindedness.

However, Charlotte's excessive crying in the second episode over Big's death is just too much. So what if she feels guilty for "forcing" Carrie to attend the concert and thus not be home when Big had his heart attack? Carrie is justified in not wanting her around; it is Carrie's right to grieve over Big's death. This is not the time for Charlotte to make it all about her. There is irony in this situation. As Alex Abad-Santos points out in a Vox article, in episode 4.16 of *Sex and the City*, "Ring a Ding Ding," Carrie's inner narcissist comes out and is there to stay. Twice, when she should be celebrating a big moment for Charlotte, Carrie barrels over her to make herself the center of attention—in this episode when Charlotte doesn't offer Carrie the money to buy her apartment and again in episode 6.7, "Paper Covers Rock," "in which Carrie bulldozes the news of Charlotte's new engagement by bemoaning a recent breakup."[27] So in that respect, Charlotte's behavior in the first two episodes of *And Just Like That . . .* has a slight ring of poetic justice.

Carrie is still very much herself, complete with a drool-worthy closet and a fabric rose on her coat lapel, but even she lacks her usual verve. Even before Big's death, she just seems worn out, like the last twenty years sucked everything out of her. Suddenly she's this old woman who can't talk about masturbation on a podcast when her younger self discussed "funky spunk" openly with Samantha. Come on, this is a former sex columnist! Granted, as she admits, she used to write about it, not talk about it, but the sudden prudishness makes it seem like the writers feel like a woman has to get more conservative with age. And I don't buy that for Carrie.

As for the missing fourth Musketeer, the show's excuse for what happened to Samantha is one of the most unconvincing moments of all. Carrie explains that she no longer needed Samantha's PR services because the book industry was tanking, so she severed their professional relationship. In response, Samantha up and moved to London and stopped talking to all four girls like a wounded teenager. That is not the Samantha Jones we know and love. She would have been able to separate business and friendship as easily as she separated sex and love. Unless something else happened that is yet to be revealed, this excuse for Samantha's absence doesn't only fail the credibility test, but it also—like so many other changes in the show—undermines everything that *Sex and the City* built. Carrie makes the point that not all friendships last, and that is true, even for a show in which those friendships are the glue, but there has to be ways to write out the character without it feeling like there was real-life drama involved.

This new show is way too self-aware and clearly trying too hard to make up for the sins of its past. Writing for Vulture, Jen Chaney says, "[I]t comes across as desperate to seem cool and relevant in a very different TV landscape. . . . Nothing about the show feels organic; so much about it is painfully forced."[28] From everyone mentioning their age at least once to other gags about getting old, it is as though the writers didn't trust the audience to understand that the characters, like the viewers, are now twenty years older than they were before. On top of that, the show goes over the top trying to "be of this moment," just like it was "of the moment" in the 1990s, with way too many references to COVID—no one wants to be reminded of the pandemic they are still living through, especially not when watching a TV show, and in past tense at that.[29] "If *Sex and the City* once drove the culture, it's playing catch-up now," the *Washington Post* observes.[30]

But perhaps even worse are the "woke moment" and "trigger warning" interruptions to the podcast Carrie now is a part of. These are literal breaks in the conversation in which Che, Carrie's boss and the host of the podcast, explains something to the audience about sexual orientation, gender fluidity, racism, or some similar sensitive subject. *Rolling Stone* characterizes them as "self-conscious and clumsy," which is perhaps the nicest way one can refer to a show literally preaching at its audience in an effort to how show much it has moved on.[31]

The second episode is primarily Big's funeral, which is stark in every way possible. Instead of invoking Big—the rich, complex man who loved cigars, expensive whiskey, and the finer things in life—the venue looks more like the minimalist backdrop for a high-end fashion show. Carrie claims she is doing it for Big and that she wants it exactly perfect for him, but it comes off as more of *her* ideal funeral. Even the remarks given by Big's older brother and Miranda—written by Carrie—are not moving and are delivered more robotically than with genuine emotion. There is more sentiment in the revelation that Samantha sent the verboten flowers on Big's casket than there is in any part of the service itself. It is a terse, unauthentic sendoff for a character who deserves so much more.

The cast, especially Nixon, have vehemently defended the changes in the characters and the show. In February 2020, Nixon said to *Radio Andy* of the original show, "Because people know it so well, they have enshrined it in nostalgia. . . . If I could do anything differently, I would have made sure we said to people in letters 10 feet tall: This is not *Sex and the City*. If you're looking for *Sex and the City*, you should watch the reruns. This is a new show for this moment and for the moment in these original characters' lives."[32] But that isn't how it was presented, and that's the big reason, in general, fans and critics alike have had a mixed reaction to the series.[33] Based on online reviews and people I talked to about the show, women in their fifties and sixties have a more positive view, being able to relate to the massive change these women are undergoing, their desire to shake up their lives, and even some of their parenting woes (like Charlotte dealing with accepting a nonbinary daughter). Younger viewers, like me, feel how hard the show is trying to be relevant and are turned off by it. As with all art, it will stick with some people and not with others.

As for this viewer, I wish they would have left our girls where the series ends—or at the very least, started *And Just Like That . . .* with the tone and storylines of the season finale. Perhaps the second season will be more like the original. I know I'm raising my cosmo to that hope!

CONCLUSION

Sex and the City in a Post-#MeToo World

A lot has changed since *Sex and the City* ended its run in 2004. We've been through a Great Recession and a pandemic, both of which put an end to the consumerism the show so highly values. We experienced an LGBTQIA+ revolution with the legalization of gay marriage, are more aware (or woke) than ever of the portrayal and rights of people of color thanks to the Black Lives Matter movement, and are less willing to quietly dismiss sexual harassment because of the #MeToo movement.

All this means that some aspects of *Sex and the City* (like other shows of its time) that were once permissible or even funny strike a discordant note today. As the previous chapters show, the show's portrayal of people of color and the LGBTQIA+ community leaves, well, everything to be desired. "No one could argue that *Sex and the City* didn't help the world see that LGBTQ+ people, you know, exist," writes Brabaw. "But, while LGBTQ+ visibility might have been enough to call a show 'groundbreaking' in 1998, LGBTQ+ people now expect more from queer characters."[1] Unfortunately, that "more" isn't what the people behind the show gave them in *And Just Like That . . .* As lovely as Che is, they feel very much like a token queer and gender-fluid character, set down in the show so that the writers and producers can check a box—just like they did with Stanford and Anthony back in the day. Their messages about tolerance and wokeness, while noble in intention, go beyond preachy into hit-you-over-the-head territory.

If people are going to learn from a show, it is not through strategies like that. *Sex and the City* may have had to be loud and obvious in its aims in 1998 to get people's attention, but that is not the case today. In our technologically connected, woke world, people are well aware of injustice.

Today's viewers respond better to a subtle, nuanced plot that shows people from the LGBTQIA+ community as regular people going about their lives; they just happen to be gay, just like others happen to be straight. Yes, they may face discrimination and other situations foreign to some, but we have been watching storylines about straight White people's problems for years; why can't we see the same for those of color and other gender and sexual orientations?

"There's no getting around the fact that much of *SATC* looks extremely un-woke by 2017 standards," writes film and television writer Ellen Jones.[2] Somehow, a show that felt so real and fresh at the time now looks like a ridiculous fantasy, one that at times is very poorly written. Much of the feminist shine has worn off (except for Miranda—no wonder she has become an icon; we're still fighting the same fight she was twenty years ago) as times have changed and audiences have moved on to a feminism that embraces *all* women, including those who are trans, and battles a rapid reduction in female rights that was as unthinkable to us a few years ago as it would have been to the characters in 1998. Today's feminism is active. Women are marching, testifying, protesting, writing e-mails, making phone calls, and joining together to save their rights. The ladies of *Sex and the City* avoid politics like the plague; Carrie isn't even registered to vote! "The show is very much a creation of the late '90s and early '00s: and as such—while it might still be clever, insightful, and funny—it is no longer thought of as the feminist tour de force it was considered to be at the time," Dray writes. "We've come a long way since 1998, and today's pop-culture climate is much more enlightened."[3]

"Enlightened" might be questionable, but we are at least more aware. And much of that is due to technology. In the beginning of *Sex and the City*, Carrie doesn't even have a cell phone, and e-mail was new and exciting technology, but today everyone practically has their cell phones grafted to their palms, and social media has, in so many ways, replaced e-mail. It is now how we keep up with friends, hold our social discourse (uncivil as it has become), and find out new information. It's also a place where everyone, for good or for ill, has a voice, can share their opinions, and find (or create) a community of like-minded individuals. Sorry, Carrie, but no one has to rely on a newspaper column anymore, and your tone-deaf podcast on *And Just Like That . . .* doesn't cut it, either. "Where *Sex and the City* could claim to set the agenda for representations of women in 1998, now, online cultural criticism has provided a greater diversity of women with their own voices; we now live in a climate where it's impossible for anything from video games to Beyoncé videos to escape feminist analysis," writes Faye.[4]

"The show's landmark portrayal of women's sexual freedom is exactly what can make it feel anachronistic now, in the age of #MeToo," writes Armstrong of *Vanity Fair*. "Amid the four main characters' many encounters with men, very few involve danger, nonconsensual sex, or even harassment. Such incidents that do occur are played off as jokes, 'bad sex,' or occasions warranting no more than an eyeroll."[5] And then there are Samantha's very problematic "rape fantasy" and other power-based sex-capades with Smith.

At the time *Sex and the City* aired, sexual harassment of women from (usually older) men in power over them (the basis of the #MeToo movement) was accepted without much thought as just part of boys being boys and one of the perils of being a female in the workplace. Look at Samantha and Richard. There are certainly some cringey vibes there in the beginning before they give in and get together (4.10, "Belles of the Balls"), which is another issue all its own today. Then there is Julian, Carrie's boss/mentor at *Vogue* who is such a sweet guy until he drops trou in the accessories closet and declares his love for her (4.17, "A Vogue Idea"). But when something is considered acceptable in your world, you just go with it, which is what the characters of *Sex and the City* do.

Is it really fair to judge a show made from 1998–2004 by 2022 standards? I ask myself that question any time I see an article picking apart a movie or TV show I dearly love—and yet, here I am doing the exact same thing. So my answer is yes and no. Yes, it is fair because just as the show was a product of its time, we as viewers are constantly products of our own time, one that changes with world and personal events. If we have grown and changed (and I hope everyone has in more than twenty years), then we can't help but look at things differently now. Also yes, because it is important to learn from our past. The more cultural analysis we engage in, the more we can see what we got right in the past and should continue, how far we have come over time, and what we definitely need to change. That is what books like this one hope to achieve. However, it's a little disingenuous to the show and everyone involved to impose today's standards on a show that had no knowledge of them. To ask them to do otherwise is like asking them to predict the future, which no one can do.

It would be interesting to see what the Carrie of today would say if she were to reread her old columns.[6] Would she, like so many of us, see the shortsightedness of some of the opinions of her younger self? Would she cringe at her word choice or laugh at how trivial the world's concerns were at the time? Or would she shake her head and offer pity to her thirty-something self for her ignorance and forgiveness for her missteps? Maybe, just maybe, she'd see some prescience in a few of her words, roots of wisdom that grew into trees over time and still stand tall in the woman she is today. And on the outside chance she would, maybe she'd pass it on to a twenty- or thirty-something woman wrestling with the same questions in 2022 as she was in 1998.

SEX FOR A NEW GENERATION

While the creators, writers, and producers may have bungled the reboot, fans have found their own ways of making *Sex and the City* relevant today. The leaders of this movement are Fairless and Garroni, the masterminds behind two of the hottest *Sex and the City* Instagram phenomena: @everyoutfitonsatc and #WokeCharlotte. The home base of the duo's quest to visually memorialize every single outfit worn by Carrie, Charlotte, Miranda, and Samantha over the course of the show's six-year run is @everyoutfitonsatc. This account is fun for its nostalgia value alone, but the captions are guaranteed to fill your laughter quotient for the day. Written in a witty, irreverent style, they say all the things viewers were dying to say during the show's run, from "What the hell was she thinking?" to "Oh, where can I get that now?"

The Instagram account is a way of keeping late '90s and early '00s fashion relevant while also giving it the reality check that fashion magazines often didn't. While some of the outfits were stunning, others elevated fashion to new heights, and some inspired a new generation of fashionistas and designers, there were a few that were just plain ugly. We are allowed to say that now that twenty years have passed.

More importantly, @everyoutfitonsatc's offshoot hashtag #WokeCharlotte and its associated meme are taking problematic lines and scenes from the original show and rewriting them to correct its missteps. In it, Fairless and Garroni take an image or series of images from the show and have Charlotte, the least woke of the original characters, check the privilege, racism, homophobia, transphobia, and misogyny of the series by rewriting her reaction to what it would be today. The result is a meme that is funny, educational, and instructive.

For example, one meme shows two images: On the top is Trey in bed looking at Charlotte in her slinky red lingerie dress from episode 3.16, "Frenemies," with his original line "Charlotte, you're my wife. That's not you, take it off." The bottom image is a still of Charlotte in the dress with the reimagined line "Your Madonna-whore complex does not get to dictate how I dress. And I strongly encourage you to examine how sexist belief systems about the roles of women have impacted your ability to get it up."

This particular example "has gathered thousands of likes and even the praise of actor Kristin Davis, who played Charlotte."[7] Journalist Meghan McKenna says that "by using a critical lens to look at this outdated piece of pop culture, they're reclaiming it for today's audiences. Which means, yes, of course you're still able to watch *Sex and the City*. If anything, the #WokeCharlotte meme makes watching *Sex and the City* even more enjoyable for the single, sexually-liberated women of [today]."[8]

SEX AND THE CITY'S LASTING LEGACY

Carrie Bradshaw, Miranda Hobbes, Charlotte York, and Samantha Jones couldn't exist today, at least not the same way as they did twenty years ago; times have changed too much. But I couldn't help but wonder, "Could we, as modern women, exist without them?" I don't think so. At least not in the same way. It is important that we keep them around so we can learn from their triumphs as well as their missteps. To cancel them completely would be to undo all the magnificent strides that *Sex and the City* made:

- the freedom it brought to a generation of women to live proudly as singles over the age of thirty, forty, and beyond;
- the discussion it engendered around third-wave feminism, without which we wouldn't be in the fourth wave today;
- the permission it gave women to explore, voice, and rejoice in their own sexuality;
- the validity it lent to a variety of choices surrounding motherhood (and non-motherhood);
- the importance it gave to the idea of female friendship and women's collective power to engender change;
- the small amount of visibility it gave to the LGBTQIA+ community, leading to much greater representation and tolerance; and
- even the brands it built that shaped our youth, the fashion trends it started, and the enduring love of the city of New York that its fans still hold in their hearts.

For all this and so much more, the fans thank you.

APPENDIX

Episode Guide

A summary of all ninety-four episodes of *Sex and the City* is beyond the scope of this book, but here are the thirty-one most important episodes of the series. If you are only going to watch some, these are key to understanding the plot. Each episode is summarized, along with the question Carrie asks in her column that week, a rationale of why that episode is included, and any memorable quotes from it.

SEASON I

1.1, "Sex and the City"

Carrie's Question

Were women in New York really giving up on love and throttling up on power?

Synopsis

The episode begins with a modern-day fairy tale of an English woman who journeys to New York, falls in love, and ends up getting her heart broken. Then the show jumps to the present day at Miranda's birthday party. Samantha suggests that women should "have sex like a man"; that is, "without feelings." Carrie decides to try this idea out on one of her exes. As she is leaving his apartment, she literally runs into a handsome man on the street, scattering the contents of her purse all over the sidewalk. Sparks fly as they pick up the items, but the two part. Later, at a club called Chaos, Carrie sees the guy again, whom Samantha calls "Mr. Big," for his business success and bank account. When Carrie leaves, she has trouble finding a cab, but Mr. Big swoops in with his limo and offers her a ride home.

Meanwhile, Charlotte applies her "playing hard to get" rule to her new date, who says he understands why she doesn't want to have sex with him yet, but he needs to get laid, so he goes to Chaos and ends up leaving with Samantha, who has no trouble with one-night stands.

Why This Episode Is Important

Obviously, this is the pilot, the episode that introduces the characters and sets up the thesis of the show: that women have gained enough money and power for the first time in history that they don't need to rely on men; they can finally have sex without emotions. Yet it also sets up the fairy-tale element of the series by beginning with "once upon a time," having the damsel in distress (Carrie) meet the handsome prince (Big), and showing him rescue her for the first time.

Memorable Quotes

- "Welcome to the age of uninnocence. No one has breakfast at Tiffany's, and no one has affairs to remember. Instead, we have breakfast at 7 a.m. and affairs we try to forget as soon as possible. Self-protection and closing the deal are paramount. Cupid has flown the co-op."—Carrie
- "Sweetheart, this is the first time in the history of Manhattan that women have had as much money and power as men, plus the equal luxury of treating men like sex objects."—Samantha
- "You know, I'm beginning to think the only place one can find true love in New York is in the gay community. It's straight love that has become closeted."—Stanford
- "Abso-fucking-lutely!"—Mr. Big

1.6, "Secret Sex"

Carrie's Question

How many of us out there are having great sex with people we're ashamed to introduce to our friends?

Synopsis

Carrie has her first official date with Mr. Big, but they never go to the restaurant, making out in the limo and having sex on the floor of his apartment instead. When they do actually go out, Big takes her to an out-of-the-way Chinese place, so Carrie thinks he's embarrassed to be seen with her. On top of that, he doesn't call her for a few days, cancels his plans to join them for a celebration of her bus advertisement, and doesn't introduce her when they run into someone he knows on the street. A few days later, a drunken Carrie shows up on his doorstep, demanding to know why he doesn't want to be seen with her. He explains that she is wrong—he just loves the Chinese place, really did have something come up, and couldn't remember the guy's name so introducing her would have meant revealing that. Carrie is mollified, and the two of them are officially dating.

Miranda accidently kicks a guy in her kickboxing class and gets a date out of it. Charlotte declares that she always waits at least five dates to have sex with a man, but then the ladies find out that isn't always true—she slept with a Hassidic Jewish man right after meeting him.

Why This Episode Is Important

This is the first glimpse into how Big treats Carrie with utter disregard for her feelings, a pattern that continues throughout the series. It also shows the origins of Carrie's neurosis related to Big, which she struggles to shed throughout the entire series.

Memorable Quotes

- "You can have good sex with someone you don't even like or respect or remember."—Samantha
- "[That bus sign] is the best personal ad I've ever seen."—Samantha

1.11, "The Drought"

Carrie's Question

How often is normal?

Synopsis

Carrie and Big's relationship has progressed to the point where they are spending the night together after having sex. One morning, she farts in bed. He thinks it is funny, but she is mortified he saw her as something other than perfect. She goes on to obsess for a week that he is going to leave her. She decides to replace the farting memory in his mind with a sexy one and so shows up unannounced at his apartment to try to seduce him; she fails because he's watching the fight, which is more important to him. Later, he comes by her apartment for the first time, and they make up.

Miranda is going through a dry spell; she hasn't had sex in three months. Charlotte's boyfriend has a low sex drive because of the Prozac he is on.

Why This Episode Is Important

This episode really highlights Carrie's unhealthy reaction to Big. She doesn't know who she is around him, yet she's scared to death to be without him.

Memorable Quotes

- "There's a moment in every relationship where romance gives way to reality."—Carrie
- "Men aren't that complicated; they're kind of like plants."—Samantha
- "You should see me around him. I'm not me. I'm 'together Carrie.' I wear little outfits, you know, 'sexy Carrie' and 'casual Carrie.' Sometimes I catch myself posing. It's exhausting."—Carrie

1.12, "Oh Come All Ye Faithful"

Carrie's Question

Are relationships the religion of the '90s?

Synopsis

By this point, Carrie and Big have been going out for about a year. Carrie finds out that Big takes his mom to church every Sunday, and she wants to meet her. But Big doesn't want to introduce her because church is their mother-son thing, so Carrie goes to the church and spies on Big and his mom. All is well until she drops her book from the balcony; then he knows she is there. Big introduces her to his mother as "my friend Carrie." Not only does he not call her his girlfriend, but also his mom hasn't ever heard of her. Carrie is obviously upset by this. Big tells her he "has to do things on his time frame." Later, Carrie and Big are supposed to go on vacation, but before she leaves, she feels she needs a sign, so she asks Big to tell her she's the one. He can't, so they break up.

The other ladies are having their own issues with love. Charlotte consults a tarot-card reader and a Santerían mystic in her quest to find "the one"; neither see marriage in her future. Miranda's boyfriend has to shower right after sex because he feels like it cleanses him from sin. Samantha declares she's in love with James, even though his penis is so small she can't feel it when they have sex.

Why This Episode Is Important

This is Carrie and Big's first breakup, and it reemphasizes how little he cares about her; even after a year, he's keeping important parts of his life from her and not even mentioning her name to his family. Also, James is Samantha's first love and monogamous relationship on the show.

Memorable Quotes

- "But then I realized, I did have faith: faith that someday I would meet someone who was sure I was the one."—Carrie

SEASON 2

2.8, "The Man, the Myth, the Viagra"

Carrie's Question

Are we willing to believe anything to date?

Synopsis

After seeing Big in secret for a while, he and Carrie are finally publicly a couple again. He introduces her as his girlfriend for the first time. Carrie wants her friends to get to know Big better, but then she flakes on a dinner with Miranda to stay in with Big. Mad, Miranda takes out her aggression on the bartender at the bar where she was going to meet Carrie. That is Steve. He disarms her by being unfailingly nice and making her laugh. They have sex that night. Miranda thinks it is just a one-night stand, but Steve asks for her number. Later, when he stops by her apartment to ask her out, Miranda is very mean to him.

Big finally agrees to meet Carrie's friends. He's late, so they think he is going to stand them up, but when he does show up, Miranda is shaken and runs out after Steve in the rain.

Why This Episode Is Important

This is the episode where Miranda and Steve meet.

Memorable Quotes

- "Why do you hate guys so much?"—Steve to Miranda

2.10, "The Caste System"

Carrie's Question

Can we date outside our caste?

Synopsis

Carrie realizes she loves Big. The next time they see each other, he gives her an ugly purse. Instead of saying thank you, she says, "I love you." In response, he tells her she can take the purse back if she doesn't like it. Later, at a party, Carrie sees that all of the Upper East Side women have the same brand of purse and realizes that Big thinks she is interchangeable with them; he doesn't really know her at all.

Miranda asks Steve to be her date for an office function, but he needs a new suit, so she takes him to buy one. He feels like she is emasculating him by paying for it, so he uses multiple credit cards even though he can't afford it. He can't handle that she makes more money than he does. Miranda claims it doesn't matter to her, and she doesn't want it to matter to him. Steve returns the suit and tells Miranda she needs to be with a guy on her level.

At the same time, Samantha dates a guy who has an actual servant, and Charlotte dates a celebrity.

Why This Episode Is Important

This episode shows just how little Big knows about Carrie. It also shows the class-difference problems that keep Miranda and Steve apart.

Memorable Quotes

- "I want to enjoy my success, not apologize for it."—Miranda

2.12, "La Douleur Exquise!"

Carrie's Question

When it comes to relationships, how do you know when enough is enough?

Synopsis

Carrie finds out that Big may have to move to Paris for seven months to a year for business, and she is upset that he doesn't bother to tell her until the last minute—again. She realizes that she is in a sadomasochistic relationship with him. She is addicted to the pain, and he is terrified of being tied down.

Carrie gets drunk, calls Big in Paris, yells at him for not being able to factor her into his life in any major way, and breaks up with him.

Meanwhile, Miranda dates a guy who likes to have sex in situations where he could get caught, and Charlotte indulges her shoe fetish with a salesman who has a foot fetish.

Why This Episode Is Important

This is Carrie's second breakup with Mr. Big. Yet again, it shows how he doesn't have room for her in his life and doesn't bother to share important information—like a possible international move—with her.

2.15, "Shortcomings"

Carrie's Question

When you sleep with someone, are you screwing the family?

Synopsis

Broken up with Big again, Carrie is dating a fiction writer, whose family she loves, especially his mother. But he has a problem with premature ejaculation.

Charlotte's brother, Westley, who is separated from his wife, Leslie, is in New York visiting Charlotte. He ends up sleeping with Samantha, which is Charlotte's worst nightmare. Charlotte and Samantha get into a huge fight, and Charlotte says very mean things to Samantha. Later, when she realizes how out of line she was, Charlotte bakes Samantha muffins to apologize.

Meanwhile, Miranda, who doesn't like children, dates a guy who has an unruly child.

Why This Episode Is Important

This episode shows the vast differences between Charlotte and Samantha regarding sex and contains one of the most explicit fights between the two. It also shows how strong the bond between the women is.

Memorable Quotes

- "Is your vagina in the New York City guidebooks? Because it should be! It's the hottest spot in town. It's always open!"—Charlotte to Samantha
- "She has so many notches on her bedpost, it's practically whittled down to a toothpick."—Charlotte about Samantha

- "The most important thing in life is family. There are days you love them and others you don't, but in the end, they're the people you always come home to. Sometimes it's the family you're born into, and sometimes it's the one you make for yourself."—Carrie

2.17, "20-Something Girls vs. 30-Something Women"

Carrie's Question

Twenty-something girls: friend or foe?

Synopsis

The girls head to a cottage in the Hamptons for August. Charlotte hooks up with a younger guy who thinks she is in her twenties. He gives her crabs. Carrie meets a younger girl who is a fan of hers and wants to be her mentee but ends up driving her crazy. The ladies attend a beach party thrown by Samantha's ex-assistant who stole her Rolodex, and they realize those were a lot more fun when they were younger. At the party, Carrie sees Big, who is back from Paris because his deal fell through. The catch? He's going out with a twenty-six-year-old named Natasha, whom he met in Paris.

Why This Episode Is Important

The revelation about Big and Natasha is key to understanding the next season.

Memorable Quotes

- "Good on paper, bad in bed."—Samantha
- "The biggest threat twenty-something girls posed was to themselves." —Carrie
- "They were simply our youthful doppelgängers who needed our compassion more than anything."—Carrie

2.18, "Ex and the City"

Carrie's Question

Can you be friends with an ex?

Synopsis

Carrie calls Big, but Natasha answers, so she hangs up. She and Big meet for a friendly lunch, which goes well until he tells her he's engaged to Natasha.

She is upset because they had been together for two years, and he wouldn't commit to her, but he's only known Natasha five months, and they are getting married. She makes a scene on the way out of the restaurant.

Later, Big calls Carrie and apologizes to her machine for what happened while she is listening. She picks up, apologizes for her part in the whole thing, and wishes them the best. Then she gets an invitation to their engagement brunch and knows she can't go. It would be too much. She ends up being in the area and decides to stop by the party. She doesn't go in but sees Big outside. Carrie asks him, "Why wasn't it me?" Then she tells him he never did understand her.

Miranda sees Steve on the street and runs away; Steve is hurt by this because they are trying to be friends. When she is talking to Carrie about it, she cries because she missed him when she saw him. Later, Miranda and Steve end up sleeping together and decide to be friends with benefits.

Samantha meets a hot guy on the street and gets asked out. When they get ready to have sex, she finds out he is very well endowed and views that as a personal challenge. He ends up being too much for her physically but becomes her first male friend.

Why This Episode Is Important

This is a solid ending for Carrie and Mr. Big. While they get back together many times in the future, it is never the same after this moment. Miranda and Steve becoming friends with benefits is also an important step in the evolution of their relationship.

Memorable Quotes

- "We keep dresses we'll never wear again, and we throw away our boyfriends."—Carrie
- "When did you stop calling her the 'idiot stick figure with no soul'?" —Miranda
- "Who are you, Goldicocks?"—Carrie
- "Maybe some women aren't meant to be tamed. Maybe they need to run free until they find someone just as wild to run with."—Carrie

CARRIE [quoting *The Way We Were*]: Your girl is lovely, Hubble.
BIG: I don't get it.
CARRIE: And you never did.

SEASON 3

3.1, "Where There Is Fire"

Carrie's Question

Do women just want to be rescued?

Synopsis

Carrie and the girls go to Staten Island to judge the FDNY contest. There, Carrie meets Bill Kelly, a local politician. He wants to go out with her, but she says no. When she gets home, he's sitting on her front stoop. Not ready to give up, he asks her out again. She agrees. On the night of the date, she gets dressed but doesn't come down when his car gets there. She realizes she is afraid of getting hurt again, and that shouldn't keep her from something potentially good, so she takes the ferry over to Staten Island to meet him. When she leaves, she misses the ferry and loses her shoe like Cinderella. Bill pulls up in his car and rescues her from being stranded.

Samantha meets a fireman named Ricky who isn't very bright, but he fulfills her fireman fantasies. Charlotte gets drunk and shouts about how she wants to get married. She starts dating a guy who seems like her knight in shining armor after he punches a guy who insults her. But it ends up that he just likes to pick fights. Miranda has laser eye surgery and doesn't bring anyone to help her home because she thinks she can do everything herself. Steve wants to help her, so he shows up to escort her home and take care of her until she can see again. That is when she truly appreciates him for the first time.

Why This Episode Is Important

This episode is important to the overall theme of *Sex and the City* being a modern fairy tale. Carrie literally calls this their "Staten Island Ferry tale" at the end of the episode because each of them is rescued by a man in their own way. It is a key moment in Miranda's character arc when she realizes that she can't do everything on her own and sometimes needs people, even Steve.

Memorable Quotes

- "I've been dating since I was fifteen. Where is he?"—Charlotte
- "Charlotte, honey, did you ever think that maybe we're the white knights and we're the ones that have to save ourselves?"—Carrie
- "Inside every confident, driven single woman, is there a delicate, fragile princess just waiting to be saved?"—Carrie
- "Stop, no, no rescue."—Miranda

3.4, "Boy, Girl, Boy, Girl"

Carrie's Question

If we can take the best of the other sex and make it our own, has the opposite sex become obsolete?

Synopsis

Carrie is dating a younger guy named Sean. He tells her that he's bisexual, and Carrie can't handle it. She becomes obsessed with the idea of him checking out other guys, even though by her own admission, she doesn't believe bisexuality is a real sexual orientation. Later, they go to a party with his friends, most of whom are also bi, and Carrie gets confused about who has been with whom. She reluctantly agrees to play spin the bottle. When the bottle lands on her and she has to kiss another woman, Carrie does but then leaves, feeling very uncomfortable and blaming her age for her inability to handle bisexuality.

Meanwhile, Steve is around so much that he is cramping Miranda's style, and she's about to blow her lid. He wants to move in, and that is too much for her. She tells him she feels like she can't breathe, and Steve gets her to admit she is scared that he won't like her because she'll never be a "girly-girl," and he'll leave when he sees she is imperfect and vulnerable. Steve assures her that will never happen.

Charlotte's gallery hosts a drag kings art show. The photographer, Barret, on whom Charlotte has a crush, wants her to pose for him. She does, and it gives her the courage to make the first move. She sleeps with Barret as a one-night stand, something she never does.

Why This Episode Is Important

This episode, as hard as it can be to watch, is important because it highlights how far off the mark *Sex and the City* is when it comes to being open-minded about sexualities other than gay or straight. This is also the first time we really see Charlotte do something a little daring and risqué.

Memorable Quotes

- "Gender is an illusion."—Barret
- "I'm a try-sexual. I'll try anything once."—Samantha

3.5, "No Ifs, Ands, or Butts"

Carrie's Question

In relationships, what are the "deal breakers"?

Synopsis

Samantha begins dating Chivon, a Black man whose sister Adeena can't handle him going out with a White woman. She's fine with them sleeping together, but when it becomes clear they are starting to become more—Samantha invites him to spend the night, which she never does—Adeena demands Samantha break up with him.

Elsewhere, Carrie meets a furniture designer named Aidan and begins dating him. He doesn't like that she smokes, so she says she will quit, only to rush outside on her first date to sneak a smoke. Aidan catches her and tells her to get back to him once she's able to control it.

Steve gets the chance to try to make a million-dollar shot at Madison Square Garden that Saturday and is very excited, but Miranda doesn't share his excitement. He asks her to be there when he tries to make the shot, but she says she has to work. He points out that this is the only thing he's ever asked her for, and he needs her to believe in him. She puts away her work to watch him practice and is there for the actual shot. He doesn't win the money, but in having her be there for him, he wins everything.

Why This Episode Is Important

This is the only episode until season 6 to feature a Black person as a main character. Like the previous episode does with sexuality, this one highlights how *Sex and the City* royally messes up representation of people of color on the series. It is also the one where Carrie meets Aidan and is important to Miranda and Steve's arc as a couple because it shows that Miranda tends to take Steve for granted, but when he points it out, she reforms.

Memorable Quote

- He was "warm, masculine, and classic American, just like his furniture."
  —Carrie about Aidan

3.7, "Drama Queens"

Carrie's Question

Do we need drama to make a relationship work?

Synopsis

Carrie keeps waking up with a start in the middle of the night. After a few days, she realizes it's because she's in a relationship for the first time where nothing is wrong; she's reacting to the lack of drama. When Aidan tells Carrie he wants her to meet his parents, she freaks out and pushes him away, only to realize Aidan is acting exactly the way she wished Big would have and she is acting like Big. When she doesn't hear from Aidan, she stops by the store, and his parents are there. She meets them, and he tells her that he wasn't mad; he was just trying to be less available for her like she asked.

Charlotte's married friend Phil offers to set her up on a blind date with his friend Dennis, and Charlotte becomes obsessed with who Dennis is and the idea that he might be "the one." Their date is delayed several times, but when Charlotte shows up, it is Phil there instead. He admits he is in love with her, and there is no Dennis. Shocked, she runs out of the restaurant and trips, falling into the street and nearly getting hit by a cab. The passenger gets out, and it is the man of her dreams: Dr. Trey MacDougal.

Why This Episode Is Important

This episode clearly illustrates that Carrie can't handle a normal relationship and is used to the codependence she had with Big. It is also the one where Charlotte meets Trey.

3.9, "Easy Come, Easy Go"

Carrie's Question

When it comes to relationships, is it better to follow your heart or your head?

Synopsis

At the New Designer Showcase, where Carrie is working Aidan's booth, she runs into Big and Natasha. While Natasha is off looking at things, Big gets drunk and tells Carrie his marriage isn't working, and he wants a divorce. But then he calls her a few days later and tells her that it's too expensive to get divorced, so he's not going to. A little while later he tells her he made a mistake, and he loves her. And that's how they start cheating.

Charlotte is blissfully happy with Trey, which Miranda thinks is suspicious because they haven't known each other long. Charlotte meets Trey's mother, Bunny, who pretty much runs his life because he will do anything she says. Later, Charlotte, caught up in the moment of thinking Trey is going to propose, says, "Maybe we should get married," and Trey responds, "Alrighty."

Samantha dates a guy whose cum tastes funny. She tries to do everything she can to subtly fix it, but nothing works. She finally tells him if he can stand it, so can she.

Why This Episode Is Important

This is a juicy episode all the way around. Not only did it give us the phrase "funky spunk," but also it is a great example of how Big jerks Carrie around. It's also the one where Charlotte accidently proposes and the first time we get an inkling of the weird relationship between Trey and Bunny.

Memorable Quotes

- "Funky spunk."—Samantha

3.11, "Running with Scissors"

Carrie's Question

Is sex ever safe?

Synopsis

Carrie and Big are sneaking around, having an affair in hotels that "went from elegant with crystal to seedy with paper cups." All the while Carrie can't stop cheating with Big, she is scared to death that Aidan will find out, and she hates herself, especially when she is mistaken for a hooker in a hotel lobby and Charlotte catches her with Big. In her stressed state, Carrie literally pushes Aidan away, saying she can't breathe. Yet she doesn't stop until Natasha comes home early and catches Carrie in her house. When Carrie flees, Natasha chases her and ends up falling down the stairs. Carrie takes her to the hospital and breaks up with Big for the third time in the emergency room waiting area.

Meanwhile, Samantha meets the male version of herself, but he insists she get tested for sexually transmitted diseases (STDs) before they have sex. She has never been tested before, and she is scared to death, but she does it anyway. Samantha faints out of fear when they call her back to get her results, but she is fine. Charlotte is being a bridezilla, so Samantha suggests she hire a wedding stylist, and that is how Anthony joins the show. Miranda is harassed on the street by a guy dressed as a sandwich.

Why This Episode Is Important

This is one of only three episodes that directly addresses STDs (the first is 2.17, "20-Something Girls vs. 30-Something Women," where Charlotte gets crabs, and the other is 3.6, "Are We Sluts?" where Miranda discovers she has chlamydia) and the only one that links them to Samantha's zealous sex life, so it sends an important message. It is also the one to expose the seedy side of Carrie and Big cheating and just how low she is willing to go for him, even at the risk of a great relationship.

Memorable Quotes

- "I can't have sex with a sandwich!"—Miranda

3.12, "Don't Ask, Don't Tell"

Carrie's Question

In relationships, is honesty really the best policy?

Synopsis

Carrie is obsessing over the right time to tell Aidan she cheated on him. Even when he catches her smoking at 3 a.m. and says he can live with it because he loves her, she can't get herself to say the words. Right before Charlotte and Trey's wedding, Carrie spills her secret that she was cheating on Aidan with Big. Aidan is heartbroken, and he tells her this isn't the kind of thing he can get over. They break up.

Elsewhere in Manhattan, Charlotte and Trey are preparing for their wedding, but they haven't slept together yet. Charlotte decides to take Samantha's advice and goes to Trey's hotel room just after midnight on their wedding day to have sex with him. The only problem is that he can't perform. Despite serious reservations, Charlotte goes through with her wedding to Trey because it is the right thing to do.

Why This Episode Is Important

It is key in both Carrie's and Charlotte's plot arcs.

Memorable Quote

- "It's hard to find people who will love you no matter what. I was lucky enough to find three of them."—Carrie

SEASON 4

4.7, "Time and Punishment"

Carrie's Question

Can you ever really forgive if you can't forget?

Synopsis

Back together again, Carrie and Aidan are having sex when Big calls and leaves a message on her machine (which they can hear) that he's back in town. For Carrie, this is a sign that she needs to talk to Aidan about Big.

Now a happily wedded wife, Charlotte thinks about quitting her job. When she tells the ladies, her announcement is met with silence because they can't comprehend not working. She tells them that Trey suggested that she might quit because she has been driving herself crazy, which sets Miranda off. Later, Charlotte calls Miranda and accuses her of being judgmental.

Miranda throws her neck out in the bathroom and gets stuck naked on the floor. She calls Carrie for help. Because she has a meeting, Carrie asks Aidan to go to Miranda's and check on her. Aidan does his best to preserve Miranda's modesty and takes her to the hospital. That night, when Aidan is out with his friends, Carrie shows up and finds him playing jacks with the bartender at the bar he and Steve own. He doesn't come home that night. The next day, Carrie brings Miranda bagels, ostensibly to cheer her up, but then proceeds to complain about Aidan. Miranda calls her on it and on not being there when she needed her. She is upset that Aidan saw her naked and vulnerable. Carrie apologizes. And then goes on talking. When Carrie sees Aidan again at their apartment, she's upset to find that the bartender is there, too. She and Aidan fight, and he tells her he doesn't want to see her again. She demands that he forgive her (over and over), even if he can't forget what she has done. They get back together.

Why This Episode Is Important

This episode contains one of the best examples of Carrie being a crappy friend and focusing on herself when her friends need her. It also shows the mistrust at the heart of Carrie and Aidan's rekindled relationship.

Memorable Quote

- "The women's movement is supposed to be about choice, and if I choose to quit my job, that is my choice."—Charlotte

4.8, "My Motherboard, Myself"

Carrie's Question

If giving a man the keys to your apartment means unlocking the door to home cooking and great sex, why were so many independent women— [Carrie's computer crashes before she can finish the question.]

Synopsis

Carrie and Aidan have exchanged keys and are back on track with their relationship. Unfortunately, the same can't be said for her computer, which crashes while she is working. Carrie freaks out because it contains everything she's ever written, and she has no backup. Aidan tries to help her fix it, and Carrie gets very touchy.

Carrie gets a phone call from Miranda, who is in Philadelphia because her mother had a heart attack. That night, while the family is at home, Miranda's mom dies; Miranda is upset that they weren't at the hospital because she wasn't able to say goodbye, and her mom was alone. Carrie, Charlotte, and Samantha make plans to go to the funeral to support Miranda. Aidan offers to go with them, but Carrie says no. He still shows up with Steve because he knows they need him.

Still trying to help, Aidan gets Carrie a new computer, but she doesn't want it. He begins to realize that she is resistant to letting him into her life.

Why This Episode Is Important

This episode is the beginning of the darkest period in Miranda's life, one that becomes a real turning point for her. It is also a wonderful example of how the four ladies pull together when one of them is in need.

Memorable Quote

• "She did open her eyes just long enough to veto my lipstick."—Miranda talking about her mom after her heart attack

4.10, "Belles of the Balls"

Carrie's Question

Are men just women with balls?

Synopsis

Aidan answers the phone at Carrie's apartment, and it's Big, which leads to a fight between Aidan and Carrie. Carrie has an idea to get Aidan and Big together so they can see what is really going on. While Carrie is at Aidan's cabin the country, Big calls her to complain that his celebrity girlfriend broke it off. She accidently invites him there, and Aidan gets mad because he (rightfully) doesn't want Big in his house. Big is two hours late and then makes Carrie go out in the rain to talk to her in the car. He ends up having dinner with them and gets too drunk to drive, so Aidan reluctantly offers him the couch. The next morning, they start out playing basketball and end up in a fistfight that only ends when Aidan's dog bites Big in the butt.

Samantha runs into an old flame who knows Richard Wright, whom Samantha really wants to land as a client. He gets her an interview, and Richard is a sexist jerk, but she still wants the job because she considers him a challenge. However, he doesn't want to give it to her because her old flame is an architect there and she previously slept with him. She tells him off because he is holding her to a double standard he wouldn't enforce on a man. He hires her the next day because he likes that she isn't afraid of him.

Steve tells Miranda he had testicular cancer and had to have one of his balls removed. It's clear he feels insecure about it. She tries to convince him women don't care and likely won't notice. She even goes with him to look into getting a fake testicle. Finally, to make her point, Miranda sleeps with Steve in what she calls a "mercy fuck."

Why This Episode Is Important

This episode shows how little regard Big has for Carrie's life—going so far as to drive to Aidan's cabin when he knows Carrie and Aidan are together. This is also the episode where Samantha meets Richard, one of the great loves of her life, and where Miranda gets pregnant, though she doesn't know it yet.

4.11, "Coulda, Woulda, Shoulda"

Carrie's Question

Are we there yet?

Synopsis

Miranda finds out she is pregnant from her night with Steve and considers having an abortion. In the course of conversation, it comes to light that Samantha has had two abortions and Carrie has had one. Carrie questions her decision all those years ago and goes back to the diner where the guy who got her pregnant used to work. He still works there and doesn't even recognize her, so she knows she made the right choice. Carrie goes with Miranda to her appointment to have an abortion, but when she is called back to have the procedure done, Miranda can't go through with it and decides to have the baby.

Right about the same time Miranda makes her announcement, Charlotte finds out her body has high antisperm antibodies so she needs IVF if she has any hope of getting pregnant. She is very mad at Miranda for not even wanting the one thing she would give anything to have. Miranda shows her support by walking behind Charlotte when she tries to run away from her on the street.

Samantha has her heart set on a $4,000 red Birkin bag so she uses her client's name, Lucy Liu, name to try to get one. Lucy finds out and fires her for being unprofessional to the Hermes rep. She also keeps the Birkin because it was in her name anyway.

Why This Episode Is Important

This is the controversial episode about abortion. It is the first in recent years to speak about it so openly and to have two main characters admit they had one. It is also an important crossroads for all the characters: Miranda makes a life-changing decision, Charlotte finds out she's infertile, Carrie faces her past, and Samantha has to deal with the consequences of her actions.

4.12, "Just Say Yes"

Carrie's Question

In matters of love, how do you know when it is right?

Synopsis

Carrie finds out her building is going co-op and gets upset because she doesn't have the money to buy her apartment. Aidan offers to buy it and the one next door for both of them, if he can move in, which he does. Carrie is cleaning up after him while he is in the shower, and she finds a ring in his bag. Realizing its an engagement ring and meant for her, she vomits—and not just because the ring is really traditional and totally not her. She has a second panic attack when it seems like Aidan is going to ask her to marry him.

Later, she is trying to get a taxi when Big pulls up. She tells him what is going on, and he says she's not the marrying kind and she is never going to be ready. When Aidan isn't looking, Carrie digs through his bag where she found the ring, but it isn't there. That night, Aidan and Carrie take Pete out for a walk, and he gets down on one knee like he is petting Pete. He looks up at her and proposes with a ring that is much more her style. Carrie says yes—not because she really wants to but because she feels like she has to.

In addition to taking hormones for IVF, Charlotte puts herself and Trey on the list to adopt a Mandarin baby. When Bunny finds out, she tells Charlotte in no uncertain terms that she will not accept an adopted grandchild, especially not a Mandarin one. Trey and Charlotte have a very public, very loud fight at the Highland Fling, a major social event for his set, about having a baby. When they get home, Trey tells her he is exhausted from trying to make their marriage work and doesn't want a baby anymore. He could be happy with just the two of them.

Miranda tells Steve she's pregnant and that she's not ready, but she'll never be ready. A few days later, she opens her door to find Steve on one knee with the first ring Aidan bought for Carrie. She asks him if he is crazy, and he says he wants to do right by her. They discuss it and realize that is not the right reason to get married.

Why This Episode Is Important

This episode shows how Carrie has internalized her misgivings about Aidan being "the one" to the point that her body rebels at the idea of marrying him. It's also a turning point in Charlotte's marriage to Trey and an important stepping stone for Miranda and Steve.

Memorable Quote

- "Who needs a wife when you have a life?"—Richard

4.15, "Change of a Dress"

Carrie's Question

Do we really want these things, or are we just programmed?

Synopsis

Aidan keeps hinting around that he wants to make wedding plans with Carrie, even though she isn't ready yet. She doesn't even want to look for a dress. Miranda takes her fake wedding-dress shopping to try to help her, but Carrie has a panic attack with a serious case of hives when she sees herself in a wedding dress.

Back home, Carrie is looking at bridal magazines while Aidan works on the apartment next door. He puts the first hole in the adjoining wall, and she tells him to stop. She gets very upset and tells him she's not ready for marriage yet. Aidan is willing to give her the time she needs—until he's not. He suggests eloping to avoid the wedding madness and tells her she's just scared. Carrie tells him again she's not ready. He realizes that there is trust missing between them and gives her an ultimatum: "If you don't want to marry me right now, you'll never want to marry me." Even though they go to bed together that night, they know it is their last night. He moves out the next day.

While this is happening, Miranda gets her first sonogram and finds out she's having a boy. Soon she feels a baby kick. Samantha realizes she's falling for Richard and wants to be monogamous with him, but he is still having sex with another woman. He tries to convince her that he doesn't do monogamy for anyone, even her.

Why This Episode Is Important

This is the end of Carrie and Aidan's relationship, this time for good. Samantha also reaches a turning point when she realizes she loves Richard and doesn't want to see anyone else. The moment the baby kicks is when Miranda bonds with him and starts seeing him as real.

Memorable Quotes

- "My body is literally rejecting the idea of marriage. . . . I'm missing the bride gene."—Carrie
- "I think I have monogamy. I must have caught it from you people." —Samantha
- "We're not the monotonous—er, monogamous, kind."—Richard

4.18, "I Heart NY"

Carrie's Question

Can you make a mistake and miss your fate?

Synopsis

Having ended things with Aidan, Carrie is lonely, so she calls Big. She goes over to his apartment to keep him company and finds all his stuff packed up. He's moving to Napa, California, but didn't tell her. She decides they need to have a "proper New York goodbye." Carrie is kissing Big during a carriage ride in Central Park when Miranda calls to tell her she is in labor. When she gets to the hospital, Miranda's water breaks on Carrie's designer shoes. After the baby is born healthy, Carrie tries to catch Big before he leaves for his flight, but she's too late. She finds he left her plane tickets in case she ever gets lonely. Carrie walks home to "Moon River," in a black dress, much like Holly Golightly.

Meanwhile, Samantha has a feeling Richard is cheating on her, even though he promised they wouldn't see other people, so she stalks him while wearing a wig. She catches him in the act with another woman. Samantha's heart breaks, and she yells at him that it is over between them.

Why This Episode Is Important

This episode is full of big events: Miranda has her baby, Mr. Big moves across the country, and Samantha has her heart broken.

Memorable Quote

- "Hello, lover!"—Carrie to a pair of Christian Louboutin shoes she is admiring in a store window

SEASON 5

5.8, "I Love a Charade"

Carrie's Question

Is a relationship a relationship without the zsa-zsa-zsu?

Synopsis

At the beginning of the episode, Charlotte is still getting used to being with Harry. She's doesn't want to be seen in public with him, everything he does annoys her, and he has a hairy back. But none of it bothers him. At a friend's wedding, they confess their love for one another, but then Harry drops a bomb: He can only marry a woman who is Jewish.

Carrie's old friend Bobby—whom everyone is pretty sure is gay—is getting married to Bitsy von Muffling, a woman, much to everyone's shock. They get invited to the wedding in the Hamptons. In the middle of nowhere on the way to there, Carrie runs into Jack Berger, who is now single and is riding a motorcycle. Carrie yammers on about Aidan and scares Berger, so she's convinced she'll never see him again, but he shows up at the wedding and asks her out.

Why This Episode Is Important

This episode shows the main obstacle in Charlotte and Harry's relationship: She has to convert to Judaism for him. It is also the beginning of Carrie's relationship with Berger.

Memorable Quotes

- "Maybe we should stop looking for a great relationship and settle for a fine one."—Carrie
- "Some people refuse to settle for anything less than butterflies."—Carrie

SEASON 6

6.9, "A Woman's Right to Shoes"

Carrie's Question

When did we stop being free to be you and me?

Synopsis

Carrie and Stanford attend a baby shower for Kyra and Chuck Bronson, where they are asked to remove their shoes at the door. When she goes to leave, Carrie discovers that her Manolos were stolen. Kyra loans her shoes to walk home in, but otherwise she doesn't seem to care that these expensive, designer shoes were stolen. Miranda tells Carrie that legally, Kyra owes her for them, and Samantha mentions that if someone stole Kyra's baby, there would be payback.

Carrie returns Kyra's shoes and checks to see if anyone returned the shoes or said anything about them. Kyra offers to pay for the shoes until she hears they are worth $485. She is willing to give Carrie $200. Carrie points out that Kyra should know what they are worth because she also used to wear them, but Kyra says that was before she became a mother and had better things to spend her money on. Flabbergasted, Carrie leaves.

Later, she figures out she has spent over $2,300 on gifts for Kyra between wedding and baby gifts, but as a single woman without children, she gets nothing in return. Carrie calls Kyra to tell her she's getting married to herself and is registered at Manolo Blahnik. That way, Kyra is socially pressured into paying for a replacement.

Meanwhile, Miranda is on the co-op board of her apartment building, and they are trying to find the perfect tenant for a unit. They interview Dr. Robert Leeds, a doctor for the Knicks. He's handsome, funny, and interesting. He and Miranda hit it off right away. When she gets the chicken pox from Brady, he takes care of her. Charlotte is dealing with Harry's eccentricities—like leaving used teabags all over the house and walking around the house naked—but trying not to be too much of nag.

Why This Episode Is Important

This episode is dear to single women everywhere because it dares to place them on equal footing with people who are married and have children—those whom society deems more valuable. It is also the episode where Miranda meets Dr. Leeds, her next love interest, and is only the third in the whole series to feature a person of color as a love interest.

Memorable Quotes

- "I don't like any children but my own."—Miranda
- "She shoe-shamed me."—Carrie
- "We stopped celebrating each other's life choices and started qualifying them."—Carrie
- "If I don't ever get married or have a baby, what? I get bubkes? If you are single after graduation, there isn't one occasion when people celebrate you. I am talking about the single gal. Hallmark doesn't make a 'Congratulations! You didn't marry the wrong guy!' card, and where's the flatware for going on vacation alone?"—Carrie
- "The fact is, sometimes it's hard to walk in a single woman's shoes. That's why we need really special ones now and then—to make the walk a little more fun."—Carrie

6.12, "One"

Carrie's Question

When will waiting for "the one" be done?

Synopsis

Carrie and Charlotte go to see a performance artist in Chelsea and meet artist Aleksandr Petrovsky, who is charmed by Carrie's lack of interest in art and asks her out. They go on a very strange date, where he already begins showing controlling tendencies.

At Miranda's place, Robert drops by with a pizza but gets called out to go to work. Miranda opens the smaller box with it and sees a cookie pizza that says, "I love you," spelled out in chocolate chips. Not wanting to deal with it, she eats the evidence and avoids answering when Robert asks her about it. Miranda throws Brady a first-birthday party, and Steve, his mom, and Debbie all attend. Debbie tells Miranda that she loves Steve, and it about does Miranda in. She goes into the laundry room, where Brady's cake is being stored, to collect herself and light the candles. Steve comes in, and Miranda tells him she loves him but it's too late. He says he loves her, too.

Charlotte finds out she is pregnant but has a miscarriage shortly thereafter. She doesn't think she can attend Brady's first-birthday party after this loss, so she stays home and cries. While flipping through the channels, she comes upon a documentary on Elizabeth Taylor, her idol. It shows her that Elizabeth, too, overcame much adversity, so Charlotte finds the strength to get dressed and go to Miranda's party.

Why This Episode Is Important

This episode changes the lives of three of the women: Carrie meets Aleksandr, Miranda and Steve finally declare their love, and Charlotte overcomes her worst nightmare.

6.14, "The Ick Factor"

Carrie's Question

Have we become romance-intolerant?

Synopsis

Miranda asks Steve to marry her. She only wants a simple ceremony, which they hold in a community garden with their closest friends in attendance. Samantha considers getting her breasts enlarged after seeing photos of herself in a tabloid. The plastic surgeon finds a lump, and she is diagnosed with breast cancer.

Aleksandr woos Carrie with old-world romance, something she doesn't like but also doesn't want to tell him. He insists on going to the opera, even though she doesn't want to, and he gives her a dress. Outside the venue, Carrie passes out when Aleksandr asks her to dance, another panic attack because she is in a situation she isn't comfortable with—just like with Aidan. They never make it into his high-class world of the opera, going to McDonald's instead, which is her world.

Why This Episode Is Important

This is another life-changing episode for Miranda and Samantha—and the ladies are there for them in joy and sorrow. It also shows how uncomfortable Carrie is in Aleksandr's world and how not right for each other they are.

6.18, "Splat!"

Carrie's Question

Is it time to stop questioning. (Carrie originally writes this with a question mark, but then changes it to a period. This is the final question of the series.)

Synopsis

While he and Carrie are preparing to throw a dinner party for her friends, Alexsandr invites her to move to Paris with him. Before she can comprehend what he said, much less answer, their guests arrive. A very awkward dinner ensues, during which it becomes clear Aleksandr thinks Carrie's friends are low-class and proves himself to be arrogant.

He tells them Carrie is moving with him to Paris before she even makes the decision. Naturally, they have a lot of questions and concerns, and Carrie gets defensive when she can't answer them. Later, she talks with Alexsandr, and his answer is that she should let him handle everything, which means she will be completely under his control in Paris. Carrie suggests they could do a long-distance relationship, but he says no.

A few days later, Carrie's former editor at *Vogue*, Enid, invites her and Aleksandr to a party she is throwing. There they see Lexi Featherston, an old party girl from their twenties. She is still single and acting the same as she did then: being loud, smoking, and doing drugs like nothing has changed. Standing by an open window while she's smoking, Lexi has a meltdown about how no one is fun anymore and New York is over. She trips and falls out the window to her death. Her last words: "I'm so bored I could die." Frightened by this event, Carrie decides to go to Paris—to live her life while she still can because, like Lexi, she's not getting any younger or less single.

Why This Episode Is Important

This is the huge turning point in Carrie's life and sets up the series finale. This episode has also been called the most shocking in *Sex and the City* history by critics.

Memorable Quotes

- "Your column is all about New York. You're all about New York."—Miranda
- "If you're a successful fifty-something woman, there's a small pool. It's very small; it's a wading pool really."—Enid
- "See? You have to be a couple just to order lunch in this town."—Enid
- "Ladies, if you are single in New York after a certain point, there is nowhere to go but down."—Carrie

6.19, "An American Girl in Paris, Part Une"

Carrie's Question

No question.

Synopsis

As Carrie is preparing to leave New York for Paris, Miranda tries one more time to get her to change her mind. Big leaves her a message that he is in town and wants to see her. She deletes his message. When she leaves with her luggage, Carrie finds that Big is sitting outside her building in his car. He tries to apologize for his overreaction last time they were together, but Carrie won't let him talk. She tells him she is leaving for Paris and says goodbye. She gets out of the car, but Big follows her, and she tells him off for always doing something to mess up her happiness. She ends by telling him to forget he ever knew her name.

In Paris, Carrie gets to the hotel, only to find Aleksandr with his daughter Chloe. Carrie thought they were going to spend the day together, but he tells her he is going to spend it instead with Chloe and then meet some work people for dinner, but they can go out afterward. Ten hours later, he is still not there, and Carrie falls asleep in her ballgown. She asks him why he didn't at least call, and he said he did, but she had on the "do not disturb" setting on her phone, which may or may not be true.

A week later, she goes shopping in Dior, slips on a puddle made by her wet her umbrella, and falls on her face. As in the first episode, she has to pick up the contents of her purse. Later that night, she realizes her "Carrie" necklace is missing and must have fallen out of her purse at Dior.

Carrie walks through Paris and sees other groups of women and misses her friends, so she calls Miranda and tells her she feels lost. Miranda once again tries to get her to come home. When she gets back to the hotel, Aleksandr gives her a diamond necklace to replace her Carrie necklace. He promises it will be just the two of them once the exhibit opens, but two seconds later, a group of his friends interrupt them. They all speak French, and no one translates, so Carrie once again feels left out.

Back in New York, Samantha is on the board of a breast cancer benefit, and when she suggests giving the survivors something they can actually use, not just a cookie, she gets volun-told to speak. At the event, she gives her prepared generic speech while roasting under the lights. Finally, she can't take it anymore. She takes off her wig and speaks from her heart, encouraging other survivors to also remove their wigs.

A few days later, Charlotte picks up Carrie's mail, and while she is there, Big leaves a message on her answering machine about not wanting to lose her again and tells her he loves her. Charlotte hears it, and the girls agree to meet with him. He admits he screwed things up with Carrie many times; repeats that he loves her; and tells them that if they think he has the slightest chance, he'll be on the next flight to Paris and will roam the streets until he finds her. But if they think Carrie is really happy, he doesn't want to wreck that for her, and he'll be history. Miranda tells him to go get her.

Why This Episode Is Important

It sets up the second part and positions Carrie to need rescuing and Big to be her white knight, as any good fairy tale should.

Memorable Quotes

- "You are the loves of her life, and a guy is just lucky to come in fourth." —Big to the ladies
- "Go get our girl."—Miranda to Big

6.20, "An American Girl in Paris, Part Deux"

Carrie's Question

No question.

Synopsis

During her second week in Paris, Carrie meets with Aleksandr and his ex-wife, Juliet, for lunch—or at least she is supposed to. He ends up phoning that there is a crisis at the museum, and he can't make it. Juliet tells Carrie that she always came in second during their marriage and Aleksandr was never supportive of her work. While she is walking through Paris alone, Carrie sees her book in a shop window. She goes in, and the staff recognize her because they are big fans. They decide to host a book party for her with their friends Saturday night. Carrie goes back to the hotel and excitedly tells Aleksandr, but he says he can't make it because of a preview of his work at the museum.

On Saturday night, Aleksandr has an anxiety attack over the installation and asks Carrie to go with him to the museum instead of her party, which she reluctantly does. He makes her promise not to let go of his hand all night, but as soon as the curator calls him a genius, he lets go and leaves her behind for the rest of the evening. While searching in her purse for her cigarettes,

Carrie finds her necklace in the ripped lining of her bag. Now that she has her identity back, she is inspired to go to her own party. However, she is too late; it's already over.

Carrie returns to the hotel and confronts Aleksandr about abandoning her in the museum. He tries to put her off by saying he is tired, and she knew all along who he is. But Carrie keeps pushing. When she tries to get him to turn around and face her, he hits her accidently, and the necklace he gave her breaks, along with his hold on her. She tells him he isn't what she is looking for and leaves.

Down in the lobby, while she is trying to get another room, Big comes in. She tells him Paris is a mess, and she shouldn't have come. When he finds out Aleksandr hit her, he charges up to the room to hit him back. Carrie trips him, and they both fall to the ground giggling, while she informs him that she's already handled it and doesn't need him to rescue her. Outside the hotel, Big tells her he loves her, and they kiss. Carrie says, "I miss New York. Take me home."

Back in New York, Samantha and Smith are dealing with her cancer treatment, the fact that she has no sex drive, and that he is going to be on location for two months. Samantha gives him permission to have sex with others while he is gone, which he doesn't intend to do. While on location, he sends Samantha daffodils that will bloom in spring, with the assurance she will, too. When the shoot is over, Smith gets home early and surprises Samantha by telling her he loves her. She says to him, "You have meant more to me than any man I've never known," which is the most powerful thing she could say. They kiss and make love, and we see the flowers blooming.

Not far away, Charlotte and Harry meet the couple from North Carolina whose baby they are supposed to adopt. It turns out they have no intention of giving up the baby; they just wanted the chance to see New York. Charlotte is crushed, and Harry is at his wit's end. But a few weeks later, Charlotte comes home to the news that they are getting a Chinese baby in six months.

In Brooklyn, Steve's mom, Mary, is showing signs of dementia, so he takes her to the doctor and finds out she had a small stroke with memory loss. He and Miranda go over to Mary's apartment to get some things, only to see that it is a mess, with bugs and dirty dishes all over. Miranda helps Steve clean it up, and Miranda says Mary can live with them. Not long after Mary moves in, she wanders off, and Miranda finds her eating out of the garbage. Miranda takes her back home and gives her sponge bath like a child. Magda sees them and says to Miranda, "What you did, that is love. You love."

It is late when Carrie arrives back at her apartment in Manhattan. Big reminds her he doesn't have anywhere to stay, and she asks if he wants to come up. He answers, "Abso-fucking-lutely," just like in the first episode. The next morning, Carrie meets the girls for brunch and starts writing her column again. All is back to normal. Then Big calls her as she's walking down the street. His name appears on her phone for the first time: John. He tells her he's moving back to New York and will be there soon.

Why This Episode Is Important

It's the finale. It wraps up the series neatly, with a happy ending for everyone.

Memorable Quotes

- "Nothing else exists when art does."—Juliet
- "I believe a relationship is like couture; if it doesn't fit perfectly, it's a disaster."—Juliet
- "I am someone who is looking for love, real love, ridiculous, inconvenient, consuming, can't-live-without-each-other love."—Carrie
- "It took me a really long time to get here, but I'm here. Carrie, you're the one."—Big

NOTES

INTRODUCTION

1. There's an alternate version of the *Sex and the City* opening. In this version, Carrie wears a fashionable blue sheath dress and trips (but only slightly) after seeing her ad on the side of the bus instead of getting splashed with water. As unusual as the actual opening is, this one pales in comparison and says little about the show or its main character. The opening can be seen on YouTube at https://www.youtube.com/watch?v=RUVZoKlPiVw.

2. Marissa Blanchard, "Sarah Jessica Parker Gets Candid about Carrie," HBO, accessed April 27, 2022, https://www.hbo.com/sex-and-the-city/anniversary-sarah-jessica-parker-interview.

3. Cameron Michael Tufino, "*Sex and the City*: A Promotion of Modern American Feminism" (master's thesis, University of the Incarnate Word, 2012), 1, http://athenaeum.uiw.edu/uiw_etds/292.

4. Susan Faludi, *Backlash: The Undeclared War against American Women* (New York: Crown, 2009), 169.

5. Emily Nussbaum, "Difficult Women: How *Sex and the City* Lost Its Good Name," *New Yorker*, July 23, 2013, https://www.newyorker.com/magazine/2013/07/29/difficult-women.

6. Wendy Burns-Ardolino, *TV Female Foursomes and Their Fans* (Jefferson, NC: McFarland, 2016), 163.

7. Melanie Hamlett, "*Designing Women* Was a Series Ahead of Its Time. In 2019 It's Still Revolutionary," *Glamour*, August 26, 2019, https://www.glamour.com/story/designing-women-hulu.

8. Burns-Ardolino, *TV Female Foursomes*, 13.

9. Benie Viera, "Why Living Single Is the Blueprint," Vibe, September 24, 2013, https://www.vibe.com/features/vixen/why-living-single-is-the-blueprint-288093/.

10. Librarians at George A. Spiva Library, "Fairy Tale Conventions," Research and Course Guides, George A. Spiva Library, Southern Missouri State University, December 3, 2021, https://libguides.mssu.edu/c.php?g=185298&p=1223898.

11. Librarians at George A. Spiva Library, "Fairy Tale Conventions."

12. The fool, or the first card in the Major Arcana of tarot cards, is often associated with the hero of a story, according to Joseph Campbell's *The Hero's Journey* (Novato, CA: New World Library, 1990), a way of analyzing and understanding the way stories are created.

13. Librarians at George A. Spiva Library, "Fairy Tale Conventions."

14. Jeana Jorgensen, "A Wave of the Magic Wand: Fairy Godmothers in Contemporary American Media," *Marvels and Tales* 21, no. 2 (2007): 216, http://www.jstor.org/stable/41388835.

15. Beatriz Oria, *Talking Dirty on "Sex and the City": Romance, Intimacy, Friendship* (New York: Rowman and Littlefield, 2014), 183.

16. Jennifer Lind-Westbrook, *"Sex and The City:* 10 Biggest Ways Miranda Changed from Season 1 to the Finale," Screenrant, March 4, 2020, https://screenrant.com/sex-city-hbo-biggest-ways-miranda-changed-season-1-finale/.

17. Kim Handysides, "Sex in the City, Carrie Bradshaw Is the Female Narrator of the 90s," Blast, November 12, 2021, https://theblast.com/118034/sex-in-the-city-carrie-bradshaw-the-female-narrator-of-the-90s/.

18. Michael Hauge, "Love Stories: The 6 Categories of Romantic Comedy," Story Mastery, September 22, 2014, https://www.storymastery.com/love-stories/6-categories-romantic-comedy/.

19. Hauge, "Love Stories."

20. Cindy Royal, "Narrative Structure in *Sex and the City*: 'I Couldn't Help but Wonder . . . ,'" (doctoral dissertation, University of Texas at Austin, 2003), 11.

21. Joanna Di Mattia, "'What's the Harm in Believing?': Mr. Big, Mr. Perfect, and the Romantic Quest for Sex and the City's Mr. Right," in *Reading "Sex and the City,"* ed. Kim Akass and Janet McCabe (London: I. B. Tauris, 2006), 17.

22. Masterclass Staff, "Writing 101: The 12 Literary Archetypes," Masterclass, August 30, 2021, https://www.masterclass.com/articles/writing-101-the-12-literary-archetypes.

23. Masterclass Staff, "Writing 101."

24. Campbell, *Hero's Journey.*

25. Anne K. Kaler, *"Golden Girls*: Feminine Archetypal Patterns of the Complete Woman," *Journal of Popular Culture* 24, no. 3 (Winter 1990): 49.

26. Janet M. Cramer, "Discourses of Sexual Morality in *Sex and the City* and *Queer as Folk*," *Journal of Popular Culture* 40, no. 3 (June 2007): 413, https://doi.org/10.1111/j.1540-5931.2007.00401.x.

27. Chelsea Fairless and Lauren Garroni, *We Should All Be Mirandas: Life Lessons from "Sex and the City's" Most Underrated Character* (New York: Houghton Mifflin Harcourt, 2019), 2.

28. Burns-Ardolino, *TV Female Foursomes*, 4.

I. CARRIE

1. Chelsea Fairless and Lauren Garroni, *We Should All Be Mirandas: Life Lessons from "Sex and the City's" Most Underrated Character* (New York: Houghton Mifflin Harcourt, 2019), 2.

2. Bonnie Fuller, "What the Creators of *Sex and the City* Know about Marketing That You Don't," *AdAge*, June 9, 2008, https://adage.com/article/madisonvine-case-study/creators-sex-city-marketing/127610.

3. Quoted in Ellen E. Jones, "'That Show Was as White as It Gets!' *Sex and the City*'s Problematic Legacy," *Guardian*, April 28, 2018, https://www.theguardian.com/tv-and-radio/2018/apr/21/that-show-was-as-white-as-it-gets-sex-and-the-citys-problematic-legacy.

4. Marissa Blanchard, "Sarah Jessica Parker Gets Candid about Carrie," HBO, accessed April 27, 2022, https://www.hbo.com/sex-and-the-city/anniversary-sarah-jessica-parker-interview.

5. Quoted in Amy Sohn, *"Sex and the City": Kiss and Tell* (New York: Pocket Books, 2002), 22.

6. Quoted in Sohn, *"Sex and the City,"* 19.

7. Saim Cheeda, *"And Just Like That:* 5 Reasons Fans Are Excited for the *Sex and the City* Reboot (and 5 They're Worried)," Screenrant, January 22, 2021, https://screenrant .com/satc-and-just-like-that-excited-worried-revival/.

8. Sohn, *"Sex and the City,"* 19.

9. Emily Nussbaum, "Difficult Women: How *Sex and the City* Lost Its Good Name," *New Yorker*, July 23, 2013, https://www.newyorker.com/magazine/2013/07/29 /difficult-women.

10. Quote in Sohn, *"Sex and the City,"* 37.

11. Quoted in Maria Popova, "Ways of Seeing: John Berger's Classic 1972 BBC Critique of Consumer Culture," Marginalian, accessed April 27, 2022, https://www.the marginalian.org/2012/09/28/ways-of-seeing-john-berger/#:~:text=To%20be%20born%20 a%20woman,within%20such%20a%20limited%20space.

12. Ron Simon, *"Sex and the City,"* in *The Essential HBO Reader*, ed. Gary R. Edgerton and Jeffrey P. Jones, American Popular Culture, no. 15 (Lexington: University Press of Kentucky, 2008), 202, https://uknowledge.uky.edu/upk_american_popular_culture/15.

13. Molly St. Louis, "Research Shows That the Clothes You Wear Actually Change the Way You Perform," Inc., June 8, 2017, https://www.inc.com/molly-reynolds/research -shows-that-the-clothes-you-wear-actually-change-the-way-you-perform.html.

14. Lynn Gibbs, *"Sex and the City*: 10 Hidden Details You Never Noticed about Carrie's Apartment," Screenrant, April 18, 2020, https://screenrant.com/sex-the-city -hidden-details-carries-apartment/.

15. Beatriz Oria, *Talking Dirty on "Sex and the City": Romance, Intimacy, Friendship* (New York: Rowman and Littlefield, 2014), 72.

16. Quoted in Kayleigh Dray, *"Sex and the City*: What Happened When I Rewatched Every Episode of *SATC*," Stylist, January 15, 2021, https://www.stylist.co.uk/life/sex -and-the-city-tv-film-carrie-bradshaw-feminism-sexism/210642.

17. Anna König, *"Sex and the City*: A Fashion Editor's Dream?" in *Reading "Sex and the City,"* ed. Kim Akass and Janet McCabe (London: I. B. Tauris, 2006), 140.

18. Cindy Royal, "Narrative Structure in *Sex and the City*: 'I Couldn't Help but Wonder . . . ,'" (doctoral dissertation, University of Texas at Austin, 2003), 10.

19. Delancy Broderick, "Interpreting Womanhood through *Sex and the City*," in *Culture and the Sitcom: Student Essays*, vol. 1, Summer 2017, ed. Mary M. Dalton (Winston-Salem, NC: Library Partners Press, 2017), https://librarypartnerspress.pressbooks.pub/stu dentessaysculturesitcomv1/chapter/interpreting-womanhood-through-sex-and-the-city/.

20. Emphasis in the original. Michael Hauge, "Inner Conflict," Story Mastery, February 9, 2017, https://www.storymastery.com/character-development/inner-conflict/.

21. Andrea Francese, *"The Carrie Diaries* Got Everything Wrong about Carrie Bradshaw's Upbringing," Showbiz CheatSheet, January 6, 2021, https://www.cheatsheet .com/entertainment/the-carrie-diaries-got-everything-wrong-about-carrie-bradshaws-up bringing.html/.

2. CHARLOTTE

1. Amy Sohn, *"Sex and the City": Kiss and Tell* (New York: Pocket Books, 2002), 41.

2. Leah Thomas, "Charlotte York Is Anti-Feminist, and We've Outgrown Her," *Marie Claire*, June 29, 2017, https://www.marieclaire.com/culture/news/a27933/sex-and-the-city-charlotte-york-anti-feminist/.

3. Andrea Francese, "*Sex and the City*: Which Character Dated the Most Men?" Showbiz CheatSheet, April 29, 2020, https://www.cheatsheet.com/entertainment/sex-and-the-city-which-character-had-the-most-partners.html/.

4. Calvin Motley, "*Sex and the City* Alternate Opening Credits Has Carrie Tripping Clumsily," Showbiz CheatSheet, January 11, 2021, https://www.cheatsheet.com/entertainment/sex-and-the-city-alternate-opening-credits-has-carrie-tripping-clumsily.html/.

5. Beth Montemurro, "Charlotte Chooses Her Choice: Liberal Feminism on *Sex and the City*," *Feminist Television Studies: The Case of HBO* 3, no. 1 (Fall 2004), http://sfon line.barnard.edu/hbo/printbmo.htm.

6. In episode 2.2, "The Awful Truth," Charlotte opens up her "hope box," which contains a photo of John F. Kennedy Jr. and two homes just like these.

7. Leigh Anderson, "The Rules, 20 Years Later," Vox, April 8, 2015, https://www.vox.com/2015/4/8/8353915/rules-dating-advice.

8. Molly Mulshine, "All of the *Sex and the City* Boyfriends, Ranked," *Elle*, May 7, 2018, https://www.elle.com/culture/movies-tv/a20140092/sex-and-the-city-boyfriends-ranked/.

9. Sohn, *"Sex and the City,"* 41.

10. Richard Lawson, "*Sex and the City* 10 Years Later: The Final Rankings," *Vanity Fair*, February 14, 2014, https://www.vanityfair.com/hollywood/2014/02/sex-and-the-city-season-rankings.

11. Princess Weekes, "Charlotte York Is the Best Character on *Sex and the City*," Mary Sue, March 20, 2018, https://www.themarysue.com/charlotte-york-sex-and-the-city/.

12. US Department of Health and Human Services, Office on Women's Health, "Infertility," April 1, 2019, https://www.womenshealth.gov/a-z-topics/infertility#:~:text=Is%20infertility%20a%20common%20problem,Control%20and%20Prevention%20(CDC).

13. WebMD, "What We've Learned From *Sex and the City*," accessed April 28, 2022, https://www.webmd.com/sex-relationships/features/what-weve-learned-from-sex-city.

14. Quoted in Amy Clark, "What *Sex and the City* Taught Us about Infertility," MamaMia, May 10, 2017, https://www.mamamia.com.au/sex-and-the-city-infertility/.

15. Thomas, "Charlotte York Is Anti-Feminist."

16. Delaney Broderick, "Interpreting Womanhood through *Sex and the City*," in *Culture and the Sitcom: Student Essays*, vol. 1, Summer 2017, ed. Mary M. Dalton (Winston-Salem, NC: Library Partners Press, 2017), https://librarypartnerspress.pressbooks.pub/stu dentessaysculturesitcomv1/chapter/interpreting-womanhood-through-sex-and-the-city/.

17. Oxford Reference, "Post-Feminism," accessed April 28, 2022, https://www.ox fordreference.com/view/10.1093/oi/authority.20110803100339445.

18. Judith Stacey, "The New Conservative Feminism," *Feminist Studies* 9, no. 3 (1983): 559, https://doi.org/10.2307/3177616.

19. Stacey, "New Conservative Feminism," 561–63.

20. Stacey, "New Conservative Feminism," 562.

21. Cameron Michael Tufino, "*Sex and the City*: A Promotion of Modern American Feminism" (master's thesis, University of the Incarnate Word, 2012), 53, http://athenaeum .uiw.edu/uiw_etds/292.

22. Montemurro, "Charlotte Chooses Her Choice."

23. Andrea Francese, *"Sex and the City*: Charlotte York Was Different from Her Friends in 1 Big Way," Showbiz CheatSheet, May 31, 2021, https://www.cheatsheet.com/entertainment/sex-and-the-city-charlotte-york-was-different-from-her-friends-in-1-big-way.html/.

24. Emily Nussbaum, "Difficult Women: How *Sex and the City* Lost Its Good Name," *New Yorker*, July 23, 2013, https://www.newyorker.com/magazine/2013/07/29/difficult-women.

25. Sohn, *"Sex and the City,"* 41.

26. Weekes, "Charlotte York."

3. MIRANDA

1. Andrea Francese, *"Sex and the City*: Miranda Hobbes Had Some Pretty Bad Personality Traits, Too," Showbiz CheatSheet, February 17, 2021, https://www.cheatsheet.com/entertainment/sex-and-the-city-the-main-characters-biggest-character-development-moment.html/.

2. Eva O'Beirne, "Carrie Bradshaw Is Not the Feminist Icon We Want Her to Be," *Trinity News*, June 21, 2020, http://trinitynews.ie/2020/06/carrie-bradshaw-is-not-the-feminist-icon-we-want-her-to-be/.

3. This particular hobby, as revealed in 2.12, "La Douleur Exquise!" could be seen to imply that Miranda has a lot of free time on her hands, as these books are rarely short.

4. Ron Simon, *"Sex and the City,"* in *The Essential HBO Reader*, ed. Gary R. Edgerton and Jeffrey P. Jones, American Popular Culture, no. 15 (Lexington: University Press of Kentucky, 2008), 196, https://uknowledge.uky.edu/upk_american_popular_culture/15; Andrea Francese, *"Sex and the City*: Which Character Dated the Most Men?" Showbiz CheatSheet, April 29, 2020, https://www.cheatsheet.com/entertainment/sex-and-the-city-which-character-had-the-most-partners.html/; Kyle Kim, Kate Stanhope, and Chris Keller, "Every Single Person Carrie, Miranda, Charlotte and Samantha Dated," *Los Angeles Times*, June 1, 2018, https://www.latimes.com/projects/la-et-sex-and-the-city-every-person-they-dated/.

5. Amy Sohn, *"Sex and the City": Kiss and Tell* (New York: Pocket Books, 2002), 83.

6. Delaney Broderick, "Interpreting Womanhood through *Sex and the City*," in *Culture and the Sitcom: Student Essays*, vol. 1, Summer 2017, ed. Mary M. Dalton (Winston-Salem, NC: Library Partners Press, 2017), https://librarypartnerspress.pressbooks.pub/studentessaysculturesitcomv1/chapter/interpreting-womanhood-through-sex-and-the-city/.

7. I don't recall this being a real thing when I signed my own papers in 2006, but maybe it was in the 1990s.

8. Sohn, *"Sex and the City,"* 85.

9. Chelsea Fairless and Lauren Garroni, *We Should All Be Mirandas: Life Lessons from "Sex and the City's" Most Underrated Character* (New York: Houghton Mifflin Harcourt, 2019), 12.

10. Clifford N. Lazarus, "Think Sarcasm Is Funny? Think Again," *Psychology Today*, June 26, 2012, https://www.psychologytoday.com/us/blog/think-well/201206/think-sarcasm-is-funny-think-again.

11. Quoted in Soraya Chemaly, "All Teachers Should Be Trained to Overcome Their Hidden Biases," *Time*, February 12, 2015, https://time.com/3705454/teachers-biases-girls-education/.

12. American Bar Association, "First Year and Total J.D. Enrollment by Gender: 1947–2011," accessed April 28, 2022, https://www.americanbar.org/content/dam/aba

/administrative/legal_education_and_admissions_to_the_bar/statistics/jd_enrollment_1yr
_total_gender.authcheckdam.pdf.

13. Global Legal Post, "Male Lawyers Get Promoted over Women, McKinsey Says," November 1, 2017, https://www.globallegalpost.com/news/male-lawyers-get-promoted-over-women-mckinsey-says-56167958.

14. Fairless and Garroni, *We Should All Be Mirandas*, 3.

15. Francese, "*Sex and the City*: Miranda Hobbes."

16. Harling Ross, "If *Sex and the City* Came Out Today, Miranda Would Be the Protagonist," Repeller, April 13, 2018, https://repeller.com/miranda-hobbes-best-character-satc/.

17. Lilith Fair was an all-female touring music festival organized by singer Sarah McLachlan after she noticed how few female artists were played on the radio and booked at festivals. She was also reacting to the normalization of harassment of female fans at festivals; she wanted to create a safe place for women to see live music. See Jessica Hopper, "Building a Mystery: An Oral History of Lilith Fair," *Vanity Fair*, September 30, 2009, https://www.vanityfair.com/style/2019/09/an-oral-history-of-lilith-fair.

18. Afua Hirsch, "As a 1990s Teenager, the World Gave Us Girl Power and Pornification," *Guardian*, January 21, 2018, https://www.theguardian.com/lifeandstyle/2018/jan/31/as-a-1990s-teenager-the-world-gave-us-girl-power-and-pornification; Allison Yarrow, "How the '90s Tricked Women into Thinking They'd Gained Gender Equality," *Time*, June 13, 2018, https://time.com/5310256/90s-gender-equality-progress/.

19. Georgina Isbister, "*Sex and the City*: A Postfeminist Fairy Tale," Online Proceedings of "Sustaining Culture" (2008), annual conference of the Cultural Studies Association of Australia (CSAA) University of South Australia, Adelaide, December 6–8, 2007, 7, http://unisa.edu.au/com/csaa/onlineproceedings.htm.

20. Isbister, *"Sex and the City,"* 5–6.

21. Leah Thomas, "Charlotte York Is Anti-Feminist, and We've Outgrown Her," *Marie Claire*, June 29, 2017, https://www.marieclaire.com/culture/news/a27933/sex-and-the-city-charlotte-york-anti-feminist/.

22. Jonah Engel Bromwich, "Cynthia Nixon Confronts Miranda on the Campaign Trail," *New York Times*, July 19, 2018, https://www.nytimes.com/2018/07/19/style/cynthia-nixon-governor-sex-and-the-city-instagram.html.

23. Ross, "If *Sex and the City* Came Out Today."

24. Fairless and Garroni, *We All Should Be Mirandas*, x–xi.

25. Broderick, "Interpreting Womanhood."

26. Fairless and Garroni, *We All Should Be Mirandas*, 80.

27. Fairless and Garroni, *We All Should Be Mirandas*, 76.

28. Sohn, *"Sex and the City,"* 83.

29. Sohn, *"Sex and the City,"* 83.

30. Wendy A. Burns-Ardolino, *TV Female Foursomes and Their Fans* (Jefferson, NC: McFarland, 2016), 150.

31. Women and Hollywood, "Being Miranda Hobbes: Why Women Really Love *Sex and the City*," July 23, 2013, https://womenandhollywood.com/being-miranda-hobbes-why-women-really-love-sex-and-the-city/.

32. Fairless and Garroni, *We All Should Be Mirandas*, 3.

4. SAMANTHA

1. The Take, "*Sex and the City*: Why No One Wants to Be a Samantha (but They Should)," accessed April 28, 2022, https://the-take.com/watch/sex-and-the-city-why-no-one-wants-to-be-a-samantha-but-they-should.

2. Ron Simon, *"Sex and the City,"* in *The Essential HBO Reader*, ed. Gary R. Edgerton and Jeffrey P. Jones, American Popular Culture, no. 15 (Lexington: University Press of Kentucky, 2008), 196, https://uknowledge.uky.edu/upk_american_popular_culture/15.

3. Quoted in Simone Torn, *"Sex and the City*: Kim Cattrall Wasn't Happy with Samantha's Fate in the Series Finale," Showbiz CheatSheet, May 30, 2021, https://www.cheatsheet.com/entertainment/sex-and-the-city-kim-cattrall-wasnt-happy-with-samanthas-fate-in-the-series-finale.html/.

4. Quoted in Amy Sohn, *"Sex and the City": Kiss and Tell* (New York: Pocket Books, 2002), 103.

5. Beatriz Oria, *Talking Dirty on "Sex and the City": Romance, Intimacy, Friendship* (New York: Rowman and Littlefield, 2014), 118.

6. Delaney Broderick, "Interpreting Womanhood through *Sex and the City*," in *Culture and the Sitcom: Student Essays*, vol. 1, Summer 2017, ed. Mary M. Dalton (Winston-Salem, NC: Library Partners Press, 2017), https://librarypartnerspress.pressbooks.pub/studentessaysculturesitcomv1/chapter/interpreting-womanhood-through-sex-and-the-city/.

7. Broderick, "Interpreting Womanhood."

8. The Take, *"Sex and the City."*

9. The Take, *"Sex and the City."*

10. The Take, *"Sex and the City."*

11. Quoted in Sohn, *"Sex and the City,"* 108.

12. Sohn, *"Sex and the City,"* 105.

13. Sohn, *"Sex and the City,"* 105.

14. Sohn, *"Sex and the City,"* 105.

5. CARRIE'S TWO BIG LOVES

1. Joanna Di Mattia, "'What's the Harm in Believing?': Mr. Big, Mr. Perfect, and the Romantic Quest for *Sex and the City*'s Mr. Right," in *Reading "Sex and the City,"* ed. Kim Akass and Janet McCabe (London: I. B. Tauris, 2006), 20.

2. Quoted in Alice Wignall, "Can a Feminist Really Love *Sex and the City?*" *Guardian*, April 16, 2008, https://www.theguardian.com/lifeandstyle/2008/apr/16/women.film.

3. Di Mattia, "'What's the Harm,'" 20.

4. Chelsea Fairless and Lauren Garroni, *We Should All Be Mirandas: Life Lessons from "Sex and the City's" Most Underrated Character* (New York: Houghton Mifflin Harcourt, 2019), 74.

5. Di Mattia, "'What's the Harm,'" 18.

6. Di Mattia, "'What's the Harm,'" 19.

7. Jennifer, "Alpha-Male vs. Alpha-Hole Romance Heroes: Why One of Them *Has to Go*," *Romance Rehab* (blog), April 15, 2019, https://www.romancerehab.com/blog/alpha-male-vs-alpha-hole-romance-heroes-why-one-of-them-has-to-go.

8. Jennifer, "Alpha-Male vs. Alpha-Hole."

9. Jennifer, "Alpha-Male vs. Alpha-Hole."

10. Mandi, "The Alpha-Hole Hero: Hot or Not?" Smexy Books, August 8, 2013, https://smexybooks.com/2013/08/the-alpha-hole-hero-hot-or-not.html.

11. Amy Sohn, *"Sex and the City": Kiss and Tell* (New York: Pocket Books, 2002), 111.

12. Both Carrie and Big are toxic to one another. Carrie's contribution is discussed in a later chapter.

13. Emily Nussbaum, "Difficult Women: How *Sex and the City* Lost Its Good Name," *New Yorker*, July 23, 2013, https://www.newyorker.com/magazine/2013/07/29/difficult-women.

14. Wignall, "Can a Feminist Really Love."

15. Sohn, *"Sex and the City,"* 112.

16. Andrea Francese, *"Sex and the City'*: 3 Times Carrie Bradshaw Should Have Really Ended Her Romance with Mr. Big," Showbiz CheatSheet, December 27, 2021, https://www.cheatsheet.com/entertainment/sex-and-the-city-3-times-carrie-bradshaw-really-ended-romance-mr-big.html/.

17. Francese, *"Sex and the City'*: 3 Times."

18. Emma Clarke, "Mr. Big Might Be Dead, but Let's Face It—He Was Never 'the One' for Carrie," *Newsweek*, December 9, 2021, https://www.newsweek.com/mr-big-sex-city-trash-1657436.

19. Sohn, *"Sex and the City,"* 112.

20. Di Mattia, "'What's the Harm,'" 27.

21. Clarke, "Mr. Big Might Be Dead."

22. Sohn, *"Sex and the City,"* 110.

23. Sohn, *"Sex and the City,"* 114.

24. Quoted in Sohn, *"Sex and the City,"* 114.

25. Amanda Diehl, "Romance 101: Beta Heroes," Bookriot, October, 15, 2014, https://bookriot.com/romance-101-beta-heroes/.

26. Di Mattia, "'What's the Harm,'" 24; Georgina Isbister, *"Sex and the City*: A Postfeminist Fairy Tale," Online Proceedings of "Sustaining Culture" (2008), annual conference of the Cultural Studies Association of Australia (CSAA), University of South Australia, Adelaide, December 6–8, 2007, 9, http://unisa.edu.au/com/csaa/onlineproceedings.htm.

27. Sohn, *"Sex and the City,"* 114.

28. Di Mattia, "'What's the Harm,'" 28.

29. Sohn, *"Sex and the City,"* 114.

30. Di Mattia, "'What's the Harm,'" 29.

6. ALEKSANDR

1. Chelsea Fairless and Lauren Garroni, *We Should All Be Mirandas: Life Lessons from "Sex and the City's" Most Underrated Character* (New York: Houghton Mifflin Harcourt, 2019), 75.

2. Lisa Aronson Fontes, "How Domestic Abusers Groom and Isolate Their Victims," *Psychology Today*, February 19, 2019, https://www.psychologytoday.com/us/blog/invisible-chains/201902/how-domestic-abusers-groom-and-isolate-their-victims.

3. Amy Sohn, *"Sex and the City": Kiss and Tell* (New York: Pocket Books, 2002), 19.

4. Fontes, "How Domestic Abusers Groom"; Lisa Aronson Fontes, "When Relationship Abuse Is Hard to Recognize," *Psychology Today*, August 26, 2015, https://www.psychologytoday.com/us/blog/invisible-chains/201508/when-relationship-abuse-is-hard-recognize.

5. Emily Nussbaum, "Difficult Women: How *Sex and the City* Lost Its Good Name," *New Yorker*, July 23, 2013, https://www.newyorker.com/magazine/2013/07/29/difficult-women.

6. Sohn, *"Sex and the City,"* 129.

7. Sohn, *"Sex and the City,"* 128–29.

8. Additional discussion of the possible interpretations of the series finale is available in chapter 9.

7. THE OTHER GIRLS' MEN

1. Eliza Thompson, "What Happened to Miranda's Boyfriend Skipper? A *Sex and the City* Investigation," *Cosmopolitan*, June 8, 2018, https://www.cosmopolitan.com /entertainment/tv/a20978994/skipper-sex-and-the-city/.

2. Amy Sohn, *"Sex and the City": Kiss and Tell* (New York: Pocket Books, 2002), 116.

3. Sohn, *"Sex and the City,"* 116.

4. Sohn, *"Sex and the City,"* 116.

5. Princess Weekes, "Charlotte York Is the Best Character on *Sex and the City*," Mary Sue, March 20, 2018, https://www.themarysue.com/charlotte-york-sex-and-the-city/.

6. Sohn, *"Sex and the City,"* 118.

7. Chelsea Fairless and Lauren Garroni, *We Should All Be Mirandas: Life Lessons from "Sex and the City's" Most Underrated Character* (New York: Houghton Mifflin Harcourt, 2019), 72.

8. THE SINGLE GIRL

1. Obviously this is a broad brush of history and doesn't reflect the experiences of all races or classes of women.

2. One business that was almost exclusively female until the early sixteenth century was brewing.

3. Beth Montemurro, "Charlotte Chooses Her Choice: Liberal Feminism on *Sex and the City*," *Feminist Television Studies: The Case of HBO* 3, no. 1 (Fall 2004), http://sfon line.barnard.edu/hbo/printbmo.htm.

4. Helen McCarthy, "The Rise of the Working Wife," History Today, May 5, 2020, https://www.historytoday.com/history-matters/rise-working-wife.

5. Montemurro, "Charlotte Chooses Her Choice."

6. Tamala Edwards, "Who Needs a Husband?" *Time*, July 5, 2007, http://content .time.com/time/subscriber/article/0,33009,997804,00.html.

7. Montemurro, "Charlotte Chooses Her Choice."

8. Astrid Henry, "Orgasms and Empowerment: *Sex and the City* and the Third Wave Feminism," in *Reading "Sex and the City,"* ed. Kim Akass and Janet McCabe (London: I. B. Tauris, 2006), 82.

9. Edwards, "Who Needs a Husband?"

10. Beatriz Oria, *Talking Dirty on "Sex and the City": Romance, Intimacy, Friendship* (New York: Rowman and Littlefield, 2014), 197.

11. Quoted in Amy Sohn, *"Sex and the City": Kiss and Tell* (New York: Pocket Books, 2002), 44.

12. Edwards, "Who Needs a Husband?"

13. Quoted in Marissa Blanchard, "Darren Star Reflects Back on *Sex and the City*," HBO, accessed May 23, 2022, https://www.hbo.com/sex-and-the-city/anniversary -darren-star-interview.

14. Quoted in Sohn, *"Sex and the City,"* 36.

15. Sohn, *"Sex and the City,"* 36.

16. Quoted in Edwards, "Who Needs a Husband?"

17. Edwards, "Who Needs a Husband?"

18. Henry, "Orgasms and Empowerment," 73.

19. Nisha Gopalan, "'Splat!': The Oral History of *Sex and the City*'s Most Shocking Episode," Vulture, June 6, 2018, https://www.vulture.com/2013/12/sex-and-the-city-oral -history-splat-episode.html.

20. Quoted in Sohn, *"Sex and the City,"* 38.

21. Chelsea Fairless and Lauren Garroni, *We Should All Be Mirandas: Life Lessons from "Sex and the City's" Most Underrated Character* (New York: Houghton Mifflin Harcourt, 2019), 97.

22. Oria, *Talking Dirty*, 177–78.

23. Esme Mazzeo, "The *Sex and the City* Episode Where Carrie Was Forced to Leave Her Shoes at the Door Matters 18 Years Later Because Women Are Still Shamed for Being Single," Insider, August 17, 2021, https://www.insider.com/sex -and-the-city-single-shaming-episode-still-relevant-today-2021-8?amp.

24. Edwards, "Who Needs a Husband?"

25. Faima Bakar, "If You're an Unmarried Woman over the Age of 26, You're Not a Spinster, You're a Thornback," Metro UK, March 14, 2019, https://metro.co.uk/2019/03/14 /if-youre-an-unmarried-woman-over-the-age-of-26-youre-not-a-spinster-youre-a-thorn back-8902030/#:~:text=The%20word%20spinster%20was%20used,single%2C%20 never%2Dmarried%20woman.

26. Oria, *Talking Dirty*, 149.

27. Gopalan, "Splat!"

28. Oria, *Talking Dirty*, 149.

29. Oria, *Talking Dirty*, 86.

30. Quoted in Ellen E. Jones, "'That Show Was as White as It Gets!': *Sex and the City*'s Problematic Legacy," *Guardian*, April 28, 2018, https://www.theguardian.com/tv -and-radio/2018/apr/21/that-show-was-as-white-as-it-gets-sex-and-the-citys-problematic -legacy.

31. Fairless and Garroni, *We Should All Be Mirandas*, 97–98.

32. Jones, "'That Show.'"

33. Mazzeo, "*Sex and the City* Episode."

34. Mazzeo, "*Sex and the City* Episode."

9. FEMINISM

1. bell hooks, "Dissident Heat: Fire with Fire," in *"Bad Girls"/"Good Girls": Women, Sex and Power in the Nineties*, ed. Nan Bauer Maglin and Donna Perry (New Brunswick, NJ: Rutgers University Press, 1996), 58.

2. Julie D'Acci, "Television, Representation and Gender," in *The Television Studies Reader*, ed. Robert C. Allen and Annette Hill (London: Routledge, 2004), 373.

3. Claire Perkins and Michele Schreiber, "Independent Women: From Film to Television," *Feminist Media Studies* 19, no. 7 (2019): 919, https://doi.org/10.1080/1468 0777.2019.1667059.

4. Kim Akass and Janet McCabe, introduction to *Reading "Sex and the City,"* ed. Kim Akass and Janet McCabe (London: I. B. Tauris, 2006), 9.

5. Alice Wignall, "Can a Feminist Really Love *Sex and the City*?" *Guardian*, April 16, 2008, https://www.theguardian.com/lifeandstyle/2008/apr/16/women.film.

6. Estelle B. Freedman, *No Turning Back: The History of Feminism and the Future of Women* (London: Random House, 2007), 7.

7. Angela Chiang, "Coffee Shop Dialogics: *Sex and the City* and Third Wave Feminism" (master's thesis, Carleton University, Ottawa, Ontario, 2007), 4.

8. History.com Editors, "Abigail Adams Urges Husband to 'Remember the Ladies,'" March 30, 2020, https://www.history.com/this-day-in-history/abigail-adams-urges-hus band-to-remember-the-ladies; National Women's Hall of Fame, "Susan B. Anthony," accessed April 29, 2022, https://www.womenofthehall.org/inductee/susan-b-anthony/#:~: text=Its%20motto%20was%20%E2%80%9CMen%20their,and%20fined%20for%20 voting%20illegally.

9. The wave model implies that there were periods when feminism wasn't active, which isn't true. It has never stopped; it is only that it was more publicly visible during some periods than during others.

10. A note on terminology: *Postfeminism* is used in multiple ways. Some scholars see it as one and the same as the third wave; others see it as synonymous with anything after the third wave; while still others use it as I have here: for a period of time in the late 1990s and early 2000s, when feminism was believed to be dead. It makes reading feminist literature on this period very difficult.

11. These are my own recollections of the waves, but for a strong, nonacademic primer, see Constance Grady, "The Waves of Feminism, and Why People Keep Fighting over Them, Explained," Vox, July 20, 2018, https://www.vox.com/2018/3/20/16955588 /feminism-waves-explained-first-second-third-fourth.

12. Astrid Henry, "Orgasms and Empowerment: *Sex and the City* and the Third Wave Feminism," in *Reading "Sex and the City,"* ed. Kim Akass and Janet McCabe (London: I. B. Tauris, 2006), 66.

13. Cameron Michael Tufino, "*Sex and the City*: A Promotion of Modern American Feminism" (master's thesis, University of the Incarnate Word, 2012), 1, http://athenaeum .uiw.edu/uiw_etds/292.

14. Laura Brunell and the Editors of *Encyclopaedia Brittanica*, "The Third Wave of Feminism," Brittanica.com, https://www.britannica.com/topic/feminism/The-third-wave -of-feminism.

15. Beatriz Oria, *Talking Dirty on "Sex and the City": Romance, Intimacy, Friendship* (New York: Rowman and Littlefield, 2014), 102.

16. Princess Weekes, "Charlotte York Is the Best Character on *Sex and the City*," Mary Sue, March 20, 2018, https://www.themarysue.com/charlotte-york-sex-and-the-city/.

17. Quoted in Kim McCabe and Janet Akass, "What Has HBO Ever Done for Women?" in *The Essential HBO Reader*, ed. Gary R. Edgerton and Jeffrey P. Jones, American Popular Culture, no. 15 (Lexington: University Press of Kentucky, 2008), 306, https://uknowledge.uky.edu/upk_american_popular_culture/15.

18. Ron Simon, "Sex and the City," in *The Essential HBO Reader*, ed. Gary R. Edgerton and Jeffrey P. Jones, American Popular Culture, no. 15 (Lexington: University Press of Kentucky, 2008), 195, https://uknowledge.uky.edu/upk_american_popular_culture/15.

19. Quoted in Henry, "Orgasms and Empowerment," 66–67.

20. Catherine Harnois, "Re-Presenting Feminisms: Past, Present, and Future," *NWSA Journal* 20, no. 1 (2008): 133, http://www.jstor.org/stable/40071255.

21. Naomi Wolf, "Carrie Bradshaw: Icons of the Decade," *Guardian*, December 21, 2009, https://www.theguardian.com/world/2009/dec/22/carrie-bradshaw-icons-of-decade.

22. Wolf, "Carrie Bradshaw." As an early twenty-something at the time, I can attest to this being true.

23. Rosemarie Tong, *Feminist Thought: A More Comprehensive Introduction* (New York: Routledge, 2018), 285.

24. Eva O'Beirne, "Carrie Bradshaw Is Not the Feminist Icon We Want Her to Be," *Trinity News*, June 21, 2020, http://trinitynews.ie/2020/06/carrie-bradshaw -is-not-the-feminist-icon-we-want-her-to-be/.

25. Camilla Long, "Decade in Review: You Are a Very Noughtie and Unhappy Girl," *Times of London*, December 20, 2009, https://www.thetimes.co.uk/article/decade -in-review-you-are-a-very-noughtie-and-unhappy-girl-296dw9k96ht; Tracy Clark-Flory, "Carrie Bradshaw: Feminist Icon?" Salon, December 22, 2019, https://www.salon.com /2009/12/22/wolf_carrie_bradshaw/.

26. Delaney Broderick, "Interpreting Womanhood through *Sex and the City*," in *Culture and the Sitcom: Student Essays*, vol. 1, Summer 2017, ed. Mary M. Dalton (Winston-Salem, NC: Library Partners Press, 2017), https://librarypartnerspress.pressbooks.pub/stu dentessaysculturesitcomv1/chapter/interpreting-womanhood-through-sex-and-the-city/.

27. Rebecca, the daughter of second-wave feminist icon and author Alice Walker, is widely credited with coining the term *third wave* and is considered one of the post prominent voices of this generation of feminism. Kathleen was the lead singer of the feminist band Bikini Kill, who, along with Riot Grrrl, helped initiate third-wave feminism. Alanis was a popular grunge-alternative rock singer in the 1990s known for her outspoken feminist views. She also guest starred on *Sex and the City* as the woman Carrie kisses in "Boy, Girl, Boy, Girl."

28. The Bechdel Test was a test created in 1985 for fictional stories regardless of medium that rates whether its female characters place too much focus on men. If a story fits these three criteria, it passes: "(1) It has to have at least two [named] women in it (2) who talk to each other (3) about something besides a man." See Bechdel Test Movie List, accessed April 30, 2022, https://bechdeltest.com/.

29. Chiang, "Coffee Shop Dialogics," 43.

30. Chiang, "Coffee Shop Dialogics," 46–47.

31. Chiang, "Coffee Shop Dialogics," 12–13.

32. Quoted in Dana Micucci, "Redefining Feminism," *Chicago Tribune*, December 12, 1993, https://www.chicagotribune.com/news/ct-xpm-1993-12-12-9312120158-story. html.

33. R. Claire Snyder-Hall, "Third-Wave Feminism and the Defense of 'Choice,'" *Perspectives on Politics* 8, no. 1 (2010): 255, http://www.jstor.org/stable/25698533.

34. Beth Montemurro, "Charlotte Chooses Her Choice: Liberal Feminism on *Sex and the City*," *Feminist Television Studies: The Case of HBO* 3, no. 1 (Fall 2004), http://sfon line.barnard.edu/hbo/printbmo.htm.

35. Broderick, "Interpreting Womanhood."

36. Broderick, "Interpreting Womanhood."

37. Chiang, "Coffee Shop Dialogics," 17.

38. Anna Quindlen, "And Now, Babe Feminism," in *"Bad Girls"/"Good Girls": Women, Sex and Power in the Nineties*, ed. Nan Bauer Maglin and Donna Perry (New Brunswick, NJ: Rutgers University Press, 1996), 4.

39. Henry, "Orgasms and Empowerment," 76.

40. Wolf, "Carrie Bradshaw."

41. Quindlen, "And Now, Babe Feminism," 4.

42. David Caballero, "*Sex and the City*: 10 Major Flaws of the Show That Fans Chose to Ignore," Screenrant, January 26, 2021, https://screenrant.com/sex-and-the-city -biggest-series-flaws-problems/.

43. Montemurro, "Charlotte Chooses Her Choice."

44. McCabe and Akass, "What Has HBO Ever Done?" 305.

45. McCabe and Akass, "What Has HBO Ever Done?" 307.

46. Harnois, "Re-Presenting Feminisms," 121–22.

47. Quoted in Nan Bauer Maglin and Donna Perry, eds., introduction to *"Bad Girls"/"Good Girls": Women, Sex and Power in the Nineties* (New Brunswick, NJ: Rutgers University Press, 1996), xv.

48. Quoted in Jonah Engel Bromwich, "Cynthia Nixon Confronts Miranda on the Campaign Trail," *New York Times*, July 19, 2018, https://www.nytimes.com/2018/07/19/style/cynthia-nixon-governor-sex-and-the-city-instagram.html.

49. Oria, *Talking Dirty*, 62.

50. Oria, *Talking Dirty*, 190.

51. Oria, *Talking Dirty*, 190–91.

52. Caballero, "*Sex and the City.*"

53. Quoted in Oria, *Talking Dirty*, 190.

54. Oria, *Talking Dirty*, 138.

55. Quoted in Ariana Bacle, "How *Sex and the City* Recast the World in a Pink Light," HBO, accessed April 30, 2022, https://www.hbo.com/sex-and-the-city/anniversary-michael-patrick-king-interview.

56. Emily Nussbaum, "Difficult Women: How *Sex and the City* Lost Its Good Name," *New Yorker*, July 23, 2013, https://www.newyorker.com/magazine/2013/07/29/difficult-women.

57. Quoted in Oria, *Talking Dirty*, 190.

58. Oria, *Talking Dirty*, 191.

59. Quoted in Oria, *Talking Dirty*, 189–90.

60. Oria, *Talking Dirty*, 209; Caballero, "*Sex and the City.*"

61. Georgina Isbister, "*Sex and the City*: A Postfeminist Fairy Tale," Online Proceedings of "Sustaining Culture" (2008), annual conference of the Cultural Studies Association of Australia (CSAA), University of South Australia, Adelaide, December 6–8, 2007, 8, http://unisa.edu.au/com/csaa/onlineproceedings.htm

62. Oria, *Talking Dirty*, 86; Caballero, "*Sex and the City.*"

10. FRIENDSHIP

1. Gail Markle, "Can Women Have Sex Like a Man? Sexual Scripts in *Sex and the City*," *Sexuality and Culture* 12 (2008): 49, https://doi.org/10.1007/s12119-007-9019-1.

2. Astrid Henry, "Orgasms and Empowerment: Sex and the City and the Third Wave Feminism," in *Reading "Sex and the City,"* ed. Kim Akass and Janet McCabe (London: I. B. Tauris, 2006), 68.

3. Henry, "Orgasms and Empowerment," 69.

4. Beatriz Oria, *Talking Dirty on "Sex and the City": Romance, Intimacy, Friendship* (New York: Rowman and Littlefield, 2014), 143.

5. Wendy A. Burns-Ardolino, *TV Female Foursomes and Their Fans* (Jefferson, NC: McFarland, 2016), 158–59.

6. Delaney Broderick, "Interpreting Womanhood through *Sex and the City*," in *Culture and the Sitcom: Student Essays*, vol. 1, Summer 2017, ed. Mary M. Dalton (Winston-Salem, NC: Library Partners Press, 2017), https://librarypartnerspress.pressbooks.pub/studentessaysculturesitcomv1/chapter/interpreting-womanhood-through-sex-and-the-city/.

7. Amy Sohn, *"Sex and the City": Kiss and Tell* (New York: Pocket Books, 2002).

8. Andrea Francese, *"Sex and the City*: How Did Carrie Bradshaw Meet Her 3 Best Friends?" Showbiz CheatSheet, August 8, 2020, https://www.cheatsheet.com/en tertainment/sex-and-the-city-how-did-carrie-bradshaw-meet-her-3-best-friends.html/; Eliza Thompson, "What Happened to Miranda's Boyfriend Skipper? A *Sex and the City* Investigation," *Cosmopolitan*, June 8, 2018, https://www.cosmopolitan.com/entertainment /tv/a20978994/skipper-sex-and-the-city/.

9. Sohn, *"Sex and the City,"* 12–13.

10. Jane Gerhard, "The Personal Is Still Political: The Legacy of 1970s Feminism," in *"Bad Girls"/"Good Girls": Women, Sex and Power in the Nineties*, ed. Nan Bauer Maglin and Donna Perry (New Brunswick, NJ: Rutgers University Press, 1996), 46.

11. Oria, *Talking Dirty*, 145.

12. Oria, *Talking Dirty*, 143.

13. Quoted in Sohn, *"Sex and the City,"* 86.

14. Oria, *Talking Dirty*, 144.

15. Oria, *Talking Dirty*, 144.

16. Burns-Ardolino, *TV Female Foursomes*, 163.

17. Henry, "Orgasms and Empowerment," 67.

18. Deborah Jermyn, *"Sex and the City"* (Detroit: Wayne State University Press, 2009), 210.

19. Quoted in Sohn, *"Sex and the City,"* 29.

11. LGBTQIA+ AND RACE ISSUES

1. Quoted in Kasandra Brabaw, "How LGBTQ+ People Really Feel about *Sex and the City*," Refinery29, June 4, 2018, https://www.refinery29.com/en-us/2018/06/200625 /sex-and-the-city-gay-characters-lgbt-response.

2. Julie D'Acci, "Television, Representation and Gender," in *The Television Studies Reader*, ed. Robert C. Allen and Annette Hill (London: Routledge, 2004), 376.

3. Cassie Da Costa, "When *Sex and the City* Returns, Will It Finally Get Queer People Right?" *Vanity Fair*, January 13, 2021, https://www.vanityfair.com/hollywood /2021/01/when-sex-and-the-city-returns-will-it-finally-get-queer-people-right.

4. Hunter Harris, "For Women of Color Who Love *Sex and the City*," Refinery 29, June 6, 2018, https://www.refinery29.com/en-us/2016/07/117151/sex-and-the-city-racism.

5. Tari Ngangura, "Looking Back, *Sex and the City* Was Seriously Problematic for Black Women," *Fashion Magazine*, June 5, 2018, https://fashionmagazine.com/flare /sex-and-the-city-black-women/.

6. Maria was in three episodes, and Dr. Robert Leeds was in five.

7. Harris, "For Women of Color."

8. Jill Filipovic, *"Sex and the City* Faces Reality . . . Finally," CNN, August 24, 2021, https://www.cnn.com/2021/08/24/opinions/sex-and-the-city-filipovic/index.html.

9. Kayleigh Dray, *"Sex and the City*: What Happened When I Rewatched Every Episode of *SATC*," Stylist, January 15, 2021, https://www.stylist.co.uk/life/sex -and-the-city-tv-film-carrie-bradshaw-feminism-sexism/210642.

10. Yohana Desta, "Being One of the Only Black Actresses on *Sex and the City* Was a 'Surreal' Experience," *Vanity Fair*, June 8, 2018, https://www.vanityfair.com /hollywood/2018/06/sex-and-the-city-sundra-oakley.

11. Grace Barber-Plentie, "The Conflict of Loving *Sex and the City* When You're Not a Straight White Woman," Vice, June 7, 2018, https://i-d.vice.com/en_uk/article/7xm78g /the-conflict-of-loving-sex-and-the-city-when-youre-not-a-straight-white-woman.

12. Desta, "Being One of the Only Black Actresses."

13. Quoted in Desta, "Being One of the Only Black Actresses."

14. Shon Faye, "*Sex and the City* Is Embarrassing Now, but It Was Everything Then," Dazed, June 6, 2018, https://www.dazeddigital.com/film-tv/article/40272/1 /sex-and-the-city-20th-anniversary.

15. Quoted in Desta, "Being One of the Only Black Actresses."

16. Quoted in Kate Erbland, "15 Fabulous Facts about *Sex and the City*," Mental Floss, June 6, 2018, https://www.mentalfloss.com/article/64729/15-fabulous-facts-about -sex-and-city.

17. Brabaw, "How LGBTQ+ People Really Feel."

18. Quoted in Jess Glass, "*Sex and the City*'s Sarah Jessica Parker Admits That the Show Failed to Represent LGBT People," PinkNews, May 14, 2018, https://www.pink news.co.uk/2018/05/14/sex-and-the-city-sarah-jessica-parker-lgbt-entertainment/.

19. David Caballero, "*Sex and the City*: 10 Major Flaws of the Show That Fans Chose to Ignore," Screenrant, January 26, 2021, https://screenrant.com/sex-and-the-city -biggest-series-flaws-problems/.

20. Quoted in Dana Schuster, "26 Ways *Sex and the City* Left Its Mark," *New York Post*, May 27, 2018, https://nypost.com/2018/05/27/26-ways-sex-and-the-city-left-its-mark/.

21. Ella Alexander, "*Sex and the City*: What It Got Right vs. What It Really Didn't," *Harper's Bazaar*, January 12, 2021, https://www.harpersbazaar.com/uk/culture /a21093577/sex-and-the-city-what-it-got-right-vs-what-it-really-didnt/.

22. Ron Simon, "*Sex and the City*," in *The Essential HBO Reader*, ed. Gary R. Edgerton and Jeffrey P. Jones, American Popular Culture, no. 15 (Lexington: University Press of Kentucky, 2008), 199–200, https://uknowledge.uky.edu/upk_american_popular _culture/15; Amy Sohn, *"Sex and the City": Kiss and Tell* (New York: Pocket Books, 2002), 110.

23. Sohn, *"Sex and the City,"* 130.

24. Sohn, *"Sex and the City,"* 130.

25. Sohn, *"Sex and the City,"* 131.

26. Sohn, *"Sex and the City,"* 131.

27. Lisa Respers France, "Mark Ronson Isn't Sapiosexual after All and Apologizes for Identifying as Such," CNN, September 27, 2019, https://www.cnn.com/2019/09/27 /entertainment/mark-ronson-not-sapiosexual/index.html.

28. Kyli Rodriguez-Cayro, "5 Myths about Bisexuality That Contribute to Bi Erasure," Bustle, September 21, 2017, https://www.bustle.com/p/5-myths-about-bisexuality -that-contribute-to-bi-erasure-2418689.

29. GLAAD, "Bisexual Erasure," accessed May 1, 2022, https://www.glaad.org/accor dionview/bisexual-erasure.

30. Rodriguez-Cayro, "5 Myths."

31. Dray, "*Sex and the City*."

32. Caballero, "*Sex and the City*."

33. Beatriz Oria, *Talking Dirty on "Sex and the City": Romance, Intimacy, Friendship* (New York: Rowman and Littlefield, 2014), 129.

34. Astrid Henry, "Orgasms and Empowerment: *Sex and the City* and the Third Wave Feminism," in *Reading "Sex and the City,"* ed. Kim Akass and Janet McCabe (London: I. B. Tauris, 2006), 81.

35. Kim Akass and Janet McCabe, introduction to *Reading "Sex and the City,"* ed. Kim Akass and Janet McCabe (London: I. B. Tauris, 2006), 8.

36. Mandy Merck, "Sexuality in the City," in *Reading "Sex and the City,"* ed. Kim Akass and Janet McCabe (London: I. B. Tauris, 2006), 54.

37. Da Costa

38. Caballero, *"Sex and the City."*

39. Da Costa, "When *Sex and the City* Returns."

40. Quoted in Brabaw, "How LGBTQ+ People Really Feel."

41. Merriam-Webster, "Metrosexual," https://www.merriam-webster.com/dictionary/metrosexual.

42. Alex Williams, "'Metrosexuals' Were Just Straight Men Who Loved Self-Care. Right?" *New York Times*, June 15, 2018, https://www.nytimes.com/2018/06/15/style/metrosexuals.html.

43. Henry, "Orgasms and Empowerment," 81–82.

44. Frank DeCaro, "Drag Kings Are Ready to Rule," *New York Times*, March 4, 2021, https://www.nytimes.com/2021/03/04/style/drag-kings.html.

45. Brabaw, "How LGBTQ+ People Really Feel."

46. Brabaw, "How LGBTQ+ People Really Feel."

47. Brabaw, "How LGBTQ+ People Really Feel."

48. Brabaw, "How LGBTQ+ People Really Feel."

49. Anonymous, interview by the author, December 25, 2021.

50. Quoted in Brabaw, "How LGBTQ+ People Really Feel."

51. Barber-Plentie, "Conflict of Loving."

52. Anonymous, interview by the author, December 25, 2021.

53. Oria, *Talking Dirty*, 129–30.

54. Quoted in Oria, *Talking Dirty*, 164.

55. Quoted in Oria, *Talking Dirty*, 164.

12. SEX AND MOTHERHOOD

1. Beatriz Oria, *Talking Dirty on "Sex and the City": Romance, Intimacy, Friendship* (New York: Rowman and Littlefield, 2014), 101.

2. Quoted in Ariana Bacle, "How *Sex and the City* Recast the World in a Pink Light," HBO, accessed April 30, 2022, https://www.hbo.com/sex-and-the-city/anniversary-michael-patrick-king-interview.

3. Quotes in Amy Sohn, *"Sex and the City": Kiss and Tell* (New York: Pocket Books, 2002), 36.

4. Andrew Thompson, "Stats and the City," Ceros, accessed May 1, 2022, https://www.ceros.com/inspire/originals/sex-and-the-city/.

5. Ashli LeeAnn Dykes, "Situation Comedies and the Single Woman on Television" (doctoral dissertation, Louisiana State University and Agricultural and Mechanical College, 2011), 37, 166, 170, https://digitalcommons.lsu.edu/gradschool_dissertations/325.

6. Christy Smith, "In *Sex and the City*, Number of Sex Partners True to New York Life," *New York Daily News*, May 28, 2008, https://www.nydailynews.com/entertainment/sex-city-number-sex-partners-true-new-york-life-article-1.326644.

7. Andrew Thompson, "Stats and the City," Ceros, accessed May 1, 2022, https://www.ceros.com/inspire/originals/sex-and-the-city/.

8. Smith, "In *Sex and the City.*"

9. Smith, "In *Sex and the City*."

10. Quoted in Smith, "In *Sex and the City*."

11. Astrid Henry, "Orgasms and Empowerment: *Sex and the City* and the Third Wave Feminism," in *Reading "Sex and the City,"* ed. Kim Akass and Janet McCabe (London: I. B. Tauris, 2006), 75.

12. Quoted in Sohn, *"Sex and the City,"* 38.

13. Emily Nussbaum, "Difficult Women: How *Sex and the City* Lost Its Good Name," *New Yorker*, July 23, 2013, https://www.newyorker.com/magazine/2013/07/29/difficult-women.

14. Dictionary.com, "Slut-Shaming," September 10, 2018, https://www.dictionary.com/e/slang/slut-shaming/. No one knows for certain when the term was first used, but it is often associated with the SlutWalk, an international movement of marches founded in 2011 in Toronto "after a police officer told women to stop dressing like sluts if they wanted to avoid sexual assault." It was revived in 2014 by model Amber Rose in Los Angeles. Jessica Valenti, "SlutWalks and the Future of Feminism," *Washington Post*, June 3, 2011, https://www.washingtonpost.com/opinions/slutwalks-and-the-future-of-feminism/2011/06/01/AGjB9LIH_story.html; Nadja Sayej, "'It's My Ass and My Instagram': Amber Rose Is over Your Slut-Shaming," *Harper's Bazaar*, September 25, 2018, https://www.harpersbazaar.com/culture/features/a23357956/amber-rose-slutwalk-interview/.

15. Kevin O'Keeffe, "No, Carrie Bradshaw Was Not 'Such a Whore,'" *Atlantic*, October 15, 2014, https://www.theatlantic.com/entertainment/archive/2014/10/no-chris-noth-carrie-bradshaw-was-not-such-a-whore/381482/.

16. Quoted in Eliana Dockterman, "Chris Noth (Sort of Jokingly) Calls Carrie Bradshaw a 'Whore,'" *Time*, October 15, 2014, https://time.com/3510859/chris-noth-mr-big-carrie-bradshaw-whore-satc/.

17. Quoted in Claire Hodgson, "*Sex and the City* Creator Defends Chris Noth's 'Whore' Comment about Carrie Bradshaw," *Cosmopolitan*, October 16, 2014, https://www.cosmopolitan.com/uk/entertainment/news/a30475/sex-and-the-city-chris-noth-whore-carrie/.

18. Dockterman, "Chris Noth."

19. Dana Schuster, "26 Ways *Sex and the City* Left Its Mark," *New York Post*, May 27, 2018, https://nypost.com/2018/05/27/26-ways-sex-and-the-city-left-its-mark/.

20. Quoted in Sohn, *"Sex and the City,"* 44.

21. Oria, *Talking Dirty*, 103.

22. Schuster, "26 Ways."

23. Oria, *Talking Dirty*, 133.

24. Jennifer Wright, "#MeToo Couldn't Exist without Carrie Bradshaw," *Body+Soul*, May 14, 2018, https://www.bodyandsoul.com.au/mind-body/wellness/metoo-couldnt-exist-without-carrie-bradshaw/news-story/2b6d46fba55cad3c14a41b0ee52e0254.

25. Henry, "Orgasms and Empowerment," 75, 76.

26. Grace Barber-Plentie, "The Conflict of Loving *Sex and the City* When You're Not a Straight White Woman," Vice, June 7, 2018, https://i-d.vice.com/en_uk/article/7xm78g/the-conflict-of-loving-sex-and-the-city-when-youre-not-a-straight-white-woman.

27. Please note this section was written prior to the Supreme Court of the United States overturning *Roe v. Wade* on June 24, 2022, making abortion illegal in the United States for the first time since 1973.

28. Ackass, "Throwing,"

29. Sarah Erdreich, "More than 40 Years after *Maude*, Abortion Remains Taboo on TV," TalkingPointsMemo, May 19, 2014, https://talkingpointsmemo.com/cafe/cristina -yang-grey-s-anatomy-abortion.

30. Hillary Busis, "*Girls* Tackles Abortion; How Does It Compare to *Sex and the City*'s Abortion Episode?" *Entertainment Weekly*, April 23, 2012, https://ew.com /article/2012/04/23/girls-abortion-sex-and-the-city/.

31. Tanya Melendez, "How TV Lied about Abortion," Vox, October 14, 2021, https:// www.vox.com/culture/22715333/tv-abortion-plot-storyline-lies.

32. As a woman who is child-free by choice, she is my hero in this regard.

33. Lindsay Pugh, "Television's Representation of Childfree Women Sucks," *Woman in Revolt* (blog), 2020, https://www.womaninrevolt.com/televisions-represen tation-of-childfree-women-sucks/; Diana T. Meyers, "Gendered Work and Individual Autonomy," in *Recognition, Responsibility, and Rights: Feminist Ethics and Social Theory*, ed. Robin N. Foire and Hilde Lindemann Nelson (Lanham, MD: Rowman and Littlefield, 2003), 31.

34. Delaney Broderick, "Interpreting Womanhood through *Sex and the City*," in *Culture and the Sitcom: Student Essays*, vol. 1, Summer 2017, ed. Mary M. Dalton (Winston-Salem, NC: Library Partners Press, 2017), https://librarypartnerspress.pressbooks.pub/stu dentessaysculturesitcomv1/chapter/interpreting-womanhood-through-sex-and-the-city/.

35. Laura Tropp, "'Faking a Sonogram': Representations of Motherhood on *Sex and the City*," *Journal of Popular Culture* 39 (2006): 864, https://doi.org/10.1111/j.1540 -5931.2006.00309.x.

36. Tropp, "'Faking a Sonogram,'" 864.

37. Wendy A. Burns-Ardolino, *TV Female Foursomes and Their Fans* (Jefferson, NC: McFarland, 2016), 150.

38. Tropp, "'Faking a Sonogram,'" 862–63.

39. Tropp, "'Faking a Sonogram,'" 866.

40. Tropp, "'Faking a Sonogram,'" 869.

41. Kim Akass, "Throwing the Baby Out with the Bath Water: Miranda and the Myth of Maternal Instinct on *Sex and the City*," *Feminist Television Studies: The Case of HBO* 3, no. 1 (Fall 2004), http://sfonline.barnard.edu/hbo/printkak.htm.

42. Tropp, "'Faking a Sonogram,'" 874.

43. Cameron Michael Tufino, "*Sex and the City*: A Promotion of Modern American Feminism" (master's thesis, University of the Incarnate Word, 2012), 55, http://athenaeum .uiw.edu/uiw_etds/292.

44. Akass, "Throwing the Baby Out."

45. Akass, "Throwing the Baby Out."

13. BUILDING BRANDS AND EXPECTATIONS

1. Alex Hayes, "Sarah Jessica Parker: Product Placement Never Happened on *Sex and the City*," Mumbrella, June 16, 2014, https://mumbrella.com.au/sarah -jessica-parker-product-placement-never-happened-sex-city-2-232861.

2. Michelle Nichols, "*Sex and the City* Film a Marketing Dream," Reuters, May 15, 2008, https://www.reuters.com/article/us-sexandthecity/sex-and-the-city-film-a-marketing -dream-idUSN1530121420080515.

3. Nichols, "*Sex and the City*."

4. Nichols, "*Sex and the City*."

5. Hayes, "Sarah Jessica Parker."

6. For those interested in the history of the cosmo, see Simon Difford, "Cosmopolitan Cocktail," Difford's Guide, accessed May 1, 2022, https://www.diffordsguide.com /encyclopedia/462/cocktails/cosmopolitan-cocktail; Priya Krishna, "The Definitive History of the Cosmopolitan," Punch, September 11, 2019, https://punchdrink.com/arti cles/definitive-history-cosmopolitan-cosmo-vodka-cranberry-cocktail/; Cait Munro, "The Birth, Death and Inevitable Comeback of the Cosmo, *SATC*'s Greatest Icon," Refinery29, June 6, 2018, https://www.refinery29.com/en-us/2018/06/200515/sex-and-the-city-cosmo politan-drink-popularity; and Adam Teeter, "The History of the Cosmopolitan and the Birth of Craft Cocktail Culture," Vinepair, December 28, 2014, https://vinepair.com/wine -blog/history-cosmopolitan-birth-craft-cocktail-culture/, from whose websites the information for this section is taken unless otherwise noted.

7. Krishna, "Definitive History."

8. Krishna, "Definitive History."

9. Teeter, "History of the Cosmopolitan."

10. Quoted in Female.com.au, "*Sex and the City*'s Cosmopolitan Cocktail," accessed May 1, 2022, https://www.female.com.au/cosmopolitan-cocktail.htm.

11. Quoted in Krishna, "Definitive History of the Cosmopolitan."

12. Jennifer Keishin Armstrong, "How *Sex and the City* Holds Up in the #MeToo Era," *Vanity Fair*, June 6, 2018, https://www.vanityfair.com/style/2018/06/sex -and-the-city-me-too.

13. Chelsea Fairless and Lauren Garroni, *We Should All Be Mirandas: Life Lessons from "Sex and the City's" Most Underrated Character* (New York: Houghton Mifflin Harcourt, 2019), 186.

14. Teeter, "History of the Cosmopolitan."

15. NewsCenterMaine.com, "'I Lost My Choo!': 20 Years of Jimmy Choo in Pop Culture," July 25, 2017, https://www.newscentermaine.com/article/news/nation-now/i -lost-my-choo-20-years-of-jimmy-choo-in-pop-culture/465-959742d0-be2d-4ffe-ae84 -aacfc9fb58df.

16. Quoted in Dana Schuster, "26 Ways *Sex and the City* Left Its Mark," *New York Post*, May 27, 2018, https://nypost.com/2018/05/27/26-ways-sex-and-the-city-left-its-mark/.

17. Quoted in Helen Coster, "The Sex (and the City) Economy," *Forbes*, May 22, 2008, https://www.forbes.com/2008/05/22/twx-hbo-movies-biz-media-cz_hc_0522sexinc .html?sh=664824985c81.

18. Amy Sohn, *"Sex and the City": Kiss and Tell* (New York: Pocket Books, 2002), 158–59.

19. Johnell Gipson, "Sarah Jessica Parker Owns 'Well over 100 Pairs' of Manolo Blahnik Shoes," Showbiz CheatSheet, January 12, 2021, https://www.cheatsheet.com /entertainment/sarah-jessica-parker-owns-well-over-100-pairs-of-manolo-blahnik-shoes .html/.

20. Sohn, *"Sex and the City,"* 158.

21. Jack Houston and Irene Anna Kim, "Why Hermès Birkin Bags Are So Expensive, According to a Handbag Expert," *Insider*, June 30, 2021, https://www.businessinsider .com/hermes-birkin-bag-realreal-handbag-expert-so-expensive-2019-6.

22. Sarah Burke, "Uncovering the Cultural History of the Nameplate Necklace," Vice, May 23, 2018, https://www.vice.com/en/article/3k4dmn/uncovering -a-cultural-history-of-the-nameplate-necklace.

23. Quoted in Burke, "Uncovering the Cultural History."

24. Piper Weiss, "Carrie Bradshaw's Back in Bloom with Her Signature Flower," *New York Daily News*, May 5, 2008, https://www.nydailynews.com/life-style/carrie -bradshaw-back-bloom-signature-flower-article-1.329525.

25. Faran Krentcil, "Carrie Bradshaw Flowers Hit a Major Milan Runway," *Elle*, September 24, 2017, https://www.elle.com/fashion/a12459019/carrie-bradshaw-flower -shop/. Camellias were sewn onto Chanel blouses as far back as 1922, so even this is not a new idea. See Danièle Bott, *Chanel: Collections and Creations* (London: Thames and Hudson, 2007), 63.

26. Quoted in Sohn, *"Sex and the City,"* 159.

27. Kristen Pyszczyk, "Purses of *Sex and the City*: Where Are They Now?" *Purse Blog* (blog), February 26, 2019, https://www.purseblog.com/the-many-bags /purses-of-sex-and-the-city-where-are-they-now/.

28. Marion Fasel, "The Most Memorable Jewels on *Sex and the City*," Aventurine, accessed May 1, 2022, https://theadventurine.com/culture/movies-tv/the-most-memora- ble-jewels-on-sex-and-the-city/. A rhinestone imitation was one of the many *Sex and the City*–branded items available at the Warner Brothers Studio gift shop in Los Angeles to tourists after taking the studio tour in 2011. Yes, I bought one, along with a pink *Sex and the City* tank top.

29. Fasel, "Most Memorable Jewels."

30. Julie Wiener, "Magnolia Cupcakes Banished from *Sex and the City* Tour," *Vanity Fair*, May 26, 2010, https://www.vanityfair.com/culture/2010/05/magnolia-cupcakes -banished-from-sex-and-the-city-tour.

31. Jessica Tyler, "A Cupcake Shop That Sparked a Nationwide Craze with Its Appearance on *Sex and the City* Is Gearing Up to Take over America," *Business Insider*, May 11, 2018, https://www.businessinsider.com/sex-and-the-city-cupcake-shop -magnolia-bakery-expands-2018-5.

32. Nichols, *"Sex and the City."*

33. Schuster, "26 Ways."

34. Schuster, "26 Ways."

35. Sohn, *"Sex and the City,"* 158–59; Schuster, "26 Ways."

36. Quoted in Schuster, "26 Ways."

37. Schuster, "26 Ways."

38. Giles Turner, "Embarrassing Plot Twist for Peloton," CBS News, December 10, 2021, https://www.cbsnews.com/news/peloton-stock-death-by-peloton-just-like-that -mr-big/. For additional information on the Peloton fallout, see David Griner, "Ryan Reynolds Just Made an Official Peloton Ad about Its Big *And Just Like That* Moment," *AdWeek*, December 12, 2021, https://www.adweek.com/convergent-tv/ryan-reynolds-just -made-an-official-peloton-ad-about-its-big-and-just-like-that-moment; Amber Picchi, "Pe- loton Stock Slumps after Morbid Product Placement in *Sex and the City*," CBS News, December 10, 2021, https://www.cbsnews.com/news/peloton-stock-death-by-peloton -just-like-that-mr-big/; and Lauren Thomas and Sarah Whitten, "Peloton Removes Viral Chris Noth Ad after Sexual Assault Allegations against Him Surface," CNBC, December 16, 2021, https://www.cnbc.com/2021/12/16/peloton-removes-viral-chris-noth-ad-after-sexual -assault-allegations.html.

39. Turner, "Embarrassing Plot Twist."

40. Matt Hansen, "Peloton Just Had the Worst Product Placement Imaginable in the New *Sex and the City* Show," *Cycling Magazine*, December 10, 2021, https://cyclingmag azine.ca/sections/news/peloton-just-had-the-worst-product-placement-imaginable-in-the -new-sex-in-the-city-show/.

41. Clemence Dumoulin, "The Impact of the TV Show *Sex and the City* on the Audience," Circular, April 17, 2017, https://thecircular.org/impact-tv-show-sex-city-audience/.

42. Antonio Marazza and Stefania Saviolo, *Lifestyle Brands: A Guide to Aspirational Marketing* (Houndsmill, UK: Palgrave Macmillan, 2012).

43. Dumoulin, "Impact of the TV Show."

44. Bonnie Fuller, "What the Creators of *Sex and the City* Know about Marketing That You Don't," *AdAge*, June 9, 2008, https://adage.com/article/madisonvine-case-study/creators-sex-city-marketing/127610.

45. Hindman Network, "The Original Influencer: How Coco Chanel Forever Changed Women's Fashion," May 8, 2020, https://hindmanauctions.com/blog/chanel-costume-jewelry; IZEA, "The History of Influencer Marketing," accessed May 1, 2022, https://izea.com/history-influencer-marketing/.

46. David Schwab, "Why Lifestyle Influencers Are the Next 'It' Endorser," *Forbes*, May 11, 2016, https://www.forbes.com/sites/davidschwab/2016/05/11/why-lifestyle-influencers-are-the-next-it-endorser/?sh=5204a50c524f.

47. Certiorli, "Carrie Bradshaw, the First Prototype of Fashion Influencer," *Certiorli* (blog), May 6, 2020, https://certiorli.wordpress.com/2020/05/06/carrie-bradshaw-the-first-prototype-of-fashion-influencer/.

48. Certiorli, "Carrie Bradshaw."

49. Certiorli, "Carrie Bradshaw."

50. Schwab, "Why Lifestyle Influencers."

51. Certiorli, "Carrie Bradshaw."

52. Naomi Wolf, "Carrie Bradshaw: Icons of the Decade," *Guardian*, December 21, 2009, https://www.theguardian.com/world/2009/dec/22/carrie-bradshaw-icons-of-decade.

53. Hunter Harris, "For Women of Color Who Love *Sex and the City*," Refinery 29, June 6, 2018, https://www.refinery29.com/en-us/2016/07/117151/sex-and-the-city-racism.

54. Jill Di Donato, "Was Carrie Bradshaw the Original Influencer?" Huffington Post, December 7, 2021, https://www.huffpost.com/entry/carrie-bradshaw-original-influencer_l_61a51432e4b07fe2011cbab6.

55. Naomi Wolf, *The Beauty Myth: How Images of Beauty Are Used against Women* (New York: HarperCollins, 2009), 27.

56. Beatriz Oria, *Talking Dirty on "Sex and the City": Romance, Intimacy, Friendship* (New York: Rowman and Littlefield, 2014), 133.

57. Sarah Niblock, "'My Manolos, My Self': Manolo Blahnik, Shoes and Desire," in *Reading "Sex and the City,"* ed. Kim Akass and Janet McCabe (London: I. B. Tauris, 2006), 144.

58. Wendy A. Burns-Ardolino, *TV Female Foursomes and Their Fans* (Jefferson, NC: McFarland, 2016), 28.

59. Glenn Garner, "*SATC*'s Candace Bushnell Reveals Her Columnist Salary—Maybe Carrie's Lifestyle Wasn't Unrealistic!" *People*, February 17, 2020, https://people.com/tv/candace-bushnell-reveals-salary-vogue-columnist-90s/.

60. Sara Nachlis, "What Would It Cost to Live Like Carrie Bradshaw in 2018?" Girlboss, June 6, 2018, https://www.girlboss.com/read/carrie-bradshaw-expenses.

61. The Freelance Creative, "Rates Database," accessed May 1, 2022, https://contently.net/rates-database/rates/.

62. Andrea Francese, "*Sex and the City*: Candace Bushnell May Have Just Revealed That Carrie Bradshaw Could Afford Her Lifestyle," Showbiz CheatSheet, February 16, 2022, https://www.cheatsheet.com/entertainment/sex-and-the-city-candace-bushnell-may-have-just-revealed-that-carrie-bradshaw-could-afford-her-lifestyle.html/.

63. Andrea Francese, "*Sex and the City*: Which Characters Could Actually Afford Their Lifestyles?" Showbiz CheatSheet, November 14, 2019, https://www.cheatsheet.com/enter tainment/sex-and-the-city-which-characters-could-actually-afford-their-lifestyles.html/.

64. Francese, "*Sex and the City*: Which Characters?"

65. Carina Hsieh, "I Lived Like Carrie Bradshaw for a Week," *Cosmopolitan*, June 4, 2018, https://www.cosmopolitan.com/entertainment/tv/a20978854/carrie-bradshaw-sex -and-the-city-real-life/.

66. Hsieh, "I Lived Like Carrie."

67. Hsieh, "I Lived Like Carrie."

68. Krentcil, "Carrie Bradshaw Flowers"; Faran Krentcil, "How Much Did It Cost to Dress Carrie Bradshaw in *Sex and the City*?" *Elle*, May 29, 2018, https://www.elle.com /culture/movies-tv/a20829475/carrie-bradshaw-wardrobe-cost-sex-and-the-city.

69. Cameron Michael Tufino, "*Sex and the City*: A Promotion of Modern American Feminism," (master's thesis, University of the Incarnate Word, 2012), 31, http://athen aeum.uiw.edu/uiw_etds/292.

70. Bambi Haggins and Amanda D. Lotz, "Comedy Overview: At Home on the Cutting Edge," in *The Essential HBO Reader*, ed. Gary R. Edgerton and Jeffrey P. Jones, American Popular Culture, no. 15 (Lexington: University Press of Kentucky, 2008), 164, https://uknowledge.uky.edu/upk_american_popular_culture/15.

71. Ron Simon, "*Sex and the City*," in *The Essential HBO Reader*, ed. Gary R. Edgerton and Jeffrey P. Jones, American Popular Culture, no. 15 (Lexington: University Press of Kentucky, 2008), 194, https://uknowledge.uky.edu/upk_american_popular_culture/15.

72. Simon, "*Sex and the City*," 195.

73. Quoted in Coster, "Sex (and the City) Economy."

74. Gary R. Edgerton, introduction to *The Essential HBO Reader*, ed. Gary R. Edgerton and Jeffrey P. Jones, American Popular Culture, no. 15 (Lexington: University Press of Kentucky, 2008), 17, https://uknowledge.uky.edu/upk_american_popular_culture /15; Gary R. Edgerton and Jeffrey P. Jones, "HBO's Ongoing Legacy," in *The Essential HBO Reader*, ed. Gary R. Edgerton and Jeffrey P. Jones, American Popular Culture, no. 15 (Lexington: University Press of Kentucky, 2013), 323, https://uknowledge.uky.edu /upk_american_popular_culture/15.

75. Coster, "Sex (and the City) Economy."

76. Coster, "Sex (and the City) Economy."

77. Genevieve Ang, "Bitten Clothing Line," Love to Know, accessed May 16, 2022, https://womens-fashion.lovetoknow.com/Bitten_Clothing_Line.

78. Kim Bhasin, "Sarah Jessica Parker Is Building a Stiletto Empire," Bloomberg, October 4, 2018, https://www.bloomberg.com/news/articles/2018-10-04/sarah-jessica -parker-is-building-a-stiletto-empire.

79. Mehera Bonner, "Sarah Jessica Parker's Net Worth Is Massive Thanks to the *Sex and the City* Revival, *And Just Like That . . .*," *Cosmopolitan*, November 18, 2021, https:// www.cosmopolitan.com/entertainment/celebs/a35191075/sarah-jessica-parker-net-worth/.

80. Jessica Sager, "SJP Can Certainly Afford Fancy Shoes! How *Sex and the City* Star Sarah Jessica Parker Made Her Millions," *Parade*, December 9, 2021, https://parade .com/1150411/jessicasager/sarah-jessica-parker-net-worth/.

81. Invivo SJP, accessed May 1, 2022, https://shop.invivoxsjp.com/.

82. Kim Bhasin, "John Cena, Sarah Jessica Parker Get into the Cocktail Business," Bloomberg, May 2, 2022, https://www.bloomberg.com/news/articles/2022-05-02/thomas -ashbourne-cocktails-debut-with-sarah-jessica-parker-john-cena.

83. Bonner, "Sarah Jessica Parker's Net Worth."

84. Stella Bruzzi and Pamela Church Gibson, "'Fashion Is the Fifth Character': Fashion, Costume and Character in *Sex and the City*," in *Reading "Sex and the City,"* ed. Kim Akass and Janet McCabe (London: I. B. Tauris, 2006), 126.

85. Conspicuous Consumption, "What Is Conspicuous Consumption?" accessed May 1, 2022, https://conspicuousconsumption.org/#:~:text=Conspicuous%20consumption%20 is%20a%20term,real%20needs%20of%20the%20consumer.

86. T. H. Breen, *Tobacco Culture: The Mentality of the Great Tidewater Planters on the Eve of Revolution* (Princeton, NJ: Princeton University Press, 1985), 36.

87. Susan Zieger, "Sex and the Citizen in *Sex and the City*'s New York," in *Reading "Sex and the City,"* ed. Kim Akass and Janet McCabe (London: I. B. Tauris, 2006), 110.

88. Zieger, "Sex and the Citizen."

89. Chris Isidore, "Where the Current Economic Boom Ranks in American History," CNN, January 30, 2018, https://money.cnn.com/2018/01/30/news/economy/us-economy -boom-history/index.html.

90. Ronald Brownstein and Nina J. Easton, "The New Status Seekers: In the 1980s, People Have Been Forced to Find Ever More Creative Ways of Showing They've Arrived," *Los Angeles Times*, December 27, 1987, https://www.latimes.com/archives/la-xpm-1987 -12-27-tm-31245-story.html.

91. Delaney Broderick, "Interpreting Womanhood through *Sex and the City*," in *Culture and the Sitcom: Student Essays*, vol. 1, Summer 2017, ed. Mary M. Dalton (Winston-Salem, NC: Library Partners Press, 2017), https://librarypartnerspress.pressbooks.pub/stu dentessaysculturesitcomv1/chapter/interpreting-womanhood-through-sex-and-the-city/.

92. Oria, *Talking Dirty*, 109.

93. Broderick, "Interpreting Womanhood."

94. Sharon Marie Ross, "Comparison Shopping through Female Conversation in HBO's *Sex and the City*," in *The Sitcom Reader: America Viewed and Skewed*, ed. Mary M. Dalton and Laura R. Linder (Albany: State University of New York Press, 2005), 118.

95. Ross, "Comparison Shopping," 112, 118.

14. FASHION AND HOW WE VIEW OURSELVES

1. Kim Akass and Janet McCabe, introduction to *Reading "Sex and the City,"* ed. Kim Akass and Janet McCabe (London: I. B. Tauris, 2006), 10; Amy Sohn, *"Sex and the City": Kiss and Tell* (New York: Pocket Books, 2002), 67.

2. Chelsea Fairless and Lauren Garroni, Every Outfit, accessed May 1, 2022, https:// www.everyoutfitinc.com/; quoted in Chelsea Fairless and Lauren Garroni, *We Should All Be Mirandas: Life Lessons from "Sex and the City's" Most Underrated Character* (New York: Houghton Mifflin Harcourt, 2019), x,

3. Anna König, *"Sex and the City*: A Fashion Editor's Dream?" in *Reading "Sex and the City,"* ed. Kim Akass and Janet McCabe (London: I. B. Tauris, 2006), 130.

4. *Vogue*, "Sex and the City: Best Episodes, Fashion, Memes, and More," accessed May 1, 2022, https://www.vogue.com/tag/misc/sex-and-the-city.

5. König, *"Sex and the City."*

6. Quoted in Sohn, *"Sex and the City,"* 67.

7. Quoted in Sohn, *"Sex and the City,"* 67.

8. Quoted in Akass and McCabe, introduction, 10.

9. Stella Bruzzi and Pamela Church Gibson, "'Fashion Is the Fifth Character': Fashion, Costume and Character in *Sex and the City*," in *Reading "Sex and the City,"* ed. Kim Akass and Janet McCabe (London: I. B. Tauris, 2006), 115, 116.

10. Quoted in Sohn, *"Sex and the City,"* 67.

11. Dana Schuster, "26 Ways *Sex and the City* Left Its Mark," *New York Post*, May 27, 2018, https://nypost.com/2018/05/27/26-ways-sex-and-the-city-left-its-mark/.

12. Sohn, *"Sex and the City,"* 67.

13. Quoted in Sohn, *"Sex and the City,"* 68.

14. Patricia Field, *"SATC* Collection," Patricia Field Art Fashion, accessed May 1, 2022, https://patriciafield.com/collections/patricia-field-satc-collection.

15. Simone de Beauvoir, *The Second Sex*, trans. Constance Borde and Sheila Malovany-Chevallier (New York: Vintage, 2011), 572, 573.

16. Angela Carter, "Notes for a Theory of Sixties Style," in *Shaking a Leg: Collected Journalism and Writings*, ed. Jenny Uglow (London: Chatto and Windus, 1997), 105.

17. Eric W. Dolan, "Study Suggests Women Dress Modestly to Defend Themselves against Aggression from Other Women," PsyPost, January 5, 2020, https://www.psypost .org/2020/01/study-suggests-women-dress-modestly-to-defend-themselves-against-ag gression-from-other-women-55157.

18. Adam D. Pazda, Pavol Prokop, and Andrew J. Elliot, "Red and Romantic Rivalry: Viewing Another Woman in Red Increases Perceptions of Sexual Receptivity, Derogation, and Intentions to Mate-Guard," *Personality and Social Psychology Bulletin* 40, no. 10 (October 2014): 1260–69, https://doi.org/10.1177/0146167214539709; Jenny Kutner, "Women in Red Are Sexy—And They Make Other Women Jealous," Salon, July 11, 2014, https://www.salon.com/2014/07/11/women_in_red_are_sexy_and_they_make_other _women_jealous/.

19. Bruzzi and Gibson, "'Fashion Is the Fifth Character,'" 116.

20. PT Staff, "The Value of Style," *Psychology Today*, July 1, 2005, https://www .psychologytoday.com/us/articles/200507/the-value-style.

21. Quoted in Sohn, *"Sex and the City,"* 78–79.

22. Quoted in Sohn, *"Sex and the City,"* 78–79.

23. Jonah Engel Bromwich, "Cynthia Nixon Confronts Miranda on the Campaign Trail," *New York Times*, July 19, 2018, https://www.nytimes.com/2018/07/19/style/cynthia -nixon-governor-sex-and-the-city-instagram.html.

24. Quoted in Sohn, *"Sex and the City,"* 78.

25. Andrea Francese, *"Sex and the City* Costume Designer, Patricia Field, Explains Why Miranda Was the Worst Dressed," Showbiz CheatSheet, October 4, 2020, https:// www.cheatsheet.com/entertainment/sex-and-the-city-costume-designer-patricia-field -explains-why-miranda-was-the-worst-dressed.html/.

26. Jonah Waterhouse, "Controversial Opinion: Miranda Had the Best Style on *Sex and the City*," *Elle Australia*, January 27, 2020.

27. Jessica Davis, "How to Make Your Look a Little More Miranda Hobbes," *Harper's Bazaar*, January 28, 2021, https://www.harpersbazaar.com/uk/fashion/what-to -wear/g21079575/how-to-dress-like-miranda-sex-and-the-city/#:~:text=Although%20 Miranda%20was%20never%20considered,way%20ahead%20of%20its%20time.

28. Jessica Davis, "How to Keep Your Wardrobe as Classic and Preppy as Charlotte York's," *Harper's Bazaar*, February 2, 2021, https://www.harpersbazaar.com/uk/fashion /what-to-wear/g21070531/how-to-dress-like-charlotte-sex-and-the-city/.

29. Davis, "How to Keep Your Wardrobe."

30. Bruzzi and Gibson, "'Fashion Is the Fifth Character,'" 116.

31. Quoted in Sohn, *"Sex and the City,"* 76.

32. Penny Goldstone, "Why Charlotte Was the Real *Sex and the City* Style Queen," *Marie Claire UK*, March 30, 2017, https://www.marieclaire.co.uk/fashion/charlotte-sex-and-the-city-best-outfits-488094.

33. Quoted in Sohn, *"Sex and the City,"* 74.

34. Quoted in Sohn, *"Sex and the City,"* 74.

35. Quoted in Cameron Michael Tufino, *"Sex and the City*: A Promotion of Modern American Feminism" (master's thesis, University of the Incarnate Word, 2012), 64–65, http://athenaeum.uiw.edu/uiw_etds/292.

36. Charles Manning, "Can We Finally Admit the Outfits on *Sex and the City* Were a Big Hot Mess?" Daily Front Row, June 7, 2018, https://fashionweekdaily.com/sex-and-the-city-bad-outfits/.

37. Quoted in Sohn, *"Sex and the City,"* 70.

38. Sohn, *"Sex and the City,"* 68–69.

39. Amelia Langas, "Carrie Bradshaw's Best and Worst Outfits," *People*, accessed May 1, 2022, https://people.com/webstory/carrie-bradshaws-best-and-worst-outfits/.

40. Emily Alford, "Carrie's 'Bad' Outfits on *Sex and the City* Were the Series at Its Best," *Jezebel*, September 8, 2021, https://jezebel.com/carries-bad-outfits-on-sex-and-the-city-were-the-series-1847434654.

41. Interestingly, this is not the first time Carrie thinks she loses it. In episode 6.3, "The Perfect Present," Big mentions that Carrie once thought she lost it in one of the jets of the hot tub at the Four Seasons. This correlates perfectly with the idea of her losing her identity every time she is around Big, as well.

15. NEW YORK CITY

1. Dana Schuster, "26 Ways *Sex and the City* Left Its Mark," *New York Post*, May 27, 2018, https://nypost.com/2018/05/27/26-ways-sex-and-the-city-left-its-mark/; quoted in Ron Simon, *"Sex and the City,"* in *The Essential HBO Reader*, ed. Gary R. Edgerton and Jeffrey P. Jones, American Popular Culture, no. 15 (Lexington: University Press of Kentucky, 2008), 196, https://uknowledge.uky.edu/upk_american_popular_culture/15.

2. Simon, *"Sex and the City,"* 149.

3. Simon, *"Sex and the City,"* 197.

4. Joanna Di Mattia, "'What's the Harm in Believing?': Mr. Big, Mr. Perfect, and the Romantic Quest for *Sex and the City*'s Mr. Right," in *Reading "Sex and the City,"* ed. Kim Akass and Janet McCabe (London: I. B. Tauris, 2006), 22.

5. Quoted in Marissa Blanchard, "Darren Star Reflects Back on *Sex and the City*," HBO, accessed May 23, 2022, https://www.hbo.com/sex-and-the-city/anniversary-darren-star-interview.

6. Blanchard, "Darren Star."

7. Quoted in Blanchard, "Darren Star."

8. Beatriz Oria, *Talking Dirty on "Sex and the City": Romance, Intimacy, Friendship* (New York: Rowman and Littlefield, 2014), 115.

9. Quoted in Amy Sohn, *"Sex and the City": Kiss and Tell* (New York: Pocket Books, 2002), 146–47.

10. Quoted in Sohn, *"Sex and the City,"* 39.

11. Quoted in Sohn, *"Sex and the City,"* 39.

12. Oria, *Talking Dirty*, 148.

13. Sohn, *"Sex and the City,"* 19.

14. Wendy A. Burns-Ardolino, *TV Female Foursomes and Their Fans* (Jefferson, NC: McFarland, 2016), 119.

15. Simon, *"Sex and the City,"* 197.

16. Quoted in Sohn, *"Sex and the City,"* 147.

17. Quoted in Sohn, *"Sex and the City,"* 146–47.

18. Quoted in Blanchard, "Darren Star."

19. Sohn, *"Sex and the City,"* 146–47.

20. Oria, *Talking Dirty*, 156.

21. Kate Erbland, "15 Fabulous Facts about *Sex and the City*," *Mental Floss*, June 6, 2018, https://www.mentalfloss.com/article/64729/15-fabulous-facts-about-sex-and-city; Oria, *Talking Dirty*, 156.

22. Oria, *Talking Dirty*, 156–57.

23. Sohn, *"Sex and the City,"* 146.

24. Helen Coster, "The Sex (And the City) Economy," *Forbes*, May 22, 2008, https://www.forbes.com/2008/05/22/twx-hbo-movies-biz-media-cz_hc_0522sexinc.html?sh=664824985c81.

25. Zieger, 99.

26. Disclaimer: These were up and running at the time this book was written, but tours change, close, and open regularly, so please do your research before traveling.

27. Free Tours by Foot, *"Sex and the City* Tour Sights," November 27, 2021, https://freetoursbyfoot.com/sex-and-the-city-tour/.

28. Viator, *"Sex and the City* Night Out," accessed May 1, 2022, https://www.viator.com/tours/New-York-City/Sex-and-the-City-Night-Out/d687-6390P4.

29. Sarah Jessica Parker, *"SATC* NYC Tour," SJP by Sarah Jessica Parker, https://sjpbysarahjessicaparker.com/pages/satc-nyc-tour

30. On Location Tours, "Sex and the City Hotspots," accessed, May 1, 2022, https://onlocationtours.com/new-york-tv-and-movie-tours/sex-and-the-city-hotspots-tour/?gclid=Cj0KCQiA5aWOBhDMARIsAIXLlkffjnOp6224yqajVELXiZfeY-cL3d2pE3cJxkU6LNsvIvPKgF0nCr0aAoj8EALw_wcB.

31. Heather Cross, "A *Sex and the City* Tour through New York City," TripSavvy, June 6, 2019, tripsavvy.com/nyc-sex-and-the-city-tour-1613352.

16. AN ENDURING FRANCHISE

1. Beatriz Oria, *Talking Dirty on "Sex and the City": Romance, Intimacy, Friendship* (New York: Rowman and Littlefield, 2014), 1–2.

2. Associated Press, *"Sex and the City"* at 40 and Even (Gasp) 50," Today, May 6, 2008, https://www.today.com/popculture/sex-city-40-even-gasp-50-wbna24489675.

3. Helen Coster, "The Sex (and the City) Economy," *Forbes*, May 22, 2008, https://www.forbes.com/2008/05/22/twx-hbo-movies-biz-media-cz_hc_0522sexinc.html?sh=664824985c81.

4. Oria, *Talking Dirty*, 203.

5. Saim Cheeda, *"And Just Like That*: 5 Reasons Fans Are Excited for the *Sex and the City* Reboot (& 5 They're Worried)," Screenrant, January 22, 2021, https://screenrant.com/satc-and-just-like-that-excited-worried-revival/.

6. Oria, *Talking Dirty*, 203.

7. Oria, *Talking Dirty*, 202–3.

8. Rotten Tomatoes, "Sex and the City 2," accessed May 2, 2022, https://www.rotten tomatoes.com/m/sex_and_the_city_2.

9. Roger Ebert, "Sex, about the Same. City, Abu Dhabi," May 25, 2010, https://www.rogerebert.com/reviews/sex-and-the-city-2-2010.

10. Cheeda, *"And Just Like That."*

11. Andrea Francese, *"The Carrie Diaries* Got Everything Wrong about Carrie Bradshaw's Upbringing," Showbiz CheatSheet, January 6, 2021, https://www.cheatsheet .com/entertainment/the-carrie-diaries-got-everything-wrong-about-carrie-bradshaws-up bringing.html/.

12. Matt Zoller Seitz, "Seitz on *The Carrie Diaries*: Everything about This *Sex and the City* Prequel Feels Wrong," Vulture, January 14, 2013, https://www.vulture.com/2013/01 /tv-review-the-carrie-diaries.html.

13. Cassie Da Costa, "When *Sex and the City* Returns, Will It Finally Get Queer People Right?" *Vanity Fair*, January 13, 2021, https://www.vanityfair.com/hollywood/2021/01 /when-sex-and-the-city-returns-will-it-finally-get-queer-people-right.

14. Cheeda, *"And Just Like That."*

15. Princess Weekes, "It's So Frustrating That a *Sex and the City* Revival Is Really Happening," Mary Sue, January 11, 2021, https://www.themarysue.com/hbo -max-sex-and-the-city-revival-officially-frustrating/.

16. Quoted in Joyann Jeffery, "Kim Cattrall Talks Publicly about the *Sex and the City* Reboot for First Time Ever," Today, May 4, 2022, https://www.today.com/popculture /tv/kim-cattrall-sex-and-the-city-reboot-samantha-jones-rcna27319?fbclid=IwAR0zHsPz W67d_qsbJRhV-Nx4KOGldYoU3rWxS-5f_pRLFEPyJ1FNwWdn-jo.

17. Quoted in Jeffery, "Kim Cattrall."

18. Quoted in Jeffery, "Kim Cattrall."

19. Ryan Gajewski, "Sara Ramirez Responds to Criticism of *And Just Like That* Character: 'I Don't Recognize Myself in Che,'" *Hollywood Reporter*, February 2, 2022, https://www.hollywoodreporter.com/tv/tv-news/sara-ramirez-and-just-like-that-che -diaz-1235086293/.

20. Cheeda, *"And Just Like That."*

21. Alan Sepinwall, *"And Just Like That . . .* Is Missing the Funk and the Spunk," *Rolling Stone*, December 9, 2021, https://www.rollingstone.com/tv/tv-reviews/and-just -like-that-review-1269034/.

22. Joey Nolfi, "Sarah Jessica Parker on Why We Didn't See Carrie Call 911 after Big's Heart Attack," *Entertainment Weekly*, February 16, 2022, https://ew.com/tv /sarah-jessica-parker-why-carrie-didnt-call-911-after-mr-big-heart-attack/.

23. In case you are wondering why I am qualified to give PR advice, I have twenty years of experience in PR and marketing as my day job and am certified by the International Association of Business Communicators (IABC).

24. Cheeda, *"And Just Like That."*

25. Lucy Mangan, *"And Just Like That* Review: *Sex and the City* Sequel Has a Mouthful of Teething Troubles," *Guardian*, December 9, 2021, https://www.the guardian.com/tv-and-radio/2021/dec/09/and-just-like-that-review-sex-and-the-city -reboot-has-a-mouthful-of-teething-troubles.

26. Quoted in Julia Emmanuele, "Cynthia Nixon and More *And Just Like That* Stars Respond to Meghan McCain's Criticism of Show," *Us Weekly*, February 21, 2022,

https://www.usmagazine.com/entertainment/news/and-just-like-that-cast-responds-to
-meghan-mccains-criticism/.

27. Alex Abad-Santos, "Main Character Syndrome, Explained by Carrie Bradshaw,"
Vox, December 9, 2021, https://www.vox.com/2021/12/9/22825492/carrie-bradshaw-satc
-main-character-syndrome.

28. Jen Chaney, "*And Just Like That* . . . Is Sexless in the City," Vulture, December 9,
2021, https://www.vulture.com/article/and-just-like-that-review-sexless-in-the-city.html.

29. Sepinwall, "*And Just Like That.*"

30. Inkoo Kang, "*And Just Like That* . . . Is *Sex and the City* for 2021: A Bloated,
Laugh-Free Comedy about Grief," *Washington Post*, December 9, 2021, https://www
.washingtonpost.com/tv/2021/12/09/and-just-like-that-review/.

31. Sepinwall, "*And Just Like That.*"

32. Emmanuele, "Cynthia Nixon and More."

33. Katherine Stinson, "Critics Are Just as Divided as Fans on *And Just Like That*,"
Distractify, December 27, 2021, https://www.distractify.com/p/and-just-like-that-ratings.

CONCLUSION

1. Kasandra Brabaw, "How LGBTQ+ People Really Feel about *Sex and the
City*," Refinery29, June 4, 2018, https://www.refinery29.com/en-us/2018/06/200625
/sex-and-the-city-gay-characters-lgbt-response.

2. Ellen E. Jones, "'That Show Was as White as It Gets!' *Sex and the City*'s Problematic
Legacy," *Guardian*, April 28, 2018, https://www.theguardian.com/tv-and-radio/2018/apr
/21/that-show-was-as-white-as-it-gets-sex-and-the-citys-problematic-legacy.

3. Kayleigh Dray, "*Sex and the City*: What Happened When I Rewatched
Every Episode of *SATC*," Stylist, January 15, 2021, https://www.stylist.co.uk/life/sex
-and-the-city-tv-film-carrie-bradshaw-feminism-sexism/210642.

4. Shon Faye, "*Sex and the City* Is Embarrassing Now, but It Was Everything
Then," Dazed, June 6, 2018, https://www.dazeddigital.com/film-tv/article/40272/1/sex
-and-the-city-20th-anniversary.

5. Jennifer Keishin Armstrong, "How *Sex and the City* Holds Up in the #MeToo
Era," *Vanity Fair*, June 6, 2018, https://www.vanityfair.com/style/2018/06/sex-and-the
-city-me-too.

6. Jess Glass, "*Sex and the City*'s Sarah Jessica Parker Admits That the Show
Failed to Represent LGBT People," PinkNews, May 14, 2018, https://www.pinknews
.co.uk/2018/05/14/sex-and-the-city-sarah-jessica-parker-lgbt-entertainment/.

7. Dray, "*Sex and the City.*"

8. Meghan McKenna, "How Does *Sex and the City* Hold Up 20 Years after Its
Debut?" *Fashion Magazine*, June 6, 2018, https://fashionmagazine.com/culture/woke
-charlotte-sex-city/.

BIBLIOGRAPHY

Abad-Santos, Alex. "Main Character Syndrome, Explained by Carrie Bradshaw." Vox. December 9, 2021. https://www.vox.com/2021/12/9/22825492/carrie-bradshaw-satc -main-character-syndrome.

Akass, Kim. "Throwing the Baby Out with the Bath Water: Miranda and the Myth of Maternal Instinct on *Sex and the City*." *Feminist Television Studies: The Case of HBO* 3, no. 1 (Fall 2004). http://sfonline.barnard.edu/hbo/printkak.htm.

Akass, Kim, and Janet McCabe. Introduction to *Reading "Sex and the City."* Edited by Kim Akass and Janet McCabe. London: I. B. Tauris, 2006.

———. "What Has HBO Ever Done for Women?" In *The Essential HBO Reader.* Edited by Gary R. Edgerton and Jeffrey P. Jones. American Popular Culture, no. 15. Lexington: University Press of Kentucky, 2008. https://uknowledge.uky.edu /upk_american_popular_culture/15.

Alexander, Ella. "*Sex and the City*: What It Got Right vs. What It Really Didn't." *Harper's Bazaar*, January 12, 2021. https://www.harpersbazaar.com/uk/culture/a21093577 /sex-and-the-city-what-it-got-right-vs-what-it-really-didnt/.

Alford, Emily. "Carrie's 'Bad' Outfits on *Sex and the City* Were the Series at Its Best." *Jezebel*, September 8, 2021. https://jezebel.com/carries-bad-outfits-on-sex -and-the-city-were-the-series-1847434654.

American Bar Association. "First Year and Total J.D. Enrollment by Gender: 1947–2011." Accessed April 28, 2022. https://www.americanbar.org/content/dam/aba/administra tive/legal_education_and_admissions_to_the_bar/statistics/jd_enrollment_1yr_total _gender.authcheckdam.pdf.

Anderson, Leigh. "The Rules, 20 Years Later." Vox. April 8, 2015. https://www.vox. com/2015/4/8/8353915/rules-dating-advice.

Ang, Genevieve. "Bitten Clothing Line." Love to Know. Accessed May 16, 2022. https:// womens-fashion.lovetoknow.com/Bitten_Clothing_Line.

Armstrong, Jennifer Keishin. "How *Sex and the City* Holds Up in the #MeToo Era." *Vanity Fair*, June 6, 2018. https://www.vanityfair.com/style/2018/06/sex-and-the -city-me-too.

Associated Press. "*Sex and the City* at 40 and Even (Gasp) 50." Today. May 6, 2008. https://www.today.com/popculture/sex-city-40-even-gasp-50-wbna24489675.

Bacle, Ariana. "How *Sex and the City* Recast the World in a Pink Light." HBO. Accessed April 30, 2022. https://www.hbo.com/sex-and-the-city/anniversary-michael-patrick -king-interview.

Bakar, Faima. "If You're an Unmarried Woman over the Age of 26, You're Not a Spinster, You're a Thornback." Metro UK. March 14, 2019. https://metro.co.uk/2019/03/14/if -youre-an-unmarried-woman-over-the-age-of-26-youre-not-a-spinster-youre-a -thornback-8902030/#:~:text=The%20word%20spinster%20was%20used,single %2C%20never%2Dmarried%20woman.

Barber-Plentie, Grace. "The Conflict of Loving *Sex and the City* When You're Not a Straight White Woman." Vice. June 7, 2018. https://i-d.vice.com/en_uk/article/7xm78g/the -conflict-of-loving-sex-and-the-city-when-youre-not-a-straight-white-woman.

Beauvoir, Simone de. *The Second Sex*. Translated by Constance Borde and Sheila Malovany-Chevallier. New York: Vintage, 2011.

Bechdel Test Movie List. Accessed April 30, 2022. https://bechdeltest.com.

Bhasin, Kim. "John Cena, Sarah Jessica Parker Get into the Cocktail Business." Bloomberg. May 2, 2022. https://www.bloomberg.com/news/articles/2022-05-02 /thomas-ashbourne-cocktails-debut-with-sarah-jessica-parker-john-cena.

———. "Sarah Jessica Parker Is Building a Stiletto Empire." Bloomberg. October 4, 2018. https://www.bloomberg.com/news/articles/2018-10-04/sarah-jessica-parker-is -building-a-stiletto-empire.

Blanchard, Marissa. "Darren Star Reflects Back on *Sex and the City*." HBO. Accessed May 23, 2022. https://www.hbo.com/sex-and-the-city/anniversary-darren-star-interview.

———. "Sarah Jessica Parker Gets Candid about Carrie." HBO. Accessed April 27, 2022. https://www.hbo.com/sex-and-the-city/anniversary-sarah-jessica-parker-interview.

Bonner, Mehera. "Sarah Jessica Parker's Net Worth Is Massive Thanks to the *Sex and the City* Revival, *And Just Like That . . .*" *Cosmopolitan*, November 18, 2021. https://www .cosmopolitan.com/entertainment/celebs/a35191075/sarah-jessica-parker-net-worth/.

Bott, Danièle. *Chanel: Collections and Creations*. London: Thames and Hudson, 2007.

Brabaw, Kasandra. "How LGBTQ+ People Really Feel about *Sex and the City*." Refinery29. June 4, 2018. https://www.refinery29.com/en-us/2018/06/200625/sex-and -the-city-gay-characters-lgbt-response.

Breen, T. H. *Tobacco Culture: The Mentality of the Great Tidewater Planters on the Eve of Revolution*. Princeton, NJ: Princeton University Press, 1985.

Broderick, Delaney. "Interpreting Womanhood through *Sex and the City*." In *Culture and the Sitcom: Student Essays*, vol. 1, Summer 2017. Edited by Mary M. Dalton. Winston-Salem, NC: Library Partners Press, 2017. https://librarypartnerspress.press books.pub/studentessaysculturesitcomv1/chapter/interpreting-womanhood-through -sex-and-the-city/.

Bromwich, Jonah Engel. "Cynthia Nixon Confronts Miranda on the Campaign Trail." *New York Times*, July 19, 2018. https://www.nytimes.com/2018/07/19/style/cynthia-nixon -governor-sex-and-the-city-instagram.html.

Brownstein, Ronald, and Nina J. Easton. "The New Status Seekers: In the 1980s, People Have Been Forced to Find Ever More Creative Ways of Showing They've Arrived." *Los Angeles Times*, December 27, 1987. https://www.latimes.com/archives/la-xpm -1987-12-27-tm-31245-story.html.

Brunell, Laura, and the Editors of *Encyclopaedia Brittanica*. "The Third Wave of Feminism." Brittanica.com. https://www.britannica.com/topic/feminism/The-third -wave-of-feminism.

Bruzzi, Stella, and Pamela Church Gibson. "'Fashion Is the Fifth Character': Fashion, Costume and Character in *Sex and the City*." In *Reading "Sex and the City."* Edited by Kim Akass and Janet McCabe. London: I. B. Tauris, 2006.

Burke, Sarah. "Uncovering the Cultural History of the Nameplate Necklace." Vice. May 23, 2018. https://www.vice.com/en/article/3k4dmn/uncovering-a-cultural-history-of -the-nameplate-necklace.

Burns-Ardolino, Wendy A. *TV Female Foursomes and Their Fans.* Jefferson, NC: McFarland, 2016.

Busis, Hillary. "*Girls* Tackles Abortion: How Does It Compare to *Sex and the City*'s Abortion Episode?" *Entertainment Weekly*, April 23, 2012. https://ew.com/article/2012/04/23 /girls-abortion-sex-and-the-city/.

Caballero, David. "*Sex and the City*: 10 Major Flaws of the Show That Fans Chose to Ignore." Screenrant. January 26, 2021. https://screenrant.com/sex-and-the-city -biggest-series-flaws-problems/.

Campbell, Joseph. *The Hero's Journey.* Novato, CA: New World Library, 1990.

Carter, Angela. "Notes for a Theory of Sixties Style." In *Shaking a Leg: Collected Journalism and Writings*. Edited by Jenny Uglow. London: Chatto and Windus, 1997.

Certiorli. "Carrie Bradshaw, the First Prototype of Fashion Influencer." *Certiorli* (blog). May 6, 2020. https://certiorli.wordpress.com/2020/05/06/carrie-bradshaw -first-prototype-of-fashion-influencer/.

Chaney, Jen. "*And Just Like That . . .* Is Sexless in the City." Vulture. December 9, 2021. https://www.vulture.com/article/and-just-like-that-review-sexless-in-the-city.html.

Cheeda, Saim. "*And Just Like That*: 5 Reasons Fans Are Excited for the *Sex and the City Reboot* (and 5 They're Worried)." Screenrant. January 22, 2021. https://screenrant .com/satc-and-just-like-that-excited-worried-revival/.

Chemaly, Soraya. "All Teachers Should Be Trained to Overcome Their Hidden Biases." *Time*, February 12, 2015. https://time.com/3705454/teachers-biases-girls-education/.

Chiang, Angela. "Coffee Shop Dialogics: *Sex and the City* and Third Wave Feminism." Master's thesis, Carleton University, Ottawa, Ontario, 2007.

Clark, Amy. "What *Sex and the City* Taught Us about Infertility." MamaMia. May 10, 2017. https://www.mamamia.com.au/sex-and-the-city-infertility/.

Clarke, Emma. "Mr. Big Might Be Dead, but Let's Face It—He Was Never 'the One' for Carrie." *Newsweek*, December 9, 2021. https://www.newsweek.com/mr-big-sex -city-trash-1657436.

Clark-Flory, Tracy. "Carrie Bradshaw: Feminist Icon?" Salon. December 22, 2019. https:// www.salon.com/2009/12/22/wolf_carrie_bradshaw/.

Conspicuous Consumption. "What Is Conspicuous Consumption?" Accessed May 1, 2022. https://conspicuousconsumption.org/#:~:text=Conspicuous%20consumption%20 is%20a%20term,real%20needs%20of%20the%20consumer.

Coster, Helen. "The Sex (And the City) Economy." *Forbes*, May 22, 2008. https:// www.forbes.com/2008/05/22/twx-hbo-movies-biz-media-cz_hc_0522sexinc.html ?sh=664824985c81.

Cramer, Janet M. "Discourses of Sexual Morality in *Sex and the City* and *Queer as Folk*." *Journal of Popular Culture* 40, no. 3 (June 2007). https://doi.org/10.1111/j.1540 -5931.2007.00401.x.

Cross, Heather. "A *Sex and the City* Tour through New York City." TripSavvy. June 6, 2019. tripsavvy.com/nyc-sex-and-the-city-tour-1613352.

D'Acci, Julie. "Television, Representation and Gender." In *The Television Studies Reader.* Edited by Robert C. Allen and Annette Hill. London: Routledge, 2004.

Da Costa, Cassie. "When *Sex and the City* Returns, Will It Finally Get Queer People Right?" *Vanity Fair*, January 13, 2021. https://www.vanityfair.com/hollywood/2021/01 /when-sex-and-the-city-returns-will-it-finally-get-queer-people-right.

Davis, Jessica. "How to Keep Your Wardrobe as Classic and Preppy as Charlotte York's." *Harper's Bazaar*, February 2, 2021. https://www.harpersbazaar.com/uk/fashion/what-to-wear/g21070531/how-to-dress-like-charlotte-sex-and-the-city/.

———. "How to Make Your Look a Little More Miranda Hobbes." *Harper's Bazaar*, January 28. 2021. https://www.harpersbazaar.com/uk/fashion/what-to-wear/g21079575/how-to-dress-like-miranda-sex-and-the-city/#:~:text=Although%20Miranda%20was%20never%20considered,way%20ahead%20of%20its%20time.

DeCaro, Frank. "Drag Kings Are Ready to Rule." *New York Times*, March 4, 2021. https://www.nytimes.com/2021/03/04/style/drag-kings.html.

Desta, Yohana. "Being One of the Only Black Actresses on *Sex and the City* Was a 'Surreal' Experience." *Vanity Fair*, June 8, 2018. https://www.vanityfair.com/hollywood/2018/06/sex-and-the-city-sundra-oakley.

Dictionary.com. "Slut-Shaming." September 10, 2018. https://www.dictionary.com/e/slang/slut-shaming/.

Di Donato, Jill. "Was Carrie Bradshaw the Original Influencer?" Huffington Post. December 7, 2021. https://www.huffpost.com/entry/carrie-bradshaw-original-influencer_l_61a51432e4b07fe2011cbab6.

Diehl, Amanda. "Romance 101: Beta Heroes." Bookriot. October 15, 2014. https://bookriot.com/romance-101-beta-heroes/.

Difford, Simon. "Cosmopolitan Cocktail." Difford's Guide. Accessed May 1, 2022. https://www.diffordsguide.com/encyclopedia/462/cocktails/cosmopolitan-cocktail.

Di Mattia, Joanna. "'What's the Harm in Believing?': Mr. Big, Mr. Perfect, and the Romantic Quest for *Sex and the City*'s Mr. Right." In *Reading "Sex and the City."* Edited by Kim Akass and Janet McCabe. London: I. B. Tauris, 2006.

Dockterman, Eliana. "Chris Noth (Sort of Jokingly) Calls Carrie Bradshaw a 'Whore.'" *Time*, October 15, 2014. https://time.com/3510859/chris-noth-mr-big-carrie-bradshaw-whore-satc/.

Dolan, Eric W. "Study Suggests Women Dress Modestly to Defend Themselves against Aggression from Other Women." PsyPost. January 5, 2020. https://www.psypost.org/2020/01/study-suggests-women-dress-modestly-to-defend-themselves-against-aggression-from-other-women-55157.

Dray, Kayleigh. "*Sex and the City*: What Happened When I Rewatched Every Episode of *SATC*." Stylist. January 15, 2021. https://www.stylist.co.uk/life/sex-and-the-city-tv-film-carrie-bradshaw-feminism-sexism/210642.

Dumoulin, Clemence. "The Impact of the TV Show *Sex and the City* on the Audience." Circular. April 17, 2017. https://thecircular.org/impact-tv-show-sex-city-audience/.

Dykes, Ashli LeeAnn. "Situation Comedies and the Single Woman on Television." Doctoral dissertation, Louisiana State University and Agricultural and Mechanical College, 2011. https://digitalcommons.lsu.edu/gradschool_dissertations/325.

Ebert, Robert. "Sex, about the Same. City, Abu Dhabi." May 25, 2010. https://www.rogerebert.com/reviews/sex-and-the-city-2-2010.

Edgerton, Gary R. Introduction to *The Essential HBO Reader*. Edited by Gary R. Edgerton and Jeffrey P. Jones. American Popular Culture, no. 15. Lexington: University Press of Kentucky, 2008. https://uknowledge.uky.edu/upk_american_popular_culture/15.

Edgerton, Gary R., and Jeffrey P. Jones. "HBO's Ongoing Legacy." In *The Essential HBO Reader*. Edited by Gary R. Edgerton and Jeffrey P. Jones. American Popular Culture, no. 15. Lexington: University Press of Kentucky, 2013. https://uknowledge.uky.edu/upk_american_popular_culture/15.

Edwards, Tamala. "Who Needs a Husband?" *Time*, July 5, 2007. http://content.time.com/time/subscriber/article/0,33009,997804,00.html.

Emmanuele, Julia. "Cynthia Nixon and More *And Just Like That* Stars Respond to Meghan McCain's Criticism of Show." *Us Weekly*, February 21, 2022. https://www.usmagazine.com/entertainment/news/and-just-like-that-cast-responds-to-meghan-mccains-criticism/.

Erbland, Kate. "15 Fabulous Facts about *Sex and the City*." Mental Floss. June 6, 2018. https://www.mentalfloss.com/article/64729/15-fabulous-facts-about-sex-and-city.

Erdreich, Sarah. "More than 40 Years after *Maude*, Abortion Remains Taboo on TV." TalkingPointsMemo. May 19, 2014. https://talkingpointsmemo.com/cafe/cristina-yang-grey-s-anatomy-abortion.

Fairless, Chelsea, and Lauren Garroni. Every Outfit. Accessed May 1, 2022. https://www.everyoutfitinc.com/

———. *We Should All Be Mirandas: Life Lessons from "Sex and the City's" Most Underrated Character.* New York: Houghton Mifflin Harcourt, 2019.

Faludi, Susan. *Backlash: The Undeclared War against American Women.* New York: Crown, 2009.

Fasel, Marion. "The Most Memorable Jewels on *Sex and the City*." Aventurine. Accessed May 1, 2022. https://theadventurine.com/culture/movies-tv/the-most-memorable-jewels-on-sex-and-the-city/.

Faye, Shon. "*Sex and the City* Is Embarrassing Now, but It Was Everything Then." Dazed. June 6, 2018. https://www.dazeddigital.com/film-tv/article/40272/1/sex-and-the-city-20th-anniversary.

Female.com.au. "*Sex and the City*'s Cosmopolitan Cocktail." Accessed May 1, 2022. https://www.female.com.au/cosmopolitan-cocktail.htm.

Field, Patricia. "*SATC* Collection." Patricia Field Art Fashion. Accessed May 1, 2022. https://patriciafield.com/collections/patricia-field-satc-collection.

Filipovic, Jill. "*Sex and the City* Faces Reality . . . Finally." CNN. August 24, 2021. https://www.cnn.com/2021/08/24/opinions/sex-and-the-city-filipovic/index.html.

Fontes, Lisa Aronson. "How Domestic Abusers Groom and Isolate Their Victims." *Psychology Today*, February 19, 2019. https://www.psychologytoday.com/us/blog/invisible-chains/201902/how-domestic-abusers-groom-and-isolate-their-victims.

———. "When Relationship Abuse Is Hard to Recognize." *Psychology Today*, August 26, 2015. https://www.psychologytoday.com/us/blog/invisible-chains/201508/when-relationship-abuse-is-hard-recognize.

Francese, Andrea. "*The Carrie Diaries* Got Everything Wrong about Carrie Bradshaw's Upbringing." Showbiz CheatSheet. January 6, 2021. https://www.cheatsheet.com/entertainment/the-carrie-diaries-got-everything-wrong-about-carrie-bradshaws-upbringing.html/.

———. "*Sex and the City*: 3 Times Carrie Bradshaw Should Have Really Ended Her Romance with Mr. Big." Showbiz CheatSheet. December 27, 2021. https://www.cheatsheet.com/entertainment/sex-and-the-city-3-times-carrie-bradshaw-really-ended-romance-mr-big.html/.

———. "*Sex and the City*: Candace Bushnell May Have Just Revealed That Carrie Bradshaw Could Afford Her Lifestyle." Showbiz CheatSheet. February 16, 2022. https://www.cheatsheet.com/entertainment/sex-and-the-city-candace-bushnell-may-have-just-revealed-that-carrie-bradshaw-could-afford-her-lifestyle.html/.

————. "*Sex and the City*: Charlotte York Was Different from Her Friends in 1 Big Way." Showbiz CheatSheet. May 31, 2021. https://www.cheatsheet.com/entertainment/sex -and-the-city-charlotte-york-was-different-from-her-friends-in-1-big-way.html/.

————. "*Sex and the City* Costume Designer, Patricia Field, Explains Why Miranda Was the Worst Dressed." Showbiz CheatSheet. October 4, 2020. https://www.cheatsheet .com/entertainment/sex-and-the-city-costume-designer-patricia-field-explains-why -miranda-was-the-worst-dressed.html/.

————. "*Sex and the City*: How Did Carrie Bradshaw Meet Her 3 Best Friends?" Showbiz CheatSheet. August 8, 2020. https://www.cheatsheet.com/entertainment/sex-and-the -city-how-did-carrie-bradshaw-meet-her-3-best-friends.html/.

————. "*Sex and the City*: Miranda Hobbes Had Some Pretty Bad Personality Traits, Too." Showbiz CheatSheet. February 17, 2021. https://www.cheatsheet.com/entertainment /sex-and-the-city-the-main-characters-biggest-character-development-moment.html/.

————. "*Sex and the City*: Which Character Dated the Most Men?" Showbiz CheatSheet. April 29, 2020. https://www.cheatsheet.com/entertainment/sex-and-the-city-which -character-had-the-most-partners.html/.

————. "*Sex and the City*: Which Characters Could Actually Afford Their Lifestyles?" Showbiz CheatSheet. November 14, 2019. https://www.cheatsheet.com/entertainment /sex-and-the-city-which-characters-could-actually-afford-their-lifestyles.html/.

Freedman, Estelle B. *No Turning Back: The History of Feminism and the Future of Women*. London: Random House, 2007.

The Freelance Creative. "Rates Database." Accessed May 1, 2022. https://contently.net /rates-database/rates/.

Free Tours by Foot. "*Sex and the City* Tour Sights." Accessed May 1, 2022. https://freetours byfoot.com/sex-and-the-city-tour/.

Fuller, Bonnie. "What the Creators of *Sex and the City* Know about Marketing That You Don't." *AdAge*, June 9, 2008. https://adage.com/article/madisonvine-case-study /creators-sex-city-marketing/127610.

Gajewski, Ryan. "Sara Ramirez Responds to Criticism of *And Just Like That* Character: 'I Don't Recognize Myself in Che.'" *Hollywood Reporter*, February 2, 2022. https:// www.hollywoodreporter.com/tv/tv-news/sara-ramirez-and-just-like-that-che-diaz -1235086293/.

Garner, Glenn. "*SATC*'s Candace Bushnell Reveals Her Columnist Salary—Maybe Carrie's Lifestyle Wasn't Unrealistic!" *People*, February 17, 2020. https://people .com/tv/candace-bushnell-reveals-salary-vogue-columnist-90s/.

Gerhard, Jane. "The Personal Is Still Political: The Legacy of 1970s Feminism." In *"Bad Girls"/"Good Girls": Women, Sex and Power in the Nineties*. Edited by Nan Bauer Maglin and Donna Perry. New Brunswick, NJ: Rutgers University Press, 1996.

Gibbs, Lynn. "*Sex and the City*: 10 Hidden Details You Never Noticed about Carrie's Apartment." Screenrant. April 18, 2020. https://screenrant.com/sex-the -city-hidden-details-carries-apartment/.

Gipson, Johnell. "Sarah Jessica Parker Owns 'Well Over 100 Pairs' of Manolo Blahnik Shoes." Showbiz CheatSheet. January 12, 2021. https://www.cheatsheet.com/entertain ment/sarah-jessica-parker-owns-well-over-100-pairs-of-manolo-blahnik-shoes.html/.

GLAAD. "Bisexual Erasure." Accessed May 1, 2022. https://www.glaad.org/accordion view/bisexual-erasure.

Glass, Jess. "*Sex and the City*'s Sarah Jessica Parker Admits That the Show Failed to Represent LGBT People." PinkNews. May 14, 2018. https://www.pinknews .co.uk/2018/05/14/sex-and-the-city-sarah-jessica-parker-lgbt-entertainment/.

Global Legal Post. "Male Lawyers Get Promoted over Women, McKinsey Says." November 1, 2017. https://www.globallegalpost.com/news/male-lawyers-get-promo ted-over-women-mckinsey-says-56167958.

Goldstone, Penny. "Why Charlotte Was the Real *Sex and the City* Style Queen." *Marie Claire UK*, March 30, 2017. https://www.marieclaire.co.uk/fashion/char lotte-sex-and-the-city-best-outfits-488094.

Gopalan, Nisha. "'Splat!': The Oral History of *Sex and the City*'s Most Shocking Episode." Vulture. June 6, 2018. https://www.vulture.com/2013/12/sex-and-the-city-oral-history -splat-episode.html.

Grady, Constance. "The Waves of Feminism, and Why People Keep Fighting over Them, Explained." Vox. July 20, 2018. https://www.vox.com/2018/3/20/16955588 /feminism-waves-explained-first-second-third-fourth.

Griner, David. "Ryan Reynolds Just Made an Official Peloton Ad about Its Big *And Just Like That* Moment." *AdWeek*, December 12, 2021. https://www.adweek.com/conver gent-tv/ryan-reynolds-just-made-an-official-peloton-ad-about-its-big-and-just-like -that-moment/.

Haggins, Bambi, and Amanda D. Lotz. "Comedy Overview: At Home on the Cutting Edge." In *The Essential HBO Reader*. Edited by Gary R. Edgerton and Jeffrey P. Jones. American Popular Culture, no. 15. Lexington: University Press of Kentucky, 2008. https://uknowledge.uky.edu/upk_american_popular_culture/15.

Hamlett, Melanie. "*Designing Women* Was a Series Ahead of Its Time. In 2019 It's Still Revolutionary." *Glamour*, August 26, 2019. https://www.glamour.com/story /designing-women-hulu.

Handysides, Kim. "Sex in the City, Carrie Bradshaw Is the Female Narrator of the 90s." Blast. November 12. 2021. https://theblast.com/118034/sex-in-the-city-carrie -bradshaw-the-female-narrator-of-the-90s/.

Hansen, Matt. "Peloton Just Had the Worst Product Placement Imaginable in the New *Sex and the City* Show." *Cycling Magazine*, December 10, 2021. https://cyclingmagazine .ca/sections/news/peloton-just-had-the-worst-product-placement-imaginable-in-the -new-sex-in-the-city-show/.

Harnois, Catherine. "Re-Presenting Feminisms: Past, Present, and Future." *NWSA Journal* 20, no. 1 (2008): 120–45. http://www.jstor.org/stable/40071255.

Harris, Hunter. "For Women of Color Who Love *Sex and the City*." Refinery29. June 6, 2018. https://www.refinery29.com/en-us/2016/07/117151/sex-and-the-city-racism.

Hauge, Michael. "Inner Conflict." Story Mastery. February 9, 2017. https://www.storymas tery.com/character-development/inner-conflict/.

———. "Love Stories: The 6 Categories of Romantic Comedy." Story Mastery. September 22, 2014. https://www.storymastery.com/love-stories/6-categories-romantic-comedy/.

Hayes, Alex. "Sarah Jessica Parker: Product Placement Never Happened on *Sex and the City*." Mumbrella. June 16, 2014. https://mumbrella.com.au/sarah-jessica-parker -product-placement-never-happened-sex-city-2-232861.

Henry, Astrid. "Orgasms and Empowerment: *Sex and the City* and the Third Wave Feminism." In *Reading "Sex and the City."* Edited by Kim Akass and Janet McCabe. London: I. B. Tauris, 2006.

Hindman Network. "The Original Influencer: How Coco Chanel Forever Changed Women's Fashion." May 8, 2020. https://hindmanauctions.com/blog/chanel-costume-jewelry.

Hirsch, Afua. "As a 1990s Teenager, the World Gave Us Girl Power and Pornification." *Guardian*, January 21, 2018. https://www.theguardian.com/lifeandstyle/2018/jan/31 /as-a-1990s-teenager-the-world-gave-us-girl-power-and-pornification.

History.com Editors. "Abigail Adams Urges Husband to 'Remember the Ladies.'" History.com. March 30, 2020. https://www.history.com/this-day-in-history/abigail -adams-urges-husband-to-remember-the-ladies.

Hodgson, Claire. "*Sex and the City* Creator Defends Chris Noth's 'Whore' Comment about Carrie Bradshaw." *Cosmopolitan*, October 16, 2014. https://www.cosmopolitan.com /uk/entertainment/news/a30475/sex-and-the-city-chris-noth-whore-carrie/.

hooks, bell. "Dissident Heat: Fire with Fire." In *"Bad Girls"/"Good Girls": Women, Sex and Power in the Nineties*. Edited by Nan Bauer Maglin and Donna Perry. New Brunswick, NJ: Rutgers University Press, 1996.

Hopper, Jessica. "Building a Mystery: An Oral History of Lilith Fair." *Vanity Fair*, September 30, 2009. https://www.vanityfair.com/style/2019/09/an-oral-history-of-lilith-fair.

Houston, Jack, and Irene Anna Kim. "Why Hermès Birkin Bags Are So Expensive, According to a Handbag Expert." *Insider*, June 30, 2021. https://www.businessin sider.com/hermes-birkin-bag-realreal-handbag-expert-so-expensive-2019-6.

Hsieh, Carina. "I Lived Like Carrie Bradshaw for a Week." *Cosmopolitan*, June 4, 2018. https://www.cosmopolitan.com/entertainment/tv/a20978854/carrie-bradshaw -sex-and-the-city-real-life/.

Invivo SJP. Accessed May 1, 2022. https://shop.invivoxsjp.com/.

Isbister, Georgina. "*Sex and the City*: A Postfeminist Fairy Tale." Online proceedings of "Sustaining Culture," annual conference of the Cultural Studies Association of Australia (CSAA), University of South Australia, Adelaide, December 6–8, 2007. http://unisa.edu.au/com/csaa/onlineproceedings.htm.

Isidore, Chris. "Where the Current Economic Boom Ranks in American History." CNN. January 30, 2018. https://money.cnn.com/2018/01/30/news/economy/us-economy -boom-history/index.html.

IZEA. "The History of Influencer Marketing." Accessed May 1, 2022. https://izea.com /history-influencer-marketing/.

Jeffery, Joyann. "Kim Cattrall Talks Publicly about the *Sex and the City* Reboot for First Time Ever." Today. May 4, 2022. https://www.today.com/popculture/tv/kim -cattrall-sex-and-the-city-reboot-samantha-jones-rcna27319?fbclid=IwAR0zHsPz W67d_qsbJRhV-Nx4KOGldYoU3rWxS-5f_pRLFEPyJ1FNwWdn-jo.

Jennifer. "Alpha-Male vs. Alpha-Hole Romance Heroes: Why One of Them *Has to Go*." Romance Rehab. April 15, 2019. https://www.romancerehab.com/blog/alpha-male-vs -alpha-hole-romance-heroes-why-one-of-them-has-to-go.

Jermyn, Deborah. *"Sex and the City."* Detroit: Wayne State University Press, 2009.

Jones, Ellen E. "'That Show Was as White as It Gets!': *Sex and the City*'s Problematic Legacy." *Guardian*, April 28, 2018. https://www.theguardian.com/tv-and-radio/2018 /apr/21/that-show-was-as-white-as-it-gets-sex-and-the-citys-problematic-legacy.

Jorgensen, Jeana. "A Wave of the Magic Wand: Fairy Godmothers in Contemporary American Media." *Marvels and Tales* 21, no. 2 (2007): 216–27. http://www.jstor.org /stable/41388835.

Kaler, Anne K. "*Golden Girls*: Feminine Archetypal Patterns of the Complete Woman." *Journal of Popular Culture* 24, no. 3 (Winter 1990): 49.

Kang, Inkoo. "*And Just Like That . . .* Is *Sex and the City* for 2021: A Bloated, Laugh-Free Comedy about Grief." *Washington Post*, December 9, 2021. https://www.washington post.com/tv/2021/12/09/and-just-like-that-review/.

Kim, Kyle, Kate Stanhope, and Chris Keller. "Every Single Person Carrie, Miranda, Charlotte and Samantha Dated." *Los Angeles Times*, June 1, 2018. https://www.latimes .com/projects/la-et-sex-and-the-city-every-person-they-dated/.

König, Anna. "*Sex and the City*: A Fashion Editor's Dream?" In *Reading "Sex and the City."* Edited by Kim Akass and Janet McCabe. London: I. B. Tauris, 2006.

Krentcil, Faran. "Carrie Bradshaw Flowers Hit a Major Milan Runway." *Elle*, September 24, 2017. https://www.elle.com/fashion/a12459019/carrie-bradshaw-flower-shop/.

———. "How Much Did It Cost to Dress Carrie Bradshaw in *Sex and the City*?" *Elle*, May 29, 2018. https://www.elle.com/culture/movies-tv/a20829475/carrie -bradshaw-wardrobe-cost-sex-and-the-city/.

Krishna, Priya. "The Definitive History of the Cosmopolitan." Punch. September 11, 2019. https://punchdrink.com/articles/definitive-history-cosmopolitan-cosmo -vodka-cranberry-cocktail/.

Kutner, Jenny. "Women in Red Are Sexy—And They Make Other Women Jealous." Salon. July 11, 2014. https://www.salon.com/2014/07/11/women_in_red_are_sexy _and_they_make_other_women_jealous/.

Langas, Amelia. "Carrie Bradshaw's Best and Worst Outfits." *People*, accessed May 1, 2022. https://people.com/webstory/carrie-bradshaws-best-and-worst-outfits/.

Lawson, Richard. "*Sex and the City* 10 Years Later: The Final Rankings." *Vanity Fair*, February 14, 2014. https://www.vanityfair.com/hollywood/2014/02/sex-and-the-city -season-rankings.

Lazarus, Clifford N. "Think Sarcasm Is Funny? Think Again." *Psychology Today*, June 26, 2012. https://www.psychologytoday.com/us/blog/think-well/201206/think -sarcasm-is-funny-think-again.

Librarians at George A. Spiva Library. "Fairy Tale Conventions." Research and Course Guides, George A. Spiva Library, Southern Missouri State University. December 3, 2021. https://libguides.mssu.edu/c.php?g=185298&p=1223898.

Lind-Westbrook, Jennifer. "*Sex and the City*: 10 Biggest Ways Miranda Changed from Season 1 to the Finale." Screenrant. March 4, 2020. https://screenrant.com /sex-city-hbo-biggest-ways-miranda-changed-season-1-finale/.

Long, Camilla. "Decade in Review: You Are a Very Noughtie and Unhappy Girl." *Times of London*, December 20, 2009. https://www.thetimes.co.uk/article/decade -in-review-you-are-a-very-noughtie-and-unhappy-girl-296dw9k96ht.

Maglin, Nan Bauer, and Donna Perry, eds. Introduction to *"Bad Girls"/"Good Girls": Women, Sex and Power in the Nineties*. New Brunswick, NJ: Rutgers University Press, 1996.

Mandi. "The Alpha-Hole Hero: Hot or Not?" Smexy Books. August 8, 2013. https:// smexybooks.com/2013/08/the-alpha-hole-hero-hot-or-not.html.

Mangan, Lucy. "*And Just Like That* Review: *Sex and the City* Sequel Has a Mouthful of Teething Troubles." *Guardian*, December 9, 2021. https://www.theguardian.com /tv-and-radio/2021/dec/09/and-just-like-that-review-sex-and-the-city-reboot-has-a -mouthful-of-teething-troubles.

Manning, Charles. "Can We Finally Admit the Outfits on *Sex and the City* Were a Big Hot Mess?" Daily Front Row. June 7, 2018. https://fashionweekdaily.com/sex -and-the-city-bad-outfits/.

Marazza, Antonio, and Stefania Saviolo. *Lifestyle Brands: A Guide to Aspirational Marketing*. Houndsmill, UK: Palgrave Macmillan, 2012.

Markle, Gail. "Can Women Have Sex Like a Man? Sexual Scripts in *Sex and the City*." *Sexuality and Culture* 12 (2008): 45–57. https://doi.org/10.1007/s12119-007-9019-1.

Masterclass Staff. "Writing 101: The 12 Literary Archetypes." Masterclass. August 30, 2021. https://www.masterclass.com/articles/writing-101-the-12-literary-archetypes.

Mazzeo, Esme. "The *Sex and the City* Episode Where Carrie Was Forced to Leave Her Shoes at the Door Matters 18 Years Later Because Women Are Still Shamed for Being Single." Insider. August 17, 2021. https://www.insider.com/sex-and -the-city-single-shaming-episode-still-relevant-today-2021-8?amp.

McCarthy, Helen. "The Rise of the Working Wife." History Today. May 5, 2020. https:// www.historytoday.com/history-matters/rise-working-wife.

McKenna, Meghan. "How Does *Sex and the City* Hold Up 20 Years after Its Debut?" *Fashion Magazine*, June 6, 2018. https://fashionmagazine.com/culture/woke-charlotte -sex-city/.

Melendez, Tanya. "How TV Lied about Abortion." Vox. October 14, 2021. https://www .vox.com/culture/22715333/tv-abortion-plot-storyline-lies.

Merck, Mandy. "Sexuality in the City." In *Reading "Sex and the City."* Edited by Kim Akass and Janet McCabe. London: I. B. Tauris, 2006.

Merriam-Webster. "Metrosexual." Accessed May 1, 2022. https://www.merriam-webster .com/dictionary/metrosexual.

Meyers, Diana T. "Gendered Work and Individual Autonomy." In *Recognition, Responsibility, and Rights: Feminist Ethics and Social Theory.* Edited by Robin N. Foire and Hilde Lindemann Nelson. Lanham, MD: Rowman and Littlefield, 2003.

Micucci, Dana. "Redefining Feminism." *Chicago Tribune*, December 12, 1993. https:// www.chicagotribune.com/news/ct-xpm-1993-12-12-9312120158-story.html.

Montemurro, Beth. "Charlotte Chooses Her Choice: Liberal Feminism on *Sex and the City.*" *Feminist Television Studies: The Case of HBO* 3, no. 1 (Fall 2004). http://sfon line.barnard.edu/hbo/printbmo.htm.

Motley, Calvin. "*Sex and the City* Alternate Opening Credits Has Carrie Tripping Clumsily." Showbiz CheatSheet. January 11, 2021. https://www.cheatsheet.com/entertainment /sex-and-the-city-alternate-opening-credits-has-carrie-tripping-clumsily.html/.

Mulshine, Molly. "All of the *Sex and the City* Boyfriends, Ranked." *Elle*, May 7, 2018. https:// www.elle.com/culture/movies-tv/a20140092/sex-and-the-city-boyfriends-ranked/.

Munro, Cait. "The Birth, Death and Inevitable Comeback of the Cosmo, *SATC*'s Greatest Icon." Refinery29. June 6, 2018. https://www.refinery29.com/en-us/2018/06/200515 /sex-and-the-city-cosmopolitan-drink-popularity.

Nachlis, Sara. "What Would It Cost to Live Like Carrie Bradshaw in 2018?" Girlboss. June 6, 2018. https://www.girlboss.com/read/carrie-bradshaw-expenses.

National Women's Hall of Fame. "Susan B. Anthony." Accessed April 29, 2022. https:// www.womenofthehall.org/inductee/susan-b-anthony/#:~:text=Its%20motto%20 was%20%E2%80%9CMen%20their,and%20fined%20for%20voting%20illegally.

NewsCenterMaine.com. "'I Lost My Choo!': 20 Years of Jimmy Choo in Pop Culture." July 25, 2017. https://www.newscentermaine.com/article/news/nation-now/i-lost -my-choo-20-years-of-jimmy-choo-in-pop-culture/465-959742d0-be2d-4ffe-ae84 -aacfe9fb58df.

Ngangura, Tari. "Looking Back, *Sex and the City* Was Seriously Problematic for Black Women." *Fashion Magazine*, June 5, 2018. https://fashionmagazine.com/flare/sex -and-the-city-black-women/.

Niblock, Sarah. "'My Manolos, My Self': Manolo Blahnik, Shoes and Desire." In *Reading "Sex and the City."* Edited by Kim Akass and Janet McCabe. London: I. B. Tauris, 2006.

Nichols, Michelle. "*Sex and the City* Film a Marketing Dream." Reuters. May 15, 2008. https://www.reuters.com/article/us-sexandthecity/sex-and-the-city-film-a-mar keting-dream-idUSN1530121420080515.

Nolfi, Joey. "Sarah Jessica Parker on Why We Didn't See Carrie Call 911 after Big's Heart Attack." *Entertainment Weekly*, February 16, 2022. https://ew.com/tv/sarah -jessica-parker-why-carrie-didnt-call-911-after-mr-big-heart-attack/.

Nussbaum, Emily. "Difficult Women: How *Sex and the City* Lost Its Good Name." *New Yorker*, July 23, 2013. https://www.newyorker.com/magazine/2013/07/29/dif ficult-women.

O'Beirne, Eva. "Carrie Bradshaw Is Not the Feminist Icon We Want Her to Be." *Trinity News*, June 21, 2020. http://trinitynews.ie/2020/06/carrie-bradshaw-is-not -the-feminist-icon-we-want-her-to-be/.

O'Keeffe, Kevin. "No, Carrie Bradshaw Was Not 'Such a Whore.'" *Atlantic*, October 15, 2014. https://www.theatlantic.com/entertainment/archive/2014/10/no-chris-noth -carrie-bradshaw-was-not-such-a-whore/381482/.

On Location Tours. "*Sex and the City* Hotspots." Accessed May 1, 2022. https://onlo cationtours.com/new-york-tv-and-movie-tours/sex-and-the-city-hotspots-tour/?g clid=Cj0KCQiA5aWOBhDMARIsAIXLlkffjnOp6224yqajVELXiZfeY-cL3d2pE3c JxkU6LNsvIvPKgF0nCr0aAoj8EALw_wcB.

Oria, Beatriz. *Talking Dirty on "Sex and the City": Romance, Intimacy, Friendship*. New York: Rowman and Littlefield, 2014.

Oxford Reference. "Post-Feminism." Accessed April 28, 2022. https://www.oxfordrefer ence.com/view/10.1093/oi/authority.20110803100339445.

Parker, Sarah Jessica. "*SATC* NYC Tour." SJP by Sarah Jessica Parker. Accessed May 1, 2022. https://sjpbysarahjessicaparker.com/pages/satc-nyc-tour.

Pazda, Adam D., Pavol Prokop, and Andrew J. Elliot. "Red and Romantic Rivalry: Viewing Another Woman in Red Increases Perceptions of Sexual Receptivity, Derogation, and Intentions to Mate-Guard." *Personality and Social Psychology Bulletin* 40, no. 10 (October 2014): 1260–69. https://doi.org/10.1177/0146167214539709.

Perkins, Claire, and Michele Schreiber. "Independent Women: From Film to Television." *Feminist Media Studies* 19, no. 7 (2019): 919–27. https://doi.org/10.1080/14680777 .2019.1667059.

Picchi, Amber. "Peloton Stock Slumps after Morbid Product Placement in *Sex and the City*." CBS News. December 10, 2021. https://www.cbsnews.com/news/peloton -stock-death-by-peloton-just-like-that-mr-big/.

Popova, Maria. "Ways of Seeing: John Berger's Classic 1972 BBC Critique of Consumer Culture." Marginalian. Accessed April 27, 2022. https://www.themarginalian.org /2012/09/28/ways-of-seeing-john-berger/#:~:text=To%20be%20born%20a%20 woman,within%20such%20a%20limited%20space.

PT Staff. "The Value of Style." *Psychology Today*, July 1, 2005. https://www.psychology today.com/us/articles/200507/the-value-style.

Pugh, Lindsay. "Television's Representation of Childfree Women Sucks." *Woman in Revolt* (blog). 2020. https://www.womaninrevolt.com/televisions-representation-of -childfree-women-sucks/.

Pyszczyk, Kristen. "Purses of *Sex and the City*: Where Are They Now?" *Purse Blog* (blog). February 26, 2019. https://www.purseblog.com/the-many-bags/purses-of-sex -and-the-city-where-are-they-now/.

Quindlen, Anna. "And Now, Babe Feminism." In *"Bad Girls"/"Good Girls": Women, Sex and Power in the Nineties*. Edited by Nan Bauer Maglin and Donna Perry. New Brunswick, NJ: Rutgers University Press, 1996.

Respers France, Lisa. "Mark Ronson Isn't Sapiosexual after All and Apologizes for Identifying as Such." CNN. September 27, 2019. https://www.cnn.com/2019/09/27/entertainment/mark-ronson-not-sapiosexual/index.html.

Rodriguez-Cayro, Kyli. "5 Myths about Bisexuality That Contribute to Bi Erasure." Bustle. September 21, 2017. https://www.bustle.com/p/5-myths-about-bisexuality-that-contribute-to-bi-erasure-2418689.

Ross, Harling. "If *Sex and the City* Came Out Today, Miranda Would Be the Protagonist." Repeller. April 13, 2018. https://repeller.com/miranda-hobbes-best-character-satc/.

Ross, Sharon Marie. "Comparison Shopping through Female Conversation in HBO's *Sex and the City*." In *The Sitcom Reader: America Viewed and Skewed*. Edited by Mary M. Dalton and Laura R. Linder. Albany: State University of New York Press, 2005.

Royal, Cindy. "Narrative Structure in Sex and the City: 'I Couldn't Help But Wonder . . .'" Doctoral dissertation, University of Texas at Austin, 2003.

Rotten Tomatoes. "*Sex and the City 2*." Accessed May 2, 2022. https://www.rottentomatoes.com/m/sex_and_the_city_2.

Sager, Jessica. "SJP Can Certainly Afford Fancy Shoes! How *Sex and the City* Star Sarah Jessica Parker Made Her Millions." *Parade*, December 9, 2021. https://parade.com/1150411/jessicasager/sarah-jessica-parker-net-worth/.

Sayej, Nadja. "'It's My Ass and My Instagram': Amber Rose Is over Your Slut-Shaming." *Harper's Bazaar*, September 25, 2018. https://www.harpersbazaar.com/culture/features/a23357956/amber-rose-slutwalk-interview/.

Schuster, Dana. "26 Ways *Sex and the City* Left Its Mark." *New York Post*, May 27, 2018. https://nypost.com/2018/05/27/26-ways-sex-and-the-city-left-its-mark/.

Schwab, David. "Why Lifestyle Influencers Are the Next 'It' Endorser." *Forbes*, May 11, 2016. https://www.forbes.com/sites/davidschwab/2016/05/11/why-lifestyle-influencers-are-the-next-it-endorser/?sh=5204a50c524f.

Seitz, Matt Zoller. "Seitz on *The Carrie Diaries*: Everything about This *Sex and the City* Prequel Feels Wrong." Vulture. January 14, 2013. https://www.vulture.com/2013/01/tv-review-the-carrie-diaries.html.

Sepinwall, Alan. "*And Just Like That . . .* Is Missing the Funk and the Spunk." *Rolling Stone*, December 9, 2021. https://www.rollingstone.com/tv/tv-reviews/and-just-like-that-review-1269034/.

Simon, Ron. "*Sex and the City*." In *The Essential HBO Reader*. Edited by Gary R. Edgerton and Jeffrey P. Jones. *American Popular Culture*, no. 15. Lexington: University Press of Kentucky, 2008. https://uknowledge.uky.edu/upk_american_popular_culture/15.

Smith, Christy. "In *Sex and the City*, Number of Sex Partners True to New York Life." *New York Daily News*, May 28, 2008. https://www.nydailynews.com/entertainment/sex-city-number-sex-partners-true-new-york-life-article-1.326644.

Snyder-Hall, R. Claire. "Third-Wave Feminism and the Defense of 'Choice.'" *Perspectives on Politics* 8, no. 1 (2010): 255–61. http://www.jstor.org/stable/25698533.

Sohn, Amy. *"Sex and the City": Kiss and Tell*. New York: Pocket Books, 2002.

Stacey, Judith. "The New Conservative Feminism." *Feminist Studies* 9, no. 3 (1983): 559–83. https://doi.org/10.2307/3177616.

Stinson, Katherine. "Critics Are Just as Divided as Fans on *And Just Like That*." Distractify. December 27, 2021. https://www.distractify.com/p/and-just-like-that-ratings.

St. Louis, Molly. "Research Shows That the Clothes You Wear Actually Change the Way You Perform." Inc. June 8, 2017. https://www.inc.com/molly-reynolds

/research-shows-that-the-clothes-you-wear-actually-change-the-way-you-perform.
html.

The Take. "*Sex and the City*: Why No One Wants to Be a Samantha (But They Should)."
Accessed April 28, 2022. https://the-take.com/watch/sex-and-the-city-why-no-one
-wants-to-be-a-samantha-but-they-should.

Teeter, Adam. "The History of the Cosmopolitan and the Birth of Craft Cocktail
Culture." Vinepair. December 28, 2014. https://vinepair.com/wine-blog/history
-cosmopolitan-birth-craft-cocktail-culture/.

Thomas, Lauren, and Sarah Whitten. "Peloton Removes Viral Chris Noth Ad after Sexual
Assault Allegations against Him Surface." CNBC. December 16, 2021. https://www
.cnbc.com/2021/12/16/peloton-removes-viral-chris-noth-ad-after-sexual-assault-alle
gations.html.

Thomas, Leah. "Charlotte York Is Anti-Feminist, and We've Outgrown Her." *Marie
Claire*, June 29, 2017. https://www.marieclaire.com/culture/news/a27933/sex-and-the
-city-charlotte-york-anti-feminist/.

Thompson, Andrew. "Stats and the City." Ceros. Accessed May 1, 2022. https://www
.ceros.com/inspire/originals/sex-and-the-city/.

Thompson, Eliza. "What Happened to Miranda's Boyfriend Skipper? A *Sex and the
City* Investigation." *Cosmopolitan*, June 8, 2018. https://www.cosmopolitan.com
/entertainment/tv/a20978994/skipper-sex-and-the-city/.

Tong, Rosemarie. *Feminist Thought: A More Comprehensive Introduction.* New York:
Routledge, 2018.

Torn, Simone. "*Sex and the City*: Kim Cattrall Wasn't Happy with Samantha's Fate in the
Series Finale." Showbiz CheatSheet. May 30, 2021. https://www.cheatsheet.com/en
tertainment/sex-and-the-city-kim-cattrall-wasnt-happy-with-samanthas-fate-in-the
-series-finale.html/.

Tropp, Laura. "Faking a Sonogram: Representations of Motherhood on *Sex and the
City*." *Journal of Popular Culture* 39 (2006): 861–77. https://doi.org/10.1111
/j.1540-5931.2006.00309.x.

Tufino, Cameron Michael. "*Sex and the City*: A Promotion of Modern American Feminism."
Master's thesis, University of the Incarnate Word, 2012. http://athenaeum.uiw.edu
/uiw_etds/292.

Turner, Giles. "Embarrassing Plot Twist for Peloton." CBS News. December 10, 2021. https://
www.cbsnews.com/news/peloton-stock-death-by-peloton-just-like-that-mr-big/.

Tyler, Jessica. "A Cupcake Shop That Sparked a Nationwide Craze with Its
Appearance on *Sex and the City* Is Gearing Up to Take over America."
Business Insider, May 11, 2018. https://www.businessinsider.com/sex-and-the-city
-cupcake-shop-magnolia-bakery-expands-2018-5.

US Department of Health and Human Services, Office on Women's Health. "Infertility."
April 1, 2019. https://www.womenshealth.gov/a-z-topics/infertility#:~:text=Is%20
infertility%20a%20common%20problem,Control%20and%20Prevention%20
(CDC).

Valenti, Jessica. "SlutWalks and the Future of Feminism." *Washington Post*, June 3, 2011.
https://www.washingtonpost.com/opinions/slutwalks-and-the-future-of-feminism
/2011/06/01/AGjB9LIH_story.html.

Viator. "*Sex and the City* Night Out." Accessed May 1, 2022. https://www.viator.com
/tours/New-York-City/Sex-and-the-City-Night-Out/d687-6390P4.

Viera, Benie. "Why Living Single Is the Blueprint." Vibe. September 24, 2013. https://www.vibe.com/features/vixen/why-living-single-is-the-blueprint-288093/.

Vogue. "*Sex and the City*: Best Episodes, Fashion, Memes, and More." Accessed May 1, 2022. https://www.vogue.com/tag/misc/sex-and-the-city.

Waterhouse, Jonah. "Controversial Opinion: Miranda Had the Best Style on *Sex and the City*." *Elle Australia*, January 27, 2020.

WebMD. "What We've Learned from *Sex and the City*." Accessed April 28, 2022. https://www.webmd.com/sex-relationships/features/what-weve-learned-from-sex-city.

Weekes, Princess. "Charlotte York Is the Best Character on *Sex and the City*." Mary Sue. March 20, 2018. https://www.themarysue.com/charlotte-york-sex-and-the-city/.

———. "It's So Frustrating That a *Sex and the City* Revival Is Really Happening." Mary Sue. January 11, 2021. https://www.themarysue.com/hbo-max-sex-and-the-city-revival-officially-frustrating/.

Weiss, Piper. "Carrie Bradshaw's Back in Bloom with Her Signature Flower." *New York Daily News*, May 5, 2008. https://www.nydailynews.com/life-style/carrie-bradshaw-back-bloom-signature-flower-article-1.329525.

Wiener, Julie. "Magnolia Cupcakes Banished from *Sex and the City* Tour." *Vanity Fair*, May 26, 2010. https://www.vanityfair.com/culture/2010/05/magnolia-cupcakes-banished-from-sex-and-the-city-tour.

Wignall, Alice. "Can a Feminist Really Love *Sex and the City*?" *Guardian*, April 16, 2008. https://www.theguardian.com/lifeandstyle/2008/apr/16/women.film.

Williams, Alex. "'Metrosexuals' Were Just Straight Men Who Loved Self-Care. Right?" *New York Times*, June 15, 2018. https://www.nytimes.com/2018/06/15/style/metrosexuals.html.

Wright, Jennifer. "#MeToo Couldn't Exist without Carrie Bradshaw." Body+Soul. May 14, 2018. https://www.bodyandsoul.com.au/mind-body/wellness/metoo-couldnt-exist-without-carrie-bradshaw/news-story/2b6d46fba55cad3c14a41b0ee52e0254.

Wolf, Naomi. *The Beauty Myth: How Images of Beauty Are Used against Women*. New York: HarperCollins, 2009.

———. "Carrie Bradshaw: Icons of the Decade." *Guardian*, December 21, 2009. https://www.theguardian.com/world/2009/dec/22/carrie-bradshaw-icons-of-decade.

Women and Hollywood. "Being Miranda Hobbes: Why Women Really Love *Sex and the City*." July 23, 2013. https://womenandhollywood.com/being-miranda-hobbes-why-women-really-love-sex-and-the-city/.

Yarrow, Allison. "How the '90s Tricked Women into Thinking They'd Gained Gender Equality." *Time*, June 13, 2018. https://time.com/5310256/90s-gender-equality-progress/.

Zieger, Susan. "Sex and the Citizen in *Sex and the City*'s New York." In *Reading "Sex and the City."* Edited by Kim Akass and Janet McCabe. London: I. B. Tauris, 2006.

INDEX

ABOUT THE AUTHOR

Nicole Evelina is a Carrie, with her moon in Charlotte and Miranda rising. She's been a fan of *Sex and City* since the late 1990s and drank her fair share of cosmopolitans while watching the ladies during the show's original run. She's also a *USA Today* best-selling author of historical fiction, nonfiction, and women's fiction who tells the stories of strong women from history and today, with a focus on biographical historical fiction and little-known figures of women's history. When she's not writing, she can be found reading; enjoying theater, dance, and music; and dreaming of living in downtown Chicago—which is to her what Manhattan is to the ladies of *Sex and the City*.

CPSIA information can be obtained
at www.ICGtesting.com
Printed in the USA
BVHW082331060822
643984BV00003B/3